C++ in Actio

C++ in Action
Industrial-Strength Programming Techniques

Bartosz Milewski

Addison-Wesley

Boston • San Francisco • New York • Toronto • Montreal
London • Munich • Paris • Madrid
Capetown • Sydney • Tokyo • Singapore • Mexico City

Many of the designations used by manufacturers and sellers to distinguish their products are claimed as trademarks. Where those designations appear in this book, and Addison-Wesley was aware of a trademark claim, the designations have been printed with initial capital letters or in all capitals.

The author and publisher have taken care in the preparation of this book, but make no expressed or implied warranty of any kind and assume no responsibility for errors or omissions. No liability is assumed for incidental or consequential damages in connection with or arising out of the use of the information or programs contained herein.

The publisher offers discounts on this book when ordered in quantity for special sales. For more information, please contact:

Pearson Education Corporate Sales Division
One Lake Street
Upper Saddle River, NJ 07458
(800) 382-3419
corpsales@pearsontechgroup.com

Visit AW on the Web: www.awl.com/cseng/

Library of Congress Cataloging-in-Publication Data

Milewski, Bartosz.
  C++ in action : industrial-strength programming techniques / Bartosz Milewski.
     p. cm.
Includes bibliographical references and index.
  ISBN 0-201-69948-6
  1. C++ (Computer program language) I. Title.
  QA76.73.C153 M55 2001
  005.13'3—dc21

                                        00-054877

ISBN 0-201-69948-6
Text printed on recycled paper
1 2 3 4 5 6 7 8 9 10—CRS—0504030201
First printing, June 2001

Contents

Part 2: Techniques

Part 3: Windows

Part 4: Scaling Up

Appendices

To Pam

Preface

Why This Book?

Indeed, why YABOC++ (Yet Another Book on C++)? There are already many excellent books describing all imaginable aspects of C++. As far as learning the language and all kinds of programming tricks, the market is pretty much saturated. This book is not a language reference or a collection of clever tricks and patterns. This book is about *programming*.

Teaching programming is very different from teaching a language. A programmer is usually faced with a problem that he or she has to solve by writing a program—not with a language feature whose use he or she wants to illustrate. In this book I try to show, as much as possible, how to use the language as a tool to solve programming problems.

I center the presentation around various software projects. In each project I first describe a problem to be solved. Then I discuss what the program should do, what it should look like, and how it should react to user input. Based on that I build a scaffolding that captures the structure of the program without implementing its functionality. Finally, I implement the functionality, component by component.

But programming doesn't stop there. What follows in this book is a long series of code reviews each followed by a rewrite. "How can this be done better?" is a question a programmer asks himself or herself constantly. And then another question becomes more and more relevant, "How do I write code that can be easily revised?"

In programming, as in life, there is never a single way to do something. That's why being able to argue about various solutions is extremely important. Programmers who don't know how to argue end up bitter and frustrated. I remember my own frustrations when faced with an argument like, "Because it's always been done like this." In this book I argue a lot. I try to find the pros and cons of every solution, and in many cases I manage to settle on something I consider "elegant." However, I never use elegance as an objective criterion. I believe that one can always uncover some very practical arguments that are hidden behind the subjective impression of "elegance." An elegant solution in many cases catches a very good abstraction or generalization. It results in code that is easy to understand, modify, and debug.

Finally, in this book I emphasize the human factor in programming. My credo is "programs are written for programmers, not computers." Programmers want to write better programs not in order to make them more understandable to computers, but to make them more readable to humans. Program maintenance is impossible without program understanding. This may seem like an obvious thing to say, but many programmers overlook this self-evident truth.

Why You?

Who are you, the reader of this book? You might be a relative beginner who has picked up some programming but wants to learn C++. You might be a student who wants to supplement his or her college education. You might be a well-trained programmer who is trying to make a transition from the academic to the industrial environment. Or you might be a seasoned programmer in search of new ideas. I hope this book will satisfy you no matter which category you are in.

Why Me?

Why should I, of all people, write a book about programming in C++? You, the potential reader of this book, have the right to ask about my credentials, especially because I'm not a computer scientist by education.

I have a Ph.D. in theoretical physics—my thesis was about supersymmetric nonlinear sigma models. I used to be pretty good at calculating supersymmetric Feynman diagrams. Then, around 1986 I fell in love with computers, quit my postdoc position, and began programming.

A physicist is somebody who's in between a mathematician and an engineer. A physicist is used to constantly moving between theory and practice. He or she is not expected to believe in a theory unless it has proven itself in practice, and will always try to generalize every aspect of experience in order to find an underlying principle. And, most of all, a physicist is not supposed to take anything for granted.

Unlike a mathematician, a physicist has to be more realistic and care more about the *process* than the formal theory. The process in physics is performing calculations. In programming, it's software maintenance. So, since I'm a physicist, it should come as no surprise that this book focuses more on rewriting programs than on creating them.

I started teaching C++ and writing this book in 1994, while still working at Microsoft. I took a sabbatical to visit my alma mater, the University of Wroclaw in Poland. It turned out that I would visit that institution several more times, and each visit would prompt me to write a few more chapters. At some point I started converting the book to HTML and posting it on the web. Since C++ was still evolving, I had to rewrite many chapters over and over again. For example, when STL became part of the C++ standard library, I had to go back and rethink the implementation of most code examples in the book.

A lot of techniques described in this book were developed while I was working at Microsoft, designing and leading the development of the Index Server. After that, my new company, Reliable Software, turned out to be a great lab for testing new programming methodologies. All the techniques described in this book have been incorporated into our own products. In fact, we keep rewriting our code every time a new, better idea comes along.

Being a physicist makes me both a good programmer and a bad programmer. Good, because I constantly revise my techniques, search for new generalizations, and discuss every aspect of programming to death. Bad, because when I find a better solution I want to rewrite everything (I will try to convince you that it's actually not such a bad idea). Managers on my previous jobs always had problems with me, because I questioned every decision, convention, and custom. I hope the same qualities will make me a good writer.

If you, the reader, find a better way of doing something described in this book, please let me know, so I can start rewriting this book for the nth time. My e-mail address is bartosz@relisoft.com.

Acknowledgments

I am most grateful to my students from the University of Wroclaw and from the Digipen Institute of Technology, because the best way to learn something is to teach it. Thanks go to Professor Jerzy Lukierski, who invited me back to the university to teach computer science. I am also indebted to my coworkers at Microsoft and Reliable Software, who were the first to try and improve many techniques described in this book. My wife, Pam, besides supporting me in all my endeavors, helped me edit the first chapter of this book, making it so much easier to understand. Many thanks to editors from Addison-Wesley, especially Debbie Lafferty.

Introduction

I divided this book into four parts: Language, Techniques, Windows, and Scaling Up. Let me briefly describe the goal and the structure of each section.

Language

The first part of the book concentrates on teaching C++, the language of choice for general-purpose programming. But it is not your usual C++ tutorial.

For the beginner who doesn't know much about C or C++, it just introduces C++ as an object-oriented language (although C++ is more than just that). It doesn't concentrate on syntax or grammar; it shows how to express certain ideas in C++. It is like teaching a foreign language through conversation rather than through memorizing words and rules of grammar. (When I was teaching it to students, I called this part "Conversational C++.") After all, this is what the programmer needs: to be able to express ideas in the form of a program written in a particular language. When I learn a foreign language, the first thing I want to know is how to ask, "How much does it cost?" I don't need to learn the whole conjugation of the verb "to cost" in past, present, and future tenses. I just want to be able to walk into a store in a foreign country and buy something.

For a C programmer who doesn't know much about C++ (other than it's slow and cryptic—the popular myth in the C subculture), this is an exercise in unlearning C in order to effectively program in C++. Why should a C programmer unlearn C? Isn't C++ a superset of C? Unfortunately, yes! The decision to make C++ compatible with C was a purely practical marketing decision. And it worked! Instead of being a completely new product that would take decades to gain marketshare, it became "Version 3.1" of C. This is both good and bad. It's good because backward C compatibility allowed C++, and some elements of object-oriented programming, to quickly gain a foothold in the programming community. It's bad because it doesn't require anybody to change his or her programming habits.

Instead of having to rewrite existing code all at once, many companies were, and still are, able to gradually phase in C++. The usual path for such a phase-in is to introduce C++ as a "stricter" C. In principle, all C code could be recompiled as C++. In practice, C++ has somewhat stricter type checking, and the compiler is able to detect more bugs and issue more warnings. So recompiling C code using a C++ compiler is a good method of cleaning up existing code. The changes that have to be introduced into the source code at that stage are mostly bug fixes and stricter type enforcement. If the code was written in pre-ANSI C, the prototypes of all functions have to be generated. It is surprising how many bugs are detected during this "ANSI-zation" procedure. All that work is definitely worth the effort. A C compiler should only be used when a good C++ compiler is not available (a rare occurrence nowadays).

Once the C++ compiler becomes part of the programming environment, programmers sooner or later start learning new tricks and eventually develop some kind of C++ programming methodology, either on their own or by reading various self-help books. This is where the bad news starts. There is a subset of C++ (I call it the "C ghetto") where many former C programmers live. A lot of C programmers start hating C++ after a glimpse of the C ghetto. They don't realize that C++ has as many good uses as misuses.

I want to make one thing clear in the Introduction to this book. For a C-ghetto programmer this book should be a shock (I hope). It essentially says, "Whatever you did up to now was wrong," and "Kernighan and Ritchie are not gods." (Brian Kernighan and Dennis Ritchie are the creators of C and the authors of the influential book *The C Programming Language*.) I understand that the first, quite natural, reaction of such a programmer is to close the book immediately and ask for a refund. Please don't! The iconoclastic value of this book is not intended to hurt anybody's feelings; seeing that a different philosophy exists is supposed to prompt readers to rethink their beliefs.

For a C++ programmer, the Language section offers a new look at C++. It shows how to avoid the pitfalls of C++ and use the language according to the way it probably should have been designed in the first place. I would be lying if I said that C++ is a beautiful programming language. However, it is going to be, at least for some time, the most popular language for writing serious software. We might as well try to take advantage of its expressive power to write better software rather than use it to find so many more ways to hurt ourselves. For a C++ programmer, this part of the book should be mostly easy reading. And, although the constructs and the techniques introduced here are widely known, I have tried to show them from a different perspective. My overriding philosophy was to create a system that promotes a maintainable, human-readable coding style. That's why I took every opportunity not only to show various programming options, but also to explain why I considered some of them superior to others.

Finally, for a Java programmer, this book should be an eye-opener. It shows that, with some discipline, it is possible to write safe and robust code in C++. Everything Java can do, C++ can do too, and then much more. Plus, it can deliver unmatched performance.

But performance is not the only reason to stick with C++. The kind of elegant resource management that can be implemented in C++ is impossible in Java because of Java's reliance on garbage collection. In C++ you can have objects whose lifetimes are precisely defined by the scopes they live in. You are guaranteed that those objects will be destroyed when exiting those scopes. That's why you can entrust C++ objects with the care of such vital resources as semaphores, file handles, database transactions, and so on. Java objects have undefined life spans—they are deallocated only when the runtime decides to collect them. So the way you deal with resources in Java harks back to the old C exception paradigm, where the `finally` clause had to do all the painfully explicit garbage collection.

There are no "native" speakers of C++. When "speaking" C++, we all have some accent that reveals our programming background. Some of us have a strong C accent, some use Smalltalk-like expressions, others LISP. The goal of the Language section is to bring you as close as possible to being a native speaker of C++. Language is a tool for expressing ideas. Therefore my emphasis is not on syntax and grammar but on ways to express yourself. It is not "Here's a cute C++ construct, and this is how you can use it." Instead it's more like "Here's an idea. How do I express it in C++?" Initially the "ideas" take the form of simple sentences like "A star is a celestial body" or "A stack allows you to push and pop." Later the sentences are combined to form "paragraphs" and "chapters" describing the functionality of a software component. The various constructs of C++ are introduced as the need arises, in the context of a problem that needs to be solved.

Techniques

Writing good software requires much more than just knowing the language. First, the program doesn't execute in a vacuum. It has to interact with the computer. And interacting means going through the operating system. Without having some knowledge of the operating system, it is impossible to write serious programs. Second, we not only want to write programs that run—we want our programs to be small, fast, reliable, robust, and scalable. Third, we want to finish the development of a program in a sensible amount of time, and we want to be able to maintain and enhance it afterwards.

The goal of the second part of the book, Techniques, is to make possible the transition from "weekend programming" to "industrial-strength programming." I describe techniques that makes programming in C++ an order of magnitude more robust and maintainable. One of them, resource management, is centered on the idea of a program creating, acquiring, owning, and releasing various kinds of resources. For every resource, at any point in time during the execution of the program, there has to be a well-defined owner responsible for its release. This simple idea turns out to be extremely powerful in designing and maintaining complex software systems. Many a bug has been avoided or found and fixed using resource ownership analysis.

Resource management meshes very naturally with C++ exception handling. In fact, writing sensible C++ programs that use exceptions seems virtually impossible without the encapsulation of resources. So when should you use exceptions? What do they buy you? It depends on what your response is to the following simple question: Do you always check the result of new (or, for C programmers, the result of malloc)? This is a rhetorical question. Unless you are an exceptionally careful programmer, you don't! That means you are already using exceptions, whether you want to or not, because accessing a null pointer results in an exception called the General Protection Fault (GP-fault or Access Violation, as programmers call it). If your program is not exception-aware, it will die a horrible death upon such an exception. What's more, the operating system will shame you by putting up a message box, leaving no doubt that it was your application that was written using substandard programming practices (maybe not in so many words).

My point is that in order to write robust and reliable applications—and that's what this book is about—you will sooner or later have to use exceptions. Of course, there are other programming techniques that were, and still are, being successfully applied to the development of reasonably robust and reliable applications. None of them, however, comes close in terms of simplicity and maintainability to the proper use of C++ exceptions in combination with resource management.

Windows

As far as I know, this is the first book that gives Windows programming using modern C++ any serious consideration. The fact that the Windows API is a mess and that existing libraries don't make it much easier to write Windows applications doesn't mean that it's not an interesting topic. Encapsulating the Windows API into C++ classes, namespaces, and templates is a challenge that requires some deep rethinking of the whole Windows paradigm.

The main goal I set for myself in the Windows section was to find ways to make Windows programs easier to create and maintain—with very strong emphasis on *maintain.* I constantly asked myself questions like, "How easy should it be to add or modify a message handler? A new menu item? A command? A dialog box? And how to do it in such a way that the risk of a programmer's error is minimized?" Last, but not least, there was the concern of being able to port the library to other platforms, such as Linux.

The Windows section of the book reflects a work in progress. In fact, it's been a work in progress for many years. For each idea described in this section, there had been several ideas implemented, tested (often shipped in a product), and abandoned in favor of something even better.

Scaling Up

In this part of the book I touch on the large-scale aspects of software development. I concentrate on the dynamics of a software project, both from the point of view of management and planning as well as development strategies and tactics. I describe the dynamics of a project from its conception to shipment. I talk about documentation, the design process, and the development process. I do not, however, try to come up with ready-made recipes because they won't work—for exactly the reasons described below.

There is more to creating a successful application (or system) than just learning the language and mastering the techniques. Today's commercial software projects are among the most complex engineering undertakings of humankind. Programming is essentially the art of dealing with complexity. There have been many attempts to apply traditional engineering methods to control software's complexity. Modularization, software reuse, software ICs (integrated circuits), and so on—let's face it: in general, they don't work. They may be very helpful in providing low-level building blocks and libraries, but they can hardly be used as guiding principles in the design and implementation of complex software projects.

The simple reason is that there is very little repetition in a piece of software. Try to visually compare a printout of a program with, say, a picture of a microprocessor wafer. You'll see a lot of repetitive patterns in the layout of the microprocessor. Piecewise it resembles some kind of a high-tech crystal. A condensed view of a program, on the other hand, would look more like a high-tech fractal. You'd see a lot of similarities—large-scale patterns will resemble small-scale patterns. But you'd find very few exact matches or repetitions. Each little piece appears to be individually handcrafted. Repetitions in a program are not only unnecessary, but they contribute to a maintenance nightmare. If you modify, or bug-fix, one piece of code, you are supposed to find all the copies of this piece and change them as well.

This abhorrence of repetition is reflected in the production process of software. The proportion of research, design, and manufacturing in the software industry is different from other industries. Manufacturing, for instance, plays only a marginal role. Strictly speaking, electronic channels of distribution could make the manufacturing phase totally irrelevant. R&D plays a vital role, more so than in many other industries. But what really sets software development apart from other industries is the amount of design that goes into the product. Programming *is* designing. Designing, building prototypes, testing—over and over again. The software industry is the ultimate "design industry."

There is a popular unflattering stereotype of a programmer as a socially challenged nerd. Somebody who works alone at night, subsisting on Twinkies, avoiding direct eye contact, and caring very little about personal hygiene. I've known programmers like that, and I'm sure there are still some around. However, most specimens of this old culture became extinct, and for a good reason. Progress in hardware and software makes it impossible to produce any reasonably useful and reliable program while working in isolation. Teamwork is essential to software development.

Dividing the work and coordinating the development effort of a team is always a big challenge. In traditional industries, members of the team know (at least in theory) what they are doing. They know the routine. They are performing a synchronized dance and they know the steps and hear the music. In the software industry, team members improvise steps as they go and, at the same time, compose the music for the rest of the team.

I advocate a change of emphasis in software development. Instead of the usual idea that *"Programs are written for computers,"* I will try to convince you that *"Programs are written for programmers."* This statement is in fact the premise of this whole book. You can't develop industrial-strength software if you don't treat your code as a publication for other programmers to read, understand, and modify. You don't want your "code" to be an exercise in cryptography. The computer can compile and run your program, but only another human being—a fellow programmer— can understand its *meaning*. And it is crucial that they can do it with minimal effort, because, without that understanding, it's impossible to develop and maintain software.

How to Use This Book

You can't learn programming without hands-on experience. This is why the CD-ROM that accompanies this book contains source code and some software to get you started. If you have one of the recommended compilers, you'll be able to build and run all the programs described in this book. Some examples, especially in the beginning, are provided as a set of files in their own directories. You can just copy them from the CD-ROM to your disk and compile them. Most examples, however, require a version control system.

Version Control System

Most of the coding examples in this book have the form of gradual refinements of essentially one software project. The best way to present a progression of versions is to use a version control system (VCS). A VCS is one of the basic instruments of software development. It lets you keep track of your changes, restore old versions, and, most importantly, collaborate with other programmers.

A complimentary copy, courtesy of Reliable Software, of a VCS called Code Co-op is on the CD-ROM accompanying this book. Since the VCS is a commercial product, you would normally have to buy a license to use it. However, you don't need a license to be an "observer" in a project, and it's all you need to play with the projects for this book.

Code Co-op has some unique features that make it particularly appropriate for this book. During installation of Code Co-op, configure your machine as *stand-alone*. You will be "collaborating" with me, the author, on several software projects. The collaboration will be one-sided: I developed the projects, you'll get copies of synchronization scripts, each describing a set of code changes.

Notice that the installation of Code Co-op does not replace any DLLs in your system. After you run uninstall, there will be no trace of Code Co-op on your computer.

Compiler

At the time of writing this book there weren't many standard-compliant C++ compilers with a decent IDE (Interactive Development Environment). I have tested all code samples with Metrowerks CodeWarrior 6.0 and Microsoft Visual C++ 7.0 beta one (the code does not work with earlier versions of VC++).

I have provided project files for both compilers. If you're using CodeWarrior, use the files with the extension .mcp as your project files. If you're using VC++ 7.0, use the .vcproj files instead.

Once you've installed one of these compilers, double-click on a project file to open it. You can then browse through source files and build the project (use the Build button). After the project is built, you can run the resulting executable (use the Run button). Both of these IDEs have built-in debuggers that might not only help in debugging programs, but can also be used to trace (single-step) through code.

Code Samples

world1 When source code is available for a programming example described in the book, there is a margin note that specifies the code's location on the CD-ROM. For example, when you see a margin note *world1*, look for the subdirectory world1 of the directory src on the CD-ROM (you can get there by clicking the code-sample link on the CD-ROM's splash screen). Copy the contents of this directory to your hard disk, build it, and run it.

Project Calculator The examples of incremental development are given in the form of Code Co-op projects. You start a new project when you see a margin note specifying a project name. For example, when you see a note *Project Calculator*, start the CD-ROM and select project Calculator from the list that appears on the splash screen. You will be enlisted in the project and Code Co-op will show you the initial state of the project. You can view the contents of files by double-clicking on them in the *Files Area*.

Script 1 In Code Co-op's Mailbox Area you'll see a number of synchronization scripts that correspond to incremental changes. Each script has a number. When you see a margin note specifying a script number, *unpack* the corresponding script. For example, when you see a note *Script 1*, and you are in the middle of the project Calculator, go to the Code Co-op's Mailbox Area and unpack the script titled "1. Implemented Scanner." (This script will be marked as *Next*. After you've unpacked script 1, script 2 will be marked *Next* for unpacking, and so on.) Unpacking is done by pressing the button with an upside-down envelope.

After you've unpacked a script, you can visually review the changes it has made to the project. You will see a list of changed files in Code Co-op's *Synch Area*. When you double-click on such a file, you'll see a differential view with all the changes highlighted. After you are done reviewing, *accept* the synch by clicking on the "accept changes in all files" button in the *Synch Area*.

If you want to experiment with a given version of a project, you can export this version's files to a separate directory on your hard disk and modify them. Go to the *History Area* of Code Co-op, select the version you want to export (it may be the current version) and select *Export Version* from the *Selection* menu.

All this and more is described in detail in Code Co-op's help available through its Help menu.

Typeface Conventions

All code samples in the book are printed in fixed-pitch font:

```
int main () {}
```

Some elements in code samples are emphazised in bold:

```
World smallWorld;
```

These are usually newly added elements that are discussed in the surrounding text.

Names of classes, variables or functions (for example `World`, `smallWorld`, `main`) that appear in the main text are also printed in fixed font. The same font is used for file names, for example, `world.cpp`.

Part 1

Language

This part of the book is a C++ tutorial. It teaches the basics of the language, taking the reader from simple examples up to the development of a self-contained program. This program, a symbolic calculator, is used as the main software project throughout the book.

I tried to make this tutorial interesting not only for novices, but also for experienced programmers. The tutorial dives directly into object-oriented programming and language features specific to C++ (classes, constructors, references, and so on). In many cases I try to explain not only how to program, but also how *not* to program. Examples of the latter are very relevant in the teaching of such an eclectic language as C++.

Chapter 1
Objects and Scopes

What is the most important thing in the universe? Is it matter? It seems like everything is built from matter—galaxies, stars, planets, houses, cars, and even us, programmers. But what is matter without energy? The universe would be dead without it. Energy is the source of change, movement, and life. Furthermore, what are matter and energy without space and time? We need space into which matter can be put, and we need time to see matter change.

Programming is like creating universes. We need matter: data structures, objects, and variables. Objects would be dead without the code that operates on them. So we need energy, the lifeforce of the program, in the form of executable code. Objects need space to be put into so they can relate to each other. Finally, lines of code need time in which to be executed.

The space-time of the program is described by scopes. An object lives and dies by its scope. Lines of executable code operate within scopes. Scopes provide the structure to the program. And ultimately programming is about structure.

1.1 Global Scope

Class definition, object definition, constructor, destructor, output stream, include, main.

There is an old tradition in teaching C, dating back to Kernighan and Ritchie (*The C Programming Language*), to have the first program print the greeting `Hello World!` It is only appropriate that our first C++ program should respond to this greeting. The way to do it, of course, is to create "the World" and let it speak for itself.

The following program does just that, but it also serves as a metaphor for C++ programming. Every C++ program is a world unto itself. The world is a play and we define the characters in that play and let them interact. This program is, in a sense, "the mother of all C++ programs." It contains just one player, the World, and lets us witness its creation and destruction. The World interacts with us by printing messages on the computer screen. It prints Hello! when it is created, and Goodbye! when it vanishes. So here we go! Have a look at the listing of this short program and read the line-by-line explanation.

```cpp
#include <iostream>

class World
{
public:
  World ()  { std::cout << "Hello!\n"; }
  ~World () { std::cout << "Goodbye!\n"; }
};
World TheWorld;

int main () {}
```

Table 1.1 identifies the parts of the program.

Program part	Program text
include directive	`#include <iostream>`

class definition	`class World`
	`{`
	`public:`
	` World () { std::cout << "Hello!\n";}`
	`~World () { std::cout << "Goodbye!\n";}`
	`};`

object definition	`World TheWorld;`
main function	`int main () {}`

Table 1.1 Parts of the program

Let's start from the end, from main, and work our way backwards. Every C++ program has to have the main function, even if, as in this particular program, it does nothing.

You probably have a good idea of what a function is in mathematics. A function takes an argument (or arguments) and returns a value. A *sine* function takes an angle and returns the ratio of the length of two sides of a triangle built on this angle. For instance, $\sin(\pi/4)$ returns 0.7071 (or, more precisely, sqrt (2)/2). Similarly, in C++, a function takes zero or more arguments and returns a value. Arguments are enclosed in parentheses; if a function takes no arguments, the parentheses are empty. In this case, main takes no arguments.

Different functions return different *types* of values. A sine returns a *real* number, but a square root might return a *complex* number (e.g., a square root of minus one is equal to *i*, the imaginary unit). In logic, the function *not (p)* returns Boolean true if *p* is false and Boolean false if *p* is true. In C++, a function's definition must specify the *type* of the return value. We'll talk about various types later, but for now it's sufficient to say that `int` is one of the built-in types representing an integer (a whole number). In C++, function `main` must always return a value of type `int`.

A function's *definition* not only describes the arguments and the type of the return value, it also contains a prescription for calculating this value. This prescription is always enclosed within a pair of braces: { and } (also called *curly* braces). In our case there is *nothing* between the braces following `main ()`. The prescription is empty—`main` doesn't do anything in this program. Usually a function that promises to return an `int` would *have* to give some prescription of how to calculate this `int` (or simply set its value to some arbitrary number). The special function `main` is an exception to this rule. If the programmer doesn't specify what it should return, it is understood that it returns zero. (The meaning of this particular return value is a separate matter that will be discussed later.)

The formatting of a C++ program is more a matter of convention than language requirements. For example, I could have written the definition of `main` with a minimum number of spaces:

```
int main(){}
```

(notice there aren't any spaces between `main` and the parentheses and between the parentheses and the braces), or split it on many lines:

```
int
main
(
)
{
}
```

I didn't do either of these things, because formatting makes a big difference in readability. In this book I try to stick to formatting conventions that are widely accepted among C++ programmers (although they are far from universal).

So why do we need `main` in this program if it does absolutely nothing? It's because the C++ program execution must always go through three stages: pre-main, `main`, and post-main. The "real work" is supposed to be done in `main`. However, the pre-main and post-main parts may be quite productive, as we will see shortly.

The line:

```
World TheWorld;
```

defines `TheWorld` as an *object* of the class `World`. You can also say that `TheWorld` is an *instance* of class `World`. Notice that a definition of an object is followed by a semicolon.

Objects are the main actors in an object-oriented program and, in fact, this line is central to this whole program. If you showed this program to a C programmer and asked what it does, the programmer would say "Nothing!" That's because a C programmer looks at `main` and sees nothing there. The trained eye of a C++ programmer will spot the global definition of `TheWorld` and will say "Ha! It prints 'Hello!' and 'Goodbye!' " When I say *global,* I mean "outside of any braces." All this space outside of the braces is considered the *global scope* (see Figure 1.1).

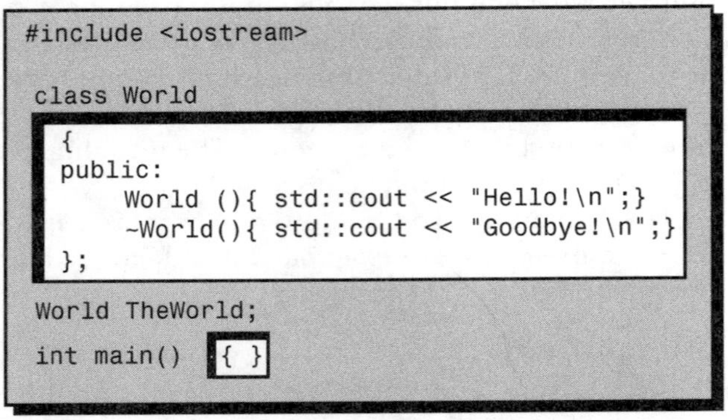

```
#include <iostream>

class World

{
public:
    World (){ std::cout << "Hello!\n";}
    ~World(){ std::cout << "Goodbye!\n";}
};

World TheWorld;

int main() { }
```

Figure 1.1 The global scope is everything outside of the braces (shaded area)

Next, following our inverted order of analysis, we'll concentrate on the definition of the class `World`. A *class* is a type defined by the programmer. We've already seen a type, `int`, that is built into the language. `World` is not a built-in type, so our program has to *define* it.

The definition of `World` is tucked inside the braces and is followed by a semicolon. The keyword `public` means that we have nothing to hide (keywords are special reserved words that are part of the C++ language—they are emphasized in bold in code examples throughout this book). Later we'll learn about the importance of data hiding, but for now let's keep everything in the open.

The first thing inside the class definition is the *constructor.*

```
World () { std::cout << "Hello!\n"; }
```

A constructor is a piece of code that is executed every time an object of this particular class is created. If you create multiple objects of the same class, the constructor will be called multiple times. The constructor looks almost like a function, except that it doesn't have a return type in front of it. A constructor's name is always the same as the name of the class. The constructor can take arguments, but in this example it doesn't—the parentheses following it are empty. This constructor actually *does* something—there is something between the braces that follow it. They contain the command

```
std::cout << "Hello!\n";
```

which means to send the string `"Hello!\n"` to the object `std::cout`. (Notice a semi-colon after a command.) The predefined object `std::cout` represents the *standard output,* presumably the computer's screen, and it prints whatever it is sent. A literal string, like `"Hello!/N"` is always enclosed in double quotation marks. The `\n` (back-slash n) at the end of the string means "print a newline," so the printout following it will start on a new line.

Next in the class definition is the *destructor,* which always has the same name as the class but is preceded by ~ (a tilde). The destructor is executed every time an object of this particular class is destroyed. If multiple objects of the same class have to be destroyed, the destructor is called multiple times. Even though a destructor looks somewhat like a function (note, however, that it doesn't have a return type in front of it), it never takes any arguments—the parentheses following a destructor's name are always empty. The destructor of `World` does something. It prints the string `"Goodbye!\n"`.

Finally, at the top of the file, we have an *include* directive:

```
#include <iostream>
```

This include directive tells the compiler to find the file called `iostream` and in-clude it right there. Strictly speaking, "standard" headers such as `iostream` don't have to be implemented as files—the compiler may just generate the appropriate code immediately. If your compiler is properly installed, it will find the file in one of the standard places where it's supposed to look. The compiler needs this file to find out what `std::cout` is and what can be done to it. This object (of the class `iostream`) is part of the C++ standard library, not part of the language. We'll see more uses of `std::cout` later.

The order in which we have analyzed this program was far from arbitrary. It is called *top-down* and is considered the correct way of looking at and analyzing pro-grams (and writing them, too). In a top-down approach you start with the most general, highest-level things and slowly descend into more specific, lower-level details.

Now, let's analyze what happens during the execution of our program.

The stage is set; the main player is a global object, `TheWorld`. Its character is defined by the class `World`. The class definition tells us that every `World` does some-thing when it is constructed and does something when it is destroyed. The play starts. Here's what happens:

- Pre-`main`: All global objects are constructed. In our case the constructor of `TheWorld` is executed and it prints `"Hello!"` on the screen.

- The `main` function is executed. In our case it does absolutely nothing (except for returning this mysterious `int`).
- Post-main: All global objects are destroyed. In our case the destructor of `TheWorld` is executed and it prints `"Goodbye!"`

That's it! Your first object-oriented C++ program.

Well, not really. If programming was really that simple, everybody would be a programmer. In order to make it difficult, there are a whole lot of magical incantations that have to be typed into the computer to make the program run. It's these incantations that provide our job security—see the sidebar.

<div markdown="1" style="border:1px solid">

This is a good time to try to compile and run your first C++ program. You'll find the source code and the necessary project files in the directory `src\world1` on the CD-ROM. Copy this directory to your hard drive to work with it. Reread the tips at the end of the Introduction on how to use the compiler. Every time there is source code available for a particular example on the CD-ROM, a note in the margin specifies the `src` subdirectory where you can find it.

One more hint. If the compiler refuses to compile your program (for instance, if you changed the source code or if you used a nonstandard-compliant compiler), look at its output. It is supposed to tell you the location and the errors it found. If you understand these error messages, you are probably an experienced programmer already. If you don't, do not despair. Only experienced programmers can understand them.

Here are some troubleshooting tips for users of nonstandard-compliant compilers:

- Your compiler complains (issues a warning) that there's a return statement missing in your `main`. Your compiler is wrong, but you might appease it by putting `return 0;` between the braces.

- Your compiler can't find the header file `iostream`. You have a very old compiler that doesn't support the new standard library. Try changing `iostream` to `iostream.h` and remove the `std::` prefixes in front of `cout`. This is a temporary fix; you need to upgrade your compiler.

- Your program prints `Hello!`, but doesn't print `Goodbye!` You have a buggy version of the standard library (unfortunately, version 6.0 of the Microsoft VC++ compiler had this flaw). Fortunately, most examples in this book don't require this feature, so don't worry too much.

</div>

world1

In most environments, after you've successfully built your program, you can single-step through it under a debugger. You'll be able to see how each statement is executed and how it changes the state of the program. Consult your compiler's documentation to find out how to use the debugger.

To summarize, we have introduced a class and an object. Think of a class as a blueprint for an object. It describes the object's structure and behavior—in our case, what happens when the object is constructed and destroyed. Once you have a blueprint, you can create objects that are based on it.

1.2   Local Scope

Scope of main, passing arguments to constructors, integer type. Private data members, initialization, embedded local scopes, the for *loop.*

world2   Global scope is anything outside of braces. It is activated (that is, global objects are constructed) before main is executed. It is deactivated (global objects are destroyed) after main is finished. Local scopes, on the other hand, are enclosed in braces (though there are some exceptions, which we'll come to soon).

Local scope is activated when the flow of the program enters it, and deactivated when the flow leaves it. Objects in local scope are constructed whenever their definition is encountered by the flow of execution, and destroyed when the local scope is exited. Such objects are also called *automatic* (because they are automatically created and destroyed), or *stack* objects (because they occupy memory that is called the program's stack).

In our first example of local scope, we will create a local World called smallWorld within the scope of main.

```
int main()
{
    World smallWorld;
    std::cout << "Hello from main!\n";
}
```

Table 1.2 shows the printouts and their sources. The smallWorld object is constructed right after entering main—that's when "Hello!" is printed by its constructor. (This is the second "Hello!," the first one was printed during the construction of the global object TheWorld.)

Printout	Source
Hello!	constructor of **TheWorld**
Hello!	constructor of **smallWorld**
Hello from main!	output in **main**
Goodbye!	destructor of **smallWorld**
Goodbye!	destructor of **TheWorld**

Table 1.2 The printouts and their sources

Next, main prints the message Hello from main! Finally, right before exiting the scope of main, the smallWorld object is destroyed. That's when its destructor prints Goodbye!

The global TheWorld is destroyed after main and it prints another Goodbye!

world3   I will make another modification to our original program. I'll make the constructor of World take an integer (the predefined type int) as an argument. This argument, also called a *formal parameter,* will serve as an identifier for the particular object being created. Inside the constructor of World, this argument, i, will be sent to the standard output (the screen).

```cpp
#include <iostream>

class World
{
public:
  World (int i)
  {
    std::cout << "Hello from" << i << ".\n";
  }
  ~World ()
  {
    std::cout << "Goodbye!\n";
  }
};

World TheWorld (1);

int main()
{
  World smallWorld (2);
  std::cout << "Hello from main!\n";
}
```

Notice how clever the std::cout object is. It accepts strings of characters and prints them as strings, and it accepts integers and prints them as numbers. And, as you can see, it's possible to chain arguments to std::cout one after another, using multiple << signs.

Since the constructor of World now expects an argument, we have to provide it when we create each object of this class. Here we just specify the values in parentheses, after the name of the object being created.

```cpp
World TheWorld (1);
```

It looks a little like a function call, because, in a sense, we *are* calling the constructor—a *function call* consists of the name of the particular function followed by a value (or list of values) in parentheses. These values are sent to the function as its arguments. Since we are passing 1 to the constructor of TheWorld, it will print Hello from 1. (see Table 1.3).

There's still something missing. Looking at the printout we can tell which object printed the first Hello and which printed the second one, but we still can't

Printout	Source
Hello from 1.	constructor of **TheWorld**
Hello from 2.	constructor of **smallWorld**
Hello from main!	output in **main**
Goodbye!	destructor of **smallWorld**
Goodbye!	destructor of **TheWorld**

Table 1.3 The printouts and their sources

tell which object printed the first Goodbye! and which printed the second one. If the numbers passed to the constructors identify our objects, these objects still aren't able to remember their identity. In the destructor, we can't just print the value of i, because i doesn't exist any more. The scope of i, the formal parameter of the constructor, ends at the closing brace of the constructor.

Before we fix that, let me digress philosophically. Here we are talking about object-oriented programming and I haven't even defined what I mean by an object. Now is a good time to do that, so here we go:

Definition: An object is something that has an identity.

If you can think of something that doesn't have an identity, it's not an object. Beauty is not an object. But if you could say "this beauty is different from the one over there," you would give the two beauties their identities and they would become objects. We sometimes define classes that have non-object names. That just means that we give an old name a new "objectified" meaning. In general, though, using non-object names is not such a great idea. If possible, you should name your objects using *countable nouns* (these are nouns in front of which you can put the indefinite articles *a* or *an*, as in "a world," "a stack," "an integer," and so on).

world4   I didn't say that our World objects didn't have an identity, because they did. They just weren't aware of it. Once we give them memory, they'll be able to remember who they are.

```cpp
#include <iostream>

class World
{
public:
  World (int id)
    : _identifier (id)
  {
    std::cout << "Hello from " << _identifier << ".\n";
  }
  ~World ()
  {
```

```
        std::cout << "Goodbye from " << _identifier << ".\n";
    }
private:
    const int _identifier;
};

World TheWorld (1);

int main ()
{
    World smallWorld (2);
    for (int i = 3; i < 6; ++i)
    {
        World aWorld (i);
    }
    World oneMoreWorld (6);
}
```

Several new things require explanation. Let's do it top-down. In main we create our local World, called smallWorld, with an argument, the object's ID, equal to 2 (but this time World will remember the argument until it's destroyed).

Next we have a for loop.

```
for (int i = 3; i < 6; ++i)
{
    World aWorld (i);
}
```

The meaning of this particular for loop is the following: For integer i starting from 3, as long as it's less than 6, incremented in steps of one after each iteration (the expression ++i increments i, by adding one to its value), do this:

1. Open the scope of the loop body.
2. Define a World called aWorld (with an ID equal to the current value of i).
3. Close the scope of the loop body.

> More precisely, the program first executes the initialization part of the loop header, int i = 3. Then it performs the test i < 6, and since it's true, it will execute the body of the loop (as explained above). Then it performs the increment part, ++i, checks the condition i < 6 again, and so on. When the increment brings i up to 6, the condition will be false and the loop will terminate.

Since each iteration opens and closes the scope of the loop's body, the constructor and destructor of aWorld are both called each time. We'll see this sequence of printouts:

```
Hello from 3.
Goodbye from 3.
Hello from 4.
Goodbye from 4.
Hello from 5.
Goodbye from 5.
```

After the loop completes its iterations, the World called oneMoreWorld is defined. It has the ID of 6, so we'll see:

```
Hello from 6.
Goodbye from 6.
```

The braces delimiting the body of the for loop can be omitted because the loop consists of a single statement (this is the exception I mentioned before). So we could have written the loop as shown in Figure 1.2 and the program would execute exactly the same way.

```
for (int i = 3; i < 6; ++i)
    World aWorld (i) ;
```

Figure 1.2 A scope without braces (shaded area)

The body of the for loop forms a separate scope within the scope of main. When the program enters this scope, the objects from the outer scope(s) are not destroyed. In fact, if there is no name conflict, they are still visible and accessible.

> There would be a name conflict if smallWorld were called aWorld, because that would conflict with the aWorld inside the for loop. It would be okay from the point of view of C++; only the outer aWorld would be temporarily inaccessible inside the for loop. The name of the outer aWorld would be *hidden* by the name of the inner aWorld. We'll see later what *accessible* means.

What is the scope of the variable i that is defined in the header of the for loop?

```
for (int i = 3; i < 6; ++i)
{
    World aWorld (i);
}
```

This is actually a nontrivial question. It used to be, in the older versions of C++, that its scope would extend beyond the scope of the loop. This is no longer true (although many compilers still support the incorrect interpretation). The scope of a variable defined in the head of a loop is that of the loop itself. Notice that it's not the same as the scope of the *body* of the loop. Objects defined in the body of the loop are reconstructed from scratch on every iteration. The variables defined in the head are initialized once, at loop entry. However, when you exit the loop, neither is accessible.

You don't need an excuse of a for loop to introduce a local subscope. A subscope is created by placing a matching pair of braces virtually anywhere inside an existing local scope. Objects defined in such a scope are destroyed when the flow of control exits it. (Consider this when solving Exercise 1.)

The class World has a *data member*, _identifier.

```
private:
    const int _identifier;
```

Its type is int and it's const and private. Why is it private? It's something I mentioned before, called *data hiding*. It means that today the private part of the class is implemented like this, but tomorrow—who knows? Maybe _identifier will be an int, maybe a string, or maybe it won't be there at all. The client of this class shouldn't care. If _identifier wasn't private, it could end up like one of those hidden functions in MS-DOS that everybody knew about. Client applications started using them and the developers of MS-DOS had to keep them forever for compatibility.

Not so in our World! The compiler will make sure that nobody, except the class World itself, has access to its private members. In C++, a class definition is divided into public and private sections. The *client* of the class, that is, the programmer who creates and interacts with objects of this class, can only use whatever is defined in the public section of the class definition. The *implementor* of the class, on the other hand, can use both the public and private sections in the implementation of the class. It's a very important distinction between the client and the implementor. We'll see examples of it throughout this book.

If the label public is omitted, the compiler defaults to private.[1] If you get the compilation error "Cannot access private members," you probably forgot to specify the public section in your class definition. Public and private sections can be interspersed in any order, although I try to follow the convention of starting a class with the public section and putting the private section at the end. After all, it's the public section that the client is interested in, so we'll try to make it as visible as possible.

The keyword const means that nobody can change the value of _identifier during the lifetime of the object. It is physically (or at least "compilatorily") impossible. But even a const variable has to be initialized once. So the compiler provides

---

1. There is one more access specifier, protected, in C++. Its use will make sense when we discuss inheritance (Chapter 4).

just one little window of opportunity when we can (and in fact *have to*) initialize a
const data member. It is in the *preamble* to the constructor. Not even in the body of
the constructor—only in the preamble itself—can we initialize a const data member.

The preamble is the part of the constructor that starts with a colon and contains a comma-separated list of data members, each followed by its initializers in
parentheses. The preamble _identifier is initialized with the value of id—the
formal parameter of the constructor.

```
World (int id)
 : _identifier (id)
{
    std::cout << "Hello from " << _identifier << ".\n";
}
```

Once _identifier is initialized, its value for the particular instance of World
never changes (later we'll learn how non-const data members can be modified).
When the destructor of this object is called, it will print the value that was passed
to it in the constructor. So when we see Goodbye from 1., we'll know that it's the
end of TheWorld, which was constructed with the ID of 1, as opposed to the end of
one of any of the aWorlds.

Why does _identifier have an underscore in front of it? It's a convention. In
this book the names of all private data members will start with an underscore followed by a lowercase letter (warning: identifiers that start with an underscore and
an *uppercase* letter are reserved for use by the libraries, so don't use them in your
code). Once you get used to this convention, it will help readability. Of course, you
can use your own convention instead. In fact, everybody can create their own conventions (which is exactly what happens all the time).

Speaking of conventions—I absolutely insist on the brace-positioning convention, and for a good reason: In the style of programming that this book promotes, scopes play a central role. It is of paramount importance for the
readability of code to make scopes stand out graphically. Therefore:

**The opening brace of any scope should be vertically aligned with the
closing brace of that scope.**

The screen and printer paper-saving convention of yesteryear

```
for (int i = 3; i < 6; ++i) {
  World aWorld (i);
}
```

is declared harmful to program maintainability.

To summarize, objects may have their own memory, or state. The data members that store the state are preferably kept private. They are best initialized in the preamble to the constructor, so that the object is in a consistent state immediately after its birth. The for *loop creates its own scope. This scope is entered and exited during every loop iteration (this is why you see all these "Goodbye from 3, 4, 5" messages).*

1.3   Embedded Objects

Embeddings, initialization of embeddings, order of construction/destruction.

world5   We've seen data members of the type int—one of the built-in types. The beauty of C++ is that it makes virtually no distinction between built-in types and the ones defined by the programmer. When a data member of some class is a user-defined type, it is called an *embedded object.* In the following example Matter is embedded in World (I will give matter identity, for example, by saying *this* matter is much more stable than *that* in a neighboring universe.) Another way to talk about it is to say World *contains* Matter.

```cpp
#include <iostream>

class Matter
{
public:
  Matter (int id)
    : _identifier (id)
  {
    std::cout << "  Matter for " << _identifier
              << " created\n";
  }
  ~Matter ()
  {
    std::cout << " Matter in " << _identifier
              << " annihilated\n";
  }
private:
  const int _identifier;
};

class World
{
public:
  World (int id)
    : _identifier (id),
      _matter (_identifier) // Initializing embeddings
  {
    std::cout << "Hello from world"
              << _identifier << ".\n";
```

```
    }

  ~World ()
  {
    std::cout << "Goodbye from world " << _identifier << ".\n";
  }
private:
  const int      _identifier;
  const Matter   _matter; // Embedded object of type Matter
};

World TheUniverse (1);

int main ()
{
  World smallWorld (2);
}
```

What's interesting in this example is the preamble to the constructor of World.

```
World (int id)
  : _identifier (id), _matter (_identifier)
```

It first initializes the _identifier and then _matter. Initializing an object means calling its constructor. The constructor of Matter requires an integer, and that's what we are passing it. We made _matter const for the same reason we made _identifier const. It is never changed during the lifetime of the World. It is initialized in the preamble and never changed or even accessed by anybody.

By the way, // (the double slash) is used for comments. The compiler ignores everything that follows // until the end of line.

And now for the surprise: The order of initialization has *nothing to do* with the order of the initializers in the preamble. In fact, if the embedded object's constructor doesn't require any arguments, it can be omitted from the preamble completely. If no explicit initializations are required, the whole preamble may be omitted. Instead, the rule of initialization is:

Data members are initialized in the order in which they appear in the class definition.

Since _identifier appears before _matter in the definition of World, it will be initialized first. That's why we could use its value in the construction of _matter. The order of embeddings in C++ is as important as the order of statements.

Embedded objects are destroyed in the reverse order of their construction. The object that was constructed last will be destroyed first, and so on. In object-oriented parlance, object embedding is called the "has-a" relationship, e.g., a World has a Matter (remember, we have objectified matter). This relationship is illustrated in Figure 1.3.

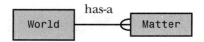

Figure 1.3 Graphical representation of the has-a relationship

To summarize, programmer-defined object types can be embedded as data members in other classes. The constructors for these embedded objects are called before the body of the object's constructor is executed. (Conceptually you can visualize them as being called in the preamble.) If these constructors need arguments, they must be initialized in the preamble. The order of construction is determined by the order of the embedded objects. The embedded objects are destroyed in the reverse order of their construction.

1.4   Inheritance

Public inheritance, initialization of the base class, order of construction/destruction, type double.

Another important relationship between objects is the "is-a" relationship. When we say that a star is a celestial body, we mean that a star has all the properties of a celestial body, and maybe some others, specific to a star. In C++ this relationship is expressed by inheritance. We can say class `Star` inherits from class `CelestialBody`, or that `CelestialBody` is the base class of `Star` (see Figure 1.4).

world6   Consider the following:

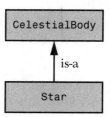

Figure 1.4 Graphical representation of the is-a relationship between objects

```cpp
#include <iostream>
class CelestialBody
{
public:
  CelestialBody (double mass)
    : _mass (mass)
  {
    std::cout << "Creating celestial body of mass "
              << _mass << "\n";
  }
  ~CelestialBody ()
  {
    std::cout << "Destroying celestial body of mass "
              << _mass << "\n";
  }
private:
  const double _mass;
};

class Star: public CelestialBody // Star is a CelestialBody
{
public:
  Star (double mass, double brightness)
    : CelestialBody (mass),
    _brightness (brightness)
  {
    std::cout << "Creating a star of brightness "
              << _brightness << "\n";
  }
  ~Star ()
  {
    std::cout << "Destroying a star of brightness "
              << _brightness << "\n";
  }
private:
  const double _brightness;
};

int main ()
{
  std::cout << "  Entering main.\n";
  Star aStar (1234.5, 0.1);
  std::cout << "  Exiting main.\n";
}
```

The line

```cpp
class Star: public CelestialBody
```

tells the compiler that Star *inherits* everything from CelestialBody. In particular, since CelestialBody has _mass, Star will have _mass too.

CelestialBody has a constructor that requires an argument of the type double, which is a built-in type corresponding to a real number. Its full name is double-precision floating-point number, which means that it has a (floating) decimal point and that it's stored with twice as many significant digits as its single-precision counterpart called `float`. (Notice that our clever object `std::cout` has no problem printing `doubles`.)

In the preamble to the constructor of `Star`, we have to pass the argument to the constructor of `CelestialBody`. Here's how we do it—we invoke the base constructor using the name of its class:

```
Star (double mass, double brightness)
    :CelestialBody (mass), _brightness (brightness)
```

The order of construction is very important.

First the base class is fully constructed, then the derived class.

The construction of the derived class proceeds in the usual order: first the embeddings, then the explicit code in the constructor. Again, the order in the preamble is meaningless, and if there are no explicit initializations the whole thing may be omitted. The order of destruction is again the reverse of the order of construction. In particular, the derived class destructor is called first, followed by the destructor of the base class.

1.5   Member Functions and Interfaces

Input stream, member functions (methods), return values, interfaces, functions returning void.

So far we have been constructing and destroying objects. What else can we do to an object? We can't access its private data members, because the compiler won't let us. Only the object itself (as specified in its class definition) can make a decision to expose some of its behavior or contents. Behavior is exposed via *member functions*, also called *methods*. If a member function is public, it can be called from any place in your program.

input1   Our first member function, GetValue, returns an `int`. From the function's implementation we can see that the returned value is the private data member _num. (Now we know what it means to have access to an object: it means to be able to invoke its member functions.)

Here, the object num of the type InputNum is defined in the scope of main, and that's where we can access it. And access it we do, calling num.GetValue(). You could also say we invoke the method GetValue() on the object num, or that we are getting the value of object num. In Smalltalk-speak, we send the *message* GetValue to the object num. What we are getting back is an `int`, which we print immediately using our old friend std::cout.

```
#include <iostream>
class InputNum
{
```

```
public:
  InputNum ()
  {
    std::cout << "Enter number ";
    std::cin >> _num;
  }

  int GetValue () const { return _num; }
private:
  int _num;
};
int main()
{
  InputNum num;
  std::cout << "The value is" << num.GetValue() << "\n";
}
```

Let me clarify the syntax. The type of the return value is always specified in front of the member function definition. A method that is supposed to return something must have a return statement at the end. (Later we'll see that a return from the middle is possible too.) If a function is *not* supposed to return anything, we must specify the return type as void.

In all our previous examples, main was declared to return an int, but in fact it had no return statement. That's because main is special, and the compiler is supposed to provide the missing return. By convention, main is expected to return 0 if the program was successful—and that's the implicit return value generated by the compiler. In the case of an error, you are supposed to return an "error level" from main—a nonzero integer whose interpretation is program-dependent.

"Return to who?" you might ask. To whoever executed the program. For instance, if you run your program from a batch file, you can check for the error level using a batch command like this:

```
if not errorlevel 1 goto end
```

When executing a program from the command line (the DOS box), you might follow its name with a list of arguments. They can be retrieved by your program in main. We'll return to this issue when we learn about pointers.

Let's talk about the keyword const following the declaration of the method GetValue.

```
int GetValue () const
```

This means that the method does not change the object's state. The compiler will not allow this method to perform assignment, increment, or decrement of any data member, or permit this method to call any nonconstant methods of that class. Moreover, only methods declared const can be called on a const object.

So far we've seen a const object _matter inside World. If Matter had a const method, like GetValue, it could be called in the context of the object _matter (that is, _matter.GetValue() would compile). We'll see examples of that later.

Note that _num cannot be declared const any more since it is *not* initialized in the preamble. The code in the body of the constructor is changing the (undefined) value of _num. Try compiling this program with a const _num and you'll get an error message.

When the object num of class InputNum is constructed in main, it prompts the user to input a number, which it then waits for and stores in its private data member _num. The input object std::cin does this by getting input from the keyboard and storing it in a variable. Depending on the type of the variable, std::cin expects different things from the keyboard. For instance, if you call it with an int, it expects an integer; if you call it with a double, it expects a floating point number, and so on.

The set of public methods is called the object's *interface*, and it defines the way clients can interact with the object. InputNum, for instance, provides read-only access to its contents. Because of that, we are guaranteed that the value of InputNum will never change once it is created. Successive calls to GetValue() will always return the same number.

It is also possible for an object to grant write-access to its contents—for example, in our case, it could be done by defining the method

```
void SetValue (int i) { _num = i; }
```

Then, after the call

```
num.SetValue (10);
```

subsequent calls to GetValue would return 10, no matter what number was input in the num constructor.

The equal sign in C++ signifies assignment. The statement

```
_num = i;
```

sets the value of _num to that of i.

Of course, the method SetValue cannot be defined const because it changes the state of the object (try it!). And if Matter had such a nonconstant method, that method couldn't be called in the context of the constant object _matter inside the World. The compiler would strongly object.

To summarize, the set of public member functions defines the interface to the object of a given class. Even more important, a well-designed and well-implemented object is able to fulfill a well-defined contract. Programming in C++ is about writing contracts and fulfilling them. An interface can, and should, be designed in such a way that the client's part of the contract is simple and well-defined. The object may even be able to protect itself from sloppy clients who break their part of the contract. We'll talk about this when we discuss the use of assertions.

1.6   **Member Function Scope**

Member function scope, strings as arrays of chars, calling other member functions.

input2   The next example shows how the body of a member function forms its own local scope. We will be able to define objects within that scope, create subscopes, and so on.
So here's a new twist in our input object.

```
#include <iostream>

class  InputNum
{
public:
  InputNum ()
  {
    std::cout << "Enter number ";
    std::cin >> _num;
  }

  int GetValue () const { return _num; }

  void AddInput ()
  {
    InputNum aNum;  // Get a number from user
    _num = _num + aNum.GetValue ();
  }

private:
  int _num;
};

int main()
{
  InputNum num;
  std::cout   < "The value is "
              < num.GetValue() < "\n";
  num.AddInput();
  std::cout   < "Now the value is "
              < num.GetValue() < "\n";
}
```

A new method called AddInput was added to InputNum. It uses a local object of type InputNum to prompt the user for a number. This number is then retrieved using GetValue and is added to the original value.

The following series of pictures visualize the execution of the program. Figure 1.5 shows the call to the constructor of the local object num in main. This constructor prompts the user for input and stores it in the data member _num.

Next, Figure 1.6 shows the call to num.GetValue() inside main. It returns the value that was input in num's constructor.

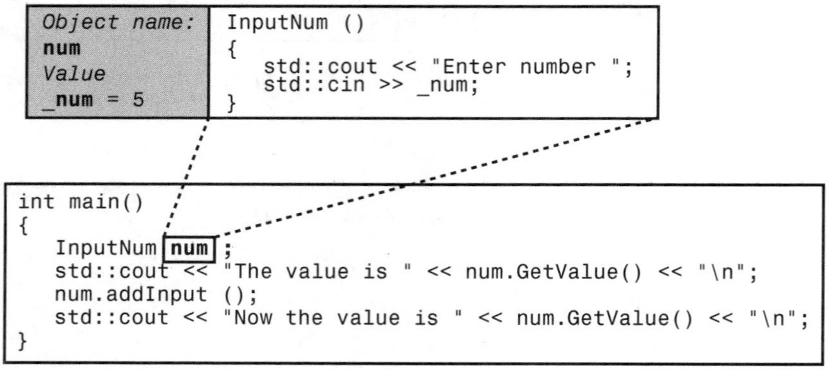

```
Object name:    InputNum ()
num             {
Value               std::cout << "Enter number ";
_num = 5            std::cin >> _num;
                }
```

```
int main()
{
    InputNum num ;
    std::cout << "The value is " << num.GetValue() << "\n";
    num.addInput ();
    std::cout << "Now the value is " << num.GetValue() << "\n";
}
```

Figure 1.5 While executing main, the constructor of object num of class InputNum is called. It prompts the user to input a number. The user inputs 5. This value is stored in num's private data member _num.

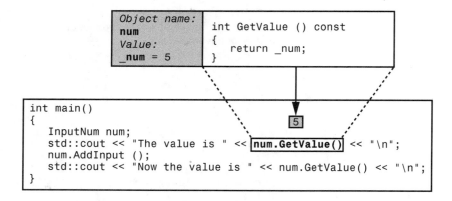

Figure 1.6 The GetValue method of the object num is called. It retrieves and returns the value stored in num's private data member _num. This value is 5.

After that, in Figure 1.7, we can see AddInput being called on the object num. The value stored in _num is initially the same.

But now, in Figure 1.8, another object, aNum, of class InputNum is created within the scope of the AddInput method. Its constructor prompts the user for another number and stores it in the _num data member of aNum. This _num is different from the _num data member of the object num.

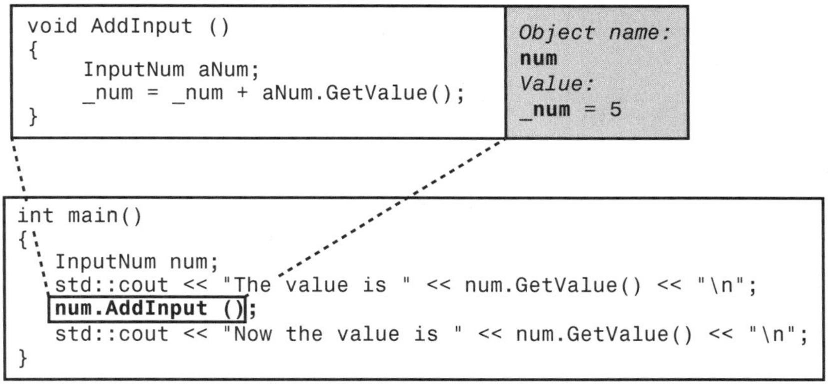

```
void AddInput ()                              Object name:
{                                             num
    InputNum aNum;                            Value:
    _num = _num + aNum.GetValue();            _num = 5
}
```

```
int main()
{
    InputNum num;
    std::cout << "The value is " << num.GetValue() << "\n";
    num.AddInput ();
    std::cout << "Now the value is " << num.GetValue() << "\n";
}
```

Figure 1.7 The AddInput method of the object num is called next.

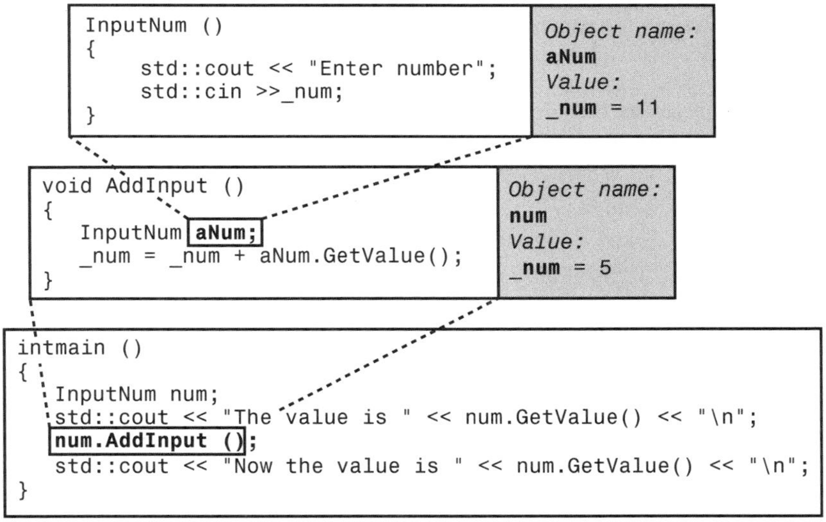

```
InputNum ()                                   Object name:
{                                             aNum
    std::cout << "Enter number";              Value:
    std::cin >>_num;                          _num = 11
}
```

```
void AddInput ()                              Object name:
{                                             num
    InputNum aNum;                            Value:
    _num = _num + aNum.GetValue();            _num = 5
}
```

```
intmain ()
{
    InputNum num;
    std::cout << "The value is " << num.GetValue() << "\n";
    num.AddInput ();
    std::cout << "Now the value is " << num.GetValue() << "\n";
}
```

Figure 1.8 The AddInput method of num creates the object aNum of the class InputNum. The constructor of aNum prompts the user to input a number. The user enters 11 and this value is stored in aNum's private data member _num.

Still inside the AddInput method of the object num, in Figure 1.9 the program calls the GetValue method of the object aNum. It returns the value stored in aNum. It's the value that's been input by the user during the construction of aNum. This value is added to the one stored inside the object num.

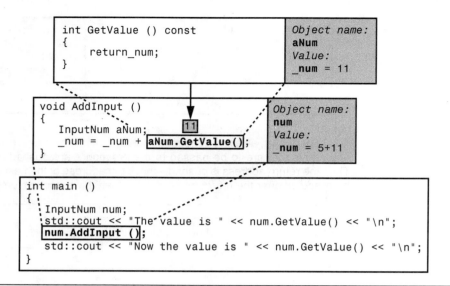

Figure 1.9 While still executing the AddInput method of num, the method GetValue of the object aNum is called. It retrieves and returns the value stored in aNum's private data member _num. This value, 11, is then added to the num's private data member _num. Its value was 5, but after the addition of 11 it changes to 16.

Finally, Figure 1.10 shows how, back in main, the program retrieves the newly incremented value from num and prints it.

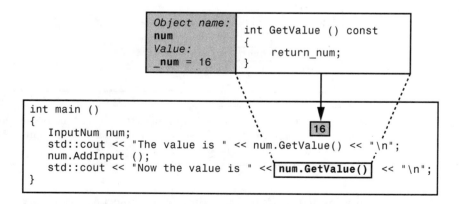

Figure 1.10 The method GetValue of the object num is called again. It retrieves and returns the value of num's private data member _num, which is now equal to 16.

You might wonder how the program executes a method, then returns to the caller and continues exactly where it has left off. Where does the program keep the information about what it was doing before it made the call? It is using the program (also called the execution) stack. Calling a procedure means pushing some data on this (invisible) stack. Returning from the procedure means popping this data from the stack and returning to the previous state and point of control.

In particular, a calling sequence might look something like this. First, all the arguments that are to be passed to the procedure are pushed on the stack. Then the return address is pushed—that's the address of the next instruction to be executed after the return from the call. Then the execution jumps to the actual code of the procedure. The procedure starts by making room on the stack for its local variables. This way, each procedure invocation gets a fresh copy of all local variables. The procedure is executed, then it pops its local variables, the return address, and the arguments passed to it, and jumps back to the return address. If there is a return value, it is usually passed in one of the processor's registers.

Take into account that this is only a conceptual model. The actual details depend on the particular *calling convention* and are both processor- and compiler-dependent.

One thing is slightly awkward in this last revision of our program. The prompt "Enter number" is always the same. The user has no idea where it's coming from. Wouldn't it be nice to vary the prompt depending on the context? Ideally we would like to have code like this in main:

```
InputNum num   ("Enter number ");
num.AddInput  ("Another one  ");
num.AddInput  ("One more     ");
```

input3   Some of the InputNum's methods would have to take strings as arguments. No problem. Here's how it's done:

```
#include <iostream>

class InputNum
{
public:
  InputNum (char msg [])
  {
    std::cout << msg;
    std::cin >> _num;
  }

  int GetValue () const { return _num; }
  void AddInput (char msg [])
```

```
      {
        InputNum aNum (msg);
        _num = GetValue () + aNum.GetValue ();
      }
    private:
      int _num;
    };

    const char SumString [] = "The sum is ";

    int main()
    {
      InputNum num ("Enter number ");
      num.AddInput  ("Another one ");
      num.AddInput  ("One more ");
      std::cout << SumString << num.GetValue () << "\n";
    }
```

Several things are going on here. A new built-in type, char, has been introduced. As the name suggests, this type is used to store characters. Unless you work on some really weird machine, you can safely assume that a char is an 8-bit quantity.

We also learn that a string is an *array* of characters—that's the meaning of the brackets, [], after the name of the string variable. What we don't see here is the fact that literal strings are zero terminated; that is, after the last explicit character, a *null* char is added by the compiler. For instance "Hi" is really an array of three characters: 'H', 'i', and 0 (or '\0' for purists). The null character is distinctly different from the character representing the digit zero. The latter is written as '0'. See the difference? Null character: 0 or '\0', zero: '0'. Since we are at it, "\n" is an array of two characters '\n' and '\0'. This terminating null tells various functions operating on strings, including our friend cout, where the end of the string is. Otherwise it would have no clue. Notice that literal strings are enclosed in double quotes, whereas character literals are in single quotes.

By the way, instead of sending the string "\n" to the output, you can get the same result sending a special thing called std::endl. The syntax is

```
    std::cout << std::endl;
```

and it works like magic (meaning, I don't want to explain it right now). The special things you send to the standard output or input are called *manipulators,* and they can, among capabilities, modify the formatting.

> There is a special std::string type defined in the C++ standard library. It's extremely useful if you're planning on doing any string manipulations. We'll get to it later.

Another curious thing about this program is the way it calls GetValue inside AddInput.

```
_num = GetValue () + aNum.GetValue ();
```

We make two calls, one with no object specified, the other targeted at aNum. We know the second one invokes GetValue on the object aNum. The first one, it turns out, invokes the GetValue method on the object we are sitting in (the "this" object, as we say in C++ parlance), and simply retrieves its own value of _num. It does this, however, in a way that isolates us from the details of its implementation. This may look like an overkill of generality (why don't we just use _num directly?), but in many situations this may mean a big win in future maintenance.

Some of you are probably wondering how expensive it is to call a member function instead of retrieving the value of _num directly. Or why not make _num public and use it as a shortcut everywhere? The syntax for accessing a public data member is

```
myNum._num
```

You won't believe it, but the call is actually free. I'm not kidding—there aren't any additional cycles. *Nada*. Nil. *Niente*. Zilch! (Later, I'll explain the meaning of *inline* functions and you'll see why.)

Since there is no runtime overhead in accessing data members using member functions, there is very little reason to use public data members in your programs. Making a data member public means releasing control over it to a client who may not only use the data, but also arbitrarily modify it. It also locks you into one particular implementation. A member function might be reimplemented, for instance, to retrieve the value from some external source on demand. You may add side effects to a function, e.g., to log every call or to increment usage count. You can't do these things with a public data member without making extensive modifications to the client code.

To summarize, the body of a member function forms a separate local scope. This is also true about the body of constructors and destructors. One can define objects within this local scope as well as create subscopes inside it.

A string is a null-terminated array of characters. Arrays are declared with rectangular brackets following their names. Arrays of characters can be initialized with explicit literal strings. Arrays may be defined within global or local scopes and passed as arguments to other functions.

1.7 Types

Built-in types, typedefs.

The following list briefly describes the built-in types.

- The Boolean type `bool` can take the predefined values `true` and `false`.
- `int` is a generic signed integral type. It is considered the most efficient implementation of an integral type for a given architecture. Its size is machine dependent, but it's guaranteed to be at least 2 bytes long, but usually is at least 4 bytes long.
- `double` is a generic signed floating point type that corresponds to a real number.
- `char` is a generic 8-bit character type used in ASCII strings. Depending on the compiler, the default *signedness* of `char` may be signed or unsigned.
- `wchar_t` is a 16-bit character type used in Unicode strings.
- `short` and `long` are a little better defined signed integral types. Usually `short` is 2 bytes long and `long` is 4 bytes long, but on a 64-bit machine `it` may be 8 bytes long (same as `int`). If you are writing your program to run on only one type of processor architecture, you can make assumptions about the sizes of `short`s and `long`s (and `char`s, for that matter). Sizes become crucial when you store data on removable disks or send them across the network.

`short` is often used as a cheap `int`, spacewise; for example, in large arrays `long` is often used when `short` or `int` may overflow. Remember, in 2 bytes you can only store numbers between –32,768 and 32,767 (or, for unsigned types, between 0 and 65,535). Your arithmetic can easily overflow such storage, and the values will quietly wrap around.

- `float` is a cheaper version of `double` (again, spacewise), but it offers less precision. It makes sense to use it in large arrays, where size really matters.
- `long double` offers more precision than `double`.
- All integral types may be prefixed by the keyword `unsigned` or `signed` (the default for all types except, as mentioned above, `char`, which is `signed`). Unsigned types of special interest include `unsigned char`, which corresponds to a machine byte, and `unsigned long`, which is often used for low-level bitwise operations.

When you are tired of typing `unsigned long` over and over again, C++ lets you define a shortcut called a `typedef`. It is a way of giving a different name for any type—built-in or user-defined. For instance, an `unsigned long` is often `typedef`'d to (given the name of) `ULONG`:

```
typedef unsigned long ULONG;
```

After you define such a `typedef`, you can use `ULONG` anywhere you would use any other type, for example,

```
ULONG SwapValue (ULONG newValue)
{
  ULONG oldValue = _ulNumber;
  _ulNumber = newValue;
  return oldValue;
}
```

Similarly, you can use `typedefs` for BYTE:

```
typedef unsigned char BYTE;
```

Like every C++ feature, typedefs can be abused. Just because you can redefine all types using your own names doesn't mean you should. What do you make of types like INT or LONG when you see them in somebody else's code? Are these typedef'd names for `int` or `long`? If so, why not just use `int` or `long`? And if not, then what the heck is going on? I can't think of any rational reason to typedef such basic data types, other than following some kind of coding standard from hell.

Besides these basic types, there is an infinite variety of derived types and user-defined types. We've had a glimpse of derived types in an array of chars. And we've seen user-defined types called classes.

1.7.1 Summary

Objects of any type (built-in, derived, or user-defined) can be defined within the global scope or local scopes. Bodies of functions (such as `main`) and member functions form local scopes. Within a given local scope, one can create subscopes that can have sub-subscopes, and so on. A subscope is usually delimited by braces, but in certain constructs, such as the for loop or the conditional if/else (we'll see examples later), a single statement body may be braceless and yet it will form a subscope.

A class is a user-defined type. Class behavior is specified by the interface—the set of member functions (including constructors and a destructor) together with the description of their behavior. A member function takes zero or more arguments and returns a value (which can be empty—the `void` return type). The implementation of the class is specified by the bodies of member functions and the types of data members. The implementation fulfills the contract declared by the interface.

Objects can be combined by embedding and inheritance—semantically corresponding to the has-a and is-a relationships. Embedding and inheritance may be combined in various ways, leading to objects containing objects that inherit from other objects, that inherit from yet other objects, and so on.

Exercises

Notice: If you have a background in C and I haven't scared you off yet, these exercises will seem trivial to you. Please do them anyway. Get used to the new way of thinking and structuring your problems. All the exercises should be solved using only the constructs introduced so far.

1. Write a program using class `World`, whose output is, in this order, "Hello from 1! Goodbye from 1. Hello from 2! Goodbye from 2." Find at least two different solutions.

2. Find a programmer's error in this class definition. Give two different ways of correcting it.

```
class Glove
{
public:
   Glove (int numFingers)
      : _n (numFingers), _hand (_n)
   {
      std::cout << "Glove with " << _n << " fingers\n";
   }
private:
   Hand   _hand;
   int    _n;
};
```

3. Define class HorBar whose constructor prints the following pattern

```
+----------+
```

where the number of minus signs is passed as an int argument to the constructor.

Similarly, class VerBar should print a vertical bar of height n, like this:

```
|
|
|
|
```

Define class Frame that contains (embedded) the upper horizontal bar, the vertical bar, and the lower horizontal bar. Its constructor should take two arguments, the horizontal and the vertical extent of the frame:

```
Frame (int hor, int ver)
```

The Frame object can be defined and initialized in the program using the following syntax:

```
Frame myFrame (10, 2);
```

4. Define class Ladder that contains two frames and a VerBar between them. The constructor should take two arguments, one for the horizontal extent and one for the vertical distance between horizontal bars. It should print the following pattern when created with (5, 2):

```
+-----+
|
|
+-----+
|
|
+-----+
|
|
+-----+
```

5. Write a program that asks for a number and calculates its factorial. The factorial of *n* is the product of all positive integers up to (and including) *n*. $n! = 1 * 2 * 3 * ... * n$. To multiply two numbers, put an asterisk, *, between them.

6. Define class `Planet` that inherits from `CelestialBody` and is characterized by an albedo (how reflective its surface is—use a `double` to store it).

7. In the following class definition, replace dummy strings with actual words in such a way that during the construction of the object, the string "program makes objects with class" is printed.

```
class One: public Two
{
public:
   One ()
   {
     Three three;
     std::cout << "dummy ";
   }
private:
   Four    _four;
};
```

Each of the classes `Two`, `Three`, and `Four` prints some dummy string in its constructor.

Design a similar class which, during construction, will print the above string, and during destruction print the same words in reverse order. The constraint is that each class has to have exactly the same code (print the same string) in its constructor and in its destructor.

8. Design, implement, and test class `Average`. An object of type `Average` should accept values that are put into it. At any point, it should be possible to retrieve their cumulative arithmetic average.

9. Design a class hierarchy (chain of inheritance) that derives a `Human` from a `LivingBeing`. Make sure you use the is-a relationship. Now add branches for a `Tomato` and an `Elephant`. Write a short test program that defines one of each inside `main`. Each class should have a constructor that prints a brief but pointed message.

10. Design a `Human` exploring the has-a relationship. A human has a head, the head has a nose, the nose has a nose hair, and so on. Derive a `Man` and a `Woman`. Implement simple classes whose constructors print messages and then create a couple of `Humans`.

1.8   Abstract Data Types

Abstract data types, include files, non-inline member functions, assertions.

It is now time to design some serious classes that actually do something useful. Let's start with something simple and easy to understand—a stack of integers. A stack is defined by its interface. Major things that you can do to a stack is to push a number into it and pop a number from it. What makes a stack a stack is its LIFO (last in, first out) behavior. You can push values into it and, when you pop them, they come up in reverse order.

By describing its behavior we have defined a stack as an *abstract data type*. We didn't have to specify how it's implemented, only what it does. Even though my description isn't very precise or complete, it is possible to have a formal mathematical definition of a stack that is independent of its implementation.

stack1   Our implementation choice is to use an array of integers. It would be nice to be able to separate the interface from the implementation into separate files. In some languages it is actually possible. Not so in C++ (or, at least, not without some gymnastics). The reasons are mostly technological. The compiler would need to know about all the files involved in the project in order to allow for such separation.[2]

The best we can do in C++ is to separate the details of the implementation of *some member functions* into the *implementation* file. The interface file, however, must contain the definition of the class, and that involves specifying all the data members. Traditionally, interfaces are defined in *header* files with the extension .h.

Here is the contents of the interface file stack.h.

```
const int maxStack = 16;

class IStack
{
public:
    IStack () :_top (0) {}
    void Push (int i);
    int  Pop ();
private:
    int _arr [maxStack];
    int _top;
};
```

The constructor of IStack initializes the top-of-the-stack index to zero—the start of the array. Yes, in C++ array elements are numbered from zero to *n*–1, where *n* is the size of the array. In our case, the size is 16. It is defined to be so in the statement

---

2. For instance, the compiler has to know the size of the object when it's allocating memory for it. This size can only be calculated by analyzing the (public as well as private) data members of the class.

```
const int maxStack = 16;
```

The modifier const tells the compiler that the value of maxStack will never change. The compiler is therefore free to substitute every use of the symbol maxStack with the actual value of 16.

The line

```
int _arr [maxStack];
```

declares _arr to be an array of maxStack integers. The size of an array has to be a constant. As we have seen in the case of strings of characters, when the array is explicitly initialized, you don't have to specify the size.

Notice that member functions Push and Pop are *declared* but not *defined* within the definition of the class IStack. The difference between function declaration and function definition is that the latter includes the code, the implementation, and is not followed by a semicolon. The former does not—it only specifies the types of parameters and the type of the return value—the so-called *signature*. So where is the implementation of Push and Pop? In the separate implementation file stack.cpp.

The first thing in that file is the include statement of the header stack.h. Next we include the new header file <cassert>. This file contains the definition of the very important function (actually a macro) assert. I will not go into the details of its implementation—suffice it to say that this magical function can be turned completely off by defining the symbol NDEBUG during compilation. However, as long as we *don't* define NDEBUG, the assertion will check its argument for logical truth, that is, for a non-zero value. In other words, it asserts the truth of its argument.

We *do* define NDEBUG after the final program is thoroughly tested and, in one fell swoop, we get rid of all the assertions, thus improving the program's speed. Many compilers distinguish between a *debug* build and a *release* build. When compiling the release build, they automatically turn on the NDEBUG flag.

What happens when the assertion's argument is not true (or is equal to zero)? In that unfortunate case the assertion will be triggered during the execution of the program—it will print a message specifying the name of the source file, the line number, and the condition that failed. Assertions are a debugging tool. When an assertion fails it signifies a programmer's error—a bug in the program.

We usually don't anticipate bugs—they appear in unexpected places all by themselves. However, there are some focal points in our code where they can be caught. These are the places where we make assumptions. It is okay to make certain assumptions—they lead to simpler and faster code. However, we should make sure, at least during development and testing, that nobody violates these assumptions.

Let's now have a look at the implementation of Push and Pop:

```
#include "stack.h"
#include <cassert>
#include <iostream>

//Compile with NDEBUG=1 to get rid of assertions
```

```
void IStack::Push (int i)
{
  assert (_top < maxStack);
  _arr [_top] = i;
  ++_top;
}

int IStack::Pop ()
{
  assert (_top > 0);
  --top;
  return _arr [_top];
}
```

The first thing worth noticing is that when the definition of a member function is taken out of the context of the class definition, its name has to be qualified with the class name followed by a double colon.

There's more to this than meets the eye, though. The methods we've defined so far were all *inline*. Member functions whose definitions are embedded inside the definition of the class are automatically made *inline* by the compiler. What does this mean? It means that the compiler, instead of generating a function call, tries to insert the actual code of the function right on the spot where it was invoked. For instance, since the method GetValue of the object input was inline, its invocation in

```
std::cout << input.GetValue ();
```

is, from the point of view of generated code, equivalent to

```
std::cout << input._num;
```

On the other hand, if the definition of the member function is taken out of the class definition, like in the case of Pop, it automatically becomes non-inline.

There is one more permutation: you can take a method out of the class definition but still make it inline. To do this, you just have to put the keyword inline in front of its definition:

```
inline void IStack::Push (int i)
{
  assert (_top < maxStack);
  _arr [_top] = i;
  ++_top;
}
```

In that case you have to remember that the compiler must have access to this definition (and not only the declaration inside the class) while it's compiling the code that calls this method. That's why definitions like this are usually put in header files that are included by the callers.

Should you use inline or non-inline methods? It depends on the complexity of the method. If the method contains a single statement, it is usually cheaper execution-wise and code-size-wise to make it inline. If it's more complex, and is invoked from many different places, it makes more sense to make the method non-inline.

In any case, inline functions are absolutely vital to programming in C++. Without inlining, it would be virtually impossible to convince anybody to use methods such as GetValue or SetValue instead of simply making _num public (even *with* inlining it is still difficult to convince some programmers). Imposing no penalty for data hiding is a tremendous strength of C++. Typing a few additional lines of code here and there, without even having to think much about it, is a price every experienced programmer is happy to pay for the convenience and power of data hiding.

Let's analyze the contract of our stack in more detail. First of all, we prevent stack overflow by requiring the client (programmer who is using our stack) to keep track of how many elements are already in it, and not to store more than maxStack elements at any one time. Second of all, we prohibit the client from calling Pop when the stack is empty, thus guarding it from underflow. These harsh requirements are enforced by strategically placed assertions.

I'm not saying that this is a particularly useful implementation of a stack of integers—the contract puts too much of a bookkeeping burden on the client. But at least the contract is clear and enforceable, which is the first step towards good design.

The main function in our stack program does a few pushes and pops to demonstrate its workings.

```
int main ( )
{
  IStack stack;
  stack.Push (1);
  stack.Push (2);
  std::cout << "Popped " << stack.Pop() << std::endl;
  std::cout << "Popped " << stack.Pop() << std::endl;
}
```

Stack 1   **Exercises**

11. Add method Top that returns the value from the top of the stack without changing its state. Add method Count that returns the count of elements in the stack.

12. Modify the main function so that one of the stack contracts is violated. See what happens when you run the program with the assertions turned on.

13. Modify the stack so that it becomes CharStack—the stack of characters. Use it to invert strings by pushing all the characters of a string, and then popping and printing them one by one.

14. Design the abstract data type Queue of doubles with methods Put and Get and the FIFO (first in, first out) behavior. Implement it using an array and two indexes: the put index, and the get index that trails the put index. The contract of this particular queue reads: The `Put` method shall never be called more than `maxPuts` times during the lifetime of the `Queue`. Thou shalt not `Get` when the `Queue` is empty.

15. Design and implement the `DblArray` data type with the methods

```
void Set (int i, double val)
```

and

```
double Get (int i) const
```

to set and get the values of the particular cells in the array identified by the index `i`. Add one more method

```
bool IsSet (int i) const
```

that returns `false` if the cell has never been set before and `true` otherwise. The contract is that no `Set`s or `Get`s shall be done with the index greater than `maxCells`; that one shall never try to get a value that hasn't been set before, and that one shouldn't try to set a value that has already been set before (write once/read many times). The array may store any values of the type `double`.

Hint: If you want to negate a Boolean result, put an exclamation mark in front of it. For instance

```
!IsSet (i)
```

is *true* when the cell is *not* set and `false` when it is.

Chapter 2
Arrays and References

An object is identified by its name in a program. But if we had to call each object by its name everywhere we want to use it, we would end up with one global soup of names. Our program would execute in a structureless global space of names. The power to give an object different names in different scopes provides a level of indirection that makes programming possible. There is an old saying in computer science: Every problem can be solved by adding a level of indirection. This indirection can be accomplished by using a reference—an alias or an alternative name that can be attached to a different object every time it enters a given scope.

Computers are great at menial tasks—they have a lot more patience than humans do. It is a punishment for a human to have to write "I will not challenge my teacher's authority" a hundred times. Tell the computer to do it a hundred times, and it won't even blink. That's the power of iteration.

2.1 References

References to objects, friends, passing by reference, initializing a reference.

So far we've been exploring the has-a and is-a types of relationships between objects. The third kind is the has-access-to relationship. What's different about the has-access-to relationship is that it's not "destructive" like the others. Objects to which A has access to are *not* destroyed when A is destroyed.

The has-access-to relationship finds its purest expression in C++ in the form of references. A reference *refers* to an object. It is like a new temporary name for an existing object—an alias. It can be used just like the original object; that is, the syntax for accessing a reference is the same as that for accessing an object. One can pass references, return references, even store them inside other objects. Whenever the contents of the object changes, all the references to this object show this change. Conversely, any reference can be used to modify the object it refers to (unless it's a const reference, which is described later).

We declare a reference variable by following the type name with an ampersand, &. Actually, the ampersand binds with the name of the variable, so if you want to declare more than one reference in the same statement, you have to precede all names with ampersands:

```
Istack & stack;
```

Once a reference is created and initialized to refer to a particular object, it will *always* refer to that object. Assignment to a reference does not make it "point" to another object; it overwrites the object it refers to with the new value. For instance, consider this code:

```
int i = 5;
int j = 10;
int & iref = i; // iref points to i
iref = j;
```

The execution of the last statement changes the value of i from 5 to 10. It will not make iref point to j. Nothing can make iref point to anything other than i.

A reference cannot be created without being initialized. If a reference is stored within an object, it must be initialized in the preamble of that object's constructor.

stack2   We'll use references in the definition and the implementation of a stack *sequencer*. A sequencer is an object that is used to present some other object as a sequence of items; it returns the values stored in that object one by one.

In order to retrieve values from the stack, the sequencer needs access to private data members of the stack (see Figure 2.1). The stack may grant such access by making the sequencer its friend. All of the stack's private data members are still invisible to the rest of the world, with the exception of its new friend, the stack sequencer. Notice that friendship is a one-way relationship: StackSeq can access private data of IStack, but not the other way around.

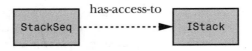

Figure 2.1 The graphical representation of the has-access-to relationship between objects

> The combination of `IStack` and `StackSeq` is an example of a larger granularity structure, a pattern that unifies several data structures into one functional unit.

```
class IStack
{
  // Give StackSeq access to IStack's private members
  friend class StackSeq;
public:
  IStack (): _top (0) {}
  void Push (int i);
  int Pop ();
private:
  int _arr [maxStack];
  int _top;
};

class StackSeq
{
public:
  StackSeq (IStack const & stack);
  bool AtEnd () const;    // Are we done yet?
  void Advance ();        // Move to next item
  int GetNum () const;    // Retrieve current item
private:
  IStack const & _stack; // Reference to stack
  int            _iCur;  // Current index into stack
};
```

The contract of `StackSeq` states that the client must not attempt to call `Advance` or `GetNum` if `AtEnd` is true.

The `StackSeq` constructor is called with a reference to a `const IStack`. One of the data members is also a reference to a `const IStack`. A `const` reference cannot be used to change the object it refers to. For instance, since `Push` is not a `const` method, the compiler will not allow `StackSeq` to call `_stack.Push()`. It also won't allow any writes into the array, or any change to `_stack._top`.

A reference to `const` can be initialized by any reference, but the converse is not true—a reference that is not `const` cannot be initialized by a reference to `const`. Hence we can pass any stack to the `StackSeq` constructor. The compiler, in accordance with the constructor's declaration, converts the stack to a reference to a `const IStack`. Then `_stack`, which is also a reference to a `const IStack`, must be initialized in the preamble of the `StackSeq` constructor (remember, references *must* be initialized in the preamble).

Data member `_iCur` stores the state of the sequencer—an index into the array `_arr` inside the referenced stack. The sequencer, friend of the class `IStack`, has full knowledge of the stack's implementation.

```
StackSeq::StackSeq (IStack const & stack )
  : _iCur (0), _stack (stack) // init reference
{}
```

The implementation of the remaining methods is rather straightforward.

```
bool StackSeq::AtEnd () const
{
  return _iCur == _stack._top; // Friend: can access _top
}

void StackSeq::Advance ()
{
  assert (!AtEnd()); // Not at end
  ++_iCur;
}

int StackSeq::GetNum () const
{
  assert (!AtEnd ());
  return _stack._arr [_iCur]; // Friend: can access _arr
}
```

Notice that the dot syntax for accessing an object's data members through a reference is the same as that of accessing the object directly. The variable _stack is a (read-only) alias for a stack object. Due to the sequencer's friend status, StackSeq can access the IStack private data members with impunity.

New logical operators have been introduced in this program as well. The exclamation point logically negates the expression that follows it. !AtEnd() is true when the sequencer is not done and false when it's done. You read it as "not at end."

The double equal sign, ==, is used for equality testing. The result is false if two quantities are different and true if they are equal.

> **Warning: The similarity between the assignment operator = and the equality operator == is a common source of serious programming mistakes.**

It is very unfortunate that, because of the heritage of C, a single typo like this can cause an almost undetectable programming error. Don't count on the compiler to flag the statement

```
x == 1;
```

or the conditional

```
if (x = 0)
```

as errors (some compilers will warn, but only at a high warning level).

Following the same logic, the *not-equal-to* relationship is expressed using the operator !=, as in x != 0. It evaluates to true if x is different from zero, and to false if they are equal.

The main procedure tests the functionality of the sequencer. It pushes a few numbers onto the stack and then iterates through it.

```
int main ()
{
  IStack TheStack;
  TheStack.Push (1);
  TheStack.Push (2);
  TheStack.Push (3);

  for (StackSeq seq (TheStack);
       !seq.AtEnd();
       seq.Advance())
  {
    std::cout << "  " << seq.GetNum() << std::endl;
  }
}
```

Notice how the object TheStack is passed to the constructor of the sequencer. The compiler knows that the programmer *really* meant reference, because it has already seen the declaration of this constructor in the class definition of IStack. Since the constructor was declared to take a reference, the reference, not a copy of the whole object, will be passed.

When a formal argument of a method is specified as a reference, we say that it is *passed by reference*. When you call a method like that, you pass it a reference to a variable, and the method may change the value of that variable. This is in contrast to passing an argument by value. When you call a method that expects to get a variable by value (no ampersand), the method will *not* change the original value of this variable. The method will operate on its copy.

Compare these two methods.

```
class Dual
{
public:
  void ByValue (int j)
  {
    ++j;
    std::cout << j << std::endl;
  }

  void ByRef (int & j)
  {
    ++j;
    std::cout << j << std::endl;
  }
};
```

```
int main ()
{
  Dual dual;
  int i = 1;
  dual.ByValue (i);
  std::cout << "After calling ByValue, i = "
      << i << std::endl;
  dual.ByRef (i);
  std::cout << "After calling ByRef, i = "
      << i << std::endl;
}
```

The first method does not change the value of i, but the second does, as can be seen in the output from this program:

```
2
After calling ByValue, i = 1
2
After calling ByRef, i = 2
```

If you are worried that from the caller's point of view it is not obvious whether a reference was meant or not—don't! As a general rule, assume that objects are passed by reference and built-in types by value (the example above notwithstanding). Only in some special cases will we pass objects by value, and it will be pretty obvious why (see Passing by Value on page 151). So, when reading most programs, you can safely assume that when an object is passed to a function, it is passed by reference.

Let us follow the path of the reference in main.

```
void main ()
{
  IStack TheStack;
  TheStack.Push (1);
  TheStack.Push (2);
  TheStack.Push (3);

  for (StackSeq seq (TheStack);
       !seq.AtEnd();
       seq.Advance())
  {
    std::cout << "  " << seq.GetNum() << std::endl;
  }
}
```

A reference to TheStack is passed to the constructor of StackSeq under the (read-only) alias of stack—the formal parameter to the StackSeq constructor.

```
StackSeq::StackSeq (IStack const & stack)
  : _iCur (0), _stack (stack) // init reference
{}
```

This is a new temporary name for the object `TheStack`. This reference cannot be used to modify `TheStack` in any way, since it is declared `const`. Next, inside the `StackSeq` constructor, we initialize the reference data member `_stack` of the object `seq`. Again, this reference cannot be used to modify `TheStack`. From the time the object `seq` is constructed until the time it is destroyed, `_stack` will be a read-only alias for `TheStack`. The sequencer will know `TheStack` under the read-only alias `_stack`.

Notice the creative use of the `for` loop. We are taking advantage of the fact that the `for` loop header contains an initialization *statement*, a test *expression*, and a post-loop action *statement*. The first statement—the loop *initialization*—is executed only once before entering the loop. In our case it contains the definition of the sequencer. The following expression—the loop *condition*—is tested every time the body of the loop is entered. If the expression is true (nonzero), the iteration starts (or continues). When it is false, the loop is exited (or never entered). In our case the condition is tested to find if the sequencer is not at the end. The third statement—the loop *increment*—is executed after every iteration. In our example it advances the sequencer. Notice that after a normal exit from the loop, the loop condition always ends up *false*.

Any of the three parts of the `for` loop header may be empty. An infinite loop, for instance, is usually written like this:

```
for (;;) // Do forever
{
    // There must be some way out of here!
}
```

(You can exit such loop using a `break` or a `return` statement.)

To summarize: A reference is always an alias for some other variable (or, strictly speaking, for something called an l-value). Modifying a reference (e.g., by assigning a value to it) changes the contents of the variable that the reference refers to (or "points to" as it's sometimes said). "Reading" a reference, e.g., using it passively in an expression, yields the value of the variable it refers to. A `const` *reference can only be used for reading.*

A reference has to be initialized at the point of creation, which is either its declaration or, in the case of member references, in the preamble to the constructor, or, when calling a method that takes a reference, at the point of call.

2.2 Operators

We've already seen examples of various operations performed on numbers and variables. You know that you can add two numbers by placing a plus sign (or a plus *operator*, as it is called in programmer-speak) between them. Addition is just one example of an arithmetic operation.

You can compare numbers using equality or inequality operators. These are the examples of logical, or Boolean, operations. They produce a true or false result.

Finally, there are operations that you can perform on individual bits—they are called bitwise logical operations.

2.2.1 Arithmetic

In C++ you can do standard arithmetic operations on numbers and variables.
Table 2.1 lists the basic arithmetic operators.

Symbol	Binary operators	Example
+	Addition	a+b
−	Subtraction	a−b
*	Multiplication	a*b
/	Division	a/b
%	Division modulo	a%b
	Unary operators	
+	Plus	+a
−	Minus	−a
	Assignment operator	
=	Assignment	a=b

Table 2.1   Basic arithmetic operators

Some of the operators require a word of explanation. For instance, why are there
two division operators?

First of all, if you are operating on floating point numbers (for instance, of the
type double), you should use the regular division operator /. Even if only one of
the two numbers or variables is a decimal fraction, like 3.14, or a double, the result
of the division will be a number of the type double. However, if *both* operands are
integers—literal numbers without a decimal point or variables defined as int (or
other integral types)—applying the operator / results in an integer equal to the
integral part of the quotient. For example, 3/2 will produce 1, which is the integral
part of 1.5. Similarly, 10/3 will produce 3, and so on.

The % operator, which can only be applied to integral types, yields the *remainder*
from the division. For instance, 3 % 2 (pronounced "3 modulo 2") is equal to 1.
Similarly, 11 % 3 yields 2, and so on.

It is always true that (as long as *b* is nonzero):

(a / b) * b + a % b is equal to a

However, the results of applying operators / and % when one of the numbers is
negative are not well defined (although they still fulfill the equality above). So
don't rely on them if you are dealing with negative numbers. If you think this is
bad, you are right. The arguments for implementing such behavior in C++ are

really lame: compatibility with C and efficient implementation in terms of processor instructions.

The unary plus essentially does nothing. It is there for symmetry with the unary minus, which inverts the sign of a number. So if $a = 2$ then $-a$ yields -2 and $+a$ yields 2.

2.2.2 Logic

Table 2.2 contains a list of comparison and equality testing operators that create Boolean values. They are mostly used inside `if` statements and as termination/continuation conditions in loops. You can also use them to initialize `bool` variables.

Symbol	Equality testing operators	Example
==	Equal to	a == b
!=	Not equal to	a != b
	Comparison operators	
>	Greater than	a > b
<	Less than	a < b
>=	Greater than or equal to	a >= b
<=	Less than or equal to	a <= b

Table 2.2   Operators producing the Boolean values `true` or `false`

You can combine simple logical expressions using logical AND, a double ampersand, and OR, a double vertical bar. You can also negate a logical expression by preceding it with an exclamation mark. Table 2.3 lists these operators.

Symbol	Logic operators	Example
&&	AND	a && b
||	OR	a || b
!	NOT	!a

Table 2.3   Logical operators

One important thing to remember about the operators && and || is that their right side is not evaluated if the value of the left side determines the outcome. For instance, suppose that x = 0. Then in the logical expression

```cpp
if (x > 5 && x < 10)
  std::cout << x << " is between 5 and 10, exclusive\n";
```

the second inequality, x < 10, will not be tested because the first one, x > 5, is already false. A false expression connected with AND to *anything* will always produce a false output. There is no need to evaluate the second expression, and a C++ program is guaranteed to skip it. The code above is therefore equivalent to the following

```cpp
if (x > 5)
{
  if (x < 10)
    std::cout << x << " is between 5 and 10, exclusive\n";
}
```

This not only results in execution speedup (the second expression might be arbitrarily complex), but also ensures that no side effects of the second expression will take place if the first one is false (for example, if you substitute ++x < 10 for the second condition you'll see that x will not be incremented if it's less than 5).

Similarly, the right side of logical OR is *not* evaluated if the left side yields true, because a true expression connected with OR to *anything* will always produce a true output.

2.2.3 Bitwise Logic

In C++ you can perform several types of bitwise operations on integral numbers (see Table 2.4). The binary bitwise operators AND and OR are denoted by a single ampersand & and a single vertical bar | respectively. The usage is

```cpp
int i = 3; // Binary 0011
int j = 5; // Binary 0101
int k = i & j; // Binary 0001
k = i | j; // Binary 0111
k = k | 8; // Binary 1111
```

The bitwise complement is denoted by a tilde, ~. For instance (on a four-bit computer), if $k = 13$ (binary 1101), then its complement j = ~k would be equal to 2 (binary 0010) (ones become zeros and zeros become ones).

Symbol	Binary bitwise operators	Example
&	Bitwise AND	a & b
|	Bitwise inclusive OR	a | b
^	Bitwise exclusive OR (XOR)	a ^ b
>>	Right shift by n bits	a >> n
<<	Left shift by n bits	a << n
	Unary bitwise operator	
~	Bitwise complement	~a

Table 2.4   Bitwise operators

The exclusive OR operator works like bitwise addition without carry. So if you XOR two 1-bits, the result is a 0-bit—you don't carry the 1 to the next position. For instance, in binary notation 0011^0101 = 0110.

The right-shift operator works differently on signed and unsigned integral types. When working on an unsigned type, it shifts bits to the right, throwing away the ones that fall off the right end and filling the empty bits on the left with zeros. For instance, in binary, 1011 >> 1 = 0101. Not so with signed types—the fill bit, in such a case, is equal to the leftmost bit of the original number. So, if in our example the number were a signed type (and we were operating on a four-bit computer), the result of 1011 >> 1 would be 1101. This actually makes sense if you know how negative numbers are stored in a computer: they always have their leftmost bit set to one. Right shifting therefore doesn't change their sign. In fact, right shift by one is always equivalent to division by two for both positive and negative numbers. Similarly, left shift by one is equivalent to multiplication by two (assuming the number doesn't overflow).

2.3   Stack-Based Calculator

Top down design, make, private member functions, if statement, do/while loop.

Our next step will be to design and implement a small but useful program using the techniques we have learned so far. It will be a simple stack-based calculator. Even though it is a very small project, we'll follow all the steps of the design and implementation process. We'll start with the external specification, then proceed with the architectural design, and finally implement the program.

2.3.1   External Specification

The stack-based calculator has a simple interface. It accepts user input in the form of numbers and operators. Numbers are stored in the LIFO type memory—they are pushed on the stack. Binary operators are applied to the two top-level numbers popped from the stack, and the result of the operation is pushed back on top of the stack. If there's only one number in the stack, it is substituted for both operands. After every action the contents of the whole stack is displayed.

Since this calculator implements the so-called "reverse Polish notation" (or post-fix notation), there is no need for parentheses. For simplicity we will implement only four basic arithmetic operations. A sample session might look like this (user input follows the > prompt and my comments are in parentheses):

```
> 3  (push 3)
3
> 2  (push 2)
3
2
> +  (add 2 + 3)
5
> +  (add 5 + 5)
10
```

2.3.2   Design

The obvious candidate for the top-level object is the *calculator* itself. It stores numbers in its memory and performs operations on them. Since we would like to be able to display the contents of the calculator's stack after every action, we need access to a stack *sequencer*. Finally, in order to completely decouple input/output operations from the calculator, we should have an *input* object that obtains input from the user and does some preprocessing (tokenization) to distinguish between numbers and operators.
We'll use the standard cout object for output.

The following list describes the minimum lifetimes of these three objects:

- The calculator has to be alive during the whole session, since it has long-term memory.
- The input object is associated with a single input operation.
- The scope of the sequencer is associated with every stack-display operation that follows a successful calculator action.

The input object obtains a string from the standard input. It can distinguish between numbers and operators, returning different tokens depending on the input. If the token is a number, the string is converted to an int and the input object remembers its value.

The calculator object accepts the input object, from which it can get predigested data, and executes the command. If the data is a number, the calculator stores it on the stack; if the data is an operator, the calculator performs the operation. The results are displayed by creating a stack sequencer and printing out its contents. The calculator simply gives access to its stack for the purpose of iteration.

Notice that we have only three types of objects interacting at the top level. There is also one object, the stack, that we can treat as a black box (we don't call any of its methods, we just pass access to it from one component to another). This is not just a reflection of the simplicity of our project—we should always strive to have only a small number of top-level objects. Once the top level is established, we can start the top-down descent. In our design we now go one level deeper and dive into the *calculator* object. We already know that it has a stack, and the stack object will be embedded in it. We will re-use the stack that we designed previously.

2.3.3 Stubbed Implementation

The top-down design will be followed by the top-down implementation. Based on our architectural specification, we can start writing the `main` procedure.

```
int main ()
{
  Calculator TheCalculator;
  bool status;
  do
  {
    // Prompt for input
    std::cout << "> ";
    Input input;
    status = TheCalculator.Execute (input);
    if (status)
    {
      for (StackSeq seq (TheCalculator.GetStack ());
                         !seq.AtEnd ();
                         seq.Advance ())
      {
        std::cout << "  " << seq.GetNum () << std::endl;
      }
    }
  } while (status);
}
```

We have introduced some new constructs here: the do/while loop and the if statement. The execution of the body of the do/while loop is repeated as long as the condition in the while clause remains true. Notice that, unlike the body of the for loop, the body of the do/while loop is always executed at least once.

There is also a version of the while loop that checks the condition *before* executing the body. In fact, any for loop can be rewritten as a while loop. For instance:

```
for (int i = 0; i < n; ++i)
{
  std::cout << i << "\n";
}
```

is equivalent to:

```
{
  int i = 0; // Initialization
  while (i < n) // Condition
  {
    std::cout << i << "\n";
    ++i; // Increment
  }
}
```

The additional braces around the whole construct are needed to restrict the scope of the loop variable, i.

As with the for loop, the body of the while loop forms a separate local scope (even if it is a single statement and the braces are omitted).

The body of the if statement is entered only if the condition in the if clause (the thing within parentheses) is true, otherwise it is skipped altogether. The condition can yield a bool true, directly, like in our case, or something that evaluates to a nonzero value. A nonzero value is automatically converted to Boolean true.

Using expressions that evaluate to numbers rather than Boolean values inside the if clause is considered bad style—a relic from C, which didn't have the Boolean type. Remember that you can always convert a number to a Boolean by comparing it to zero. For instance, instead of the terse

```
if (x)
```

you should use the much more readable

```
if (x != 0)
```

A notoriously bad example of using the result of an arithmetic expression in the if statement is

```
if (x = y)
```

This kind of code is accepted by the compiler because, in C and C++, the assignment is an expression that produces a value—in this case it will be the same value as that of y (and x, after the assignment). If you have to use an assignment as part of the if clause, at least change your code to something more obvious, like

```
if ((x = y) != 0)
```

Again, the body of the `if` statement forms a local scope even if it is only one statement—in which case the braces can be omitted.

Notice also that the variable `status` is defined without being initialized. We try to avoid such situations in C++. Here, I took the liberty of not initializing the variable, because it is always initialized inside the body of the `do`/`while` loop (and we *know* that it is executed at least once). I couldn't define the variable `status` inside the scope of the loop, because it is tested in the `while` clause that belongs to the outer scope. The `while` clause is evaluated during each iteration, after the body of the loop is executed.

Next, following the top-down approach, we'll write stub implementations for all classes. The stubs won't implement the expected functionality, but they'll let us sketch the top-level structure of the program. Moreover, we'll be able to compile and run the "sketch" and see the top-level flow of control.

The stack is passed from the calculator to the sequencer and we don't need to know anything about it (other than that the stack is an object of class `IStack`). Hence the temporary trivial implementation:

```
class IStack { };
```

The sequencer has all the methods stubbed out. I have added to it a dummy variable, _done, to simulate the finiteness of the stack. GetNum returns the arbitrarily chosen number 13.

```
class StackSeq
{
public:
  StackSeq (IStack const & stack)
    : _stack (stack), _done (false)
  {
    std::cout << "Stack sequencer created\n";
  }
  bool AtEnd () const { return _done;}
  void Advance () { _done = true; }
  int GetNum () const { return 13; }
private:
  IStack const & _stack;
  bool      _done;
};
```

At this level of detail, the class `Input` exposes only its constructor:

```
class Input
{
public:
  Input ()
  {
    std::cout << "Input created\n";
  }
};
```

The calculator, again, has a dummy variable whose purpose is to break out of the loop in main after just one iteration.

```
class Calculator
{
public:
  Calculator () : _done (false)
  {
    std::cout << "Calculator created\n";
  }
  bool Execute (Input& input)
  {
    std::cout << "Calculator::Execute\n";
    return !_done;
  }
  IStack const & GetStack () //const
  {
    _done = true;
    return _stack;
  }
private:
  IStack _stack;
  bool _done;
};
```

The method GetStack[1] returns a const reference to IStack. In other words, GetStack makes a read-only alias for the calculator's private object _stack and makes it available to the caller. The user may use this alias to access _stack, but only through its const methods; or, if it is an IStack friend, by reading the values of _top and those stored in the array _arr. This is exactly what the sequencer needs.

Notice also that the statement return _stack is interpreted by the compiler to return a *reference* to _stack. This is because GetStack was declared as returning a reference. If GetStack was declared as

```
IStack const GetStack ();
```

the compiler would return a read-only *copy* of the stack. Copying the stack is somewhat more expensive than providing a reference to it. We'll come back to this problem later, when we talk about value classes.

With all the dummies in place, we can compile and execute the test program. Its output shows that everything works as expected.

---

1. I had to comment on the const modifier of the method GetStack because in this temporary implementation GetStack modifies the member _done. (A better technique would be to add the mutable modifier, which will be disucssed later, to the declaration of _done.)

```
Calculator created
> Input created
Calculator::Execute
Stack sequencer created
  13
> Input created
Calculator::Execute
```

2.3.4   Implementation

calc2   Since our project will be growing, we should split it into separate files. We need
three header files for class definitions—calc.h, stack.h, and input.h—as well as
three implementation files—calc.cpp, stack.cpp, and input.cpp. To build an
executable program out of multiple source files one needs the help of a *linker*.
Fortunately, in an integrated environment you can create a project to which you
add all the implementation files and let the environment *build* the program for
you. However, we don't want to get too involved in such details here.

The more header files we have, the more likely it is we will include the same
file twice. How can this happen? Suppose we include input.h inside calc.h. Then
we include both calc.h and input.h inside calc.cpp, and we're in trouble. The
compiler will see two definitions of class Input (they're identical, but that doesn't
matter). The way to protect ourselves from such situations is to guard the header
files with conditional compilation directives. Let's enclose the whole body of
input.h with the pair

```
#if !defined input_h
...
#endif
```

If the symbol input_h is not defined, the compiler will process the code between these two *preprocessor directives* (as they are called). In the beginning, this
symbol is not defined by anybody. So the first time the compiler encounters the
#include "input.h" directive, it will go ahead and process input.h. However, the
first directive inside the if/endif pair defines the symbol input_h:

```
#define input_h
```

The next time the #include "input.h" directive is encountered, the compiler will
skip everything between #if !defined input_h and #endif, because input_h has
already been defined (the exclamation mark is the familiar logical NOT).

Calculator: Implementation

Starting a top to bottom descent, the first candidate for implementation is the
Calculator itself. When implementing the calculator we'll find out what we need
from the Input object. The Execute method should retrieve one of the following
tokens from the input: the number token, any of the arithmetic operator tokens,

or the *error* token. For each type we do a different thing. For the *number* token we
retrieve the value of the number from the input and push it on the stack. For the
operator we pop two numbers (or one number if there aren't two), pass them to the
`Calculate` method, and push the result.

```cpp
bool Calculator::Execute (Input const & input)
{
    int token = input.Token ();
    bool status = false; // Assume failure

    if (token == tokError)
    {
        std::cout << "Unknown token\n";
    }
    else if (token == tokNumber)
    {
        if (_stack.IsFull ())
        {
            std::cout << "Stack is full\n";
        }
        else
        {
            _stack.Push (input.Number ());
            status = true; // Success
        }
    }
    else
    {
        // Contract: Input must not produce any other tokens
        assert (token == '+' || token == '-'
                || token == '*' || token == '/');
        if (_stack.IsEmpty ())
        {
            std::cout << "Stack is empty\n";
        }
        else
        {
            int num2 = _stack.Pop ();
            int num1;
            // Special case, when only one number on the stack:
            // use this number for both operands.
            if (_stack.IsEmpty ())
                num1 = num2;
            else
                num1 = _stack.Pop ();

            _stack.Push (Calculate (num1, num2, token));
            status = true;
        }
    }
    return status;
}
```

We have introduced the extension of the conditional—the `else` clause. The body of the `else` statement is executed only if the preceding `if` statement hasn't been executed (because the condition was false).

`if`/`else` statements can be staggered like this:

```
if (A)
  ...
else if (B)
  ...
else if (C)
  ...
else
  ...
```

`Calculate` is the new method of `Calculator`. Since it is used only inside the implementation of `Calculator`, it is made private. It takes two numbers and a token and it returns the result of the operation. I have separated this code into a method because the `Execute` method was getting too large. `Calculate` has a well-defined functionality quite independent from the rest of the code.[2] It is implemented as one large staggered `if`/`else` construct.

```cpp
int Calculator::Calculate (int num1,
                           int num2,
                           int token) const
{
  int result;

  if (token == '+')
    result = num1 + num2;
  else if (token == '-')
    result = num1 - num2;
  else if (token == '*')
    result = num1 * num2;
  else if (token == '/')
  {
    if (num2 == 0)
    {
      std::cout << "Division by zero\n";
      result = 0;
    }
    else
      result = num1 / num2; // Integer division
  }
  return result;
}
```

---

2. Strictly speaking, `Calculate` should be a `static` method because it doesn't use any `Calculator` members. We'll talk about static methods later in this book.

Notice the use of character literals such as '+', '-', '*', '/'. Unlike string literals, character literals are surrounded by *single* quotes. Instead of assigning special values to *operator* tokens, we just used their character literal (ASCII) values.

Let's have a look at the modified Calculator class definition.

```
class Calculator
{
public:
  bool Execute (Input const & input);
  // Give access to the stack
  IStack const & GetStack () const { return _stack; }
private:
  int Calculate (int n1, int n2, int token) const;
  IStack _stack;

};
```

We can now add our old implementation of IStack and StackSeq, extend the dummy Input by adding dummy implementations of the methods Token and Number, define tokError and tokNumber as const integers, recompile, and run the program.

Input: Implementation

Now it's time to implement the Input class.

calc3

```
#if !defined input_h  // Prevent multiple inclusions
#define input_h

const int maxBuf = 100;

// Tokens are tokNumber, tokError, +, -, *, /.

const int tokNumber = 1;
const int tokError = 2;

// Gets input from stdin, converts to token.

class Input
{
public:
  Input ();
  int Token () const { return _token; }
  int Number () const;
private:
  int _token;
  char _buf [maxBuf];
};

#endif // input_h
```

Notice that the methods `Token` and `Number` are declared `const`. `Calculator` has read-only access to the `Input` class (through a `const` reference) and still can call these methods. The buffer `_buf` is where the string obtained from the user will be stored.

The implementation file `input.cpp` includes two new standard headers.

```
#include <cctype>
#include <cstdlib>
```

The header `cctype` contains the definitions of (very efficient) macros that recognize character type. The `isdigit` macro, for instance, returns true if the character is one of the digits between 0 and 9 and false otherwise. The other file, `cstdlib`, is needed for the declaration of the function `atoi` that converts an ASCII string representing a decimal number to an integer. You can find out more about functions like that by studying the C++ standard library. You can refer to the compiler's online Help or printed manuals (or some other books).

```
Input::Input ( )
{
  std::cin >> _buf;

  // First char of input is usually enough to decide
  // what token it is

  int c = _buf [0];

  if (std::isdigit (c))
    _token = tokNumber;
  else if (c == '+' || c == '*' || c == '/')
    _token = c;
  else if (c == '-') // Allow entering negative numbers
  {
    if (std::isdigit (_buf [1])) // Peek at next char
      _token = tokNumber;
    else
      _token = c;
  }
  else
    _token = tokError;
}
```

The constructor of `Input` reads a line of text from the standard input into a character buffer. This is yet another amazing trick performed by our friend `cin`. (By the way, for the time being, we are not even thinking about what could happen if the buffer overflows. We are still at the level of "weekend programming.")

Depending on the first character in the buffer, we decide what token to make out of it. Notice the special treatment of the minus sign. It could be a binary minus, or it could be a unary minus in front of a number. To find out which one it is, we peek at the next character in the buffer. Notice the use of one of the character classification macros I mentioned before. isdigit returns true when the character is a digit (that is, 0, 1, 2 ... or 9). The character classification macros are implemented using a very efficient *table lookup* method. It is actually more efficient to call isdigit than to execute code like this (the double ampersand, **&&,** is a logical AND, see "Logic" on page 47):

```
if (c >= '0' && c <= '9')
```

The header cctype contains other useful macros besides isdigit, like isspace, islower, and isupper.

If the token is tokNumber, the Calculator needs to know its value. The method Number converts the string in the buffer into an int value using the library function atoi declared in cstdlib.

```
int Input::Number () const
{
  assert (_token == tokNumber);
  return std::atoi (_buf);  // Convert string to integer
}
```

Exercises

1. Add bitwise operations to our calculator.

2. Add a new command, *x*, that toggles between decimal and hexadecimal outputs.

   Hint: To output a number in hexadecimal (base sixteen), send the manipulator hex to the output.

   ```
   std::cout << std::hex;
   ```

   To toggle the output back to decimal, send it the manipulator dec.

3. Create a "logical calculator" that operates on Boolean values. Instead of numbers, it accepts *t* and *f* for true and false. It performs logical *and, or,* and *not,* and accepts &, |, and ! as tokens (notice the *not* is a unary operation—it takes one argument). Send the manipulator std::boolalpha to the output stream before printing Boolean values.

Chapter 3
Pointers

Using references, we can give multiple names to the same object. Using pointers, we can have the same name refer to different objects—a pointer is a *mutable* reference.

Pointers give us power to create complex data structures. They also increase our ability to shoot ourselves in the foot. A pointer is like a plug that can be plugged into a jack. If you have too many plugs and too many jacks, you may end up with a mess of tangled cables. A programmer has to strike a balance between creating a program that looks like a breadboard or like a printed circuit.

3.1 The Evils of Pointers

A pointer variable stores the *memory address* of an object (for instance, of a variable, an array, a function, an instance of a class, and so on). Using a pointer one can access the contents of the object it points to. In this sense a pointer acts just like a reference: it is an alias of some other object. There is, however, one big difference between a pointer and a reference. Pointers are not permanently attached to objects—they can be moved. The programmer can change a pointer to point to another object (or to no object at all!). This is a very powerful feature and, at the same time, a very dangerous one. The majority of programming bugs involve, in one way or another, the use of pointers. In C++ (and C) we have the following types of pointers:

- Uninitialized pointers
- Pointers to deallocated memory
- Pointers beyond the end of an array

- Pointers that think they point to something else
- Cross-your-fingers/knock-on-wood kind of pointers

Obviously, we don't want to use such pointers. We want to use pointers that at all times point to what they think (and we think, and the next person thinks) they point to. And that requires a lot of discipline on the programmer's part. Therefore, the first rule of pointer use is:

> **Don't use pointers unless there is no other way.**

Use references instead, whenever possible. You'll definitely avoid the problem of uninitialized pointers. Using references also gives you the opportunity to fine-tune the scope of objects and variables. References, unlike pointers, have to be initialized at the point of definition. If they are inside of an object, you'll have to define this object in the right spot. It must be created within the scope where these references are available. That imposes a certain natural order of creation.

Another misuse of pointers, a heritage of C, is the use of pointers in place of array indexes. The old argument was that scanning an array using a pointer results in faster code. Not so with modern optimizing compilers. It turns out that a compiler is more likely to do some aggressive (but correct!) optimizations when the algorithm is expressed using indexes rather than pointers. So there goes another myth from the dark ages of computing. We'll discuss this issue in more detail soon.

Finally, many C programmers are used to combining pointers with error codes, that is, using a null pointer as a sign of an error. Although there are ways of faking "null references," they won't be discussed in this book for obvious reasons (they are ugly hacks!). The solution is either to separate error codes from references, or to use exceptions (see Chapter 10, Resource Management) to signal abnormal conditions. Of course, there is nothing wrong with functions that return pointers *by design* and use the null-pointer trick to signal special conditions.

> There is an opposing school of thought about dealing with pointers—fighting fire with fire. Some object-oriented languages, notably Java and C#, use pointers as the only way of accessing objects. The trick is that they don't allow C-style manipulation of pointers. In Java, pointers are treated like immutable handles. Moreover, languages like Java, C#, Smalltalk, and Eiffel implement garbage collection. The programmer is freed from the chore of keeping track of pointers and objects they point to, because the runtime system takes care of it. It reference-counts every object and automatically destroys an object when it's not referenced by any pointer. This service doesn't come for free, though—there is a runtime cost associated with it. Moreover, not having direct control over when the destructors are executed makes the methods of resource management impossible to implement in such systems. But I am getting ahead of myself. We'll discuss these topics later in more detail.

3.2 Pointers versus References

A pointer variable is declared with an asterisk between the type name and the variable name (the asterisk binds with the variable name). For instance,

```
int * pValue;
```

declares pValue to be a pointer to an integer. The pointer can be initialized with (or assigned to, using the assignment operator =) an address of some other variable. The *address of* operator is denoted by the ampersand (there is no conflict between this ampersand and the reference ampersand—they appear in different contexts). For instance,

```
int TheValue = 10;
pValue = &TheValue;
```

assigns the address of the variable TheValue to the pointer pValue. (see Figure 3.1).

If we want to access the value to which the pointer points, we use the *dereference* operator, the asterisk (again, its double meaning can't cause any confusion). For instance, in

```
int i = *pValue;
```

the value that pValue points to is assigned to the integer i. In our example, i will change its value to 10. Conversely,

```
*pValue = 20;
```

changes the value that pValue points to, that is, the value of TheValue. (The value of TheValue will now be 20.) As you can see, this is a little bit more complicated than using references.

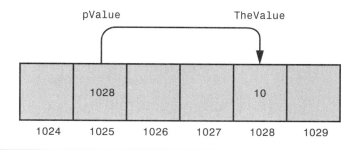

Figure 3.1 The pointer pValue stores the address of (that is, points to) the variable TheValue.

By the way, the same example with references would look like this:

```
int TheValue = 10;
int & aliasValue = TheValue; // Refers to TheValue
int i = aliasValue; // Access TheValue through an alias
aliasValue = 20; // Change TheValue through an alias
```

3.3 Pointers versus Arrays

Accessing arrays through pointers, arrays of pointers.

Arrays are passed around as pointers. In fact, a C++ array is implemented as a pointer to the first element of the array. In practical terms this means we can access a pointer as if it were an array—that is, using an index. Conversely, we can use a pointer to access elements of an array. We can increment a pointer to move from one element of the array to the next. Of course, in either case it is our responsibility to make sure that the pointer actually points to an element of an array.

A string is a good example of an array. There is a function in the standard library called strlen that calculates the length of a null-terminated string (its declaration is in the <cstring> header). Let's write our own implementation of this function, which we will call StrLen.

```
int StrLen (char const str [])
{
  int i;
  for (i = 0; str [i] != '\0'; ++i)
      continue;
  return i;
}
```

The continue keyword is used here instead of an empty body of the loop (which would be a semicolon on its own). It means to skip the rest of the body of the loop (if any) and go back to the loop-head to continue with the next iteration.

Here's the main procedure that passes an array to StrLen:

```
int main ()
{
  char aString [] = "the long string";
  int len = StrLen (aString);
  std::cout << "The length of " << aString
            << " is " << len << std::endl;
}
```

We are scanning the string for a terminating null and returning the index of this null. Pretty obvious, isn't it?

Here's a more traditional "optimized" version (see also Figure 3.2). (Warning: This extremely terse style of programming is not recommended!)

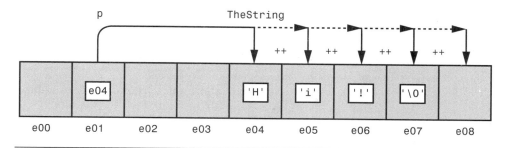

Figure 3.2 The pointer p initially points at the first character of the string "Hi!" at address 0xe04 (I use hexadecimal notation for addresses). Subsequent increments move it through the characters of the string until the null character is reached and processed.

```
int StrLen (char const * pStr)
{
  char const * p = pStr;
  while (*p++)
    ;
  return p - pStr - 1;
}
```

We initialize p to point to the beginning of the string. The while loop is a little cryptic, to say the least. We dereference the pointer, test it for Boolean truth, and *post-increment* it, all in one statement. If the character obtained by dereferencing the pointer is not zero (because zero is equivalent to Boolean false), we will continue looping.

The post-increment operator moves the pointer to the next position in the array, but only *after* it has been used in the expression (yielding true or false in our case). Table 3.1 lists all the increment and decrement operators.

In the spirit of terseness, I haven't bothered using the continue statement in the empty body of the loop—the semicolon (denoting the empty statement) is considered sufficient for the old-school C programmers.

	Increment operators (acting on i)
i++	Post-increment
++i	Pre-increment
	Decrement operators (acting on i)
i--	Post-decrement
--i	Pre-decrement

Table 3.1 Increment and decrement operators acting upon a variable i

Finally, we subtract the two pointers to get the number of array elements that we have gone through; and subtract 1, since we have overshot the null character (the last test accesses the null character, and then increments the pointer anyway). By the way, I never get this part right the first time around—I have to pay the penalty of an additional edit-compile-run cycle.

If you have problems understanding this second implementation, you're lucky. I won't have to convince you any further not to write code like this. However, if after seeing both versions you still don't prefer to write the simpler and more readable index implementation of procedures like StrLen, read the next section, Assembly Digression.

The art of programming is in a very peculiar situation. It is developing so fast, that people who started programming when C was in its infancy are still very active in the field. In other sciences such progress was usually made by generation after generation of researchers. Ideas that seemed new and revolutionary to one generation could be accepted by the next generation as common knowledge.

The computer revolution, on the other hand, has happened well within one generation and there hasn't been enough time for everybody to digest and accept all the progress. There are still many programmers who carry around their old (although only a decade or so old) bag of tricks, which they learned when they were programming XTs with 64K memory. A few of them still refuse to accept the new realities and, if they happen to be in a managerial position, might do quite a bit of harm.

There are some excellent old books that were so good that nobody could successfully outdo them. To this day new programmers learn programming from classics like Kernighan and Ritchie's *The C Programming Language.* It's a great book, don't get me wrong, but it teaches the programming style of times long gone.

The highest authority in algorithms and data structures is Donald Knuth's great classic *The Art of Programming.* It's a beautiful and very thorough series of scientific books. However, I've seen C implementations of quicksort that were based on the algorithms from these books. They were prestructured programming monstrosities.

Finally, if your compiler is unable to optimize the human-readable, maintainable version of the algorithm, and you have to double as a human compiler—*get a new compiler!* Nobody can afford human compilers anymore. So have mercy on yourself and your fellow programmers who will have to look at your code.

A multidimensional array can be implemented in C++ in two ways. If you know the dimensions of the array up front, you can declare it using more than one set of brackets. For instance, a 3-by-4 array of integers will look like this:

```
int arr2d [3][4];
```

and can be accessed by specifying two indexes:

```
for (int i = 0; i < 3; ++i)
  for (int j = 0; j < 4; ++j)
    arr2d [i][j] = i * 10 + j;
```

If, on the other hand, you're not sure what the length of the rows might be, or even let the length vary from row to row, you're better off using an *array of pointers*. In particular, a set of strings can be implemented as an array of pointers to characters.

Here's an example of a definition, complete with initialization, of an array of three strings.

```
char const * strings [] = { "one", "two", "three" };
```

These strings can be accessed using single indexing,

```
char const * oneStr = strings [0];
```

whereas individual characters can be accessed using double indexing,

```
char cInitial = strings [0][0];
```

Here's the interesting part—if you expect that your program will be called with command-line arguments, declare your main function like this:

```
int main (int argCount, char * arguments [])
```

When your program is called, the first parameter, argCount, will contain the count of strings that are stored in the second parameter, the array arguments. The first (or rather zeroth) string, arguments [0], will always contain the name used to invoke the program. The remaining strings, arguments [1] to arguments [argCount − 1], will contain the command-line arguments with which your program was invoked. For instance, if you have a program called testing.exe and you call it from the command line with three arguments,

```
testing one two three
```

your main will be called with four strings (argCount equal to 4), listed in Table 3.2.

3.3.1 Assembly Digression

"Beautiful it is not, but who cares, if it's more efficient." Well, not really. For those of you who understand the x86 assembler, Table 3.3 shows the output of the optimizing 16-bit compiler for the two implementations.

String	Value
arguments [0]	"c:\work\testing.exe"
arguments [1]	"one"
arguments [2]	"two"
arguments [3]	"three"

Table 3.2 Command-line arguments

Index	Pointer
| ```
?StrLen@@YAHPAD@Z       PROC NEAR
    push        bp
    mov         bp,sp
    push        di
;   pStr = 4
;   register bx = i
    mov         di,WORD PTR [bp+4]
    xor         bx,bx
    cmp         BYTE PTR [di],bl
    je          $FB1596
$F1594:
    inc         bx
    cmp         BYTE PTR [bx][di],0
    jne         $F1594
$FB1596:
    mov         ax,bx
    pop         di

    mov         sp,bp
    pop         bp
    ret
?StrLen@@YAHPAD@Z       ENDP
``` | ```
?StrLen@@YAHPAD@Z       PROC NEAR
    push        bp
    mov         bp,sp

;   register bx = p
;   pStr = 4
    mov         dx,WORD PTR [bp+4]
    mov         bx,dx


$FC1603:
    inc         bx
    cmp         BYTE PTR [bx-1],0
    jne         $FC1603

    mov         ax,bx
    sub         ax,dx
    dec         ax
    mov         sp,bp
    pop         bp
    ret
?StrLen@@YAHPAD@Z       ENDP
``` |

Table 3.3 Comparison of assembly code generated by an optimizing compiler for the two implementations of StrLen

In the first implementation the compiler decided to use two register variables, hence the additional push and pop. The loop is essentially the same; only the addressing mode is different. Under close scrutiny it turns out that the instruction in the second loop is longer by one byte in comparison with the first one.

80 39 00	cmp	BYTE PTR [bx][di],0	; first loop
80 7f ff 00	cmp	BYTE PTR [bx—1],0	; second loop

So for really long strings, the index implementation beats the pointers. Or does it? A lot depends on the alignment of the instructions. On my old machine, an 80486, the second loop turned out to be better aligned and therefore produced faster code.

In the pointer implementation, some additional pointer arithmetic is done at the end—in the index implementation, a test is done before entering the loop—but then the loop is executed one fewer time. Again on my machine, the overhead of the index solution turned out to be smaller than the overhead of the pointer one; therefore, for strings of up to three characters indexes beat pointers.

Frankly, it's six of one, half a dozen of another. Is it worth the complication? Have you actually done the comparison of assembly instructions and timings for all your favorite tricks? Maybe it's time to throw away all these idioms from the great era of hacking in C and learn some new tricks that are focused on the understandability and maintainability of code. You don't want to end up penny-wise and pound-foolish.

Don't use pointers where an index will do.

Exercises

1. Implement the function

    ```
    void StrCpy (char * strDest, char const * strSrc);
    ```

    that copies the source string up to, and with the terminating null, into the destination string. The destination string is assumed to have enough space (unfortunately, we can't simply assert it). Use the "indexing the array" method rather than pointers to char.

2. Implement the function

    ```
    int StrCmp (char const * str1, char const * str2);
    ```

    that lexicographically compares two strings. It returns zero when the strings are equal, returns a number greater than zero when the second string is "less" than the first one, and returns less than zero when the second string is "greater" than the first one.

    The strings are compared character-by-character until a mismatch is found. If the first differing character in str1 has an ASCII code greater than the corresponding character in str2, the return value is positive; otherwise, it's negative. The comparison stops when a null character is encountered in either string. If str1 is longer, a positive number is returned; if str2 is longer, a negative number is returned. Use the index implementation.

3. Another of these old "optimizing" tricks is to run a loop backwards. Instead of incrementing the counter, we decrement it until it becomes negative or reaches zero. (At some point every programmer gets bitten by this trick when the loop variable is of the unsigned type.)

Find a bug and rewrite the function

```
void StrNCpy (char * strDest,
              char const * strSrc, std::size_t len)
{
  while (len--)
    *strDest++ = *strSrc++;
}
```

where std::size_t is some unsigned integral type defined, for instance, in cstring.

Get rid of the "optimizing" tricks introduced here by a human compiler.

4. Write a test program that prints its command-line arguments.

3.4   Pointers and Dynamic Memory Allocation

Despite all the negative advertising in this book, pointers are invaluable whenever dynamic data structures are involved. Dynamic data structures have to be able to grow and shrink. Growing involves acquiring new areas of memory and cultivating them; shrinking means recycling them. How do we acquire new areas of memory? We have to ask the system to give us memory for a particular type of variable or object. We do it using the operator new. The memory returned by new is allocated from the so-called *heap*—the area of memory managed by the C++ runtime. How do we access this new memory? Using a *pointer* to that particular type of variable or object. For instance, to get enough memory to store a single integer[1], we'd use the following syntax:

```
int * pNumber = new int;
```

Even better, we could (and should) immediately initialize this memory with a particular value we want to store there (see Figure 3.3).

---

1. You can store an int in a local variable if its lifetime corresponds to some convenient scope. But if you need storage for an int whose lifetime it not easily confined to a scope or you can't tell up front how many ints you will need, you won't be able to use local variables for all of them, and your only choice will be to allocate space dynamically.

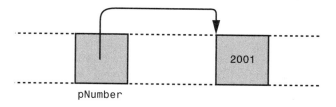

pNumber

Figure 3.3 New memory for an integer was allocated and initialized with the value of 2001. The pointer pNumber contains the address of this new memory.

```
int * pNumber = new int (2001);
```

Initialization is mandatory when allocating an object that has a constructor. There are two cases: In the first case, when a constructor doesn't take any arguments, you don't have to do anything—such a constructor is called by default. An argument-less constructor may, for instance, initialize member variables to some predefined values (e.g., zeros).

```
IStack* pStack = new IStack; // Default constructor called
```

In the second instance, when the object has a constructor that requires arguments, we have to specify their values in the call to new:

```
Star * pStar = new Star (1234.5, 10.2);
```

If we want to store *n* integers, we need to allocate an array of *n* integers (see Figure 3.4).

```
int * pNumbers = new int [n];
```

Similarly, we can allocate an array of objects that don't have constructors, for instance,

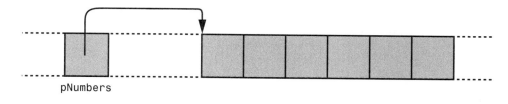

pNumbers

Figure 3.4 The result of allocating an array

```
Calculator * calcs = new Calculator [100];
```

Notice that even if an object doesn't have an explicit constructor, the compiler might have to generate some code to construct it. For instance, a `Calculator` has an `IStack` embedded in it, so the *default constructor* of a `Calculator` must call the (argument-less) constructor of `IStack`. You don't have to write (declare or define) this constructor—the compiler does it for you. The compiler always generates an invisible constructor (and destructor) when there is a need to initialize embedded objects or base classes. This means that the above code will in fact execute the `IStack` constructor a hundred times—once for each `Calculator`.

Of course, if a class has a no-argument constructor explicitly defined, this constructor will be called by the compiler for each allocation, like in this case:

```
IStack * stacks = new IStack [100]
```

But what are we to do if we want to dynamically allocate an array of objects that *do* have nontrivial constructors? Take a `CelestialBody`, for instance. It has a constructor that requires an argument—the value of the mass. If you write the line

```
CelestialBody * bodies = new CelestialBody [100];
```

the compiler will refuse to compile it. Once an object has a nontrivial constructor, the compiler (correctly) assumes that it can't just go ahead and generate a default, no-argument constructor for it.

If you want to be able to allocate arrays of `CelestialBodys`, you must provide a no-argument constructor like this, for instance:

```
CelestialBody () : _mass (0) {}
```

You can keep *both* constructors in your class definition as long as they differ by the number or types of arguments. In general, using the same name for more than one method is called *overloading*. You have to make sure that it will be clear for the compiler *which* overload to call just by looking at the number and type of arguments you're passing when making a call.

Finally, you can combine the two overloads of the constructor of `CelestialBody` by providing a default value for its parameter. In the class declaration you can write:

```
CelestialBody (double mass = 0.0) : _mass (mass) {}
```

This will be equivalent to having two overloaded constructors with zero and one argument. It will let you write code like this:

```
CelestialBody * bodies = new CelestialBody [100];
```

> You can provide default values to arguments of any method. The only limi-
> tation is that the default arguments must follow the nondefault ones. When call-
> ing such a method, you can skip any number of trailing arguments for which the
> compiler will use the defaults you have specified in the definition of the method
> (or constructor).

There is no direct way to initialize the contents of a dynamically allocated
array, because there is no way to pass initial values or arguments to objects' constructors. We just have to iterate through newly allocated arrays and set the values
by hand. For example:

```
for (int i = 0; i < n; ++i)
    pNumbers [i] = i * i;
```

To recycle, or free, the memory allocated with new, we use the operator
delete:

```
delete pNumber;
```

If the object being deleted has a destructor, it will be called automatically. For
instance,

```
delete pStar;
```

will print "Destroying a star of brightness. . . . "

In the case of arrays, we precede the pointer to be deleted with square brackets. (We put the brackets in front of the pointer name, rather than after it.)

```
delete [] pNumbers;
```

Again, if we are dealing with an array of objects, the destructor for each of them is
automatically called.

This is not the case in an *array of pointers!* When an array of pointers is deleted,
the objects pointed to by elements of the array are *not* automatically deleted. You
have to actually go through a loop and delete each of them. The rule of thumb is:
Try to allocate memory in the constructor of an object and deallocate it in its destructor. The deallocation should then reflect the allocation. If you had to call the
operator new in a loop, you'll have to call the operator delete in a similar loop.

Deleting a null pointer is safe. Hint:

> **Don't check for a null pointer before calling** delete.

```
delete will do it for you anyway.
```

What happens if we forget to call `delete` for a dynamically allocated object or array? The memory it occupies will never be recycled (at least not until the program terminates). We call it a *memory leak*. Is it a bug? During program termination all memory is freed anyway (although no destructors are called for the leaked objects), so who cares?

It depends. If the program repeatedly leaks more and more memory during its execution, it will eventually run out of memory. So that's a bug. (And a very difficult one to catch, I might add.) Good programming practice, therefore, is to *always deallocate* everything that has ever been allocated. Incidentally, there are tools and techniques to monitor memory leaks. I'll talk about these later.

3.5 Dynamic Data Structures

Linked lists, recursive type definitions, hash tables, arrays and pointers.

It is time to introduce a few fundamental data structures that will serve as building blocks for the creation of more complex objects. We will start with a dynamic array (actually a stack), a linked list, and a string buffer. Then we will introduce hash tables, and finally we'll put all these components together to form a string table—a data structure for efficient storage and retrieval of strings.

It's good to know that almost all of these data structures are available through the C++ standard library. A dynamic array is called a `vector`; there is also a `list`, a `string`, and much more. There are, however, several reasons why I'd like you to first learn to implement these data structures without using the standard library. First, it will be a good exercise and a good way to learn the language step-by-step. Second, I want you to get an idea how these data structures might be implemented in the standard library. Third, the standard library uses very advanced features of the language (e.g., templates, operator overloading, and so on), which we haven't talked about yet. We'll get there later, though.

3.5.1 Dynamic Stack

Dynamic arrays.

calc4   We will now modify the contract of our stack. There will no longer be a strict limit on how many integers can be pushed; we'll be able to keep pushing until the computer runs out of memory.

We would like our implementation not to be a memory hog (at least when it's not necessary), so we won't preallocate the largest available chunk of memory. Instead, we'll allocate some minimum number of bytes, and every time we run out of space in the stack we'll just double its size. Obviously, we'll no longer need the method `IsFull`. Other than that, the interface will be the same as that of our old stack.

Here's how our new stack works: There's a private helper function `Grow` that's used internally to double the stack size. We store the current capacity of the stack in the private data member _capacity. For the purpose of testing we'll set the initial capacity of the stack to one, so we'll be able to see the stack grow almost immediately.

```
const int initStack = 1;
class IStack
{
public:
  IStack ();
  ~IStack ();
  void Push (int i);
  int Pop ();
  int Top () const;
  bool IsEmpty () const;
private:
  void Grow ();
  int * _arr;
  int   _capacity; // Size of the array
  int   _top;
};
```

Notice that _arr is declared as a pointer rather than an array. A dynamically allocated array *must* be declared as a pointer.

We allocate the initial array in the constructor of IStack and we delete the memory in the destructor.

```
IStack::IStack ()
  : _top (0), _capacity (initStack)
{
  _arr = new int [initStack]; // Allocate memory
}

IStack::~IStack ()
{
  delete [ ]_arr; // Free memory
}
```

This illustrates a new kind of relationship between objects. Not only can we say that IStack has access to the array, we can say that IStack *owns* the array (see Figure 3.5). The *owns-a* relationship is expressed using a pointer. Object A owns

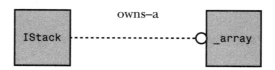

Figure 3.5 The owns-a relationship between objects

object B if object A is responsible for object B's deallocation. We'll talk much more about this when we discuss resource management.

IStack acquires the memory for the array in its constructor and deallocates the memory in its destructor. In a moment we'll see that the method Grow does some reallocation of its own.

So what happens when we Push an integer and there is no space left in the array? We call the Grow method and complete the Push.

```
void IStack::Push (int i)
{
  assert (_top <= _capacity);
  if (_top == _capacity)
      Grow ();
  _arr [_top] = i;
  ++_top;
}
```

Let's see what Grow does. It has to go through the following steps:

1. Allocate a new array twice the size of the current array.

2. Copy all entries from the old array into the first half of the new array.

3. Double the _capacity variable.

4. Delete the old array.

5. Set the pointer _arr to point to the newly allocated array.

```
void IStack::Grow ()
{
  std::cout << "Doubling stack from "
            << _capacity << ".\n";
  // Allocate new array
  int * arrNew = new int [2 * _capacity];
  // Copy all entries
  for (int i = 0; i < _capacity; ++i)
    arrNew [i] = _arr [i];
  _capacity = 2 * _capacity;
  // Free old memory
  delete []_arr;
  // Substitute new array for old array
  _arr = arrNew;
}
```

The statement

```
_arr = arrNew;
```

is a *pointer assignment.* We are changing the pointer _arr to point to the new location—the same location arrNew is pointing at. This is the one operation that we cannot do with references. Notice that we are not changing the *contents* of the location. That would be done in the statement

```
*_arr = *arrNew;
```

or its equivalent

```
_arr [0] = arrNew [0];
```

We are changing the pointer _arr itself.

```
_arr = arrNew;
```

For completeness, here are the implementations of the rest of the methods. Notice that although _arr is a pointer, it is accessed like an array.

```
int IStack::Pop ()
{
  // Do not Pop an empty stack
  assert (_top > 0);
  --top;
  return _arr [_top];
}
int IStack::Top () const
{
  // Don't call Top on an empty stack
  assert (_top > 0);
  return _arr [_top - 1];
}
bool IStack::IsEmpty () const
{
  assert (_top >= 0);
  return _top == 0;
}
```

The expression _top == 0 evaluates to Boolean true or false and this result is returned from IsEmpty. We can now substitute this new implementation of IStack in our calculator and test it. Notice that we never shrink the stack. This is called a *high water mark* type of the algorithm. It would, however, be easy to add the Shrink method that would be called by Pop every time _top gets much below _size/2.

3.5.2   Linked List

A linked list is a dynamic data structure for fast constant time, (independent of the size of the list) prepending and linear time (proportional to the size of the list) searching. Linear time searching means that as the list grows in size, so does the search time. A list consists of links. Suppose that we want to store some integer IDs in a list. A Link will contain a field for an ID and a pointer to the next link. To see how it works in practice, let's look at Figure 3.6.

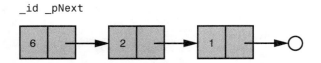

Figure 3.6 A linked list storing numbers 6, 2, and 1

The last link in the list has the null (zero) pointer _pNext. That's the list termi-
nator. A *null pointer* is never a valid pointer, that is, it cannot be dereferenced. It
can, however, be checked against zero.

list   This is the class Link:

```
class Link
{
public:
  Link (Link* pNext, int id)
    : _pNext (pNext), _id (id) {}
  Link * Next () const { return _pNext; }
  int    Id () const { return _id; }
private:
  int    _id;
  Link *_pNext;
};
```

Notice how the definition of Link is self-referencing—a Link contains a
pointer to a Link. It's okay to use *pointers* and *references* to types whose definitions
haven't been seen by the compiler. The only thing needed by the compiler in such
a case is the *declaration* of the type. In our case, the first line

```
class Link
```

serves as such a declaration (not to be confused with forward declarations—see
page 204).

A linked List stores a pointer to the first link. Conceptually, a list is a different
object than the link. To begin with, it has a different interface. One can add new
items to the list and remove them as well. One can also iterate through the list.
These operations make no sense as methods of Link. Yet, in some sense, every link
is a beginning of a list. This recursive way of looking at things is very popular in
languages like LISP. We usually try to avoid such recursive concepts in object-oriented programming. So for us, a List will be a different creature than a Link.

Starting from the first link pointed to by _pHead, we can traverse the whole list
following the pointers _pNext.

In the beginning, the list is empty and the pointer _pHead is initialized to zero.

```
class List
{
public:
  List (): _pHead (0) {}
  ~List ();
  void Add (int id);
  Link const * GetHead () const { return _pHead; }
private:
  Link* _pHead;

};
```

Adding a new ID to the list is done by allocating a new link and initializing it with the ID and the pointer to the next item. The next item is the link that was previously at the beginning of the list. (It was pointed to by _pHead.) The new link becomes the head of the list and _pHead is pointed to it (pointer assignment), as illustrated in Figure 3.7. This process is called *prepending*.

```
void List::Add (int id)
{
  // Add in front of the list
  Link * pLink = new Link (_pHead, id);
  _pHead = pLink;
}
```

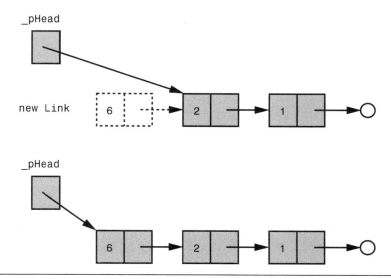

Figure 3.7 Prepending a new element in front of the list

Since the list grows dynamically, every new Link has to be allocated using the operator new. When a *new object* is allocated, its constructor is automatically called. This is why we are passing the constructor arguments in new Link (_pHead, id).

List iteration, that is, going through the whole list element by element, is simple enough. For instance, here's how we can do a search for a link containing a given ID:

```
for (Link const * pLink = list.GetHead();
     pLink != 0;
     pLink = pLink->Next ())
{
  if (pLink->Id() == id)
     break;
}
```

In pLink–>Next () we are calling a member function of an object to which we have access through a pointer. We have to dereference the pointer and then access the member function. This can be done explicitly, as in (*pLink).Next (), or using a shorthand, operator –>, which combines the two actions (dereferencing and member access).

The break statement can be used in any kind of loop to immediately exit its body. I prefer this style (even though it doesn't strictly adhere to the principles of structured programming) over the terser version of the same code

```
for (Link const * pLink = list.GetHead();
     pLink != 0 && pLink->Id () != id;
     pLink = pLink->Next ())
{
  continue; // Empty loop body
}
```

which mixes two exit conditions in the loop header. In fact (and this will also be sneered at by structural-programming purists), you can use a return statement to break from a loop. For instance, this is how one might implement a Find function:

```
bool List::Find (int id) const
{
  for (Link const * pLink = GetHead();
       pLink != 0;
       pLink = pLink->Next ())
  {
    if (pLink->Id() == id)
       return true;
  }
  return false;
}
```

The list has a destructor in which it deallocates all the links. The list *owns* the links.

```
List::~List ()
{
  // Free the list
  while (_pHead != 0)
  {
    Link* pLinkTmp = _pHead;
    _pHead = _pHead->Next(); // Unlink pLink
    delete pLinkTmp;
  }
}
```

The algorithm for deallocating a list works as follows: As long as there is something in the list, we point a temporary pointer, pLinkTmp, at the first link; point the _pHead at the next link (could be null), which is equivalent to unlinking the first link; and delete this link (see Figure 3.8). The statement

```
_pHead = _pHead->Next ();
```

is a pointer assignment. _pHead will now point at the same link that is pointed at by

```
_pHead->_pNext
```

Again, this is something we wouldn't be able to do with references.

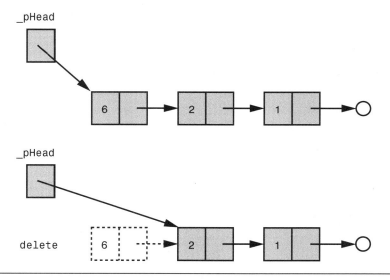

Figure 3.8 The unlinking and deleting of the first element of the list

There is a simpler, recursive implementation of the linked list destructor:

```
List::~List ()
{
  delete _pHead;
}
Link::~Link ()
{
  delete _pNext;
}
```

When a `Link` is destroyed, it deletes its successor, which in turn will delete its successor, and so on. The recursion stops automatically when it reaches the terminating null pointer, because no destructor is called on a null pointer.

Simplicity is the obvious advantage of the recursive solution. The price you pay for this simplicity is speed and memory usage. Recursive function calls are usually more expensive than looping (although there are compiler optimizations, for the so-called tail recursion, that may turn recursion into iteration). Recursive function calls also consume the program stack space. If stack is at a premium (e.g., when you're writing the kernel of an operating system), recursion is out of the question. But even if you have plenty of stack, you might still be better off using the iterative solution for really large linked lists. On the other hand, because of memory thrashing, really large linked lists are a bad idea. In any case, whichever way you go, it's good to know your trade-offs.

Notice also the use of pointers to `const` in our code. The method `GetHead` is declared to return a pointer to a `const Link`.

```
Link const * GetHead () const;
```

The variable we assign it to must therefore be a pointer to a `const Link` too.

```
Link const * pLink = list.GetHead ();
```

The meaning of a pointer to `const` is the same as the meaning of a reference to `const`—the object pointed to, or referred to, cannot be changed through such a pointer or reference. In the case of a pointer, however, we have to distinguish between a pointer to `const` and a `const` pointer. The latter is a pointer that, once initialized, cannot be pointed to anything else (just like a reference). The syntax for these two cases is

```
Link const * pLink; // Pointer to const
Link * const pLink = pInitPtr; // const pointer
```

Finally, the two can be combined to form a const pointer to const:

```
Link const * const pLink = pInitPtr; // const ptr to const
```

This last pointer can only be used for read access to a single location to which it was initialized.

There is some confusion in the naming of pointers and references when combined with const. Since there is only one possibility of const-ness for a reference, one often uses the terms reference to const and const reference interchangeably. Unfortunately, the two cases are often confused when applied to pointers. In this book const pointer will always mean a pointer that cannot be moved, and pointer to const means a pointer through which one cannot write.

But wait, there's even more to confuse you! There is an equivalent syntax for a pointer to const:

```
const Link * pLink; // Pointer to const
```

and, of course,

```
const Link * const pLink = pInitPtr; // const ptr to const
```

The source of all this confusion is our insistence on reading text from left to right (people in the Middle East will laugh at us). Since C was written for computers and not humans, the direction of reading didn't really matter. So, to this day, declarations are best read right to left.

Let's play with reversing some of the declarations. Remember that the asterisk means "pointer to a." This declaration,

```
Link const * pLink;
```

becomes Figure 3.9.

Similarly,

```
Link * const pLink;
```

turns into Figure 3.10.

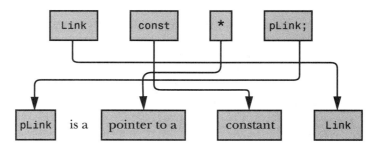

Figure 3.9 Reading type declarations: pLink is a pointer to a constant Link

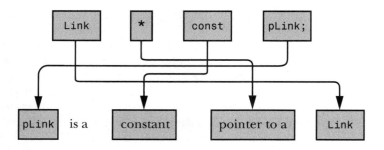

Figure 3.10 Reading type declarations: `pLink` is a constant pointer to a `Link`

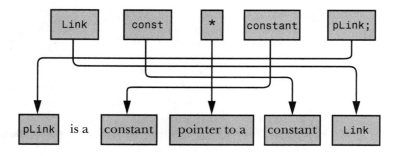

Figure 3.11 Reading type declarations: `pLink` is a constant pointer to a constant `Link`

This one,

```
Link const * const pLink = pInitPtr;
```

becomes Figure 3.11.

3.5.3 String Table

A string table maps integers to strings and strings to integers. The first mapping is easily implemented using an array of strings (pointers, or even better, offsets into a buffer). The second one is more difficult to implement efficiently.

Our goal is to have constant time access both ways. It means that, independent of how many strings there are in the table (within some reasonable limits), the mapping of an `int` into a string should always take, more or less, the same amount of time (in programmer speak, big-O of 1, or O(1), or *constant* time). The same should be true about the inverse mapping—string to `int`. Notice that in the simplest implementation—going through the list of strings and comparing each with the search string—the execution takes longer and longer as the list grows (we say, it grows linearly, or O(N)). However, there is a data structure called a *hash table* that can accomplish constant time mapping. We'll use it to implement an efficient string table.

strtab

With this performance goal in mind, we are ready to start designing the string table. Since we want to be able to add lots of strings to it, we will need a large buffer to store them. The StringBuffer object stores a string and returns an offset at which the string can be found. This offset, in turn, is stored in another data structure, an array of offsets, that maps integer IDs to string offsets. Each string is thus assigned an ID, which is simply the index into the array of offsets (see Figure 3.12).

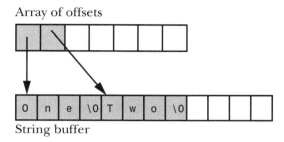

Figure 3.12 Offsets into a string buffer are stored in an array. The index into this array serves as a string ID

When adding a new string, the appropriate entry is also added to the hash table. For the moment, let's treat the hash table as a black box that maps strings into IDs.

```
const int idNotFound = -1;
const int maxStrings = 100;
// String table maps strings to ints
// and ints to strings
class StringTable
{
public:
  StringTable ();
  int ForceAdd (char const * str);
  int Find (char const * str) const;
  char const * GetString (int id) const;
private:
  HTable       _htab; // String -> IDs
  int          _offStr [maxStrings]; // ID -> offset
  int          _curId;
  StringBuffer _strBuf; // Offset -> string
};
```

The translation from an ID into a string is done in the `GetString` method, the translation from the string into an ID is done in `Find`, and the addition of new strings without looking for duplicates is done in `ForceAdd`. The design of the string table is illustrated in Figure 3.13.

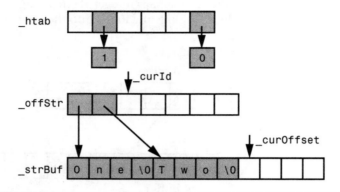

Figure 3.13 The hash table stores indexes in the offset array, the offset array stores indexes in the string buffer, and the string buffer stores strings.

```
StringTable::StringTable ()
  : _curId (0)
{}
int StringTable::ForceAdd (char const * str)
{
  int len = std::strlen (str);
  // Is there enough space?
  if (_curId == maxStrings || !_strBuf.WillFit (len))
  {
    return idNotFound;
  }
  // Point to the place where the string will be stored
  _offStr [_curId] = _strBuf.GetOffset ();
  _strBuf.Add (str);
  // Add mapping to hash table
  _htab. Add (str, _curId);
  ++_curId;
  return _curId - 1;
}
```

The hash table (still a black box for us) finds a short list of entries, one of which contains the ID of the given string. We search this list in order to find the correct ID.

```
int StringTable::Find (char const * str) const
{
  // Get a short list from hash table
  List const & list = _htab. Find (str);
  // Iterate over this list
  for (Link const * pLink = list.GetHead ();
       pLink != 0;
       pLink = pLink->Next ())
  {
    int id = pLink->Id ();
    int offStr = _offStr [id];
    if (strBuf.IsEqual (offStr, str))
      return id;
  }
  return idNotFound;
}
// Map integer into string. Must be valid ID
char const * StringTable::GetString (int id) const
{
  assert (id >= 0);
  assert (id < _curId);
  int offStr = _offStr [id];
  return _strBuf.GetString (offStr);
}
```

3.5.4 String Buffer

Our string buffer is implemented as an array of characters. We keep copying null-terminated strings into this array until we run out of space. The variable _curOffset is an index into the array and it always points at the next free area where a string can be copied. It is initialized to zero, thus pointing at the beginning of the buffer.

Before adding a string we make sure that it will fit in the remaining space. Adding a string means copying it to the place where _curOffset points to, and moving _curOffset past the string's terminating null (see Figure 3.14).

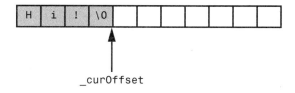

_curOffset

Figure 3.14 Current offset in the string buffer

GetOffset returns the current offset, which can be used later to access the string about to be copied. IsEqual compares the string at a given offset with a given string, and GetString returns a const string given the offset.

```cpp
const int maxBufSize=500;
class StringBuffer
{
public:
  StringBuffer () : _curOffset (0) {}
  bool WillFit (int len) const
  {
    return _curOffset + len + 1 < maxBufSize;
  }
  void Add (char const * str)
  {
    // Same as std::strcpy (_buf + _curOffset, str);
    std::strcpy (&_buf [_curOffset], str);
    _curOffset += std::strlen (str) + 1;
  }
  int GetOffset () const
  {
    return _curOffset;
  }
  bool IsEqual (int offStr, char const * str) const
  {
    // char const * strStored = _buf + offStr;
    char const * strStored = &_buf [offStr];
    // strcmp returns 0 when strings are equal
    return std::strcmp (str, strStored) == 0;
  }
  char const * GetString (int offStr) const
  {
    //Same as return _buf + offStr;
    return &_buf [offStr];
  }
private:
  char _buf [maxBufSize];
  int  _curOffset;
};
```

There are two ways to create a pointer that points to a particular entry in an array. One is to take the address of the *n*th element

```cpp
p = &arr [n]; // Address of the n'th element
```

The other is to use the capability to add an integer to a pointer in order to move it *n* entries ahead (notice, it's not *n* bytes but *n* array *entries*).

```cpp
p = arr + n; // Pointer plus integer
```

Both are correct and produce the same code—in the example above, the pointer equivalents are shown in the comments. The array notation seems less confusing, so I will keep using it.

I also used the generalized assignment operator +=, which adds the right side expression to the left side variable. For instance,

```
n += i;
```

is equivalent to

```
n = n + i;
```

The code produced is, of course, the same (although originally the += operator was introduced in C as an optimization), and the shorthand is useful once you get used to it.

Finally, I used some of the string functions from the standard library (more precisely, the part of the standard library that is common to C and C++). The header file that contains their declaration is called cstring. You can find a detailed description of these functions in your compiler's Help.

3.5.5   Table Lookup

Before explaining how the hash table works, let me digress a little about algorithms that use table lookup. Accessing a table is a very fast operation (unless the table doesn't fit in physical memory, but that's a different story). So, if we have a function whose values can be precomputed and stored in a table, we can trade memory for speed. The isdigit function (macro) is a prime example of such a trade-off. The naive implementation would be

```
inline bool IsDigitSlow (char c)
{
  return c >= '0' && c <= '9';
}
```

However, if we notice that there can only be 256 different arguments to isdigit, we can precompute them all and store them in a table. Let's define the class CharTable that stores the precomputed values.

```
class CharTable
{
public:
  CharTable ();
  bool IsDigit (unsigned char c) const
  {
    return _tab [c];
  }
private:
  bool _tab [UCHAR_MAX + 1]; // From <climits>
};
```

```
CharTable::CharTable ()
{
  for (int i = 0; i <= UCHAR_MAX; ++i)
  {
    // Use the slow method
    if (i >= '0' && i <= '9')
       _tab [i] = true;
    else
       _tab [i] = false;
  }
}
CharTable TheCharTable;
```

Now we can quickly find out whether a given character is a digit by calling

```
TheCharTable.IsDigit (c)
```

In reality, the isdigit macro is usually implemented using a lookup of a statically initialized table of bit fields (numbers whose bits are interpreted independently), where every bit corresponds to one property, such as being a digit, a white space, an alphanumeric character, and so on.

3.5.6 Hash Table

The hash table data structure is based on the idea of using a table lookup to speed up an arbitrary mapping. For our purposes, we are interested in mapping strings into integers. We cannot use strings directly as indexes into an array. However, we can define an auxiliary function that converts strings into such indexes. Such a function is called a *hash function.* Thus we could imagine a two-step process to map a string into an integer: for a given string calculate the value of the hash function and then use the result as an index to access an array that contains the precomputed values of the mapping.

Such hashing, called *perfect hashing,* is usually difficult to implement. In the imperfect world we are usually satisfied with a flawed hash function that may occasionally map two or more different strings into the same index. Such a situation is called a *collision.* Because of collisions, the hash table maps a string not into a single value but rather into a "short list" of candidates, as shown in Figure 3.15. By searching this list further, we can find the string we are interested in, as well as the value into which it is mapped.

This algorithm becomes efficient when the number of strings to be mapped is large enough. A direct linear search among n strings would require, on average, $n/2$ comparisons. On the other hand, the search in a hash table requires, on average, one comparison (plus the calculation of the hash function).

For instance, in our string table we can store at most 100 strings. Finding a given string directly in such a table would require, on average, 50 string comparisons. If we spread these strings in a 127-entry array using a hashing function that

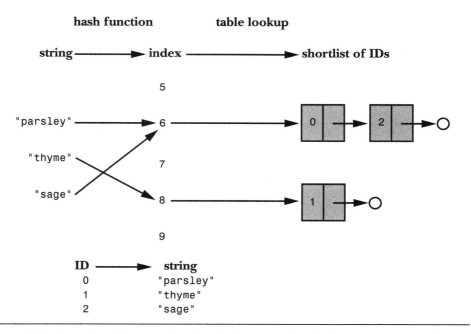

Figure 3.15 The value of the hash function for the string "parsley" is the same as for the string "sage." The collision is dealt with by creating a short list that contains the IDs for both strings. There is a separate mapping of IDs into strings.

randomizes the strings reasonably well, we can expect to find the correct string on the first try—just one comparison. That's a significant improvement.

Here is the definition of the class HashTable. The table itself is an array of lists (these are the "short lists" we were talking about). Most of them will contain zero or one element. In the rare case of a collision, that is, two or more strings hashed into the same index, some lists may be longer than that.

```
const int sizeHTable = 127;
// Hash table of strings
class HTable
{
public:
  // Return a short list of candidates
  List const & Find (char const * str) const;
  // Add another string->ID mapping
  void Add (char const * str, int id);
private:
  // The hashing function
  int hash (char const * str) const;
  List _aList [sizeHTable]; // An array of (short) lists
};
```

```
// Find the list in the hash table that may contain
// the ID of the string we are looking for
List const & HTable::Find (char const * str) const
{
  int i = hash (str);
  return _aList [i];
}
void HTable::Add (char const * str, int id)
{
  int i = hash (str);
  _aList [i].Add (id);
}
```

The choice of a hash function is important because we don't want to have too many collisions. The shift-and-add algorithm is one of the best short string randomizers.

```
int HTable::hash (char const * str) const
{
  // No empty strings, please
  assert (str != 0 && str [0] != 0);
  unsigned h = str [0];
  for (int i = 1; str [i] != 0; ++i)
    h = (h << 4) + str [i];
  return h % sizeHTable; // Remainder
}
```

The expression h << 4 is equal to h shifted left by four bits. In hexadecimal notation, shift left by four is equivalent to appending a zero to the number. For instance, 0x3F shifted left by four becomes 0x3F0. The result of the shift might not fit in the integral type where it's stored (the unsigned, in our example), in which case the leftmost bits are discarded. Notice also that shift left by four is equivalent to multiplication by sixteen. (In general, shifts are equivalent to multiplications or divisions by powers of two.)

The last step in the hashing algorithm calculates the remainder of the division of h by the size of the hash table. This value can be used directly as an index into the array of sizeHTable entries. The size of the table is also important. Powers of two are the worst—they create a lot of collisions; prime numbers are the best. Usually a power of two plus or minus one will do. In our case $127 = 2^7 - 1$, which is a prime number.

The hash value of the string "One" is 114. Table 3.4 shows how it is calculated. The remainder of the division of h by 127 is 114, so the ID of string "One" will be stored at offset 114 in the hash table array.

char	ASCII	h
'O'	0x4F	0x4F
'n'	0x6E	0x55E
'e'	0x65	0x5645

Table 3.4 The calculation of the hash value of the string "One"

3.5.7 Test Program

This is how we can test the string table:

```
int main ()
{
  StringTable strTable;
  strTable.ForceAdd ("One");
  strTable.ForceAdd ("Two");
  strTable.ForceAdd ("Three");
  int id = strTable.Find ("One");
  std::cout << "One at " << id << std::endl;
  id = strTable.Find ("Two");
  std::cout << "Two at " << id << std::endl;
  id = strTable.Find ("Three");
  std::cout << "Three at " << id << std::endl;
  id = strTable.Find ("Minus one");
  std::cout << "Minus one at " << id << std::endl;
  std::cout << "String 0 is "
            << strTable.GetString (0) << std::endl;
  std::cout << "String 1 is "
            << strTable.GetString (1) << std::endl;
  std::cout << "String 2 is "
            << strTable.GetString (2) << std::endl;
}
```

calc4 **Exercises**

5. Add a private Shrink method to the dynamic stack. Let Pop call it when _top reaches some low water mark. Caution: Make sure the stack doesn't have a size at which alternating Pushes and Pops lead to alternating allocations and de-allocations.

6. Create a two-deep stack of strings (char const *). It's a stack that remembers only the last two strings. When a new string is pushed, the next to last string is forgotten, the last string takes its place, and the new one becomes "last." Pop moves up the "next to last" string to the "last" position one and stores zero in its place. Pop doesn't return anything—use Top to access the top string.

7. Create a queue of integers with the FIFO (first in, first out) protocol. Methods `Put` and `Get` insert and retrieve elements, respectively. Use a linked list to implement it.

8. Create a sequencer for a linked list. Create another sequencer that keeps track of both the current and the previous item. Implement method `Unlink` in the second sequencer. It should remove the current item from the list that is being iterated. Test for special cases (remove first, remove last, a one-element list, and so on).

9. Create a doubly linked list item, `DLink`, with the `_pNext` as well as `_pPrev` pointers. Implement the `Unlink` method of the `DLink` object. Create a FIFO queue that uses a circular doubly linked list; that is, the last element points at the first element and the first element points back at the last element (see Figure 3.16). Always create a new `DLink` with both links closed on itself. The pointer to itself can be accessed through the keyword `this`. For instance, `_pNext = this;` will point `_pNext` at the current `DLink`.

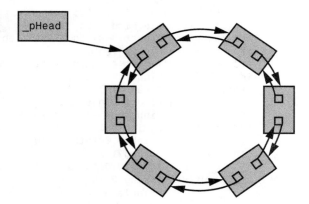

Figure 3.16 A circular doubly linked list

10. Design and implement a sequencer for the hash table. It should go through all the entries in the array and follow all the nonempty linked lists.

11. Using the hash table sequencer from the previous problem, design and implement a new `StringTable` that uses a dynamic hash table that grows by allocating a larger array, iterates through the old hash table and rehashes each element into the new array. Notice that the new array's hash function will differ from the old one (the division modulo size will use a different size).

Chapter 4
Polymorphism

Polymorphic means *multi-shaped*. A tuner, a tape deck, and a CD player come in different shapes but they all have the same *audio-out* jack. You can plug your earphones into it and listen to music no matter whether it came as a modulation of a carrier wave, a set of magnetic domains on a tape, or a series of pits in the aluminum substrate on a plastic disk. From the point of view of an audiophile, all these devices represent examples of audio sources. As long as they expose the same interface (the audio-out jack) their implementation is irrelevant.

4.1　The Meaning of is-a

The fact that a `Star` is a `CelestialBody` means not only that a `Star` has all the member variables and methods of a CelestialBody (plus more). After all, that would be just syntactic sugar over straight embedding. One could embed a `CelestialBody` as a public member of `Star` and, apart from awkward semantics of the has-a relationship, one could imitate inheritance. (As a matter of fact, this is probably how your compiler implements inheritance.)

There is one big difference: Due to inheritance, a `Star` can pass as a `CelestialBody`. What does this mean? It means that a function that expects a reference or a pointer to a `CelestialBody` will happily accept a reference or a pointer to a `Star` (computer linguists call this the Liskov substitution principle).

Here's an example: The class `BlackHole` has a method `Gobble` that accepts any CelestialBody:

```
void BlackHole::Gobble (CelestialBody * pBody);
```

Since a `Star` is a `CelestialBody`, it can be `Gobbled` by a `BlackHole`:

```
Star* pStar = new Star (1, 2);
TheBlackHole.Gobble (pStar); // Yum
```

How is the `CelestialBody` treated inside a `BlackHole`?

```
void BlackHole::Gobble (CelestialBody* pBody)
{
  delete pBody;
}
```

It is destroyed! Now the big question is: whose destructor is called? On the one hand, we know that we sent a `Star` to its fiery death, so we should see the printout "Destroying a star. . . ." On the other hand, the `BlackHole` has no idea that it is swallowing a `Star`. It will expect to see "Destroying celestial body. . . ." What's more, at compile time, the compiler has no idea what will be sent into the `BlackHole`. Imagine a situation like this:

```
Star * pStar = new Star (1, 2);
Planet * pPlanet = new Planet (3, 4);

TheBlackHole.Gobble (pStar); // Yum
TheBlackHole.Gobble (pPlanet); // Yum, yum
```

In both cases the same method `Gobble` is called and the same code is executed; therefore, it is obvious that inside `Gobble` the compiler may only insert the call to (or expand inline) `CelestialBody`'s destructor. The compiler dispatches the call based on the *type of the pointer*. Notice that the same would apply to any other method of `CelestialBody` overridden by `Star` or `Planet`. If `Gobble` called any of these, the compiler would call the `CelestialBody`'s implementation, and not the one provided by `Star` or `Planet`.

This solution is cheap and in many cases adequate. However, for a small additional fee, C++ offers a very powerful feature called *polymorphism*. If you want to hear different final cries from inside of a `BlackHole`, depending on what has fallen into it you must declare the `CelestialBody`'s destructor *virtual*. When a virtual function is overridden in a derived class, the dispatching of calls to that function is done by the *actual type* of the object pointed to, rather than by the *type of the pointer*.

4.1.1   Implementation Digression

Obviously, for polymorphism to work, the object itself must store some information about its actual type. Based on this type, the call is dispatched to the method's appropriate implementation. In fact, the object may store a pointer to a dispatch table through which virtual methods are called.

Here's how it works: Every class that has at least one virtual method (a polymorphic class) has a hidden member that is a pointer to a *virtual table*. The virtual

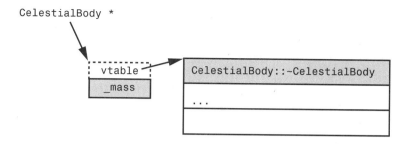

Figure 4.1 The invisible member of a celestial body—the pointer to the vtable. The first entry in the vtable is a pointer to a function that is the destructor of celestial body.

table (vtable) contains the addresses of the virtual member functions for that particular class (see Figure 4.1). When a call is made through a pointer or reference to such an object, the compiler generates code that dereferences the pointer to the object's virtual table and makes an *indirect call* using the address of a member function stored in the table (we are getting slightly ahead of ourselves—these topics, like pointers to functions and methods, will be discussed later in this book).

An object of a derived class that has overridden the implementation of the virtual method has its pointer pointed to a different virtual table (see Figure 4.2). In that table the entry corresponding to that particular method contains the address of the overridden member function.

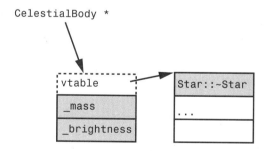

Figure 4.2 The vtable pointer of a star points to a different vtable. Its first entry is also a pointer to a function that serves as a destructor, only this time it's the destructor of a star.

4.1.2   The Overhead

Before you decide to use virtual functions everywhere, I want to make you aware of the size and speed considerations. The space overhead of polymorphism is one pointer per every object (instance of the class). There is an additional per-class overhead of a vtable, but it's not that important. One pointer per object is not a lot when dealing with a small number of relatively large objects. It becomes significant, though, when dealing with a large number of lightweight objects.

A virtual function call is slower than a direct call and significantly slower than using an inline function. Again, you can safely ignore this overhead when calling a heavyweight member function, but turning an inline function such as AtEnd into a virtual function may significantly slow down your loops.

So don't even think of creating the class Object—the mother of all objects—with a handy virtual destructor. (And maybe with one more integer field for some kind of a class ID—run time typing!—plus some conditionally compiled debugging devices, and so on). Don't try to make it the root of all classes either. In fact, if you hear somebody complaining about how slow C++ is, he or she is probably a victim of this Smalltalk-induced syndrome in C++.

Not that Smalltalk is a poor language. When size and speed are of no concern, Smalltalk beats C++ on many fronts. It is a truly object-oriented language with no shameful heritage of the hackers' C. It unifies built-in types with user-defined types much better than C++. It has a single-rooted hierarchy of objects. All methods are virtual (you can even override them at runtime!).

Java, a simplified outgrowth of C++, tries to strike a balance between object-orientation and performance. All methods in Java are virtual except when explicitly declared final (and then they cannot be overridden).

If speed and size *are* of concern to you, stick to C++ and use polymorphism wisely. Well-designed polymorphic classes will lead to C++ code that is at least as fast as the equivalent C code (and much better from the maintenance point of view).

The rule of thumb for those coming from a C background is to be on the lookout for the *switch statements* and complicated *conditionals*. It is natural in C++ to use polymorphism in their place.

4.2 Parse Tree

Virtual member functions, virtual destructors, pure virtual functions, protected data members.

tree1   I will demonstrate the use of polymorphism in an example of a very useful data structure—an arithmetic tree. An arithmetic expression can be converted into a tree structure whose nodes are arithmetic operators and leaf nodes are numbers. Figure 4.3 shows a tree that corresponds to the expression 2 * (3 + 4) + 5. Analyzing it from the root towards the leaves, we first encounter the plus-node, whose children are the two terms that are to be added. The left child is a product of two factors. The left factor is the number two and the right factor is the sum of three and four. The right child of the top level plus-node is five. Notice that the tree representation doesn't require any parentheses or the knowledge of operator precedence. It uniquely describes the calculation to be performed.

We will represent all nodes of the arithmetic tree as objects inheriting from the class Node. The direct descendants of Node are NumNode, which represents a number, and BinNode, which represents a binary operator. For simplicity, we will restrict ourselves to only two classes derived from BinNode: AddNode and MultNode. Figure 4.4 shows the class hierarchy I have just described. Abstract classes are the

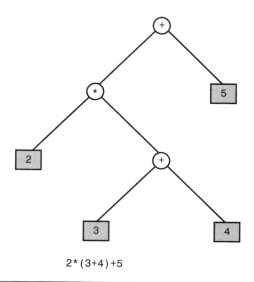

2*(3+4)+5

Figure 4.3 The arithmetic tree corresponding to the expression 2 * (3 + 4) + 5

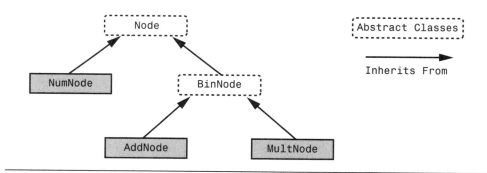

Figure 4.4 The class hierarchy of nodes

classes that cannot be instantiated; they only serve as parents for other classes. I'll explain this term in more detail in a moment.

What are the operations we would like to perform on a node? We would like to be able to calculate its value and, at some point, destroy it. The `Calc` method returns a `double` as the result of calculating the node's value. Of course, for some nodes the calculation may involve the recursive calculations of its children. This method is `const` because it doesn't change the node itself. Since each type of node has to provide its own implementation of the `Calc` method, we make this function virtual. However, there is no "default" implementation of `Calc` for an arbitrary `Node`. A function that has no implementation (inherited or otherwise) is called a *pure virtual* function. That's the meaning of `= 0` in the declaration of `Calc`.

```
class Node
{
public:
  virtual ~Node () {}
  virtual double Calc () const = 0;
};
```

A class that has one or more pure virtual functions is called an *abstract class,* and it cannot be instantiated (no object of this class can be created). Only classes that are derived from an abstract class and that provide their own implementations of all the pure virtual functions can be instantiated. Notice that our sample arithmetic tree has instances of AddNodes, MultNodes, and NumNodes, but no instances of Nodes or BinNodes.

A rule of thumb is that if a class has a virtual function, it probably needs a *virtual destructor* as well—and once we decide to pay the overhead of a vtable pointer, all subsequent virtual functions don't increase the size of the object. So, in such a case, adding a virtual destructor doesn't add any significant overhead.

In our case we can anticipate that some of the descendant nodes will have to destroy their children in their destructors, so we really need a virtual destructor. A destructor can be made a pure virtual function, but we would have to override it in every derived class, whether such a class needs it or not. That's why I gave the base-class destructor an empty body. (Even though I made it inline, the compiler will create a function body for it, because the compiler needs to stick a pointer for it into the virtual table.)

NumNode stores a double value that is initialized in its constructor. NumNode also overrides the Calc virtual function. In this case, Calc simply returns the value stored in the node.

```
class NumNode: public Node
{
public:
  NumNode (double num) : _num (num ) {}
  double Calc () const;
private:
  const double _num;
};
double NumNode::Calc () const
{
  std::cout << "Numeric node " << _num << std::endl;
  return _num;
}
```

BinNode has two children that are pointers to (abstract) Nodes. They are initialized in the constructor and deleted in the destructor—this is why I could make them const pointers. The Calc method is still a pure virtual function, inherited from Node; only the descendants of BinNode will know how to implement it.

```
class BinNode: public Node
{
```

```
public:
  BinNode (Node * pLeft, Node * pRight)
    : _pLeft (pLeft), _pRight (pRight) {}
  ~BinNode ();
protected:
  Node * const _pLeft;
  Node * const _pRight;

};
BinNode::~BinNode ()
{
  delete _pLeft;
  delete _pRight;
}
```

This is where you first see the advantage of polymorphism. A binary node can have children that are arbitrary nodes. Each of them can be a number node, an addition node, or a multiplication node. There are nine possible combinations of children—it would be silly to make separate classes for each of them (consider, for instance, AddNodeWithLeftMultNodeAndRightNumberNode). We have no choice but to accept and store pointers to children as more general pointers to Nodes. Yet, when we call destructors through them, we need to call different functions to destroy different Nodes. For instance, AddNode has a different destructor than NumNode (which has an empty one), and so on. This is why we have to make the destructors of Nodes virtual.

Notice that the two data members of BinNode are not private—they are protected. This qualification is slightly weaker than private. A private data member or method cannot be accessed from any code outside of the implementation of the given class (or its friends)—not even from the code of the *derived* class. Had we made _pLeft and _pRight private, we'd have to provide public methods to set and get them. That would be tantamount to exposing them to everybody. By making them protected we are letting classes *derived* from BinNode manipulate them, but, at the same time, bar anybody else from doing so. A short description of all three access specifiers is presented in Table 4.1. Incidentally, the same access specifiers are used in declaring inheritance. By far the most useful type of inheritance is public, and that's what we've been using so far, but if you'd like to restrict the access to the base class, you're free to use the other two types of inheritance.

Access specifier	Who can access such a member?
public	Anybody
protected	The class itself, its friends, and derived classes
private	Only the class itself and its friends

Table 4.1 The meaning of the three access specifiers

The class `AddNode` is derived from `BinNode`.

```
class AddNode: public BinNode
{
public:
   AddNode (Node * pLeft, Node * pRight)
      : BinNode (pLeft, pRight) {}
   double Calc () const;
};
```

`AddNode` provides its own implementation of `Calc`. This is where you see the advantages of polymorphism again. We let the child nodes calculate themselves. Since the `Calc` method is virtual, they will do the right thing based on their actual class, and not on the class of the pointer (`Node *`). The two results of calling `Calc` are added and the sum returned.

```
double AddNode::Calc () const
{
   std::cout << "Adding\n";
   return _pLeft->Calc () + _pRight->Calc ();
}
```

Notice how the method of `AddNode` directly accesses its parent's protected data members _pLeft and _pRight. Again, were they declared private, such access would be flagged as an error by the compiler.

For completeness, here's the implementation of `MultNode` and a simple test program.

```
class MultNode: public BinNode
{
public:
   MultNode (Node * pLeft, Node * pRight)
      : BinNode (pLeft, pRight) {}
   double Calc () const;
};
double MultNode::Calc () const
{
   std::cout << "Multiplying\n";
   return _pLeft->Calc () * _pRight->Calc ();
}
int main ()
{
   // ( 20.0 + (-10.0) ) * 0.1
   Node * pNode1 = new NumNode (20.0);
   Node * pNode2 = new NumNode (-10.0);
   Node * pNode3 = new AddNode (pNode1, pNode2);
   Node * pNode4 = new NumNode (0.1);
   Node * pNode5 = new MultNode (pNode3, pNode4);
   std::cout << "Calculating the tree\n";
   // Tell the root to calculate itself
```

```
        double x = pNode5->Calc ();
        std::cout << "Result: " << x << std::endl;
        delete pNode5; // And all children
   }
```

> Do you think you can write more efficient code by not using polymorphism? Think twice! If you're still not convinced, go on a little sidetrip into the alternative universe of C.

4.2.1 C Digression

tree2 How would the same problem be solved in C, where there are no virtual functions? A good way would be to try to implement a virtual table by hand and make calls through function pointers. You'd be surprised how often this is done. This is called object-oriented programming in C. The more traditional approach would be to define a struct Node that has enough fields to accommodate the needs of binary operators as well as numeric nodes. The identity of the node would be stored in a separate field.

```
#define NUM_NODE 1
#define ADD_NODE 2
#define MULT_NODE 3
struct Node
{
  /* Node type */
  int type;
  /* Used only in numeric nodes */
  double val;
  /* Used only in binary nodes */
  struct Node * pLeft;
  struct Node * pRight;
};
```

Virtual functions in C++ would be turned into multi-way conditionals, like this switch statement below (see page 114 for the description of a switch statement).

```
double Calc (struct Node * pNode)
{
  double x;
  x = 0.0;
  switch (pNode->type)
  {
  case NUM_NODE:
```

```
          x = pNode->val;
          break;
       case ADD_NODE:
          x = Calc (pNode->pLeft) + Calc (pNode->pRight);
          break;
       case MULT_NODE:
          x = Calc (pNode->pLeft) * Calc (pNode->pRight);
          break;
    }
    return x;
}
```

tree3   Obviously, this solution would be too expensive when applied to trees with hundreds of nodes. This is when a C programmer would fetch his or her powerful secret weapon. When the going gets tough, type safety is the first to go—use casts (I am being sarcastic here). Instead of packing everything into a single struct, the programmer creates a variety of structs:

```
struct Node
{
   int type;
};
struct NumNode
{
   int type;
   double val;
};
struct BinNode
{
   int type;
   struct Node * pLeft;
   struct Node * pRight;
};
```

Some would even use a byte to store type—trading speed for size (on many processors fetching a word-aligned value is faster than fetching a byte-aligned value). The function Calc takes a pointer to Node and, based on its type field, casts it to the appropriate pointer. (In fact, one could even get rid of the last pretense of type safety and pass Calc a void pointer.)

```
double Calc (struct Node * pNode)
{
   double x = 0.0;
   switch (pNode->type)
   {
     case NUM_NODE:
        x =((struct NumNode *)pNode)->val;
        break;
     case ADD_NODE:
     {
        struct BinNode * pN = (struct BinNode *) pNode;
```

```
      x = Calc (pN->pLeft) + Calc (pN->pRight);
      break;
   }
   case MULT_NODE:
   {
      struct BinNode * pN = (struct BinNode *) pNode;
      x = Calc (pN->pLeft) * Calc (pN->pRight);
      break;
   }
   default:
      printf ("Bad node type\n");
   }
   return x;
}
```

> I haven't explained casting yet, and I'm very reluctant to do it at this stage. *Casting* means cheating the compiler. You have an object that is declared as a pointer to Node and you are telling the compiler to treat it as a pointer to BinNode. This way, you are bypassing the compiler's elaborate mechanism of type checking. Now it's up to you, the programmer, to make sure that the pointer in question actually points to BinNode and not something else.

Notice that even the "constructor"—CreateNumNode—has to use casts. The destructor would use both casts and conditionals.

```
struct Node * CreateNumNode (double value)
{
   struct NumNode * pNode = malloc (sizeof (struct NumNode));
   pNode->type = NUM_NODE;
   pNode->val = value;
   return (struct Node *) pNode;
}
```

How do these C solutions compare with the C++ polymorphic approach? As far as the size of the data structures is concerned, C doesn't offer much in the way of savings. In fact, the first C solution is substantially more memory consuming.

As far as the speed of execution is concerned, we have to compare a multi-way conditional plus a direct call against a doubly indirect call through the vtable. The result of the comparison depends on how well the compiler optimizes conditionals. In our case, since the case labels are consecutive, the compiler will probably create a jump table indexed by the value of type. Before doing an indirect jump, the compiler will have to check whether the index is within bounds (if it's not, the compiler will jump to the default label). So in fact we have a conditional, an indirect jump, and a function call. In C++ we have a doubly indirect function call.

The C++ compiler usually optimizes the passing of the *this* pointer by putting it in a register, so the calling sequence may be simpler in C++. The bottom line is that without actually timing both versions, there is no way to tell which one will be faster.

As far as correctness and ease of maintenance is concerned, just consider what it would be like to add a new type of node to each of the implementations. Notice also that, even though we've been writing progressively more complex programs in C++, we haven't felt the need for either casts or switch statements.

Even C programmers will admit that using casts should be a last resort. C++ programmers feel the same about switch statements.

> **Use switch statements only when polymorphism cannot be used.**

Exercises

1. Design a program that calculates all prime numbers up to 100 by eliminating all numbers divisible by 2, 3, 5, and 7. Create an abstract class Sieve with one pure virtual method NextNumber. Implement SourceSieve that simply iterates over all numbers from 1 to 100 in order. Implement Sieve2 that takes a reference to a Sieve in its constructor and, when asked to give the next number, keeps retrieving numbers from its source sieve until it finds one that is not divisible by 2 and returns that number (but it should return 2, because 2 is a prime number). Do the same for 3, 5, and 7. Create all these Sieves as local objects in main, chain them by passing one to the constructor of another, and print all the numbers returned by the top Sieve. What order of Sieves is best?

2. Create an abstract class Command with the two pure virtual methods Execute and Undo. Create command classes for our stack-based calculator, corresponding to all possible calculator inputs. For every user input construct a corresponding Command object, Execute it, and push it on a two-deep stack of Commands. Add the undo (u-command) to the calculator. The u-command pops the last Command from the command stack and calls its virtual method Undo.

Chapter 5
A Small Software Project

When you write a program, you don't ask yourself, "How can I use a particular language feature?" You ask, "What language feature will help me solve my problem?"

5.1 Starting a Software Project

Top-down design and implementation. Scanner, top-down recursive parser, symbol table. Allocation and ownership of objects returned from a function. Function pointers, switch statements.

Programmers are rarely totally satisfied with their code. So after I wrote the program for this chapter—a simple parser-calculator—I immediately noticed I could have done it better. I felt the top-level view of the program was not very clear. The nodes of the parsing tree needed access to components such as the Store (the calculator's "memory"), the symbol table (to print meaningful error messages), and maybe even to the function table (to evaluate built-in functions). I could have either made all these objects global and thus known to everybody, or pass references to them to all the nodes of the tree. The order of construction of these objects was important, so I felt that maybe they should be combined into one high-level object, the Calculator. The temptation to redesign and rewrite the whole program was strong. Maybe after the *n*th iteration I could come up with something close to the ideal?

Then I decided I shouldn't do it. Part of making a program is coming up with not-so-good solutions and then improving upon them. I would have cheated if I had come up with the best, and then reverse-engineered it to fit the top-down design and implementation process. So here it is—the actual, real-life process of *creating a program*.

5.1.1 Design Specification

The purpose of the calculator program is to accept arithmetic expressions from the user, evaluate them, and display the results. The expressions are to be parsed by a simple top-down recursive descent parser[1] (if you have no idea what I'm talking about, don't panic—it's just a name for what I'm going to describe in detail later). The parser's goal is to convert the input string into an arithmetic tree. The simple grammar accepted by the parser is defined as follows:

The parser is looking for an expression.

1. An *expression*

    a. is a *term* followed by a plus or a minus sign, which is followed by another *expression*.

    b. If an expression doesn't contain any plus or minus signs, it is equal to a *term*.

    c. An *expression* can also be a *term* followed by the equal sign followed by an *expression*.

2. A *term* is

    a. a *factor* multiplied or divided by another *term*.

    b. If a term doesn't contain any multiplication or division operators, it is equal to a *factor*.

3. A *factor* can be

    a. a number

    b. an identifier corresponding to a variable

    c. a minus sign followed by a **factor** (unary minus)

    d. a whole **expression** enclosed in parentheses

For instance, the expression $1 + x * (2 - y)$ is parsed as shown in Figure 5.1 This grammar is simple and natural, but it has one flaw—the arithmetic operators are right associative instead of being left associative. That means, for example, that $a - b + c$ will be parsed as $a - (b + c)$, which is not exactly what we'd expect. There are standard ways of fixing this grammar or modifying the parser, but that's beyond the scope of this section. (We will revisit this issue later.)

Since we want our calculator to be able to use variables, we will need a symbol table. A *symbol table* remembers names of variables. We will reuse the string table described in Chapter 3.

We'll also need to be able to assign values to variables. We can do it by expanding the definition of expression to include the following clause:

---

1. In principle, the type of parser is an implementation detail and as such would not normally be mentioned in the external specification. In our case, however, the type of parser (unfortunately) influences the choice of the grammar, which *is* part of the external specification.

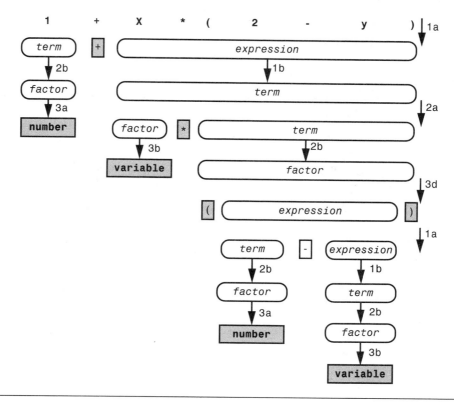

Figure 5.1 The parsing of an arithmetic expression. The arrows with numbers correspond to the rules of grammar that are used to make each parsing step.

Not every term, though, is appropriate on the left side of an assignment. It has to be an *lvalue*—something that can be on the left side of an assignment. In our case the only allowed type of lvalue will be an identifier corresponding to a variable. Similarly, things that can be put on the right side of the assignment are called *rvalues*. In our case, any expression is a valid rvalue[2].

We will also introduce a scanner, which will convert the input string into a series of tokens. It will recognize arithmetic operators, numbers, and identifiers. This way the parser will have an easier job matching sequences of tokens to grammatical productions.

---

2. One can also derive lvalue from "location value," since it represents a location where a value can be stored, and rvalue from "read value," since a value can be read from it.

5.1.2 Stubbed Implementation

I will follow the top-down implementation strategy. It means that I will run the
program first and implement it later. (Actually, I will run it as soon as I create stubs
for all the top level classes.)

> The source code for this chapter is provided in the form of Code Co-op scripts.
> The instructions are given in the Introduction on page xxiii. The project name is
> Calculator (see margin note). Occasionally I will make short digressions. You'll
> be able to find the source code for such digressions on the CD-ROM. The mar-
> gin note will name the appropriate directory (instead of the Script number).

Project
Calculator Let's start with the Scanner. It is constructed out of a buffer of text (a line of
text, to be precise). The Scanner keeps a pointer to that buffer, and later it will be
able to scan the buffer left to right and convert it to tokens. For now the constructor of the Scanner stub announces its existence to the world and prints the contents of the buffer.

```cpp
class Scanner
{
public:
    Scanner (char const * buf);
private:
    char const * const _buf;
};

Scanner::Scanner (char const * buf)
    : _buf (buf)
{
    std::cout << "Scanner with \"" << buf << "\""
        << std::endl;
}
```

Notice that in order to include a double quote in a string literal we have to
precede it by the *escape* character—the backslash. The backslash itself will not become part of the string; it is there only to tell the compiler that the following
quote is not the end of the string. If you really want a literal backslash in your
string you have to double it.

The SymbolTable stub will be really trivial for now. We will only assume that it
has a constructor.

```cpp
class SymbolTable
{
public:
    SymbolTable () {}
};
```

The `Parser` will need access to the scanner and to the symbol table. It will parse the tokens retrieved from the scanner and evaluate the resulting tree. The method `Eval` is supposed to do that and return a status code that depends on the result of the parsing. We combine the three possible statuses `stOk`, `stQuit`, and `stError`, into an *enumeration*. An enum is an integral type that can only take a few predefined values. These values are given symbolic names and are either initialized to concrete values by the programmer or by the compiler. In our case we don't really care what values correspond to the various statuses, so we leave it to the compiler. Using an enum rather than an `int` for the return type of `Eval` has the advantage of stricter type checking. It also prevents us from returning anything other than one of the three values defined by the enum.

```
enum Status
{
  stOk,
  stQuit,
  stError
};

class Parser
{
public:
  Parser (Scanner & scanner, SymbolTable & symTab);
  ~Parser ();
  Status Eval ();
private:

  Scanner      & _scanner;
  SymbolTable  & _symTab;
};

Parser::Parser (Scanner & scanner, SymbolTable & symTab)
  : _scanner (scanner), _symTab (symTab)
{
  std::cout << "Parser created\n";
}

Parser::~Parser ()
{
  std::cout << "Destroying parser\n";
}

Status Parser::Eval ()
{
  std::cout << "Parser eval\n";
  return stQuit;
}
```

Finally, here's the `main` procedure. You can see the top-level design of the program in action. The lifetime of the `SymbolTable` has to be equal to that of the whole program, since it has to remember the names of all the variables introduced by the user during one session. The scanner and the parser, though, can be created every

time a line of text is entered. The parser doesn't have any state that has to be preserved from one line of text to another. If the parser encounters a new variable
name, it will store the name in the symbol table that has a longer lifespan.

```cpp
const int maxBuf = 100;

int main ()
{
  char buf [maxBuf];
  Status status;
  SymbolTable symTab;
  do
  {
    std::cout << "> "; // Prompt
    std::cin.getline (buf, maxBuf);
    Scanner scanner (buf);
    Parser parser (scanner, symTab);
    status = parser.Eval ();
  } while (status != stQuit);
}
```

In the main loop of our program a line of text is retrieved from the standard
input using the getline method of cin. This is a standard way of extracting a
whole line of text, as opposed to extracting individual words or numbers using >>.
A scanner is constructed from the line, and a parser is created from the scanner.
The Eval method of the parser is then called to parse and evaluate the expression.
As long as the status returned by Eval is different from stQuit, the whole process is
repeated. The do/while loop introduced here differs from the while loop in that
its body is always executed at least once.

This program compiles and runs, thus proving the validity of the concept.

5.1.3 Expanding Stubs

Script 1 The first stub to be expanded into a full implementation will be that of the
Scanner. The scanner converts the input string into a series of tokens. It works like
a sequencer. Whenever the Parser needs a token, it asks the Scanner for the current token. When this token is parsed[3], the Parser accepts it by calling
Scanner::Accept. The Accept method scans the string further trying to recognize
the next token.

There is a finite, well-defined set of tokens. It is convenient to put them into
the enumeration EToken (for now we'll only use a limited number of tokens, but
we'll be adding more as the need arises).

```cpp
enum EToken
{
```

---

3. Even if the parser recognizes an error, it still usually accepts the token, so that the parsing doesn't get
   into an infinite loop.

```
     tEnd,
     tError,
     tNumber,
     tPlus,
     tMult
};
```

We would also like the Scanner to be able to convert the part of the input string recognized as a number to a floating-point value. This is done by the Number method that can be called only when the current token is tNumber (see the assertion there). Notice the use of the type char const * const—a const pointer to a const string. The pointer is initialized in the constructor and never changes again. Its contents are read-only, too.

```
class Scanner
{
public:
  Scanner (char const * buf);
  EToken Token () const { return _token; }
  void Accept ();
  double Number ()
  {
    assert (_token == tNumber);
    return _number;
  }
private:
  void EatWhite ();
  char const * const _buf;
  int              _iLook;
  EToken           _token;
  double           _number;
};
```

The constructor of the Scanner, besides initializing all member variables, calls the method Accept. Accept recognizes the first available token and positions the index _iLook past the recognized part of the buffer.

```
Scanner::Scanner (char const * buf)
  : _buf (buf), _iLook(0)
{
  std::cout << "Scanner with \"" << buf << "\""
       << std::endl;
  Accept ();
}
```

EatWhite is the helper function that skips whitespace characters in the input.

```
void Scanner::EatWhite ()
{
  while (std::isspace (_buf [_iLook]))
     ++_iLook;
}
```

Accept is just one big *switch* statement. Depending on the value of the current character in the buffer, _buf[_iLook], the control passes to the appropriate case label within the switch. For now I have implemented the recognition of the addition and the multiplication operators. When either of them is recognized, the _token variable is initialized to the corresponding enumerated value, and the variable _iLook is incremented by one.

The recognition of digits is done using the fall-through property of the case statements. Unless there is an explicit break in a switch statement, the control passes to the next case. All digit cases fall through to reach the code after case '9'. The string starting with a digit is converted to an integer (later we will change this part of the program to recognize floating-point numbers) and _iLook is positioned after the last digit.

The default case is executed when no other case matches the value passed to the switch.

```cpp
void Scanner::Accept ()
{
  EatWhite ();
  switch (_buf[_iLook])
  {
  case '+':
    _token = tPlus;
    ++_iLook;
    break;
  case '*':
    _token = tMult;
    ++_iLook;
    break;
  case '0': case '1': case '2': case '3': case '4':
  case '5': case '6': case '7': case '8': case '9':
    _token = tNumber;
    _number = std::atoi (&_buf [_iLook]);
    while (std::isdigit (_buf [_iLook]))
      ++_iLook;
    break;
  case '\0': // End of input
    _token = tEnd;
    break;
  default:
    _token = tError;
    break;
  }
}
```

You might ask, "Can this switch statement be replaced by some clever use of polymorphism?" I really don't know how one could do it. The trouble is that the incoming data stream—characters from the buffer—is *amorphous*. At the stage where we are trying to determine the meaning of the input—to give it *form*—the best we can do is to go through a multi-way conditional, in this case a switch statement.[4] Dealing with amorphous input is virtually the only time when using a switch statement is completely legitimate in C++. The parsing of user input or data stored in a file, or the processing of external events all require a switch statement or a multi-way conditional.

The dummy parser is, for now, implemented as a `for` loop that retrieves one token after another and prints the appropriate message.

```
Status Parser::Eval ()
{
  for (EToken token = _scanner.Token ();
       token != tEnd;
       _scanner.Accept ())
  {
    token = _scanner.Token ()
    switch (token)
    {
    case tMult:
      std::cout << "Times\n";
      break;
    case tPlus:
      std::cout << "Plus\n";
      break;
    case tNumber:
      std::cout << "Number: " << _scanner.Number ()
                << std::endl;
      break;
    case tError:
      std::cout << "Error\n";
      return stQuit;
    default:
      std::cout << "Error: bad token\n";
      return stQuit;
    }
  }
  return stOk;
}
```

Once more, this partially implemented program is compiled and tested. We can see the flow of control and the correct recognition of a few tokens.

Final Implementation. Not!

There is no "final" implementation. Let me reiterate:

---

4. In some cases we can bypass conditionals by using a table-driven approach. For instance, since there are only 256 possible characters, we could have defined a table of 256 entries and indexed it using the current input character. The entries could be pointers to functions (which we'll talk about later) designed specifically for processing a given type of character.

> **There is no "final" implementation.**

So how do we know when to stop? The truth is, we don't! Sometimes we just get bored with the program; sometimes we start a new interesting project and we abandon the current one (promising ourselves that we'll come back to it later). Having a delivery date planned ahead (even if we slip a little), and a manager who tells us to stop adding new features and just ship the product, might help sometimes too.

With this caveat in mind, let me go over the pseudo-final version of the calculator to show how the stubs get expanded to create a working program.

5.2 Scanner

Pointer to pointer type, passing simple types by reference, C++ identifiers, passing buffers.

Script 2   The list of tokens is enlarged to include four arithmetic operators, the assignment operator, parentheses, and a token representing an identifier. An *identifier* is a symbolic name, like *pi, sin, x,* and so on.

```
enum EToken
{
  tEnd,
  tError,
  tNumber, // Literal number
  tPlus,   // +
  tMult,   // *
  tMinus,  // −
  tDivide, // /
  tLParen, // (
  tRParen, // )
  tAssign, // =
  tIdent   // Identifier (symbolic name)
};
```

The Scanner now has the ability to recognize symbolic names. So, besides the new method GetSymbolName, it has two additional data members: _lenSymbol, which specifies the length of the currently recognized symbolic name, and _iSymbol, which marks the beginning of the name in the Scanner's buffer.

```
class Scanner
{
public:
  ...
  void GetSymbolName (char * strOut, int & len);
private:
  ...
```

```
    int         _lenSymbol;
    int         _iSymbol;
};
```

The Accept method is expanded to recognize the additional arithmetic symbols (the minus sign and the division sign), the two parentheses, the equal sign, as well as floating point numbers and identifiers. The decimal point is added to the list of digits in the scanner's switch statement, so the scanner can recognize numbers like .5 that start with the decimal point.

The library function strtod (string to double) not only converts a string to a floating point number, but it also updates the pointer to the first character that cannot possibly be part of the number. This is very useful, since it lets us easily calculate the new value of _iLook after scanning the number.

```
case '0': case '1': case '2': case '3': case '4':
case '5': case '6': case '7': case '8': case '9':
case '.':
{
  _token = tNumber;
  char * p;
  _number = std:: strtod (&_buf [_iLook], &p);
  _iLook = p − _buf; // Pointer subtraction
  break;
}
```

The function strtod has two outputs: the value of the number that it has recognized and the pointer to the first unrecognized character.

```
double strtod (char const * str, char *ppEnd);
```

How can a function have more than one output? The trick is to pass an argument that is a reference or a pointer to the value to be modified by the function. In our case the additional output is a pointer to char. We have to pass a reference or a pointer to this pointer. (Since strtod is a function from the standard C library, it uses pointers rather than references.) Let's see what happens, step-by-step. We first define the variable that is to be modified by strtod. This variable is a pointer to a char:

```
char * p;
```

Notice that we don't have to initialize it to anything; it will be overwritten in the subsequent call anyway. Next, we pass the address of this variable to strtod:

```
_number = std::strtod (&_buf [_iLook], &p);
```

The function expects a *pointer to a pointer* to a char:

```
double strtod (char const * str, char *ppEnd);
```

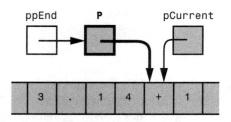

Figure 5.2 ppEnd contains the address of the pointer p. Pointer p can thus be changed through ppEnd.

By dereferencing this pointer to a pointer, strtod can overwrite the value of the pointer. For instance, it could do this:

```
*ppEnd = pCurrent;
```

This would make the original p point to whatever pCurrent was pointing to (see Figure 5.2).

In C++ we could have passed a *reference to a pointer* instead (not that it's much more readable).

```
char *& pEnd
```

It is not clear that passing simple types like char* or int by reference leads to more readable code. Consider this:

```
char * p;
_number = StrToDouble2 (&_buf [iLook], p);
```

It looks like an uninitialized variable is being passed to a function. Only by looking up the declaration of StrToDouble would you know that p is passed by a reference:

```
double StrToDouble2 (char const * str, char * rpEnd)
{
  ...
  rpEnd = pCurrent;
  ...
}
```

Although it definitely is good programming practice to look up at least the declaration of the function you are about to call, one might argue that it shouldn't be necessary to look it up when you are reading somebody else's code. Then again, how can you understand the code if you don't know what StrToDouble2 is doing? And how about a comment that will immediately explain what is going on?

```
char * p; // p will be initialized by StrToDouble2
_number = StrToDouble2 (&_buf [_iLook], p);
```

You should definitely include a comment whenever you define a variable without immediately initializing it. Otherwise the reader of your code will suspect a bug.

Taking all of this into account, my recommendation would be to go ahead and use C++ references for passing simple as well as user-defined types by reference.

Of course, if strtod was not written by a human optimizing compiler, the code would probably look more like this

```
case '0': case '1': case '2': case '3': case '4':
case '5': case '6': case '7': case '8': case '9':
case '.':
{
  _token = tNumber;
  _number = StrToDouble (_buf, _iLook); // Updates _iLook
  break;
}
```

with StrToDouble declared as follows:

```
double StrToDouble (char const * pBuf, int & iCurrent);
```

It would convert the string to a double starting from pBuf [iCurrent], and advance iCurrent past the end of the number.

Back to Scanner::Accept. Identifiers are recognized in the default statement of the big switch. The idea is that if the character is not a digit, a decimal point, or an operator, it must either be an identifier or an error. In our calculator we require an identifier to start with an uppercase or lowercase letter, or with an underscore. By the way, this is exactly the same requirement that C++ identifiers must fulfill. We use the isalpha function (really a macro) to check for the letters of the alphabet. Inside the identifier we (and C++) allow digits as well. The macro isalnum checks if the character is alphanumeric. Examples of identifiers are i, pEnd, _token, __iscsymf, Istop4digits, SERIOUS_ERROR_1, and so on.

```
default:
  if (std::isalpha (_buf [_iLook])
      || _buf [_iLook] == '_')
  {
      _token = tIdent;
      _iSymbol = _iLook;

      int cLook; // Initialized in the do loop
      do {
          ++_iLook;
          cLook = _buf [_iLook];
      } while (std::isalnum (cLook) || cLook == '_');
```

```
      _lenSymbol = _iLook - _iSymbol;
      if (_lenSymbol >= maxSymLen)
        _lenSymbol = maxSymLen - 1;
    }
    else
      _token = tError;
    break;
```

To simplify our lives as programmers, we chose to limit the size of symbols to maxSymLen. Remember, we are still weekend programmers![5]

Once the Scanner recognizes an identifier, it should be able to provide its name for use by other parts of the program. To retrieve a symbol name, we call the following method:

```
    void Scanner::GetSymbolName (char * strOut, int & len)
    {
      assert (len >= maxSymLen);
      assert (_lenSymbol <= maxSymLen);
      std::strncpy (strOut, &_buf [_iSymbol], _lenSymbol);
      strOut [_lenSymbol] = '\0';
      len = _lenSymbol;
    }
```

Notice that we *have* to make a copy of the string, since the original in the buffer is not null terminated. We copy the string to the caller's buffer strOut of length len. We do it by calling the function strncpy (string-n-copy, where *n* means that there is a maximum number of characters to be copied). The length is an in/out parameter of the method GetSymbolName. It should be initialized by the caller to the size of the buffer strOut. After GetSymbolName returns, its value reflects the actual length of the string copied. How do we know that the buffer is big enough? We make it part of the contract—see the assertions.

The method GetSymbolName is an example of a more general pattern of passing buffers of data between objects. There are three main schemes: caller's fixed buffer, caller-allocated buffer, and callee-allocated buffer. In our case the buffer is passed by the caller and its size is fixed. This allows the caller to use a local fixed buffer—there is no need to allocate or reallocate it every time the function is called. Here's the Parser code that makes this call (the buffer strSymbol is a local array):

```
    char strSymbol [maxSymLen];
    int lenSym = maxSymLen;
    _scanner.GetSymbolName (strSymbol, lenSym);
```

Notice that this method can only be used when there is a well-defined and reasonable maximum size for the buffer, or when the data can be retrieved incrementally

---

5. If you're worried about how these limits are enforced and how the errors are handled, your instincts are right! We'll deal with these issues in Part 2 of this book, Techniques, when we graduate from "weekend programming." We don't have the tools to do it right yet.

in multiple calls. Here, we were clever enough to always truncate the size of our identifiers to maxSymLen.

If the size of the data to be passed in the buffer is not limited, we have to be able to allocate the buffer on demand. In the case of a caller-allocated buffer we have two options. Optimally, the caller should be able to first ask for the size of data, allocate the appropriate buffer, and call the method to fill the buffer. There is a variation of the scheme—the caller reallocated buffer—where the caller allocates the buffer of some arbitrary size that covers, say, 99% of the cases. When the data does not fit into the buffer, the callee returns the appropriate failure code and lets the caller allocate a bigger buffer.

```
char * pBuf = new char [goodSize];
int len = goodSize;
if (FillBuffer (pBuf, len) == errOverflow)
{
    // Rarely necessary
    delete [] pBuf;
    pBuf = new char [len]; // len updated by FillBuffer
    FillBuffer (pBuf, len);
}
```

This may seem like a strange optimization until you encounter situations where the call to ask for the size of data is really expensive. For instance, you might be calling across the network, or require disk access to find the size, and so on.

The callee-allocated buffer seems a simple enough scheme. Since the called function knows how much space is needed, it allocates the buffer and returns a pointer to it. The most likely complication is a memory leak when the caller forgets to deallocate the buffer (which, we should remember, hasn't been explicitly allocated by the caller). We'll see how to protect ourselves from such problems using smart pointers (see Chapter 10, Resource Management). Other complications arise when the callee uses a different memory allocator than the caller, or when the call crosses process boundaries using, for instance, Remote Procedure Call (RPC, a protocol for programs to talk to each other). Usually we let the callee allocate memory when dealing with functions that have to return dynamic data structures (lists, trees, and so on). Here's a simple code example of callee-allocated buffer:

```
char * pBuf = AcquireData ( );
// Use pBuf
delete pBuf;
```

The following decision tree summarizes various methods of passing data to the caller:

```
if (max data size well-defined)
{
   use caller's fixed buffer
}
```

```
else if (it's cheap to ask for size)
{
  use caller-allocated buffer
}
else if ((caller trusted to free memory
          && caller uses the same allocator
          && no problems with remoting)
     || returning dynamic data structures)
{
  use callee-allocated buffer
}
else
{
  use caller-reallocated buffer
}
```

In Part 2 of this book, Techniques, we'll talk about some interesting ways of making the callee-allocated buffer a much more attractive and convenient mechanism.

5.3 Symbol Table

Implicit conversions, explicit keyword.

Script 3   With a few minor modifications, we are going to reuse the hash table and the string buffer code to implement the symbol table. But first we'll make it so the size of the hash table can be set during construction.

```
explicit HTable (int size): _size (size)
{
  _aList = new List [size];
}

~HTable ()
{
  delete []_aList;
}
```

Notice the keyword explicit in front of the constructor. I put it there to tell the compiler not to use this constructor to do implicit conversions. Normally, when you define a constructor that takes a single argument of type *T*, the compiler can use it to quietly convert an object of type *T* to an object of the class whose constructor it is. For instance, since the constructor of the hash table takes a single argument of type int, the compiler would accept a statement like this:

```
HTable table (13);
table = 5;
```

It would just "convert" an integer, 5, to a hash table as easily as it converts an integer to a double. Such implicit conversions are sometimes extremely useful, but at other times they are a source of unexpected problems. The code above makes little sense and the error would be easy to spot. Imagine, however, that somebody by mistake passed an `int` to a function expecting a `const` reference to a hash table. The compiler would actually create a temporary hash table of the size equal to the value of the integer and pass it to the function. To protect yourself from this kind of error you should make it a habit to declare single-argument constructors `explicit`—that is, unless you really want to define an implicit conversion.

The symbol table is a simple modification of our earlier string table (see Section 3.5.3). It uses a hash table to map strings into short lists of string IDs. New strings are stored in the string buffer at the first available offset and are given the first available ID, `curId`. The offset of the string in the buffer is then stored in a separate array, `_offStr`. String ID doubles as an index to this array.

```cpp
const int idNotFound = -1;

class SymbolTable
{
public:
  explicit SymbolTable (int size);
  ~SymbolTable ();
  int ForceAdd (char const * str, int len);
  int Find (char const * str) const;
  char const * GetString (int id) const;
private:
  HTable        _htab;
  int           _maxId;      // The size of _offStr
  int         * _offStr;     // Offsets of strings in buffer
  int           _curId;
  StringBuffer  _strBuf;
};
```

Here are the constructor and the destructor of the symbol table. Other methods are just copied from our earlier implementation of the string table, except for the fact that the string buffer now has a dynamically allocated buffer whose size is passed in the constructor.

```cpp
SymbolTable::SymbolTable (int size)
  : _curId (0),
    _maxId (size),
    _htab (size + 1),
    _strBuf (size * 10)
{
  _offStr = new int [size];
}

SymbolTable::~SymbolTable ()
{
  delete []_offStr;
}
```

The values used to initialize the hash table and the string buffer are a bit heuristic. We want the hash table to be slightly larger than the number of entries to be stored in it. We also want the average size of an identifier to be less than ten characters.

5.4   Store

Forward declarations.

Script 4   Our calculator can deal with symbolic variables. The user creates a variable by inventing a name for it and then using it in arithmetic operations. Every variable has to be initialized—assigned a value in an assignment expression—before it can be used in evaluating other expressions. To store the values of user-defined variables, our calculator will need some kind of "memory." We will create a class `Store` that contains a fixed number, called `size`, of memory cells. Each cell can store a value of the type `double`. The cells are numbered from zero to `size`–1. Each cell can be in either of two states—uninitialized or initialized.

```
enum { stNotInit, stInit };
```

The association between a symbolic name—a string—and the cell number is handled by the symbol table. For instance, when the user first introduces a given variable, say *x,* the string `"x"` is added to the symbol table and assigned an integer, say 3. From that point on, the value of the variable *x* will be stored in cell number 3 in the `Store` object.

We would also like to preinitialize the symbol table and the store with some useful constants like *e* (the base of natural logarithms) and *pi* (the ratio of the circumference of a circle to its diameter). We would like to do it in the constructor of `Store`, so we need to pass it a reference to the symbol table. Now here's a little snag: We want to put the definition of the class `Store` in a separate header file, `store.h`. The definition of the class `SymbolTable` is in a different file, `symtab.h`. When the compiler is looking at the declaration of the constructor of `Store`,

```
Store (int size, SymbolTable & symTab);
```

it has no idea what `SymbolTable` is. The simple-minded solution is to include the file `symtab.h` in `store.h`. There is nothing wrong with doing that, except that it burdens the compiler with the processing of one more file whenever it is processing `symtab.h` or any file that includes it. In a really big project, with a lot of header files including one another, this might become a real headache. Also, if you are using any type of dependency checker, it will assume that a change in `symtab.h` requires the recompilation of all the files that include it directly or indirectly. In particular, any file that includes `store.h` will have to be recompiled too. All this unnecessary processing would be done because we needed to let the compiler know that `SymbolTable` is a name of a class. Why don't we just say that? Indeed, the syntax of such a *forward declaration* is:

```
class SymbolTable;
```

As long as we are *only* using pointers or references to SymbolTable, this will do. We don't need to include symtab.h.

On the other hand, a forward declaration would not be sufficient if we wanted to call any of the methods of SymbolTable (including the constructor or the destructor) or if we tried to embed or inherit from SymbolTable.

Here's the definition of Store:

```
class SymbolTable; // Forward declaration

class Store
{
public:
  Store (int size, SymbolTable & symTab);
  ~Store ( )
  {
    delete []_cell;
    delete []_status;
  }
  bool IsInit (int id) const
  {
    return (id < _size && _status [id] != stNotInit);
  }
  double Value (int id) const
  {
    assert (IsInit (id));
    return _cell [id];
  }
  void SetValue (int id, double val)
  {
    if (id < _size)
    {
      _cell [id] = val;
      _status [id] = stInit;
    }
  }
private:
  int           _size;
  double       *_cell;
  unsigned char *_status;
};
```

Store contains two arrays: the array of cells and the array of statuses. The arrays are initialized in the constructor and deleted in the destructor. We also store the size of these arrays (it's used for error checking). The client of Store can check whether a given cell has been initialized, get the value stored there, as well as set (and initialize) this value.

Why am I using two arrays instead of a single array of two-field objects? I could have defined a class `Cell` as:

```
class Cell
{
  // ...
private:
  double        _value;
  unsigned char _status;
};
```

I could have had a single array of `Cell`s in `Store` instead of two separate arrays for values and statuses.

Both solutions have their merits. Using `Cell` improves code understandability and maintenance. On the other hand, using two separate arrays may be more space efficient. How come? Because of the *alignment* of data.

On most computer architectures it is cheaper to retrieve data from memory if it's aligned on a 32- or 64-bit boundary. So, unless you specify otherwise, the compiler will force the alignment of user-defined data structures on such boundaries. In particular, it might add padding to your data structures. It's very likely that the compiler will add three (or even seven) bytes of padding to every `Cell`. This way, the size of a `Cell` in memory will be guaranteed to be a multiple of 32 (or 64) bits, and accessing an array of `Cell`s will be very fast.

As long as you're dealing with reasonably small arrays, you shouldn't care. But if your program uses lots of memory, you might want to be more careful. In our implementation we tried to reduce the memory overhead by declaring the array `_status` to be an array of bytes (`unsigned chars`). In fact, we could get away with an array of bits. After all, status is a two-valued variable and can be encoded using a single bit. Implementing a bit array is nontrivial and involves explicit bitwise operations on every access, but in some cases it might save you oodles of memory.

So here's a rule of thumb: If you anticipate that you might have to shrink your data structures because of memory constraints, implementing the shrinkable part separately will give you more flexibility. In our case, we could, in the future, reimplement the _status array as a bit array without changing much code around it. On the other hand, if you anticipate that you might have to add more *undersized* variables to each element of the array, you'd be better off combining them into a single class. In our case, if we expected that we might, say, need some kind of type enumeration for every variable, we could easily add it to the `Cell` class.

Making choices like this is what makes programming interesting.

The constructor of `Store` is defined in the source file `store.cpp`. Since the constructor calls actual methods of the `SymbolTable`, the forward declaration of this class is no longer sufficient and we need to explicitly include the header `symtab.h` in `store.cpp`.

```
Store::Store (int size, SymbolTable & symTab)
  : _size (size)
{
    _cell = new double [size];
    _status = new unsigned char [size];
    for (int i = 0; i < size; ++i)
      _status [i] = stNotInit;
    // Add predefined constants
    // Note: if more needed, do a more general job
    std::cout << "e = " << std::exp (1) << std::endl;
    int id = symTab.ForceAdd ("e", 1);
    SetValue (id, std::exp (1));
    std::cout << "pi = " << 2 * std::acos (0.0)
        << std::endl;
    id = symTab.ForceAdd ("pi", 2);
    SetValue (id, 2.0 * std::acos (0.0));
}
```

We add the mapping of the string e of size 1 to the symbol table and then use the returned integer as a cell number in the call to SetValue. The same procedure is used to initialize the value of pi.

5.5 Function Table

Metaprograms, pointers to functions, explicit array initialization, explicit class initialization.

Script 5   For a good scientific calculator, built-in functions are a must. We have to be able to calculate square roots, logarithms, trigonometric functions, and so on. We are quite lucky because the standard C library implements most of the basic math functions. All we need is for the parser to recognize a function call and then call the appropriate library function. The only tricky part is to make the connection between the function name—the string recognized by the parser—and the call to the appropriate function.

One way would be to create a multiway conditional that compares the string to a list of predefined function names, and, when successful, calls the corresponding function.

```
if (std::strcmp (string, "sin") == 0)
{
    result = sin (arg);
}
else if ...
...
```

As long as the number of built-in functions is reasonably small, this solution is good enough. Let's pretend though that instead of a toy calculator, we are writing an industrial-strength program that will have to handle hundreds, if not thousands, of built-in functions. The problem then becomes: Given a string, match it against hundreds of predefined strings. Clearly, doing hundreds of string comparisons every time is unacceptable.

But wait! We already have a string-matching object—the symbol table. Since it's implemented as a hash table, it can perform a match in constant time, independent of the size of the table. The symbol table converts a string into an integer. We can prefill the table with built-in function names (just like we did with built-in constants) and dispatch the function calls based on integers rather than strings. We could, for instance, insert the string sin in the zeroth slot of the symbol table, cos in the first slot, and so on, and then dispatch calls using a switch statement:

```
case 0:
  result = sin (arg);
  break;
case 1:
  result = cos (arg);
  break;
...
```

A switch statement that uses a set of consecutive labels—0, 1, 2, and so on—is implemented by the compiler as a jump table with a constant switching time independent of the number of labels. This seems like a perfect, constant-time solution.

But how do we make sure that sin always corresponds to 0, cos to 1, and so on? Well, we can always initialize the symbol table with these strings in this particular order. After all, we know that the symbol table assigns consecutive indexes starting with zero. Is it okay, though? These are implementation secrets of the symbol table. What if the next person who maintains our program rewrites the symbol table to use an even better algorithm? One that does not assign consecutive indexes starting with zero?

And how about expandability of such code? Suppose that at some point in the future we want to add one more built-in function. What kind of changes will we have to make to this implementation? We'll have to

- Add one more case to the switch statement
- Add one more string to the symbol table
- Make sure that the string is assigned an ID that is the same as the case label of the corresponding function

Notice what we have just done. We have written a *metaprogram*—a set of instructions to be followed in order to add a new built-in function to our calculator. These are not machine instructions; these are instructions for the programmer. In fact, they don't appear anywhere in the program, not even as comments—they are implicit. This kind of invisible *metacode* adds to the hidden complexity of a program. What does metacode describe? It describes the steps to be taken to implement the most likely extension to the program, as well as the assertions that have to be preserved when making such extensions.

> **When comparing various implementations, take into account not only the complexity of the code but also the complexity of the metacode.**

Let's see if we can find a better implementation for built-in functions. Optimally, we would like to have some kind of table listing all the functions. (It is almost always a good idea to shift the complexity from code to data structures.) Adding a new function would be equivalent to adding a new entry to this table. The metaprogram for such an implementation would consist of a single statement:

Add a new entry to the function array.

In order to make a connection between data and executable code we need a new device: *pointers to functions*. A pointer to a function is just like a regular pointer, but instead of pointing to data it points to executable code. By using a pointer to data you can read or modify data; by using a pointer to a function you can call functions. Just like with any other type of pointer, we'll have to be able to

- Declare a pointer to a function
- Initialize a pointer to point to a particular function
- Make a function call through a pointer

For instance, we may declare a pointer to a function taking a `double` (as an argument) and returning a `double`. There are many such functions and we can initialize the pointer to point to any one of these. In particular, we may initialize the pointer to point to the function `double sin (double x)`. After that, if we make a function call through that pointer, we will be calling `sin`. Had we initialized the pointer to point to `double cos (double x)`, we would have called `cos` instead. The beauty of a pointer to a function is that the same pointer can point to different functions during the execution of the program. The part of the program that makes the function call doesn't have to know what function it is calling.

Let's look at some actual code to see what the syntax looks like. First, let's declare a pointer `pFun` to a function taking a `double` and returning a `double`:

```
double (* pFun) (double x);
```

Compare it with the declaration of a function `sin` taking a `double` and returning a `double`:

```
double sin (double x);
```

Why did we have to enclose the asterisk and the pointer name within parentheses? We had to do it in order to distinguish the declaration of a pointer to a function from a declaration of a function returning a pointer. Without the parentheses,

```
double * pFun (double x);
```

declares a function taking a double and returning a pointer to double. Quite a difference!

You can declare a pointer to any type of a function by taking the declaration of any function of this type and replacing the function name with (* pFun). Of course, you can use an arbitrary name instead of pFun.

Remember the function strtod? Its declaration was:

```
double strtod (char const * str, char *ppEnd);
```

A pointer to a function of this type would be declared as:

```
double (* pStrtod) (char const * str, char *ppEnd);
```

It's that simple!

Because of pointers to functions, we have to augment the rules of reading declarations. We start reading backwards, as usual: pStrtod *is a pointer.* . . . But when we hit the parenthesis, we immediately go to the matching parenthesis and change the direction of parsing. The first thing we see now is a left parenthesis that starts the argument list. A parenthesized argument list means that we are dealing with a function, so we continue reading . . . *to a function taking* str, *which is a pointer to a* const char, *and* ppEnd, *which is a pointer to a pointer to a* char. Here we hit the closing parenthesis, so we zigzag back to where we left our leftward scanning and continue: . . . *returning double.* Similarly, when we encounter a left square bracket, we know we are dealing with an array, so, for instance

```
int (* pArr) [3];
```

reads: ← pArr *is a pointer* → *to an array of three* ← *integers.* (The arrows mark the change of direction.) Let's try something more complicated:

```
double (* (* pFunArr) [6]) (double x);
```

← pFunArr *is a pointer* → *to an array of six* ← *pointers* → *to functions taking* double x ← *and returning a double.* Finally, as an exercise for the reader, a nice little declaration:

```
double (* (* pFunFunFun) (double (* pFun)(double x))) (double x);
```

Please don't try these at home!

Now for the second step: the initialization. In order to make the pointer point to a function, we have to take the address of the function and assign it to the pointer. It so happens that the name of the function *is* the address of the function. We can therefore initialize our pointer like this:

```
double (* pFun) (double x) = std::sin;
```

or do the assignment at a later point:

```
pFun = std::sin;
```

Finally, in order to invoke a function through a pointer, we dereference the pointer and pass the appropriate argument(s):

```
double x = 3.1415;
double y = (* pFun) (x);
```

Pointers to functions can be used as building blocks in more complex data structures such as arrays, classes, pointers to pointers, and so on. To simplify the declarations of such data structures, type definitions are often used.

All our built-in functions take one argument of the type `double` and return a result which is also `double`, so we start our implementation of the built-in function table with a type definition:

```
typedef double (*PtrFun) (double);
```

The connection between a function and its string name is established through the class `FunctionEntry`.

```
class   FunctionEntry
{
public:
  PtrFun   pFun;
  char*    strFun;
};
```

You might be wondering why we have made all the data members of this class public[6] but not provided a constructor to initialize them. That's because we want to be able to initialize them explicitly, like this:

```
FunctionEntry funEntry = { std::sin, "sin" };
```

This kind of initialization, where you assign values directly to the object's data members, is possible if and only if the object doesn't have both private data and a constructor. Still, I haven't explained why anyone would want to use this kind of direct initialization instead of simply providing an appropriate constructor. Here's why:

```
const int maxIdFun = 16;
FunctionEntry funArr [maxIdFun] =
{
  std::log,   "log",
```

---

6. Following the C tradition, a `class` with all public data members is often declared as a `struct` instead. The only advantage of using a `struct` in pure C++ is that you don't have to type the `public:` label at its top.

```
          std::log10,  "log10",
          std::exp,    "exp",
          std::sqrt,   "sqrt",
          std::sin,    "sin",
          std::cos,    "cos",
          std::tan,    "tan",
          CoTan,       "cotan",
          std::sinh,   "sinh",
          std::cosh,   "cosh",
          std::tanh,   "tanh",
          std::asin,   "asin",
          std::acos,   "acos",
          std::atan,   "atan",
          0,           ""
      };
```

In one fell swoop we've been able to initialize the whole array of
FunctionEntries. That's exactly what we are striving for. Notice how easy it will be
now to add a new built-in function: just add one more line with a function pointer
and string name between any two lines in this list and it'll just work (you'll need to
increment maxIdFun as well, but that's something the compiler will remind you of,
if you forget). If you want to know more about explicit initialization of aggregates
(such as classes and arrays), refer to section 5.9.

Now that we are through with the preliminaries, let's get back to our original
problem: the initialization of the symbol table with built-in function names. This
should be done in the construction stages of the program—the calculator is not
ready to be used unless the symbol table is filled in advance. We will therefore
define an object called the FunctionTable with the dual purpose of initializing the
symbol table with the names and translating symbol IDs to function pointers for all
the built-in functions.

```
class SymbolTable;

class FunctionTable
{
public:
  FunctionTable (SymbolTable & symTab,
                 FunctionEntry funArr []);
  int Size () const { return _size; }
  PtrFun GetFun (int id) const
  {
    return _pFun [id];
  }
private:
  PtrFun   _pFun [maxIdFun];
  int      _size;
};
```

The constructor of the FunctionTable takes a reference to the symbol table
and fills it with strings from our array of FunctionEntrys, funArr. At the same
time, it copies corresponding function pointers into its own array (strictly speak-

ing, the copying could be avoided if we let the function table use the function array directly—that's an optimization that is best left as an exercise to the reader).

```
FunctionTable::FunctionTable (
    SymbolTable & symTab, FunctionEntry funArr [])
  : _size (0)
{
  for (int i = 0; i < maxIdFun; ++i)
  {
    int len = std::strlen (funArr [i].strFun);
    if (len == 0)
        break;
    _pFun [i] = funArr [i].pFun;
    std::cout << funArr[i].strFun << std::endl;
    int j = symTab.ForceAdd (funArr [i].strFun, len);
    assert (i == j);
    ++_size;
  }
}
```

Notice the very important assertion in the loop. We are making sure that the assumption that the symbol table assigns consecutive indexes to our functions is indeed true. We want the string `log` to correspond to ID 0, because we store the pointer to the function `log` at offset 0, and so on.

All of the built-in functions so far have been library functions (defined in the standard C library) except for one, the cotangent. The cotangent is just the inverse of the tangent, so it is easy to write our own implementation of it. The only tricky part is dealing with the inverse of zero—division by zero causes an exception, which would terminate the program. That's why we test for zero and return `HUGE_VAL` (defined in `<cmath>`) as its inverse. That's not entirely correct (the result of division by zero is undefined), but it'll do for now:

```
double CoTan (double x)
{
  double y = std::tan (x);
  if (y == 0)
  {
      std::cout << "cotan of " << x << " undefined\n";
      return HUGE_VAL;
  }
  return 1.0 / y;
}
```

Note that the appropriate line in the initialization of `funArr`

```
CoTan, "cotan",
```

contains the pointer to our own implementation of cotangent, namely `CoTan`. To let the compiler know what `CoTan` is and how to call it correctly, I added the *declaration* of this function at the top of the file `FunTab.cpp`. The difference between a declaration and the definition is that the former doesn't provide the implementation; it only specifies the function's *signature*—the number and the types of arguments and the return type.

```
double CoTan (double x);
```

A function declaration, also called a *prototype,* is always followed by a semicolon. If you try to call (or, as in our case, assign to a pointer) a function that hasn't been prototyped, the compiler will tell you about the "missing prototype." Unlike a definition, a declaration can be repeated in the same file or in different files. You can also put declarations inside a header file.

Objects, variables, and other data structures can also be declared before being defined. However, since a definition of a data structure doesn't necessarily require its initialization, it would be hard for the compiler to distinguish them from declarations. For instance,

```
int x;
```

is always interpreted as a definition. Upon seeing this definition, the compiler will allocate storage (either global or on the stack) for the variable x. If you repeat this definition or put it in a header file that's included in more than one implementation file, you'll get an error—"symbol multiply defined."

Therefore, a declaration of *data* has to be preceded by the keyword extern. For instance, to tell the compiler that there is an integer variable called x defined in some implementation file, you'd declare it like this (no initialization is allowed):

```
extern int x;
```

Similarly, to tell everybody that there is an array funArr that can be used in other files, we'll add the following declaration to the header FunTab.h:

```
extern FunctionEntry funArr [];
```

To summarize: We went through quite a bit of trouble in order to produce an implementation that avoids some of the hidden complexities of something we called metacode. In this particular case, it was well worth the effort because we knew that the table of built-in functions would be the first thing to be modified in the future. We made sure such modifications would be easy and virtually foolproof. We have gathered them in one place (the initialization of funArr*), made trivial mistakes compiler-detectable (forgetting to update* maxIdFun*), and positioned an assertion in a strategic place (inside the* FunctionTable *constructor). The function table works, but its implementation is not yet totally satisfactory from a design point of view. We'll come back to it later.*

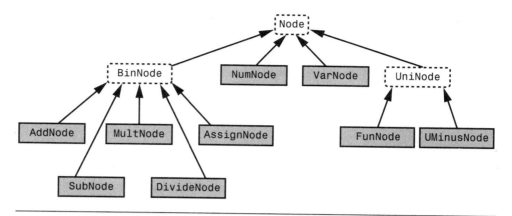

Figure 5.3 The hierarchy of node classes

5.6 Nodes

Script 6   It's time to add a few more node types (see Figure 5.3).

Corresponding to built-in functions are the objects of type FunNode.

```
class FunNode: public UniNode
{
public:
  FunNode (PtrFun pFun, Node * pNode)
    : UniNode (pNode), _pFun (pFun)
  {}
  double Calc () const;
private:
  PtrFun _pFun;
};
```

The base class UniNode is very similar to BinNode, except that it has one child instead of two (we'll also derive UMinusNode from this class). The Calc method of FunNode illustrates the syntax for the invocation of a function through a pointer.

```
double FunNode::Calc () const
{
  assert (_pFun != 0);
  return (*_pFun)(_pNode->Calc ());
}
```

By the way, there is an alternative syntax for calling a function through a pointer. You can simply treat the pointer as if it were a function name, like this:

```
return _pFun (_pNode->Calc ());
```

The assignment node is a little trickier. It is a binary node with the children corresponding to the left and right side of the assignment. For instance, the parsing of the line

```
x = 1
```

will produce an assignment node with the left node corresponding to the symbolic variable *x* and the right node corresponding to the value 1. First of all, not every node can be a left side of an assignment. For instance

```
2 = 1
```

is clearly unacceptable. We need a way of deciding whether a given node can appear on the left side of an assignment—whether it can be an *lvalue*. In our calculator, the only possible lvalue is a symbolic variable.

In order to be able to verify if a given node is an lvalue, we will add the virtual method `IsLvalue` to the base class `Node` and provide the default implementation

```
bool Node::IsLvalue () const
{
    return false;
}
```

The only type of node that will override this default will be the symbolic-variable node. We'll make the parser perform the `IsLvalue` test on the left side of the assignment before creating the `AssignNode`. Inside the assignment node, we'll only assert that the parser did its job.

```
class AssignNode : public BinNode
{
public:
    AssignNode (Node * pLeft, Node * pRight)
      : BinNode (pLeft, pRight)
    {
        assert (pLeft->IsLvalue ());
    }
    double Calc () const;
};
```

The `Calc` method calls the `Assign` method of the left child with the value calculated by the right child. Again, we will add the virtual method `Assign` to the base class `Node`, together with the default implementation that does nothing.

```
virtual void Assign (double value) {}
```

Only the *variable* node will override this implementation.

Having said that, the implementation of `AssignNode::Calc` is straightforward:

```
double AssignNode::Calc () const
{
  double x = _pRight->Calc ();
  _pLeft->Assign (x);
  return x;
}
```

Next, we have to define the node corresponding to a symbolic variable. The value of the variable is stored in the Store object. VarNode needs access to this object in order to calculate itself. But, as we have just stated, VarNode can also be used on the left side of an assignment, so it has to override the virtual methods IsLvalue and Assign.

```
class Store;

class VarNode: public Node
{
public:
  VarNode (int id, Store & store)
    : _id (id), _store (store) {}
  double Calc () const;
  bool IsLvalue () const;
  void Assign (double val);
private:
  const int _id;
  Store & _store;
};

double VarNode::Calc () const
{
  double x = 0.0;
  if (_store.IsInit (_id))
    x = _store.Value (_id);
  else
    std::cout << "Use of uninitialized variable\n";
  return x;
}

void VarNode::Assign (double val)
{
  _store.SetValue (_id, val);
}

bool VarNode::IsLvalue () const
{
  return true;
}
```

There are a few more node classes that the parser needs: SubNode for subtractions, DivideNode for divisions, and UMinusNode for unary negations. They are very simple to implement.

5.7 Parser

Private methods.

The parser requires a major makeover. Let's start with the header file, parse.h. It contains a lot of forward declarations:

```
class Node;
class Scanner;
class Store;
class FunctionTable;
class SymbolTable;
```

All these classes are mentioned in parse.h either through pointers or references—there is no need to include the header files that define them.

The class Parser has a constructor that takes references to all the major objects it will need in order to parse the stream of tokens from the Scanner. It needs Store to create VarNodes, FunctionTable to create FunNodes, and the SymbolTable to recognize variables and function names. Once the Parser is created, we can only ask it to evaluate the expression passed to it in the Scanner. The Eval method has the side effect of printing the result on the screen (if you're cringing now, I promise you'll be relieved when you read the next chapter of this book).

Parser uses a number of private methods to parse expressions, terms, and factors, and a method to execute the evaluation of the expression tree. Private methods are a useful device for code structuring. They cannot be called from outside of the class—they are just helper functions used in the implementation of other (public or private) methods.

```
class Parser
{
public:
   Parser (Scanner & scanner,
           Store & store,
           FunctionTable & funTab,
           SymbolTable & symTab);
   ~Parser ();
   Status Eval ();
private:
   void    Parse();
   Node * Expr();
   Node * Term();
   Node * Factor();
   void    Execute ();

   Scanner        & _scanner;
   Node           * _pTree;
   Status           _status;
   Store          & _store;
   FunctionTable & _funTab;
   SymbolTable    & _symTab;
};
```

The constructor (we are already looking at the implementation file `parse.cpp`) initializes all the `Parser`'s private member variables.

```cpp
Parser::Parser (Scanner & scanner,
                Store & store,
                FunctionTable & funTab,
                SymbolTable & symTab)
: _scanner (scanner),
  _pTree (0),
  _status (stOk),
  _funTab (funTab),
  _store (store),
  _symTab (symTab)
{}
```

The destructor recursively deletes the parse tree (compare with the recursive destructor of a linked list, page 82):

```cpp
Parser::~Parser ()
{
    delete _pTree;
}
```

The `Eval` method calls private methods to parse the input and execute the calculation:

```cpp
Status Parser::Eval ()
{
    Parse ();
    if (_status == stOk)
        Execute ();
    else
        _status = stQuit;
    return _status;
}
```

Execute calls the `Calc` method of the top node of the parse tree and prints the result of the (recursive) calculation:

```cpp
void Parser::Execute ()
{
    if (_pTree)
    {
        double result = _pTree->Calc ();
        std::cout << " " << result << std::endl;
    }
}
```

The parsing starts with the assumption that everything is an expression.

```cpp
void Parser::Parse ()
```

```
{
  _pTree = Expr ();
}
```

The expression starts with a term. The term can be followed by an operator that binds terms—the plus sign, minus sign, or assignment sign—or nothing at all. These correspond to the four productions (see our original description of the grammar on page 108).

```
Expression is Term + Expression
or Term − Expression
or Term = Expression   // The Term must be an lvalue
or just Term
```

As you might recall, these productions define a right-associative arithmetic operator. Unfortunately, that also means the assignment is right-associative, and an expression like this

```
1 + x = 2
```

is legal. It is parsed as

```
1 + (x = 2)
```

For the time being, we'll have to live with this flaw. It will be fixed in Part 2 of this book, section 6.6.

According to our grammar, after parsing a term we should ask the Scanner for the next token and test it against tPlus, tMinus, and tAssign.

Immediately after a token is recognized, we tell the Scanner to accept it.

```
Node * Parser::Expr ()
{
  Node * pNode = Term ();
  EToken token = _scanner.Token ();
  if (token == tPlus)
  {
    _scanner.Accept ();
    Node * pRight = Expr ();
    pNode = new AddNode (pNode, pRight);
  }
  else if (token == tMinus)
  {
    _scanner.Accept ();
    Node * pRight = Expr ();
    pNode = new SubNode (pNode, pRight);
  }
  else if (token == tAssign)
  {
    _scanner.Accept ();
    Node * pRight = Expr ();
```

```
        if (pNode->IsLvalue ())
        {
          pNode = new AssignNode (pNode, pRight);
        }
        else
        {
          _status = stError;
          delete pNode;
          pNode = Expr ();
        }
      }
      return pNode;
    }
```

Error recovery in parsers involves a bit of heuristics. Here, for instance, when we detect that the left side of an assignment is not an lvalue, we discard it and proceed to evaluate the expression on the right side. In more complex parsers it makes sense to continue parsing after the first error, if only to be able to report more errors to the user. We'll get more into error processing in Part 2 of this book.

We proceed in a similar fashion with Term, following the productions:

Term is **Factor * Term**
or **Factor / Term**
or just **Factor**

The method Term should look like this:

```
Node * Parser::Term ()
{
  Node * pNode = Factor ();
  if (_scanner.Token () == tMult)
  {
    _scanner.Accept ();
    Node * pRight = Term ();
    pNode = new MultNode (pNode, pRight);
  }
  else if (_scanner.Token () == tDivide)
  {
    _scanner.Accept ();
    Node * pRight = Term ();
    pNode = new DivideNode (pNode, pRight);
  }
  return pNode;
}
```

A Factor, in turn, can be one of these:

Factor is **(Expression)** // Parenthesized expression
or **Number** // Literal floating-point number
or **Identifier (Expression)** // Function call
or **Identifier** // Symbolic variable
or **– Factor** // Unary minus

```
Node * Parser::Factor ()
{
  Node * pNode;
  EToken token = _scanner.Token ();

  if (token == tLParen)
  {
    _scanner.Accept (); // Accept '('
    pNode = Expr ();
    if (_scanner.Token() != tRParen)
      _status = stError;
    else
      _scanner.Accept (); // Accept ')'
  }
  else if (token == tNumber)
  {
    pNode = new NumNode (_scanner.Number ());
    _scanner.Accept ();
  }
  else if (token == tIdent)
  {
    char strSymbol [maxSymLen];
    int lenSym = maxSymLen;
    // Copy the symbol into strSymbol
    _scanner.GetSymbolName (strSymbol, lenSym);
    int id = _symTab.Find (strSymbol);
    _scanner.Accept ();
    if (_scanner.Token() == tLParen) // Function call
    {
      _scanner.Accept ( ); // Accept '('
      pNode = Expr ( );
      if (_scanner.Token () == tRParen)
        _scanner.Accept (); // Accept ')'
      else
        _status = stError;
      if (id != idNotFound && id < _funTab.Size ())
      {
        pNode = new FunNode (
          _funTab.GetFun (id), pNode);
      }
      else
      {
        std::cout << "Unknown function \"";
        std::cout << strSymbol << "\"\n";
      }
    }
    else
    {
      if (id == idNotFound)
        id = _symTab.ForceAdd (strSymbol, lenSym);
      pNode = new VarNode (id, _store);
    }
  }
  else if (token == tMinus) // Unary minus
  {
```

```
      _scanner.Accept ( ); // Accept minus
      pNode = new UMinusNode (Factor ());
   }
   else
   {
     _scanner.Accept ();
     _status = stError;
     pNode = 0;
   }
   return pNode;
}
```

To see how the parser works, let's step through a simple example. Suppose that the user typed

```
x = 1
```

First, a scanner containing the input string is created. It scans the first token and decides that it's an identifier, tIdent. Next, the parser is called to Eval the expression. It starts parsing it by assuming that it is, indeed, an expression.

```
_pTree = Expr ();
```

The expression must start with a term, so Expr calls Term.

```
Node * pNode = Term ();
```

Term, on the other hand, expects to see a Factor.

```
Node * pNode = Factor ();
```

Finally, Factor looks at the first token

```
EToken token = _scanner.Token ();
```

and compares it to tLParen, tNumber, tIdent, and tMinus. In our case the first token is an identifier, tIdent. It then asks the scanner for the name of the symbol (the name is *x*) and searches for it in the symbol table. Now factor is done with the first token so it tells the scanner to accept the token.

```
// Copy the symbol into strSymbol
_scanner.GetSymbolName (strSymbol, lenSym);
int id = _symTab.Find (strSymbol, lenSym);
_scanner.Accept ();
```

The scanner scans for the next token, which is the assignment operator tAssign. The parser looks at this token to see if it's a left parenthesis—that would signify a function call. Since it isn't, the parser creates a VarNode using the ID of the symbol found in the symbol table. If this is a new symbol for which there isn't an ID, the parser just adds it to the symbol table and creates a new ID.

```
if (id == idNotFound)
  id = _symTab.ForceAdd (strSymbol, lenSym);
pNode = new VarNode (id, _store);
```

Factor is now done and it returns a pointer to the node it has just created. Back to Term. Term has a node from factor, so now it looks at the next token to see if it is either tMult or tDivide. Since it's not, Term returns the same node. Back to Expr. Again, a look at the token: is it tPlus, tMinus, or tAssign? It is tAssign! Expr accepts the token (the scanner positions itself at tNumber whose value is 1). So far, the parser has seen a node followed by an equal sign. An equal sign can be followed by an arbitrary expression, so Expr now calls itself to parse the rest of the input, which is "1".

```
_scanner.Accept ();
Node* pRight = Expr ();
```

Expr again goes through Term and Factor, which creates a NumNode.

```
pNode = new NumNode (_scanner.Number ());
_scanner.Accept ();
```

Back to Term and Expr with the new node pRight. The parser has now seen a node, pNode, followed by the equal sign and another node, pRight. It looks very much like an assignment statement, except the parser doesn't know if pNode represents an lvalue. In our case, the node, VarNode, does. An assignment node is created:

```
if (pNode->IsLvalue ())
{
  pNode = new AssignNode (pNode, pRight);
}
```

Expr returns this AssignNode to Parse. The parse tree now looks like Figure 5.4.

Since the parsing was successful, Eval calls Execute, which calls _pTree->Calc. The virtual Calc method of AssignNode calculates the value of the right node—NumNode returns 1—and calls the Assign method of VarNode with this value. VarNode has access to Store and stores the value of 1 in the slot corresponding to *x*.

5.8 Main

The main function drives the whole program. Its overall structure hasn't changed much since our last iteration—except for the addition of the function table, the symbol table, and the store.

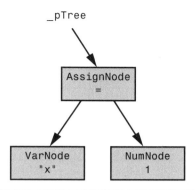

_pTree

AssignNode
=

VarNode
"x"

NumNode
1

Figure 5.4 Parse tree of the expression *x* = 1

```
const int maxBuf = 100;
const int maxSymbols = 40;

void main ()
{
  // Notice all these local objects.
  // A clear sign that there should be
  // a top-level object, say, the Calculator.
  // Back to the drawing board!

  char buf [maxBuf];
  Status status;
  SymbolTable symTab (maxSymbols);
  FunctionTable funTab (symTab, funArr);
  Store store (maxSymbols, symTab);
  do
  {
      std::cout << "> ";   // Prompt
      std::cin.getline (buf, maxBuf);
      Scanner scanner (buf);
      Parser parser (scanner, store, funTab, symTab);
      status = parser.Eval ();
  } while (status != stQuit);

}
```

Notice that for every line of input we create a new scanner and a new parser. We keep, however, the same symbol table, function table, and store. This is important because we want the values assigned to variables to be remembered as long as the program is active. The parser's destructor is called after the evaluation of every line. This call plays the important role of freeing the parse tree.

Script 7   Let's have another look at the structure of the project (see Table 5.1). You can see that most classes have their own file pairs—the header file and the implementation file. A few files contain more than one class. Closely related groups of classes

Files	Contents
`Calc.cpp`	`main`
`Parser.h, Parser.cpp`	`Parser`
`Scan.h, Scan.cpp`	`EToken, Scanner`
`FunTab.h, FunTab.cpp`	`FunctionEntry, funArr, FunctionTable`
`SymTab.h, SymTab.cpp`	`SymbolTable`
`StrBuf.h`	`StringBuffer`
`List.h, List.cpp`	`Link, List`
`HTab.h, HTab.cpp`	`HTable`
`Store.h, Store.cpp`	`Store`
`Tree.h, Tree.cpp`	`Node` and its children

Table 5.1   Project files and their contents

and data structures are sometimes combined together. The `main` function is usually put in a separate file, whose name is either `main.cpp` or is derived from the name of the application, as it is in our case.

We'll come back to this project in Part 2 of the book, Techniques, to see how it can be made into a professional, "industrial-strength" program. Before we do that, though, I'd like to tie up a few loose ends and introduce a few concepts that will be useful in what follows.

5.9   Initialization of Aggregates

Explicit initialization of classes and arrays.

Just as you can explicitly initialize an array of characters using a literal string,

```
char const string [ ] = "Literal String";
```

you can initialize other aggregate data structures—classes and arrays. An object of a given class can be explicitly initialized if and only if all its data members are public and there isn't a constructor for it. These public data members must be explicitly initializable as well (a little recursion here). For instance, if you have

```
class Initializable
{
public:
  // No constructor
  int          _val;
  char const * _string;
  Foo        * _pFoo;
};
```

you can define an instance of that class and initialize all its members at once:

```
Foo foo;
Initializable init = { 1, "Literal String", &foo };
```

Since `Initializable` can be initialized, you can use it as a data member of another initializable class.

```
class BigInitializable
{
public:
  Initializable _init;
  double       _pi;
};

BigInitializable big =
   {{1, "Literal String", &foo }, 3.14 };
```

As you can see, you can nest initializations by putting braces within braces.

You can also explicitly initialize an array of objects. They may be of a simple or aggregate type. They may even be arrays of arrays of objects. Here are a few examples.

```
char const string [] = { 'A', 'B', 'C', '\0' };
```

is equivalent to its shorthand

```
char const string [] = "ABC";
```

Here's another example:

```
Initializable init [2] = {
      { 1, "Literal String", &foo1 },
      { 2, "Another String", &foo2 } };
```

We used this method in the initialization of our array of `FunctionEntry` objects.

If objects in the array have single-argument constructors, you can specify these arguments in the initializer list. For instance,

```
CelestialBody solarSystem [] =
   { 0.33, 4.87, 5.98, 0.64, 1900, 569, 87, 103, 0.66 };
```

where masses of planets are given in units of 10^{24}kg. You couldn't use this kind of initialization if the array `solarSystem` was allocated dynamically (using `new`).

Exercises

1. Add two new built-in functions, `sqr` and `cube`, to the calculator. `Sqr` squares its argument and `cube` cubes it (raises to the third power).

2. Add the recognition of unary plus to the calculator. Make necessary modifications to the scanner and the parser. Add a new node, UPlusNode. The calculator should be able to deal correctly with such expressions as

```
x = +2
2 * + 7
1 / (+1 - 2)
```

3. Add powers to the calculator according to the following productions:

```
Factor is SimpleFactor ^ Factor // a ^ b (a to the power of b)
   or SimpleFactor

SimpleFactor is ( Expression )// Parenthesized expression
   or Number   // Literal floating-point number
   or Identifier ( Expression )// Function call
   or Identifier// Symbolic variable
   or - Factor  // Unary minus
```

4. Add a virtual method Print to all nodes in the parse tree. When Print() is called on the root of the tree, the whole tree should be displayed in some readable form. Use varying indentation (by printing a number of spaces at the beginning of every line) to distinguish between different levels of the tree. For instance,

```
void AddNode::Print (int indent) const
{
  _pLeft->Print (indent + 2);
  Indent (indent);
  std::cout << "+" << std::endl;
  _pRight->Print (indent + 2);
  std::cout << std::endl;
}
```

where Indent prints as many spaces as is the value of its argument.

5. Derivatives of some of the built-in functions are, respectively,

```
sin(x) -> cos(x)
cos(x) -> -sin(x)
exp(x) -> exp(x)
log(x) -> 1/x
sqrt(x)-> 1/(2 * sqrt(x))
```

The derivative of a sum is a sum of derivatives; the derivative of a product is given by the formula

```
(f(x) * g(x))' = f'(x) * g(x) + f(x) * g'(x)
```

where the apostrophe denotes taking a derivative. The derivative of a quotient is given by the formula

```
(f(x) / g(x))' = (f(x) * g'(x) - f'(x) * g(x)) / (g(x) * g(x))
```

and the derivative of the superposition of functions is given by

```
(f(g(x))' = g'(x) * f'(g(x)).
```

Rewrite the calculator to derive the symbolic derivative of the input by transforming the parse tree according to the formulas above. Make sure no memory is leaked in the process (that is, you must delete everything you allocate).

5.10 Procedural Programming

So far, except for some library functions, the functions we've been using and implementing were almost exclusively member functions associated with various classes. This is not how C++ is traditionally taught. Most C++ books start by teaching about so called *free functions* that are not associated with any classes. In fact, classes are usually introduced much later, preferably after covering the C subset of C++.

I chose a different approach because I've found that it's much easier to make a transition from objects to procedures than the other way around. In fact, it seems like procedural programming is the more natural one. We tend to think in terms of recipes—do this first, then this, repeat some other thing a few times, and so on. Structuring a problem in terms of interacting objects is much harder, because it requires a leap of abstraction.

Programmers coming from a procedural background, most notably C programmers, find object-oriented programming not only difficult, but also awkward, unnatural, and unnecessary. Even if they embrace object-oriented programming when implementing abstract data types, they feel reluctant to apply it when solving new problems. That's because they already see the procedural steps leading to the solution with the help of some really basic data structures. When designing a calculator, they would immediately see the process of parsing using recursive function calls, a switch statement to recognize the tokens, and maybe a hash table to store identifiers, plus a few arrays here and there.

I am not saying that procedural programming is inherently bad and object-oriented programming is always good. But I do believe that it's better to start your design and implementation from the object-oriented perspective, and eventually descend into procedures (after all, at some point you have to implement your methods, and they are, ultimately, procedures).

Doing it the other way around—starting with procedural solutions and treating data structures as an afterthought—results in nicely structured code but a shapeless, unmanageable morass of data structures.

C++ is a very eclectic language. It is as good (or bad, depending on your standards) at supporting procedural programming as it is at object-oriented programming (and, with the advent of templates, generic programming as well). Having just learned the basics of object-oriented programming, you don't have to do anything special to learn procedural programming. Let me just review some facts about free functions, compared to methods.

A free function is called without the context of an object. It only has access to its formal parameters, local variables, and global objects. A (nonstatic) member function, on the other hand, is always called in the context of a particular object, and has access to all the object's data members and methods. It also has access to a pointer called "this" that points to the object. Access to "this" is useful when writing code like

```
_next = this;
_prev = this;
```

which we've seen in one of the exercise 9, page 94.

In C++, free functions, just like member functions, can be defined inline (their definition has to be preceded by the keyword `inline`), can be overloaded by the number and type of arguments, and can have default values for trailing arguments. A free function cannot be defined `const`, since it would make no sense. As you already know, you can take an address of a free function and assign it to a pointer to a function. Pointers to members are also allowed in C++, but their syntax and usage is slightly more complicated—we'll talk about them later.

Incidentally, if you want to combine your C++ code with some existing C code, you have to tell the compiler that a function you're about to call is written in C. This is because C has a different calling convention—it puts the arguments on the stack in a different order. You do this by preceding the declaration of a C function with `extern "C"`.

Similarly, if you want your free function to be callable from C, you have to declare it as `extern "C"`:

```
extern "C" void called_from_C (int x, int y);
```

5.11 Operator Overloading

You can pretty much do any kind of arithmetic in C++ using the built-in integral and floating-point types. However, that's not always enough. Old-time engineers swear by FORTRAN, the language that has the built-in type `complex`. In a lot of engineering applications, especially in electronics, you can't really do effective calculations without the use of complex numbers.

The C++ language doesn't have a built-in complex type. Neither does it support matrix or vector calculus. Does that mean that engineers and scientists should stick to FORTRAN? Not at all! Obviously in C++ you can define new classes of objects, so defining a complex number is a piece of cake. What about adding, subtracting, multiplying, and so on? You can define appropriate methods of class `complex`. What about notational convenience? In FORTRAN you can add two complex numbers simply by putting the plus sign between them. No problem! Enter operator overloading.

In an expression like

```
double delta = 5 * 5 − 4 * 3.2 * 0.1;
```

you see several arithmetic operators: the equal sign, the multiplication symbol, and the minus sign. Their meaning is well understood by the compiler. It knows how to multiply or subtract integers or floating-point numbers. But if you want to teach the compiler to multiply or subtract objects of some user-defined class, you have to *overload* the appropriate operators. The syntax for operator overloading, which we'll discuss in a moment, requires some getting used to, but the use of overloaded operators doesn't. You simply put a multiplication sign between two complex variables and the compiler finds your definition of complex multiplication and applies it.

By the way, a `complex` type is conveniently defined for you in the standard C++ library.

An equal sign is an operator too. Like most operators in C++, it can be overloaded. Its meaning, however, goes well beyond arithmetic. In fact, if you don't do anything special about it, you can assign an arbitrary object to another object of the same class by simply putting an equal sign between them. Yes, that's right, you can, for instance, assign symbol tables:

```
SymbolTable symTab1 (100);
SymbolTable symTab2 (200);
symTab1 = symTab2;
```

Will the assignment in this case do the sensible thing? No, the assignment will most definitely be wrong, and it will result in a very nasty problem with memory management. So, even if you're not planning on overloading the standard arithmetic operators, you should still learn something about the assignment operator, including when and why you would want to overload it. And that brings us to a very important topic—passing by value and value semantics.

5.12 Passing by Value

Copy constructor, overloading the assignment operator, default copy constructor and operator =, return by value, passing by value, implicit type conversions.

So far we've been using references or pointers when passing objects from and to methods. For instance, in the following line of code

```
Parser parser (scanner, store, funTab, symTab);
```

all arguments to the `Parser`'s constructor—scanner, store, funTab, and symTab—are passed by reference. We know that, because we've seen the following declaration (and so did the compiler):

```
Parser (Scanner & scanner,
        Store & store,
        FunctionTable & funTab,
        SymbolTable & symTab);
```

When we construct the parser, we don't give it a *copy* of a symbol table. We give it *access* to an existing symbol table. If we gave it a private copy, we wouldn't be able to see the changes the parser made to it. The parser might, for instance, add a new variable to the symbol table. We want our symbol table to remember this variable even after the current parser is destroyed. The same goes for `Store`—it must remember the values assigned to symbolic variables across the invocations of the parser.

But what about the scanner? We don't really care whether the parser makes a copy of it for its private use. Neither do we care what the parser does to the function table. What we *do* care about in this case is performance. Creating a copy of a large object might be quite time consuming.

But suppose we didn't care about performance. Would the following work?

```
Parser (Scanner scanner,
        Store & store,
        FunctionTable funTab,
        SymbolTable & symTab);
```

Notice the absence of ampersands after `Scanner` and `FunctionTable`. What we are telling the compiler is this: When the caller creates a parser and passes it a scanner, make a temporary copy of this scanner and let the parser's constructor operate on that copy.

> This is, after all, the way built-in types are passed around. When you call a method that expects an integer, it's the copy of that integer that's used inside the method. You can modify that copy to your heart's content and you'll never change the original. Only if you explicitly request that the method accept a *reference* to an integer can you change the original.

There are many reasons why such an approach will not work as expected in our `Parser` example unless we make several modifications to our code. First of all, the temporary copy of the scanner (and the function table) will disappear as soon as the execution of the parser's constructor is finished. The parser will store a reference to it in its member variable, but that's useless. After the end of construction the reference will point to a nonexistent scratch copy of a scanner. That's no good.

If we decide to pass a copy of the scanner to the parser, we should also *store* a copy of the scanner inside the parser. Here's how you could do it—just omit the ampersand.

```
class Parser
{
   ...
private:
   Scanner         _scanner;
   Node         * _pTree;
   Status          _status;
   Store        & _store;
   FunctionTable  _funTab;
   SymbolTable  & _symTab;
};
```

But what is really happening inside the constructor? Now that neither the argument, scanner, nor the member variable, _scanner, are references, how is _scanner initialized with scanner? The syntax is misleadingly simple.

```
Parser::Parser (Scanner scanner,
     Store & store,
     FunctionTable funTab,
     SymbolTable & symTab)
: _scanner (scanner),
  _pTree (0),
  _status (stOk),
  _funTab (funTab),
  _store (store),
  _symTab (symTab)
{
}
```

What happens behind the scenes is that Scanner's *copy constructor* is called. A copy constructor is one that takes a const reference to an object of the same class and clones it. In our case, the appropriate constructor would be declared as

```
Scanner::Scanner (Scanner const & scanner);
```

But wait a minute! Scanner does *not* have a constructor of this signature. Why doesn't the compiler protest, like it always does when we try to call an undefined member function? The unexpected answer is that if you don't explicitly declare a copy constructor for a given class, the compiler will create one for you. If this doesn't sound scary, I don't know what does.

Beware of default copy constructors!

The copy constructor generated by the compiler is potentially wrong[7]! After all, what can a dumb compiler know about copying user-defined classes? Sure, it tries to do its best—it

- Does a bitwise copy of all the data members that are of built-in types
- Calls respective copy constructors for user-defined embedded objects

But that's it. Any time the compiler encounters a pointer it simply duplicates it; the compiler *does not* create a copy of the object pointed to by the pointer. That might be okay, or not—only the creator of the class knows for sure.

This kind of operation is called a *shallow copy*, as opposed to a *deep copy*, which follows all the pointers and copies all the objects they point to. A shallow copy is fine when the pointed-to data structures can be easily shared between multiple instances of the object.

But consider, as an example, what happens when we make a shallow copy of the top node of a parse tree. If the top node has children, a shallow copy will not clone the child nodes. We will end up with two top nodes, both pointing to the same child nodes. That's not a problem until the destructor of one of the top nodes is called. It promptly deletes its children. And what is the second top node pointing to now? A piece of garbage! The moment it tries to access the children, it will stomp over reclaimed memory with disastrous results. But even if it does nothing, eventually its own destructor is called. And that destructor will attempt to delete the same children that have already been deleted by the first top node. The result? Memory corruption!

But wait, there's more! C++ not only sneaks in a default copy constructor on you. It also provides you with a convenient default assignment operator.

Beware of default assignments!

The following code is perfectly legal:

```
SymbolTable symTab1 (100);
SymbolTable symTab2 (200);
// ...
symTab1 = symTab2;
```

Not only does it perform a shallow copy of symTab2 into symTab1, but it also clobbers whatever already was there in symTab1. All memory that was allocated in symTab1 is lost, never to be reclaimed. Instead, the memory allocated in symTab2 will be deleted twice. Now that's a bargain!

---

7. In particular, it is almost always wrong for those classes that have a nontrivial constructor (e.g., allocating some objects) and a nontrivial destructor (e.g., freeing the objects that have been allocated in the constructor).

Why does C++ quietly perform these outrageous and uncalled-for services? If you've followed this book closely, you know the answer—compatibility with C! In C you can't define a copy constructor because there aren't any constructors. So every time you want to copy something more complex than an `int`, you have to write a special function or a macro. So, in the traditional spirit of letting programmers shoot themselves in the foot, C provides this additional facility of quietly copying all the user-defined `struct`s. In C this wasn't such a big deal—a C `struct` is just raw data. There isn't data hiding, methods, or inheritance. Besides, there aren't any references in C, so you are much less likely to inadvertently copy a `struct` just because you forgot to use an ampersand. But in C++ it's a completely different story. Beware—many a bug in C++ is a result of a missing ampersand.

But wait, there's even more! C++ not only offers a free copy constructor and a free assignment, it will also quietly use these two to return objects from functions. Here's a fragment of code from our old implementation of the stack-based calculator, except for one small modification. Can you spot it?

```
class Calculator
{
public:
   int Execute (Input & input);
   IStack const GetStack () const {return _stack;}
private:
   int Calculate (int n1, int n2, int token) const;

   IStack _stack;
};
```

What happened here was that I omitted the ampersand in the return type of `Calculator::GetStack`, and now `IStack` is returned by value. Let's have a very close look at what happens during such a transfer. Also, let's assume for a moment that the compiler doesn't do any clever optimizations here. In particular, let's define `GetStack` out of line, so a regular function call has to be executed.

```
IStack const Calculator::GetStack () const
{
   return _stack;
}
//...
IStack const stk = calc.GetStack ();  // <- By value!
```

The process of *returning an object by value* consists of two steps: copy construction and assignment.

- First of all, before executing the call to GetStack, the compiler preallocates some scratch space on the stack (I'm talking here about the internal call stack, where function arguments and local variables live at runtime). This scratch space is then passed to the function being called. To copy the value of _stack into the scratch space, GetStack calls Istack's copy constructor.
- After returning from GetStack, the assignment operator is called to copy the value from the scratch space to the local variable stk.[8]

It might look pretty complicated at first, but if you think about it, this is really the only sensible foolproof way of returning an object by value, especially if the programmer took care of both defining a copy constructor and overloading the assignment operator for the class in question.

For some classes the compiler will not be able to generate a default assignment. These are the classes that contain data members that cannot be assigned outside of the constructor's preamble. This is true for any const members (including const pointers) and for references. For instance, if you tried to assign one parser to another, like this:

```
parser1 = parser;
```

the compiler would give you the error, "No assignment operator defined for class Parser." That's because it can't reinitialize all these references to Scanner, Store, FunctionTable, and SymbolTable that are inside parser1. Once a reference refers to something, you can't make it refer to something else. Notice, however, that these restrictions don't apply to the default copy constructor. The code:

```
Parser parser1 (parser);
```

will compile. The references in parser1 will be correctly initialized to refer to the same objects as the ones in parser. However, since value semantics require both—the copy constructor and the assignment—class Parser in its present form cannot be passed by value.

By the way, a small modification of the above code

```
Parser parser1 = parser;
```

will also compile, because the assignment here is understood as a shorthand for a constructor call.

---

8. A good compiler might be able to optimize this process, especially if the return object is constructed in place within the return statement. This is called "return value optimization."

5.13 Value Semantics

Let's try to make some sense of this mess. We've just learned about several features of C++ that, taken separately, may turn our code against us. It's time to find out what they can do for us when used in a proper context.

The question whether a given object should be passed by reference or by value should be decided on the level of its own class. For some objects it makes little sense to be passed by value, for others it makes a lot of sense. By designing the class properly, we can accommodate either case.

First of all, we can easily protect objects of a given class from being passed by value by declaring a private copy constructor and a private assignment operator. No implementation of these methods is necessary. They are there just to stop the compiler from doing the unwanted magic behind our backs.

Suppose we want to prevent IStack objects from being passed by value. All we have to do is add two lines to its class definition: the first one declares a copy constructor, and the second overloads the assignment operator =.

```
class IStack
{
public:
  // ...
private:
  IStack (IStack const & src);
  IStack & operator = (IStack const & src);
  // ...
};
```

Now try compiling any of the code that attempted to pass an IStack to a function, return an IStack from a function, or assign one IStack to another. It simply won't compile! If you make the mistake of omitting an ampersand following the IStack class name in any such context, the compiler will immediately catch it for you.

Should you, therefore, be adding copy constructors and assignment overloads to every class you create? Frankly, I don't think it's practical. There are definitely some classes that are being passed around a lot—these should have this type of protection in their declarations. With others, use your best judgment.

There are, however, some classes of objects for which passing by value makes a lot of sense. Such classes are said to have *value semantics*. Usually, but not always, objects of such classes have a relatively small footprint. Size is important if you care about performance.

Also, quite often the only alternative to passing some objects by value is to keep allocating new copies from the free store using new—a much more expensive choice. So you shouldn't dismiss value semantics out-of-hand even for larger objects. Such would be the case, for instance, with some algebraic classes like vectors or matrixes.

In many cases, giving a class value semantics does not require any work. As we've seen earlier, the compiler will gladly provide a default copy constructor and the default assignment operator. If the default shallow copy does an adequate job of duplicating all the relevant data stored in the object, you shouldn't look any further.

> A useful rule of thumb is that you should provide a copy constructor and overload the assignment operator if your class has a nontrivial destructor.

In cases when a shallow copy is not enough, you should provide the appropriate copy constructor and overload the assignment operator. Let's consider a simple example: the object of class `StringVal` represents a string that can be safely passed by value.

Value
```cpp
class StringVal
{
    friend StringVal operator+ (StringVal const &v1,
                                StringVal const &v2);
public:
    StringVal (char const * cstr)
      : _buf (0)
    {
        std::cout << "Constructor taking char * "
                  << cstr << std::endl;
        Init (cstr);
    }
    StringVal (StringVal const & str)
      : _buf (0)
    {
        std::cout << "Copy constructor "
                  << str.c_str () << std::endl;
        Init (str.c_str ());
    }
    ~StringVal ()
    {
        std::cout << "Destructor of " << _buf << std::endl;
        delete _buf;
    }
    StringVal & operator= (StringVal const & str);
    char const * c_str ( ) const { return _buf; }
private:
    StringVal () : _buf (0) {}
    void Init (char const * cstr)
    {
        _buf = new char [std::strlen (cstr) + 1];
        std::strcpy (_buf, cstr);
    }
private:
    char * _buf;
};
```

A lot of things are happening here. First of all, we have a bunch of constructors. Let's use this opportunity to learn more about various types of constructors.

- The *default constructor* with no arguments. You must have this if you want to
  dynamically allocate arrays of objects of this class. A default constructor could
  also be a constructor with the defaults provided for all its arguments. In the
  case of `StringVal`, the default constructor is private, so only static arrays with
  initializer lists can be defined.

- The constructor with a single argument. Unless declared as `explicit`, such a
  constructor provides *implicit conversion* from the type of its argument to the
  type represented by the class. In this case, we are giving the compiler the go-
  ahead to convert any `char*` to a `StringVal` if this conversion is required to
  make sense of our code. We'll see examples of such conversions in a moment.
  A single-argument constructor can also be used in a syntactical variation of an
  object definition that uses an equal sign to pass an argument to the constructor, as in:

  Value val = "Foo";

- The *copy constructor*. This takes a `const` reference to an object of the same class
  and clones it.

Next, we have the overloading of the assignment operator. By convention, the
assignment operator takes a `const` reference to an object and copies it into an
existing object of the same class. Unlike the copy constructor, the assignment operator must be able to deal with an already initialized object as its target. Special
precautions, therefore, are required. We usually have to deallocate whatever resources the target object stores and allocate new resources to hold the copy of the
source.

```
StringVal & StringVal::operator= (StringVal const & str)
{
  std::cout << "Operator = " << str.c_str () << std::endl;
  if (this != &str)
  {
    if (std::strlen (_buf) < std::strlen (str.c_str ()))
    {
      delete _buf;
      Init (str.c_str ());
    }
    else
      std::strcpy (_buf, str.c_str ());
  }
  return *this;
}
```

Special code is needed to take care of the following perfectly legitimate use of assignment:

```
Value val ("Foo");
val = val;
```

Here, if it weren't for our testing for "source equal to target" in the definition of the assignment operator, we could have deallocated the source before making the copy.

There's one more thing you should know: the assignment operator is *not* inherited—you have to provide a separate overload for each derived class. If you think about it, this makes perfect sense. Using base class operator= to assign objects of derived classes could lead to object slicing—copying only the part of the member data that is present in the base class. If a derived class adds any new data members, they wouldn't be copied.

Finally, to make things really interesting, I've added an overload of the *plus operator* for objects of type StringVal.

```
StringVal operator + (StringVal const &v1,
                      StringVal const &v2)
{
  std::cout << " operator + (" << v1.c_str () << ", "
    << v2.c_str ( ) << ")\n";

  StringVal result; // Empty
  int len = std::strlen (v1._buf) + std::strlen (v2._buf);
  char * buf = new char [len + 1];
  std::strcpy (buf, v1.c_str ());
  std::strcat (buf, v2.c_str ());
  result._buf = buf;
  std::cout << " Returning by value\n";
  return result;
}
```

Our operator+ takes two arguments of the type const reference to StringVal, and returns another StringVal—their "sum"—by value.

Now every time the compiler sees an expression like str1 + str2, it will call our method StringVal::operator+. In fact, the following two statements are equivalent:

```
str3 = str1 + str2;
str3.operator= (operator+ (str1, str2));
```

For us humans, the first one is usually much easier to grasp.

Notice that I haven't declared operator+ to be a method of StringVal. Instead, it is a *free function*. You can execute it outside of the context of any particular object. There is a good reason for doing that and I am about to explain it. But first, let me show you the alternative approach.

```
StringVal StringVal::operator+ (StringVal const &v)
{
  std::cout << " operator + (" << c_str () << ", "
            << v.c_str () << ")\n";
  StringVal result; // Empty
  int len = std::strlen (_buf) + std::strlen (v._buf);
  char * buf = new char [len + 1];
  std::strcpy (buf, c_str ());
  std::strcat (buf, v.c_str ());
  result._buf = buf;
  std::cout << " Returning by value\n";
  return result;
}
```

Here, operator+ is defined as a member function of StringVal, so it requires
only one argument. The first addend is implicitly the this object. The syntax for
using this version of operator+ is identical to the free function one, and the equivalence works as follows:

```
str3 = str1 + str2;
str3.operator= (str1.operator+ (str2));
```

There is just one subtle difference between these two definitions—the way the
two addends are treated in the "method" implementation is not symmetric.
Normally that wouldn't be a problem, except when you try to add a char* to a
StringVal object. Consider this:

```
StringVal str ("Foo");
StringVal vSum = str + "bar";
```

In general, you'd need to define a separate overload of operator+ to deal with
such mixed additions. For instance, if using the free function approach

```
StringVal operator+ (StringVal const & str1,
                     char const * str2);
```

or using the "method" approach

```
StringVal StringVal::operator+ (char const * str);
```

Do you see the problem, though? You can deal with adding a char* to a StringVal
using either method. But if you want to do the opposite, add a StringVal to a
char*, only the free function approach will work:

```
StringVal operator+ (char const * str1,
                     StringVal const & str2);
StringVal str ("bar");
StringVal strSum = "Foo" + str;
```

By the way, notice how smart the compiler is when parsing arithmetic expressions. It looks at the types of operands and, based on that, finds the correct overloading of the operator. Actually, it is even smarter than that!

I told you that you needed a special overloading of `operator+` to deal with mixed additions. That's not entirely true. In fact, both adding a `char*` to a `StringVal` and adding a `StringVal` to a `char*` would work without any additional overloads of `operator+`. How so? Because there is an implicit conversion from a `char*` to a `StringVal` that the compiler may, and will, use in its attempts to parse a mixed arithmetic expression. This is only a slight generalization of what happens when you add an `int` to a `double` (the `int` will be converted to a `double`). For instance, in

```
StringVal str1 ("Foo");
char * str2 = "bar"
StringVal result = str1 + str2;
```

the compiler is free to convert `str2` to a `StringVal` and use the overloaded `operator+` that takes two (const references to) `StringVals`. In case you're wondering about the *implicit conversion* from `char*` to `StringVal`, look again at the set of `StringVal` constructors. Remember:

> **A constructor that takes a single argument defines an implicit conversion from the type of its argument to its own type.**

But converting a `char*` into a `StringVal` is one thing. Here, the compiler has to do even more. It has to convert a `char*` into a *constant reference to* `StringVal`. The compiler does this by creating a temporary `StringVal`, initializing it with a `char*`, and passing a `const` reference to it to the called function. The tricky part is that the temporary `StringVal` has to be kept alive for the duration of the call. How the compiler does this is another story. Suffice it to say that *it works*.

What does *not* work is if you tried to do the same with a non-`const` reference. A function that takes a non-`const` reference expects to be able to have a side effect of changing the value of that argument. So using a temporary as a go-between is out of the question. In fact, the compiler will refuse to do implicit conversions to non-`const` references even for built-in primitive types. Consider the following example:

```
void increment (double & x) { x += 1.0; }
int n = 5;
increment (n); // <- Error!
```

There is no way the compiler could figure out that you were expecting `n` to change its value from 5 to 6. And it can't pass the address of an `int` where the address of a `double` is expected, because the two have a completely different memory layout (and possibly size). Therefore, the compiler will tell you something like, "*Error: There's no conversion from int to (non-const) reference to double.*"

In contrast, the following code compiles just fine,

```
void dontIncrement (double const & x);
int n = 5;
dontIncrement (n); // <- OK!
```

because the compiler is free to generate a temporary `double`, initialize it with the value of n, and pass a const reference to it.

One last thing. Why did I declare `operator=` to return a reference to `StringVal` and `operator+` to return `StringVal` by value? Let's start with `operator=`. It has to return something (by reference or by value) only if you like this style of programming

```
StringVal s1 ("Foo"), s2 ("Bar"), s3 ("Baz");
s1 = s2 = s3;
```

or

```
if (s1 = s2) // Notice, it's not ==
   ...
```

The chaining of assignments works, because it is interpreted as

```
s1.operator= (s2.operator= (s3));
```

and the assignment as condition works because it is equivalent to

```
if (s1.operator= (s2))
   ...
```

and the return value from `operator=` is interpreted as `true` if it's different from zero.

On the other hand, if you don't care for this style of programming, you may as well declare `operator=` to return `void`.

```
void StringVal::operator= (StringVal const & str)
```

I wouldn't recommend this when overloading `operator+`, because we are usually interested in the result of addition. Instead, let me try to explain why returning the result of addition *by value* is preferable to returning it by reference. It's simple—just ask yourself this question, "Reference to what?" It can't be the reference to any of the addends, because they are supposed to keep their original values. So you *have* to create a new object to store the result of addition. If you create it on the stack, as a local variable, it will quickly disappear after you return from `operator+`. You'll end up with a reference to some stack junk. If you create it using new, it won't disappear from under your reference, but then you'll never be able to delete it. You'll end up with a memory leak.

Think of operator+ (or any other binary operator, for that matter) as a two-argument constructor. It constructs a new entity, the sum of the two addends, and it has to put this entity somewhere. There is very little choice as to where to store the new value, especially when you're inside a complicated arithmetic expression. Return it by value and let the compiler worry about the rest.

To summarize, primitive built-in types are usually passed around by value. The same kind of value semantics for a user-defined type is accomplished by using a copy constructor and an overloaded operator=. *Unless specifically overridden, the compiler will create a default copy constructor and default assignment for any user-defined type.*

Part 2

Techniques

A programmer spends, on average, much more time improving existing code than writing new code. That's why program modification is such an important skill. Program modification involves maintenance (fixing bugs), adding new features, rewriting, and restructuring. If you keep adding new features, you have to schedule time for rewrites, otherwise your program will gradually become unmaintainable. Rewrites are the programmers' only defense against entropy.

In this part of the book I guide the reader through a number of major and minor rewrites of the symbolic calculator—the program that was created in the first part of the book. I use these rewrites as an opportunity to describe some important programming techniques and to introduce more advanced features of C++.

Chapter 6
The Cleanup

As much as we would like a program to follow a design, there is always an element of ad-libbing when filling in the details. We create auxiliary classes and functions, as well as add methods and data members to existing classes. This process is reminiscent of the growth of a yeast culture. As each cell keeps growing, it starts to bloat and bud. Eventually new buds separate and start a life of their own.

In software, the growing and (especially) the bloating happens quite naturally. It's the budding and the separation that requires conscious effort on the part of the programmer. Code reviews help this process greatly.

In what follows we'll see examples of overgrown files, methods, and classes. Our response will be to create new files, new methods, and, especially, new classes. We'll always be on the lookout for potential code reuse. When reviewing code, we will also figure out which parts require a more thorough explanation and add appropriate comments.

Project
CalcTech

Sources for this section of the book are in the Code Co-op project `CalcTech`. Select the `CalcTech` link from the CD-ROM's splash screen to create this project. Margin notes tell which script to unpack next.

6.1 Decoupling the Output

Script 1   Let's look again at the main loop of our calculator.

```
std::cout << "> "; // Prompt
std::cin.getline (buf, maxBuf);
Scanner scanner (buf);
Parser parser (scanner, store, funTab, symTab);
status = parser.Eval ();
```

The first two lines take care of user input. The next three lines do the parsing and evaluation. Aren't we missing something? Shouldn't the calculator display the result? Well, it does—inside Eval. Sending the result of the calculation to the output is a side effect of evaluation. In general,

> **Side effects are bad!**

In order to understand what the calculator is doing, somebody will have to look inside the implementation of Eval.

It does sound bad, but isn't it true in general that you have to look inside the implementation of Eval in order to know what it's doing? How would you otherwise know that it first parses and then evaluates the user input, which was passed to the parser in the form of a scanner?

Well, that's a good point! Indeed, why don't we rewrite the last line of the main loop in this more transparent way?

```
std::cout << "> ";   // Prompt
std::cin.getline (buf, maxBuf);
Scanner scanner (buf);
Parser  parser (scanner, store, funTab, symTab);
status = parser.Parse ();
double result = parser.Calculate ();
std::cout << result << std::endl;
```

Here, every statement does just one well-defined thing. I can read this code without having to know any of the implementation details of any of the objects. This is how I read it:

1. Prompt the user.
2. Get a line of input.
3. Create a scanner to encapsulate the line of input.
4. Create a parser to process this input.
5. Let the parser parse it.
6. Let the parser calculate the result.
7. Display the result.

I find this solution esthetically more pleasing, but esthetics alone aren't usually enough to convince somebody to rewrite their code. It's a good thing to learn to

translate esthetics into practical arguments. So instead I will argue that this version
is *better* than the original because:

- It separates three distinct and well-defined actions: parsing, calculation, and
  display. This decoupling will translate into easier maintenance.

- Input and output are now performed at the same level, rather than input being done at the top-level and output interspersed with the lower-level code.

- Input and output are part of the user interface, which usually evolves independently of the rest of the program. That's why it's always a good idea to have
  it concentrated in one place. I'm already anticipating the possible switch from
  command-line interface to a Windows interface.

The changes to Parser to support this new split are pretty obvious. We have to
get rid of the old Parse method and paste its code directly to the only place from
which it was called (all it did was _pTree = Expr()). Then we rename Eval to Parse
and move the calculation to the new method Calculate. We also get rid of
Execute.

As a (good) side effect, we can also fix a loophole in the error checking: the
input line should not contain any characters following the expression. Before, a
line like 1 + 1 = 1 would have been accepted without a complaint. Now the
IsDone method will return false and an error will be flagged.

```cpp
Status Parser::Parse ()
{
  // Everything is an expression
  _pTree = Expr ();
  if (!_scanner.IsDone ())
    _status = stError;
  return _status;
}

double Parser::Calculate () const
{
  assert (_status == stOk);
  assert (_pTree != 0);
  return _pTree->Calc ();
}

bool Scanner::IsDone () const
{
  return _buf [_iLook] == '\0';
}
```

My students convinced me that Calculate should not be called if the parsing
resulted in an error. As you can see, that certainly simplifies the code of Parse and
Calculate. Now we have to check for errors in main, but that's okay. We have the
status codes available there, so why not do something useful with them?

And, as long as we're at it, we can also check the scanner for an empty line
and not bother creating a parser in such a case. Incidentally, that will allow us to

use an empty line as a sign from the user to quit the calculator. Things are very nicely falling into place.

```cpp
std::cout << "\nEnter empty line to quit\n";
// Process a line of input at a time
do
{
  std::cout << "> ";  // Prompt
  std::cin.getline (buf, maxBuf); // Read a line
  Scanner scanner (buf); // Create a scanner
  if (!scanner.IsEmpty ())
  {
    // Create a parser
    Parser  parser (scanner, store, funTab, symTab);
    status = parser.Parse ();
    if (status == stOk)
    {
      double result = parser.Calculate ();
      std::cout << result << std::endl;
    }
    else
    {
      std::cout << "Syntax error.\n";
    }
  }
  else
  {
    break;
  }
} while (status != stQuit);
```

Look what we've just done! We have reorganized the top level of our program with very little effort. In traditional programming this is a big no-no. Changing the top level is synonymous with rewriting the whole program. We must have done something right if we were able to pull off such a trick. Of course, this is a small program and, besides that, *I* wrote it, so it was easy for *me* to change it. Let me assure you, I have tried these methods in a project a hundred times bigger and it worked. Even better—I would let a newcomer go right ahead and make a top-level change in the project and propagate it all the way to the lowest level. And frankly, if I weren't able to do that, I would have been stuck forever with some early design mistakes—just like the one in the calculator that we have just fixed.

Script 2   There are several other output operations throughout the program. They are mostly dealing with error reporting. Since we don't have yet a coherent plan for error reporting and error propagation, we'll just do one cosmetic change. Instead of directing error messages to the standard output cout, we'll direct them to the standard error cerr like this:

```cpp
std::cerr << "Error: division by zero\n";
```

The only practical difference is that if you redirect standard output of your program to a file, the error messages will still go to your console. Not that we care much, but when we port this program to Windows, we would like to be able to quickly search the source for `cerr` and, for instance, redirect error output to message boxes.

6.2 Fighting Defensive Programming

"Defensive programming" sounds good, doesn't it? A program written by a defensive programmer should be safer and more robust, right?

Wrong! Defensive programming is a dangerous form of engineering malpractice (in a show of self-abasement, I'll shortly expose examples of such practices in my own code). Defensive programming promotes writing code that is supposed to work even in the face of programmers' errors, a.k.a., bugs. In practice, it gives the bugs the opportunity to cover their tracks. Anybody who spent a sleepless night chasing a bug that could have been caught early on if it weren't for defensive programming will understand my indignation. In most cases, defensive programming is a result of not understanding the exact contract between various parts of the program. A confused or lazy programmer, instead of trying to understand the logic of the program, might write something that should work *no matter what.* That code will obscure the program's logic even more, making further development even sloppier. The programmer will eventually lose control of the code.

One source of confusion which is often covered up by defensive programming is the discrepancy between the length of a string and the size of the array into which it will fit. The array must have room for the terminating null that is not counted in the length of the string. Does `MAX_PATH` defined in a system header take into account the terminating null? Should one use `MAX_PATH` or `MAX_PATH + 1` when allocating a buffer?

Script 3 Now look at the confusion in our calculator. `Scanner::GetSymbolName` assumes that its argument `len` is the maximum size of a string that can fit in the buffer. So the buffer size should be one larger than `len`. Hence the assertions:

```
assert (len >= maxSymLen);
assert (_lenSymbol <= maxSymLen);
```

But when we are calling `GetSymbolName` from the parser, we are allocating a buffer of `maxSymLen` characters and pass `maxSymLen` as its length. Wait a moment, that looks like a bug, doesn't it? We have just said that `GetSymbolName` expects the buffer to be one character longer than `len`.

So how did it work? As it turns out, in the scanner we have defensively truncated the length of a symbolic name to *one fewer* than `maxSymLen`.

```
if (_lenSymbol >= maxSymLen)
  _lenSymbol = maxSymLen - 1;
```

So now it turns out that maxSymLen includes the terminating null, and Scanner::GetSymbolName expects len to be the size of the buffer, not the string. However, when it returns, GetSymbolName sets len to the actual size of the string—without the null. Hey, it works! Yes, but is such code maintainable? I don't think so.

Let's just try to rationalize our assumptions. First of all, maxSymLen should be the maximum length of a symbolic name *without* the terminating null. Null termination is an implementation detail—we should be able to switch to counted strings without having to change the value of maxSymLen. The method Scanner::Accept should therefore truncate symbolic names like this:

```
if (_lenSymbol > maxSymLen)
  _lenSymbol = maxSymLen;
```

And this is how GetSymbolName should be called

```
char strSymbol [maxSymLen + 1];
int lenSym = _scanner.GetSymbolName (strSymbol,
                                     maxSymLen + 1);
```

and this is how it should be implemented

```
int Scanner::GetSymbolName (char * strOut, int lenBuf)
{
  assert (lenBuf > maxSymLen);
  assert (_lenSymbol < lenBuf);
  std::strncpy (strOut, &_buf[_iSymbol], _lenSymbol);
  strOut [_lenSymbol] = '\0';
  return _lenSymbol;
}
```

The in-argument, lenBuf, is the length of the buffer. The return value is the length of the string copied into the buffer. That's *much* less confusing.

Another excuse for all kinds of lame coding practices is any situation that is *not really supposed to happen*. Our calculator has some built-in limitations. For instance, the size of Store is limited to maxSymbols, which is set to 40. That's plenty, and we don't expect to hit this limitation under normal circumstances. Even if we did, we have a line of defense in Store:

```
void Store::SetValue (int id, double val)
{
  if (id < _size)
  {
    _cell [id] = val;
    _status [id] = stInit;
  }
}
```

That's very fortunate, because it lets us get away with some sloppy error checking in the parser (we'll look at it shortly).

Script 4   Do you see what happens when you lower your defenses against defensive programming? You get sloppy. Sooner or later your sloppiness will catch up with you. So let's turn this method into an example of *offensive programming*—we are so sure of the correctness of our (or others') code that we're not afraid to assert it.

```
void Store::SetValue (int id, double val)
{
  assert (id < _size);
  _cell [id] = val;
  _status [id] = stInit;
}
```

We'll fix the caller's code shortly.

6.3   A Case of Paranoid Programming

Script 5   The initialization of the function table is an example of defensive programming gone berserk. First we define maxIdFun to be the size of the array of function entries. Then we define the array of size maxIdFun, but we initialize it with a smaller number of entries. We also add a sentinel with a null pointer and an empty string. Then, in the constructor of FunctionTable, we set up the loop to go from zero to maxIdFun − 1, but we break from it when we encounter the sentinel. All this mess is there to prevent the mismatch between the size of the function array and the number of entries in the function table. Instead, one simple assertion would suffice:

```
assert (maxIdFun ==
        sizeof FunctionArray/sizeof FunctionArray [0]);
```

The sizeof operator returns the size (in bytes) of its argument. When applied to a static array, it returns the size of the whole array. When applied to a pointer, even if the pointer points to an array, it returns the size of the pointer—4 bytes on a 32-bit computer. (The argument to sizeof may also be a type name; it will return the size of an object of that type.)

Notice that I had to correct an awkward naming conflict for this assertion to work. I had named the argument to FunctionTable constructor the same name as the global array—they were both called funArr. Guess what? When I first wrote the assertion, it didn't work as planned: sizeof funArr kept returning 4. I checked the language reference several times, tried using brackets—nothing worked. I was ready to blame the compiler when suddenly I realized that my sizeof was applied to the *argument passed to the constructor* and not to the global array as I had thought. The local name funArr obscured the global name funArr and, consequently, I was sizing a pointer rather than a static array.

I learned (or rather relearned for the *n*th time) two lessons: don't use the same name for different variables and, if operator `sizeof` returns 4 when applied to an array, don't blame the compiler. The irony of this situation was that I usually, but not this time, follow the convention of starting a global name with a capital letter (and also make it less abbreviated).

After changing the name of the global array to `FunctionArray`, I set `maxIdFun` correctly to 14 and let the compiler size the array by counting the initializers (I left the brackets empty).

```
const int maxIdFun = 14;
FunctionEntry FunctionArray [] =
{
  log, "log",
  ...
  atan, "atan"
};
```

Now I could finally add the assertion that would catch the mismatch between the size of `FunctionArray` and the array `FunctionTable::_pFun` was pointing to.

```
FunctionTable::FunctionTable (SymbolTable & symTab,
                              FunctionEntry * funArr)
  : _size(0)
{
  assert(maxIdFun ==
         sizeof FunctionArray / sizeof FunctionArray [0]);
  ...
}
```

When I showed this solution to my students, they immediately noticed the problem: What if the constructor of `FunctionTable` is called with a pointer to an array *different* than `FunctionArray`? There's no way to prevent it. Obviously the design was evolving away from the generality of `FunctionTable` as an object that can be initialized by any array of function entries, and towards making `FunctionArray` a very close partner of `FunctionTable`. In fact, that's what I was planning to do in the next code review. Here's the code I wrote for that purpose:

```
static FunctionEntry FunctionArray [] = { ... };
FunctionTable::FunctionTable (SymbolTable & symTab)
  : _size(0)
{
  assert (maxIdFun ==
          sizeof FunctionArray/sizeof FunctionArray [0]);
  ...
}
```

I made `FunctionArray` *static,* which means that it was invisible outside of the file `funtab.cpp` where it was defined. In this sense *static* and *extern* are on the opposite ends of the spectrum of visibility. I followed the rule:

> **Data hiding is almost always a good idea.**

By the way, the use of `static` for data hiding is being discouraged in modern C++. Its usage has been supplanted by namespaces (of which we'll talk in Chapter 7).

Is it possible to make `FunctionArray` and `FunctionTable` even more intimately related? How about making `FunctionArray` a member of the class `FunctionTable`?

Now remember, the whole idea of `FunctionArray` was to be able to *statically* initialize it—compile-time instead of run-time. It turns out that there is a construct in C++ called (notice the overloading of this keyword) a *static* member.

> A static member can be viewed as a member of the class object rather than a member of the particular instance object. In some object-oriented languages (e.g., Smalltalk), there is a clear distinction between the instance object and the class object. There can be many instances of objects of the same class, but they all share the same class object. A class object may have its own data members and methods. The values of class object data members are shared between all instances. One can access class data or call class methods without having access to any instance object. Class methods can only operate on class data, not on the data of a particular instance.
>
> Although in C++ there is no notion of class object, static data members and static methods effectively provide the equivalent functionality. There is only one instance of each static data member per class, no matter how many objects of a given class are created. (In fact, even if no instances are created, static data members are still accessible.) A static method is essentially a regular function (in that it doesn't have the `this` pointer), with the visibility restricted by its membership in the class.

This is the syntax for declaring a private static data member:

```
class FunctionTable
{
  ...
private:
  static FunctionEntry _functionArray [];
  ...
};
```

And this is how it's initialized in the implementation file:

```
FunctionEntry FunctionTable::_functionArray [] =
{
  log, "log",
  ...
};
```

Notice that even though _functionArray is private, its initialization is done within the global scope.

Unfortunately, when _functionArray is made a static member with an undefined size (look at the empty brackets in the declaration), the sizeof operator does not return the initialized size of the array as we would like it to. The compiler looks only at the declaration in FunctionTable and it doesn't find the information about the size there. When you think about it, it actually makes sense.

There was another interesting suggestion. Why not use sizeof FunctionArray/size of FunctionArray [0] as the size of the array _pFun inside the declaration of FunctionTable?

```
Pfun _pFun [sizeof FunctionArray / sizeof FunctionArray[0]];
```

In principle it's possible, but in practice we would have to initialize FunctionArray before the declaration of FunctionTable so the compiler could calculate sizeof. This would mean putting the initialization in the header file and, since the header had to be included in several implementation files, we would get a linker error (multiple definitions).

The proposed solution was then modified to make FunctionTable an array of constants, so the linker wouldn't complain that it is initialized in multiple files. After all, constructs like this

```
const int maxLen = 10;
```

are perfectly acceptable in header files, as is

```
const FunctionEntry FunctionArray [] =
{
  log, "log",
    ...
};
```

This solution is good because it makes the table of function pointers automatically adjust its size when the function array grows. That's better than hitting the assertion and having to adjust the size by hand. However, FunctionArray, which is only needed internally to initialize the function table, suddenly becomes visible to the whole world. This is exactly the opposite of the other proposal, which made the array a private static member of the function table. It violates the principle of data hiding.

Script 6   So what are we to do? Here's my solution: Let's hide the function array in the implementation file funtab.cpp. But instead of trying at all costs to size _pFun stati-

cally, let's use dynamic allocation. At the point of allocation, the static size of
FunctionTable is well-known to the compiler.

```
FunctionTable::FunctionTable (SymbolTable& symTab)
  : _size (sizeof FunctionArray / sizeof FunctionArray [0])
{
  _pFun = new PtrFun [_size];
  for (int i = 0; i < _size; ++i)
  {
    int len = std::strlen (FunctionArray[i].strFun);
    _pFun [i] = FunctionArray [i].pFun;
    std::cerr << FunctionArray[i].strFun << std::endl;
    int j = symTab.ForceAdd (FunctionArray[i].strFun, len);
    assert (i == j);
  }
}
```

Let's not forget to deallocate the array in the destructor:

```
FunctionTable::~FunctionTable ()
{
  delete []_pFun;
}
```

We have already seen examples of classes forming patterns (stack and its
sequencer). Here we see an example of a static array teaming up with a class. In
practice, such patterns will share the same header and implementation file.

What have I sacrificed by choosing this solution? I have sacrificed static allocation of an array. The drawbacks of dynamic allocation are twofold: having to remember to deallocate the object—a maintainability drawback—and an
infinitesimal increase in the cost of access, which I mention here only for the sake
of completeness, because it is *really* negligible. In return, I can keep the function
array and its initializer list hidden, which is an important maintainability gain.

The code of FunctionTable is not immediately reusable, but I could easily
make it so by changing the constructor to accept an array of function entries and
the count of entries. Since I don't see a lot of potential for reuse, I won't do it.
This way I will reduce the number of objects visible at the highest abstraction
level—at the level of main.

6.4 Fringes

Dealing with boundary cases and error paths is the area where beginning
programmers make the most mistakes. Not checking for array bounds, not testing
error returns, ignoring null pointers, and so on are the types of errors that usually
don't manifest themselves during superficial testing. The program works, except
for weird cases. Such an approach is not acceptable when writing professional

software. Weird cases are as important as the main execution path—in fact, they often contribute to the bulk of code.

Script 7   I've found an example of sloppy error checking in the parser. It so happens that the method `SymbolTable::ForceAdd` may fail if there is no more room for symbolic variables. Yet we are not testing for a failure in the parser. The code works (sort of) due to the defensive programming in the symbol table. Now that we have just replaced the defensive code with the offensive one, we must fix this fragment too:

```
// Factor := Ident
if (id == idNotFound)
{
  // Add new identifier to the symbol table
  id = _symTab.ForceAdd (strSymbol, lenSym);
  if (id == idNotFound)
  {
    std::cerr << "Error: Too many variables\n";
    _status = stError;
    pNode = 0;
  }
}
if (id != idNotFound)
  pNode = new VarNode (id, _store);
```

The rule of thumb is to check for the error as soon as possible. In this case we shouldn't have waited until `VarNode` was created and then silently break the contract of that class (`VarNode::Calc` was not doing the correct thing!).

6.5 Improving Communication between Classes

When passing a string to a function, it is sometimes advantageous to pass along its length—especially if it's already available for some other reason. On the other hand, one might calculate the length of the string inside the function. The trade-off is speed versus maintainability. Why call `strlen` if the length is already known? Then again, by passing the length we introduce one more possibility of making a mistake—passing the wrong length.

Script 8   Let's look at the method `SymbolTable::ForceAdd`. It is called from several places with a string accompanied by length. To begin with, we should be alerted by code like this:

```
int id = symTab.ForceAdd ("e", 1);
...
id = symTab.ForceAdd ("pi", 2);
```

From a performance standpoint, it makes little sense and the risk of a mistake is high, especially since it is quite likely that this code will expand in the future.

Then, in the constructor of `Function::Table`, we have code that calculates `strlen` only to pass it to `ForceAdd`.

```
int len =  std::strlen (FunctionArray[i].strFun);
...
int j = symTab.ForceAdd (FunctionArray[i].strFun, len);
```

Finally, there is one place where we might think we had a good reason for this construct—in `Parser::Factor`, where the length of the string was made available as a side effect of calling `Scanner::GetSymbolName`. But even there the savings are ridiculous—definitely not worth even an infinitesimal increase in the possibility of introducing a bug.

Therefore, it makes sense to modify the interface and the implementation of `ForceAdd`.

```
int SymbolTable::ForceAdd (char const * str)
{
  int len = std::strlen (str);
  assert (len > 0);
  ...
}
```

As a bonus, we won't need to return the size of the symbol from `Scanner::GetSymbolName`.

Script 9   Next, let's have a closer look at the interactions between various classes inside the symbol table. The hash table is an array of lists, and the search for a string in the hash table returns a short list of candidates. Symbol table code then iterates over this short list and tries to find the string using direct comparison. Here's the code that does it:

```
int SymbolTable::Find (char const * str) const
{
  // Get a short list from hash table
  List const & list = _htab.Find (str);
  // Iterate over this list
  for (Link const * pLink = list.GetHead ();
      pLink != 0;
      pLink = pLink->Next ())
  {
    int id = pLink->Id ();
    int offStr = _offStr [id];
    if (_strBuf.IsEqual (offStr, str))
      return id;
  }
  return idNotFound;
}
```

Objects of the class `List` play the role of communication packets between the hash table and the symbol table. As a code reviewer I feel uneasy about it.

Something is bothering me in this arrangement—does `HTable` have to expose the details of its implementation, namely linked lists, to its client? After all, there *could* be implementations of hash tables that don't use linked lists. As a code reviewer I can express my uneasiness even if I don't know how to fix the situation. In this case, however, I *do* know what to do. The one common feature of all implementations of hash tables is that they have to be able to deal with collisions (unless they are perfect hash tables—we won't worry about those here). So they will *always*, at least conceptually, return an overflow list. All the client has to do is sequence through this list in order to finish the search.

The key word here is *sequence*. A sequencer object for a linked list is easy to implement. It's just a repackaging of the code we see above. But a sequencer has much more potential. We've already seen a stack sequencer. One can also write a sequencer for an array, a sequencer that skips entries, and so on. We could make the hash table return a sequencer rather than a list. That way we would isolate ourselves from another implementation detail of the hash table. (If you're wondering why I'm calling it a sequencer and not an iterator, it's because I reserve the name *iterator* for the pointer-like objects of the C++ standard library—we'll get there in due time.)

Figure 6.1 shows the interaction of the client's code (`SymbolTable` code) with the hash table using the sequencer object that encapsulates the results of the hash table search.

The straightforward and simpleminded translation of Figure 6.1 into code would produce a method like this:

```
ListSeq * HashTable::Find (char const * str);// BAD!!!
```

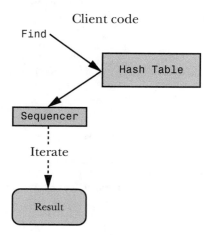

Figure 6.1 Using a sequencer for communications between the hash table and the client

The sequencer would somehow be allocated inside Find using new, and would have to be deleted once the sequencing is finished.

Never do that! We had some simple, foolproof code and it turned into a dangerous kludge. Don't laugh! You might find this kind of coding practice turned into methodology in some commercially available libraries or API sets.

Our solution to this is *object inversion*. Instead of creating an auxiliary object inside the callee and making the caller responsible for deleting it, we'll let the caller create an auxiliary *local* object (on the stack) which will be freed automatically upon exiting from the scope. The constructor of this object will take a reference to the source object (in our case, the hash table) and negotiate the transfer of data with it. In fact, we already saw this mechanism in action when we first introduced a sequencer. (It was a stack sequencer whose constructor took a reference to the stack object.)

Here's the new implementation of SymbolTable::Find that uses such a sequencer, IdSeq. It takes a reference to the hash table and obtains from it a list corresponding to the string str.

```cpp
int SymbolTable::Find (char const * str) const
{
    // Iterate over a short list from hash table
    for (IdSeq seq (_htab, str);
         !seq.AtEnd ();
         seq.Advance ())
    {
        int id = seq.GetId ();
        int offStr = _offStr [id];
        if (_strBuf.IsEqual (offStr, str))
            return id;
    }
    return idNotFound;
}
```

That's how it looks from the client's point of view. Searching through a hash table is reduced to the act of creating a sequencer corresponding to the pair: hash table, string. In other words, we have transformed a situation—where a string sent to a hash table resulted in a sequencer—into an equivalent situation, where a sequencer is created from the interaction between the hash table and a string.

I still haven't explained how the whole thing is implemented. Obviously IdSeq is a special class that knows something about the workings of the hash table. Behind our backs it still obtains a linked list from the hash table and uses it for sequencing. The difference, though, is that the hash table no longer gives linked lists away to just anybody. The HTable::Find method is private and can only be accessed by our friend—and now Htable's friend—IdSeq.

```cpp
class HTable
{
    friend class IdSeq;
    ...
```

```
private:
  List & Find (char const * str) const;
  ...
};
```

One more cosmetic issue: The linked list sequencer is really a more general class, i.e., it belongs in the file list.h and should have nothing to do with the hash table. Something general like this would be perfect:

```
// List sequencer
// Usage:
// for (ListSeq seq (list);
//        !seq.AtEnd ();
//        seq.Advance ())
// {
//      int id = seq.GetId ();
//      ...
// }
class ListSeq
{
public:
  ListSeq (List const & list)
    : _pLink (list.GetHead ()) {}
  bool AtEnd () const { return _pLink == 0; }
  void Advance () { _pLink = _pLink->Next (); }
  int GetId () const { return _pLink->Id (); }
private:
  Link const * _pLink; // Current link
};
```

However, in our particular case, we need a specialized sequencer that interacts with the hash table in its constructor.

Nothing is simpler than that. We can easily create a sequencer that inherits everything from the generic sequencer. It only adds its own constructor, which obtains the linked list from the hash table and passes it to the parent's constructor.

```
// The short list sequencer.
// The client creates this sequencer
// to search for a given string.
class IdSeq: public ListSeq
{
public:
    IdSeq (HTable const & htab, char const * str)
      : ListSeq (htab.Find (str)) {}
};
```

Let's summarize the situation. There are only five actors in this play, so it is still possible to keep them all in mind at once. Table 6.1 lists them all and explains their roles.

Class	File	Role
List	list.h	Singly linked list.
ListSeq	list.h	Generic sequencer of a singly linked list.
IdSeq	htab.h	Specialized sequencer: friend of HTable, inherits behavior from ListSeq.
HTable	htab.h	Hash table. For clients, the access is only through IdSeq. For friends, private method Find returns a List.
SymbolTable	symtab.h	The client of HTable. Accesses HTable only through specialized IdSeq.

Table 6.1 Hash table–related classes and their relationships

Notice how the classes are grouped: List and ListSeq form one team. They are generic enough to be ready for reuse. IdSeq and HTable form another team that depends for its implementation on the List team. They are also ready for reuse. SymbolTable depends on HTable and a few objects to store strings.

How do we measure our accomplishment after making these changes? Suppose that we decide to change the implementation of the hash table to something that is called *closed hashing*. In such a scheme, the overflow entries are stored in the same array as the direct entries. The overflow list is no longer a linked list, but rather a prescription how to jump around that array. It can be encapsulated in a sequencer (which, of course, has to be a friend of the hash table).

So what's the metaprogram that transforms the symbol table from one implementation of the hash table to another? Provided we named our new classes the same names as before (HTable and IdSeq), the metaprogram is *empty*. We don't have to touch a single line of code in the symbol table. That's quite an accomplishment!

6.6 Correcting Design Flaws

Script 10   As I mentioned before, our parser of arithmetic expressions has a flaw—its grammar is right associative. That means that an expression like this

    8 - 2 + 1

will be parsed as

    8 - (2 + 1) = 5

rather than, as we would expect,

    (8 - 2) + 1 = 7

We could try to correct the grammar to contain left-associative productions of the type

```
Expression := Expression '+' Term
```

but they would immediately send our recursive parser into an infinite spin (`Expr` would start by calling `Expr`, that would start by calling `Expr`, that would. . . .). There are more powerful parsing algorithms that can deal with left recursion but they are too complicated for our simple calculator. There is, however, a middle-of-the-road solution that shifts associativity from grammar to execution. In that approach, the expression parser keeps parsing term after term and stores them all in a new type of multinode. All terms that are the children of the multinode have the same status, but when it comes to calculation, they are evaluated from left to right. For instance, the parsing of the expression

```
8 - 2 + 1
```

would result in the tree shown in Figure 6.2.

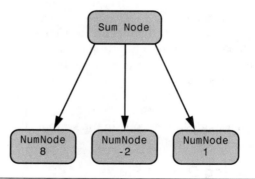

Figure 6.2 The result of parsing $8 - 2 + 1$ using a multinode

The `Calc` method of the multinode, `SumNode`, sums the terms left to right, giving the correct answer

```
8 - 2 + 1 = 7
```

We can do the same trick when parsing terms to correct the associativity of factors.

The grammar is modified to contain productions of the type (this is called the *extended* Backus-Naur Forum—BNF—notation),

```
Expr  := Term { ('+' | '-') Term }
Term  := Factor { ('*' | '/') Factor }
```

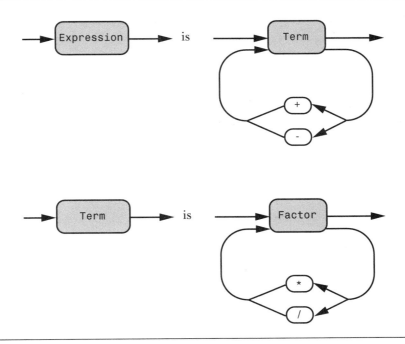

Figure 6.3   Extended productions for expressions and terms

or, in more descriptive language, Expression is a Term followed by zero or more occurrences of the combination of a sign (*plus* or *minus*) and a Term. Term, in turn, is a Factor followed by zero or more occurrences of the combination of a *multiplication* or *division* sign and a Factor. For those who like pictorial representations, Figure 6.3 illustrates these relationships using diagrams.

The phrase "zero or more occurrences," corresponding to curly braces in a production, translates directly into the do/while loop in a recursive parser. Below is the corrected implementation of Parser::Expr.

```
Node * Parser::Expr ()
{
  Node * pNode = Term ();
  EToken token = _scanner.Token ();
  if (token == tPlus || token == tMinus)
  {
    // Expr := Term { ('+' | '-') Term }
    MultiNode * pMultiNode = new SumNode (pNode);
    do
    {
      _scanner.Accept ();
      Node * pRight = Term ();
      pMultiNode->AddChild (pRight, (token == tPlus));
      token = _scanner.Token ();
```

```
      } while (token == tPlus || token == tMinus);
      pNode = pMultiNode;
   }
   else if (token == tAssign)
   {
     _scanner.Accept ();
     // Expr := Term = Expr
     Node * pRight = Expr ();
     // provided the Term is an lvalue
     if (pNode->IsLvalue ())
     {
       pNode = new AssignNode (pNode, pRight);
     }
     else
     {
       _status = stError;
       delete pNode;
       pNode = Expr ();
     }
   }
   return pNode;
}
```

The coding of `Parser::Term` undergoes a similar transformation.

```
Node * Parser::Term ()
{
   Node * pNode = Factor ();
   EToken token = _scanner.Token ();
   if (token == tMult || token == tDivide)
   {
     // Term := Factor { ('*' | '/') Factor }
     MultiNode * pMultiNode = new ProductNode (pNode);
     do
     {
       _scanner.Accept ();
       Node * pRight = Factor ();
       pMultiNode->AddChild (pRight, (token == tMult));
       token = _scanner.Token ();
     } while (token == tMult || token == tDivide);
     pNode = pMultiNode;
   }
   return pNode;
}
```

We have introduced two new types of Nodes: SumNode and ProductNode. They both share the property that they can have multiple children, and that these children have a "sign" associated with each of them. In SumNode the sign is plus or minus; in ProductNode it is the multiplication or the division sign. We will store pointers-to-children in one array and the corresponding signs in another array. The convention will be that addition and multiplication signs are stored as true while subtraction and division signs are stored as false in the _isPositive

Boolean array. The distinction will be obvious in the classes derived from the (abstract) base class MultiNode. MultiNode will represent what's common between SumNode and ProductNode. For our first sloppy implementation we will arbitrarily restrict the number of children to eight—to be fixed in Chapter 9. Sloppy or not, we will test for overflow and return an error when the user writes an expression (or term) with more than eight children nodes.

```cpp
const int MAX_CHILDREN = 8;
// Generic multiple node: an abstract class
class MultiNode: public Node
{
public:
  MultiNode (Node * pNode)
    : _isError (false)
  {
    _aChild [0] = pNode;
    _aIsPositive[0] = true;
    _iCur = 1;
  }
  ~MultiNode ();
  void AddChild (Node * pNode, bool isPositive)
  {
    if (_iCur == MAX_CHILDREN)
    {
      _isError = true;
      return;
    }
    _aChild [_iCur] = pNode;
    _aIsPositive [_iCur] = isPositive;
    ++_iCur;
  }
protected:
  bool    _isError;
  int     _iCur;
  Node *  _aChild [MAX_CHILDREN];
  bool    _aIsPositive [MAX_CHILDREN];
};
```

An array of Boolean values can be most simply implemented as an array of bool. It is, however, not the most space-efficient implementation. To store two possible values, true and false, all one needs is a bit. The standard C++ library uses this optimization in its own implementation of the Boolean array.

Here are the definitions of the two derived classes. Notice that since MultiNode is a Node, so are SumNode and ProductNode (the is-a relation is transitive).

```
// Summing
class SumNode: public MultiNode
{
public:
  SumNode (Node * pNode)
    : MultiNode (pNode) {}
  double Calc () const;
};

// Multiplying and dividing.
// Sign in this case refers to
// the exponent: positive means multiply,
// negative means divide
class ProductNode: public MultiNode
{
public:
  ProductNode (Node * pNode)
    : MultiNode (pNode) {}
  double Calc () const;
};
```

Don't forget to delete the children after we're done.

```
MultiNode::~MultiNode ()
{
  for (int i = 0; i < _iCur; ++i)
      delete _aChild [i];
}
```

And here comes our *pièce de résistance:* The Calc method that makes our algebra left associative.

```
double SumNode::Calc () const
{
  if (_isError)
  {
    std::cerr << "Error: too many terms\n";
    return 0.0;
  }

  double sum = 0.0;
  for (int i = 0; i < _iCur; ++i)
  {
    double val = _aChild [i]->Calc ();
    if (_aIsPositive [i])
     sum += val;
    else
     sum -= val;
  }
  return sum;
}
```

```
// Notice: the calculation is left associative
double ProductNode::Calc () const
{
  if (_isError)
  {
    std::cerr << "Error: too many terms\n";
    return 0.0;
  }

  double prod = 1.0;
  for (int i = 0; i < _iCur; ++i)
  {
    double val = _aChild [i]->Calc ();
    if (_aIsPositive [i])
      prod *= val;
    else if (val != 0.0)
      prod /= val;
    else
    {
      std::cerr << "Error: division by zero\n";
      return HUGE_VAL;
    }
  }
  return prod;
}
```

Notice that our change also solved the problem of expressions like

```
1 + x = 2
```

They are no longer legal, because the parsing of an expression is "greedy." It will first swallow all the terms to the left of the equal sign and make them into one node. This node, however, is not an lvalue, so the assignment node will not be created and a syntax error will follow.

Script 11   At this point you should unpack script 11, which will create a milestone label ending the cleanup phase.

Chapter 7
Hiding Implementation Details

Embedded classes, protected constructors, hiding constants, anonymous enums, namespaces.

A good software engineer is like a spy. He or she exposes information to collaborators on a need-to-know basis, because knowing too much may get them in trouble. I'm not warning here about the dangers of industrial espionage—I'm talking about the constant struggle with complexity. The more details are hidden, the simpler it is to understand what's going on.

7.1 Using Embedded Classes

Script 12 The class Link is only used internally by the linked list and its friend the sequencer. Frankly, nobody else should even know about its existence. The potential for code reuse of the class Link outside of the class List is minimal. We'll hide the definition of Link inside the private section of the class definition of List.

```
class List
{
  friend class ListSeq;
public:
  List ();
  ~List ();
  void Add (int id);
private:
  // Nested class definition
  class Link
  {
  public:
```

```
    Link (Link * pNext, int id)
        : _pNext (pNext), _id (id){}

    Link *    Next () const { return _pNext;}
    int       Id () const { return _id;}
    private:
    int       _id;
    Link    * _pNext;
  };
private:
  Link const * GetHead () const { return _pHead; }
  Link*_pHead;
};
```

The syntax of class embedding is self-explanatory. Notice that an embedded class
has no access to the embedding class' data members or methods.

The class ListSeq has a data member that is a pointer to Link. Being a friend
of List, it has no problem accessing the private definition of the class Link.
However, it has to qualify the name Link with the name of the enclosing class
List—the new name becomes List::Link.

```
class ListSeq
{
public:
  bool AtEnd () const { return _pLink == 0; }
  void Advance () { _pLink = _pLink->Next(); }
  int GetId () const { return _pLink->Id (); }
protected:
  ListSeq (List const & list)
    : _pLink (list.GetHead ()) {}
private:
  List::Link const *_pLink;
};
```

Notice that inside the definition of the class List we didn't have to qualify the
name Link. It's only outside of the definition that we have to disambiguate
between the List's internal class List::Link and, possibly, some other external
class called Link. In fact, if we wanted to access an external class Link inside List,
we would have to explicitly differentiate it from the internal Link by preceding it
with a double colon, ::Link.

> One way to look at a class declaration is to see it as a collection of methods,
> data members, and types. So far we've been dealing only with methods and
> data members; now we can see how a type—in this case, another class—can
> be defined within a class. A class may also create aliases for other types using
> typedefs. We'll see more examples of these techniques later.

The classes List and ListSeq went through some additional privatization (in the case of ListSeq, it should probably be called "protectization"). I made the GetHead method private, but I made ListSeq a friend, so it can still call GetHead. I also made the constructor of ListSeq protected, because we never create it in our program—we only use objects of the derived class, IdSeq.

I might have gone too far with privatization here, making these classes more difficult to reuse. It's important, however, to know how far you can go before you can make an informed decision on when to stop.

7.2   Combining Classes

Script 13   Conceptually, the sequencer object is very closely tied to the list object. This relationship is somehow reflected in our code by having ListSeq be a friend of List. But we can do much better than that—we can embed the sequencer class inside the list class. This time, however, we don't want to make it private—we want all clients of List to be able to use it. As you know, outside of the embedding class, the client may only access the embedded class by prefixing it with the name of the outer class. In this case, the *scope-resolution* prefix would be List::. It makes sense, then, to shorten the name of the embedded class to Seq. On the outside it will be seen as List::Seq, and on the inside of List there will be no danger of name conflict anyway.

Here's the modified declaration of List:

```
class List
{
public:
  List ();
  ~List ();
  void Add (int id);
private:
  class Link
  {
  public:
    Link (Link * pNext, int id)
      : _pNext (pNext), _id (id) {}

    Link *  Next () const { return _pNext; }
    int     Id () const { return _id; }
  private:
    Link *  _pNext;
    int     _id;
  };
public:
  class Seq
  {
  public:
    bool AtEnd () const { return _pLink == 0; }
    void Advance () { _pLink = _pLink->Next (); }
```

```
      int GetId () const { return _pLink->Id (); }

   protected:
      Seq (List const & list)
         : _pLink (list.GetHead ()) {}
   private:
   };
      Link const * _pLink; // Current link
   friend class Seq;
private:
   Link const * GetHead () const { return _pHead; }

   Link * _pHead;
};
```

Notice, by the way, that the labels public, private, and protected can be mixed in any order.

The fact that the class Seq is embedded inside the class List doesn't give it any special access privileges. In particular, it still couldn't call List's private GetHead if it weren't declared as friend.

The only client of our sequencer is the hash table sequencer, IdSeq. We have to modify its definition accordingly.

```
class IdSeq: public List::Seq
{
public:
   IdSeq (HTable const & htab, char const * str)
      : List::Seq (htab.Find (str)) {}
};
```

And, while we're at it, how about moving this class definition where it belongs, inside the class HTable? We can even shorten its name from IdSeq to Seq and make it visible outside as HTable::Seq. As before, the sequencer has to be a friend of its outer class HTable. If we announce this friendship *before* the embedded definition of the class Seq, we'll have to use the qualified name:

```
friend class HTable::Seq;
```

The same announcement *after* the definition may be abbreviated to:

```
friend class Seq;
```

The usage inside SymbolTable::Find reflects the new naming structure:

```
for (HTable::Seq seq (_htab, str);
     !seq.AtEnd ();
     seq.Advance ())
```

7.3 Combining Things Using Namespaces

There is one more example of a set of related entities that we would like to combine more tightly in our program. But this time it's a mixture of classes and data. I'm talking about the whole complex of `FunctionTable`, `FunctionEntry`, and `FunctionArray` (we can add to it also the definition of `CoTan`, which is never used outside of the context of the function table). Of course, I could embed `FunctionEntry` inside `FunctionTable`, make `CoTan` a static method, and declare `FunctionArray` a static member (we discussed this option earlier).

Script 14   There is, however, a better solution. In C++ we can create a higher-level grouping called `namespace`. Just look at the names of the objects we're trying to combine. Except for `CoTan`, they all share the same prefix, `Function`. So let's call our namespace `Function` and start by embedding the class definition of `Table` (formerly known as `FunctionTable`) in it.

```
namespace Function
{
  class Table
  {
  public:
    Table (SymbolTable & symTab);
    ~Table () { delete []_pFun; }
    int Size () const { return _size; }
    PFun GetFun (int id) { return _pFun [id]; }
  private:
    PFun * _pFun;
    int    _size;
  };
}
```

The beauty of a namespace is that you can continue it in the implementation file. Here's the condensed version of the file `funtab.cpp`:

```
namespace Function
{
  double CoTan (double x) {...}
  class Entry {...};
  Entry Array [] =
  {...};
  Table::Table (SymbolTable & symTab)
    : _size(sizeof Array / sizeof Array [0])
  {...}
}
```

As you might have guessed, the next step is to replace all occurrences of `FunctionTable` in the rest of the program by `Function::Table`. The only tricky part is the forward declaration in the header `parse.h`. You can't just say `class Function::Table;`, because the compiler hasn't seen the declaration of the `Function` namespace (remember, the point of using a forward declaration was to avoid including `funtab.h`). We have to tell the compiler not only that `Table` is a class, but also that it's declared inside the `Function` namespace. Here's how we do it:

```
namespace Function
{
  class Table;
}
class Parser
{
public:
  Parser (Scanner & scanner,
          Store & store,
          Function::Table & funTab,
          SymbolTable & symTab );
  ...
};
```

> As a general rule, a lot of traditional naming conventions for classes, functions, and objects are being replaced in modern C++ by scope resolution prefixes associated with the use of embedded classes and namespaces.

By the way, the whole C++ standard library is enclosed in a namespace. Its name is `std`. Now you can finally understand the prefixes `std::` in front of `cin`, `cout`, `endl`, and so on. There is a way to avoid these prefixes using the `using` keyword. I don't recommend this practice, but you could declare

```
using namespace std;
```

at the top of the file and forgo the use of the `std::` scope resolution prefixes. You could also be more selective and announce your use of a particular type, function, or object, as in

```
using std::cout;
```

You'll see more use of namespaces later in this book.

7.4   Hiding Constants in Enumerations

There are several constants in our program that are specific to the implementation of certain classes. It would be natural to hide the definitions of these constants inside the definitions of classes that use them. It turns out that we can do it using enumerations. We don't even have to give names to enumerations—they can be anonymous.

Look how many ways of defining constants there are in C++. There is the old-style C #define preprocessor macro, there is a type-safe global const and, finally, there is the minimum-scope enum. Which one is best? It all depends on the type. If you need a constant of a specific type, say, a double or a (user-defined) Vector, use a global const. If you just need a generic integral type constant—as in the case of an array bound—look at its scope. If it's needed by one class only, or a closely related group of classes, use an enum. If its scope is larger, use a global const int. A #define, on the other hand, is a hack that can be used to bypass type checking or type conversions—avoid it at all costs (we'll talk about macros later).

Script 15   Here's the first example of hiding constants using enumerations. The constant idNotFound is specific to SymbolTable.

```cpp
class SymbolTable
{
public:
  // Embedded anonymous enum
  enum { idNotFound = -1 };
  ...
}
```

No change is required in the implementation of Find; because it is a method of SymbolTable, Find can access idNotFound with no qualifications.

Not so with the parser. It can still use the constant idNotFound, since it is defined in the public section of SymbolTable, but it has to qualify its name with the name of the class where it's embedded.

```cpp
if (_scanner.Token () == tLParen) // Function call
{
  _scanner.Accept (); // Accept '('
  pNode = Expr ();
  if (_scanner.Token() == tRParen)
    _scanner.Accept (); // Accept ')'
  else
    _status = stError;
  // The use of embedded enum
  if (id != SymbolTable::idNotFound
      && id < _funTab.Size ())
  {
    pNode = new FunNode (
      _funTab.GetFun (id), pNode );
  }
  else
  {
    std::cerr << "Unknown function \"";
    std::cerr << strSymbol << "\"\n";
```

```
      }
    }
    else
    {
      // Factor := Ident
      if (id == SymbolTable::idNotFound)
      {
        // add new identifier to the symbol table
        id = _symTab.ForceAdd (strSymbol);
        if (id == SymbolTable::idNotFound)
        {
          std::cerr << "Error: Too many variables\n";
          _status = stError;
          pNode = 0;
        }
      }
      if (id != SymbolTable::idNotFound)
          pNode = new VarNode (id, _store);
    }
```

Maximum symbol length might be considered an internal limitation of the Scanner (although one might argue that it is a limitation of the "language" that it recognizes—we'll actually remove this limitation later).

```
class Scanner
{
public:
  // Embedded anonymous enum
  enum { maxSymLen = 80 };
  ...
};
```

7.5 Hiding Constants in Local Variables

Script 16   A constant that is only used within a single code fragment should not, in general, be exposed in the global scope; it should be defined within the scope of its usefulness. The compiler will still do inlining of such constants (that is, it will substitute the occurrences of the constant name with its literal value, rather than introducing a separate variable in memory). We have a few such constants that are only used in main:

```
int main ()
{
  const int maxBuf = 100;
  const int maxSymbols = 40;
  char buf [maxBuf];
  Status status;
  SymbolTable symTab (maxSymbols);

}
```

Script 17   This concludes our first attempt at hiding code.

Chapter 8
Sharing

Have you noticed how we oscillate between global and local perspective in our code reviews? Whenever we talk about sharing, we take a more global stance. Whenever we talk about data or implementation hiding, we take a local stance. It's time to swing the pendulum towards sharing.

8.1 Isolating Global Program Parameters

Script 18

From the global perspective, some of the constants that we've been so busily burying inside local scopes are actually tunable parameters of our program. Imagine that somebody (say, our client) wants to increase the maximum length of symbolic names. Or wants to be able to add more entries to the symbol table. Or desperately needs to increase the size of the input buffer. We'll have to dig deeper into our classes and functions to find the appropriate constants.

Fortunately, there are several ways to make such fine-tuning less cumbersome. I'll only show the most basic one—collecting all tunable constants in a single file, `Params.h`. Here's the contents of this file:

```
const int maxBuf = 100; // Size of input buffer
const int maxSymbols = 40; // Size of symbol table
const int maxSymLen = 80; // Max length of symbol name
```

There will almost always be some tunable parameters in your program whose change will require recompilation. Their place is in `Params.h`.

There usually is another set of parameters that should be tunable by the user. These are called *user preferences* and are stored persistently in some convenient

location. Even these parameters have their default values whose place is, again, in
Params.h.

8.2   Pushing the Envelope

We know that our program has built-in limitations: see Params.h. Obviously we
want to make these limitations as unobtrusive as possible. We generously allocate
space for symbols, characters in buffers, and others so that in day-to-day operation
the user doesn't hit these limits. Unfortunately, that also means that we, the programmers, are unlikely to hit these limitations in our testing. And rest assured—
whatever boundaries we don't hit, our users will!

So let's do a little experiment. Let's edit the file Params.h and set all the limits
to some relatively low values. We might even keep two sets of parameters—one for
regular operation and one for testing. I used conditional compilation directives to
switch between the two sets. Changing 0 to 1 in the #if directive will switch us back
to the regular set.

```
#if 0
const int maxBuf = 100;     // Size of input buffer
const int maxSymbols = 40;  // Size of symbol table
const int maxSymLen = 80;   // Max length of symbol name
#else
const int maxBuf = 8;       // Size of input buffer
const int maxSymbols = 5;   // Size of symbol table
const int maxSymLen = 4;    // Max length of symbol name
#endif
```

After recompiling the whole program, I ran it and immediately hit an assertion in the constructor of Function::Table. A quick inspection revealed that the
program was trying to cram 14 symbols for built-in functions into our symbol table,
whose maximum capacity was set to 5. That's good! Obviously the value of 5 for
the size of the symbol table was too small, but we were able to catch it immediately.

Is an assertion enough protection from these types of problems? In general,
yes. This particular problem might only arise when somebody changes the value of
maxSymLen or adds more built-in functions. We are safe in that case, because

> **After every code change the program will be rebuilt in the debugging
> version (with the assertions turned on) and run at least once before it's
> released to others.**

By "others" I don't mean customers—I mean other programmers on the same
team. Before releasing a program to customers, much stricter testing is required.

So now let's set the size of the symbol table to 14—just enough for built-in functions—and try to enter an expression that introduces a new symbolic variable, for instance x = 0. Kaboom! The program crashes!

What happened? Parser::Factor correctly discovered a problem, even printed out "Error: Too many variables," and then returned a null pointer. Well, what else was it supposed to do?! Unfortunately, the caller of Parser::Factor never expected a null pointer. Back to the drawing board!

Let's add checks for a null pointer to all the callers of Parser::Factor (as well as the callers of Parser::Expr, who can propagate the null obtained from Parser::Factor and Parser::Term.

One more test—this time everything works fine; that is, until we exit the program. Remember, all this time we are running a debug build of our program under the debugger. A good debug runtime will do a heap check when your program frees memory. A heap check should discover problems such as buffer overflows, double deletions, and so on. And indeed it does! The destructor of Store reported an overwritten memory block. A little more sleuthing and the culprit becomes obvious. Look at this code in the constructor of Store:

```
int id = symTab.ForceAdd ("e");
SetValue (id, std::exp (1));
std::cerr << "pi = " << 2 * std::acos (0.0) << std::endl;
id = symTab.ForceAdd ("pi");
SetValue (id, 2 * std::acos (0.0));
```

When our symbol table overflows, it returns –1. Store::SetValue is called with –1 and happily obliges.

```
void SetValue (int id, double val)
{
  assert (id < _size);
  _cell [id] = val;
  _status [id] = stInit;
}
```

We were smart enough to assert that id be less than the size of the table, but not smart enough to guard against a negative value of id.

Okay, let's change that to

```
assert (id >= 0 && id < _size);
```

and try again. This time we hit the assertion immediately. Great! One more test with maxSymbols = 16 and we're in the clear.

Now let's test the restriction on the size of the input buffer. Let's input a large expression, say, one with ten zeros. The program works, but not exactly as the user would expect. It first prints the incorrect result, then goes into an infinite loop (on other compilers it exits).

First of all, why does it go into an infinite loop? It turns out that since we didn't retrieve all the characters from the input on the first try, the next time we call cin.getline it returns immediately without filling the buffer. Some library implementations clear the buffer and our program exits; some don't and we loop forever.

But that's not our biggest problem. A program that quietly returns incorrect results is much worse than the one that crashes. Incorrect information is worse than no information at all. We have to fix it immediately. First, let me show you a very general solution that doesn't go into the specifics of the input stream.

```
char buf [maxBuf + 1];
// ...
std::cin.getline (buf, maxBuf + 1);
if (std::strlen (buf) == maxBuf)
{
  std::cerr << "Error: Input buffer overflow\n";
  status = stError;
  break;
}
```

The trick is to increase the size of the buffer by one, so that we can grab one character more than the self-imposed limit. Now we can detect if our greedy request was satisfied and, if so, we know that the input was larger than maxBuf and we can bail out.

In our particular case, there is a simpler solution. When the call to getline cannot be satisfied because the line doesn't fit in the buffer, the state of the stream, cin, changes. We can test this state and react appropriately.

```
std::cin.getline (buf, maxBuf); // Read a line
if (std::cin.fail ())
{
  std::cerr << "Error: Input buffer overflow\n";
  status = stError;
  break;
}
```

Now for the last test—maximum symbol length. Before we try that, we have to increase maxSymbols and maxBuf so that we can enter a few test symbols into our program. What we discover is that, although the program works, it quietly lies to the user. Try inputting the expression toolong = 6 and then displaying the value of the variable tool. Instead of complaining about the use of an uninitialized variable, the program quietly treats both names as representing the same variable. The least we can do is display a warning in Scanner::Accept.

```
if (_lenSymbol > maxSymLen)
{
  std::cerr << "Warning: Variable name truncated\n";
  _lenSymbol = maxSymLen;
}
```

Scary, isn't it? Why was this program so buggy? Was this the norm or an exception? The truth is that no matter how good you are, your programs will contain errors. The compiler will catch most of the simple errors—typos, type mismatches, wrong number of arguments, and so on. Many errors will become obvious after some elementary testing. The rest are the "hard bugs."

There are many techniques to eradicate hard bugs. One is testing; in particular, you can make testing easier by *instrumenting* your program—writing code whose only purpose is to catch bugs. We've done something like that by instrumenting the file Params.h. I'll show you more testing and instrumentation techniques later.

There is also the matter of attitude. I wrote this program without much concern for error checking and exceptional conditions. Normally I would be much more careful, but I wanted to show you the kind of mistakes that can result from carelessness.

Finally, there is the matter of policy. Dealing with exceptional conditions is not something you do on a whim—you have to develop some rules. We'll talk about this some more.

8.3 Templates

Script 19   We have put the class List together with its sequencer in a standalone file with code reuse in mind. At any time in the future when we need a linked list of integers we can just include this well-tested and solid code. Did I just say "a linked list of *integers*"? What if we need a list of unsigned longs or doubles or even Stars for that matter? What would be really useful is a class that is *parameterized* by a type. Enter templates!

To turn List into a template, you need to preface its class definition with

```
template<class T>
```

or, equivalently,

```
template<typename T>
```

and replace ints with Ts. We are parameterizing the definition of List with the parameter T that stands for any type. Once you have the template defined, you can *instantiate* it —use it with T substituted by any type, it doesn't even have to be a class. For instance,

```
List<int> myList;
```

will define a List of integers called myList. You are also free to declare other lists, such as a list of unsigned longs, List<unsigned long>, a list of doubles, List<double>, or a list of Stars, List<Star>.

Here's the definition of the List template.

```cpp
template<class T>
class List
{
public:
  List ();
  ~List ();
  void Add (T value);
private:
  class Link
  {
  public:
    Link (Link * pNext, T value)
      : _pNext (pNext), _value (value) {}
    Link *  Next () const { return _pNext; }
    T GetValue () const { return _value; }
  private:
    T        _value;
    Link *  _pNext;
  };
public:
  class Seq
  {
  public:
    bool AtEnd () const { return _pLink == 0; }
    void Advance () { _pLink = _pLink->Next (); }
    T GetValue () const { return _pLink->GetValue (); }
  protected:
    Seq (List const & list)
      : _pLink (list.GetHead ()) {}
  private:
    Link const * _pLink; // Current link
  };
  friend class Seq;
private:
  Link const * GetHead () const { return _pHead; }
  Link * _pHead;
};
```

To be more general, I've changed the name of the method that retrieves the stored value from GetId to GetValue.

For technical reasons, today's compilers require all template code to be visible in the place of template instantiation (this requirement might change in future compilers). What this means is that we have to put all the method implementations in the same header file as the template class definition. It doesn't make these methods inline (unless they are declared as such), nor does it imply that their code will be instantiated multiple times.

Here's how you define the constructor outside of the class definition but still in the header file List.h. Notice that only the first List, the one before the double colon, is followed by <T>.

```
template<class T>
List<T>: :List ()
  : _pHead (0)
{}
```

The same with the destructor:

```
template <class T>
List <T>::~List ()
{
  // Free linked list
  while (_pHead != 0)
  {
    Link * pLink = _pHead;
    _pHead = _pHead->Next ();
    delete pLink;
  }
}
```

Other methods follow the same pattern.

```
template <class T>
void List <T>::Add (T value)
{
  Link * pLink = new Link (_pHead, value);
  _pHead = pLink;
}
```

The second part of "templatization" is to substitute all the uses of *List of integers* with List<int>. For instance, here's our hash table:

```
class HTable
{
public:
  class Seq: public List<int>::Seq
  {
  public:
    Seq (HTable const & htab, char const * str)
      : List<int>::Seq (htab.Find (str)) {}
  };
  friend class Seq;
public:
  explicit HTable (int size): _size(size)
  {
    _aList = new List<int> [size];
  }
  ~HTable ()
  {
    delete []_aList;
  }

  void Add (char const * str, int id);
```

```
private:
  List<int> const & Find (char const * str) const;
  int hash (char const * str) const;

  List<int> *_aList;
  int        _size;
};
```

Defining a template doesn't by itself result in any code in the executable program. A template is like a set of instructions for a compiler: it tells how to generate code if the need arises. The first time the compiler sees the instantiation of a given template, it creates the necessary code. Seeing the use of List<int> inside HTable will prompt the compiler to generate the definition of the class List, which has been modified specifically for integers. The code for non-inline methods—the list's constructor, destructor, and Add—will be generated. All subsequent instantiations of List<int> in the program will share this code. But were we also to instantiate List<double>, a totally separate version of the constructor, destructor, and Add for doubles would be generated.

In general, a class template can be parameterized by more than one type. It can also be parameterized by values. For instance:

```
template<class T, int size>
class Array
{
public:
  T _arr [size];
};
```

Notice that in this case two instantiations with different values of parameters

```
Array<double, 10> a;
Array<double, 20> b;
```

will be equivalent to two separate class definitions. If these classes have code (non-inline methods) associated with them, the code will be duplicated too.

Besides class templates, C++ also provides function templates—functions parameterized by types or values. A typical example of such a function template is the definition of max:

```
template<class T>
inline T const & max (T const & a, T const & b)
{
  if (a < b)
    return b;
  else
    return a;
}
```

To calculate the maximum of two integers, we might then write code like this:

```
int i = max<int> (j, 5);
```

or omit the type completely and let the compiler figure out what version of max to instantiate based on the types of arguments:

```
int i = max (j, 5);
```

Notice that since the function max is defined inline, there is no hidden cost to using a template instead of a macro (we'll talk about macros later).

Script 20

To summarize: A class template is a definition of a class that is parameterized by one or more types. The type parameters are listed within angle brackets after the keyword template.

```
template <class type1, class type2 ...>
```

To instantiate the template, it is enough to use it with the type parameters substituted by actual types (either built-in or user-defined). You can also define function templates and templates parameterized by values.

Exercises

1. Convert our implementation of a simple stack (see the section Abstract Data Types on page 34) to a template parameterized by the type of values and the maximum size of the stack:

   ```
   template<class T, int maxSize>
   class Stack
   ```

2. Convert our implementation of dynamic stack (see the section Dynamic Stack on page 74) to a template.

3. We have defined a hash table of integers. Turn this definition into a template parameterized by the type of values to be stored in it. Instantiate this template for the type double.

Chapter 9
Removing Limitations

Dynamic arrays, overloading of the array access operator.

Don't you just hate it when you're trying to save the results of a few hours of editing only to see a message box saying "Cannot save: Too many windows open" or some such nonsense? Unfortunately, it's a common occurrence—somebody who considers himself or herself a programmer hardcoded a fixed size array to store some important program resources. With the advent of templates, it has become so easy to remove the unnecessary limits that there's hardly any justification for leaving them around.

Let's first look around to see where in our program we have managed to impose unreasonable limitations due to our ignorance of templates. There's one we introduced in MultiNode, by arbitrarily limiting the number of children to eight. The whole symbol table is infested with limitations; for example, the buffer for a string is limited and the array of offsets is finite. Finally, the storage of variable values has an arbitrary limit.

You might ask, "What's the likelihood of a user hitting one of the limitations? Is it worth going to all this trouble of writing templates in order to deal with such unlikely cases?" The answer is:

> **It is less trouble to use dynamic containers than it is to deal with limitations.**

Just think of all the error messages you'll have to display, the propagation of these errors (by the way, we'll deal with this topic separately later), and the localization of message strings. Believe me, you don't want to do it!

9.1 Dynamic Array

Script 21 Almost all cases of artificial limits can be solved by just one template—the dynamic array. Let's walk together through its design and implementation. In the process you'll not only learn more about templates and operator overloading, but you'll also prepare yourself for the general-purpose dynamic vector from the C++ standard library.

Let's first try to come up with a set of requirements for this data structure. As much as possible we would like the dynamic array to look and work just like an array. That means we would like to access its elements by indexing, both to read and to write. Adding new elements is a bit trickier. For performance reasons, we don't want the array to check for bounds on every access (except maybe in the debugging version) and extend the array if necessary. Also, in our program we never actually need to add new elements at an arbitrary offset—we always add elements to the end of an array. It would be tempting to simply keep track of the last added element and have the method Push add and extend the array.

For this particular exercise I decided to be a little more general and have a method Set that can add a new element at an arbitrary offset. I did that because I wanted to be able to use pairs of synchronized arrays that share the same insertion index—we'll see an example of it in a moment.

One more thing: in many cases it makes sense to pre-fill the array with some default values. For instance, an array of pointers could be pre-filled with null pointers, integers could be preset to zero or minus one, enumerated types to some default value, and so on. We'll store this default value in the dynamic array, so we can use it to pre-fill the new pieces of the array when we grow it.

```
template <class T>
class DynArray
{
  enum { initDynArray = 8 };
public:
  explicit DynArray (T const valDefault);
  ~DynArray ();
  void Set (int i, T const val);
  T operator [] (int i) const;
  T & operator [] (int i);
  bool InRange (int i) const { return i < _capacity; }
private:
  void Grow (int i);

  T    * _arr;
  int    _capacity; // Size of the array
  T const _valDefault;
};
```

The line

```
T operator [] (int i) const;
```

is another example of operator overloading. Here we are overloading the array access operator [] (square brackets) in order to be able to access dynamic arrays just like regular arrays.

> Notice that objects of type DynArray do not have value semantics (neither do built-in array types—you can't pass an entire array by value). They shouldn't be copied or assigned to. The default shallow copy implemented by the compiler will not work correctly—it will lead to double deletions. If you are concerned about inadvertent copying of DynArray objects, you can provide dummy unimplemented declarations of a copy constructor and an assignment operator (we talked about this in the section Value Semantics in Section 5.13, page 157.):
>
> ```
> DynArray (DynArray const & src);
> DynArray & operator = (DynArray const & src);
> ```

Here's how we can define a dynamic array of integers, add a value to it using Add, and retrieve it using an index.

```
DynArray<int> a (0); // Dynamic array with 0 default value
a.Set (3, 10);  // Add entry with value 10 at offset 3
int i = a [3];  // Access it like a regular array
```

The compiler will translate the last line into the call to operator [] like this,

```
int i = a.operator [] (3);
```

which, by the way, is also the correct alternative syntax.

Notice that we have another overloading of the same operator in the same class:

```
T & operator [] (int i);
```

How can this be done? It's the same operator, takes the same arguments, but it returns T by reference, not by value. Is it enough for the compiler to decide between these two when it sees, for instance, a[3]? The answer is no—overloads that only differ by return type are not allowed. What really matters for disambiguation here is the word const. One method is constant and the other is not. When acting on a const object, the compiler will pick the constant method, otherwise it will use the non-constant one.

The non-constant, reference-returning version of the operator allows us to use the result of array indexing as an *lvalue*. The following statement "does the right thing":

```
a [3] = 11;
```

Compare it with the more verbose version:

```
int & r = a.operator [] (3); // Reference to 3rd element
r = 11; // Change value through reference
```

In the above example, if a was defined to be const, the compiler would flag it as an error. And rightly so! You are not supposed to change the value of a const object.

That shows you why I had to define two versions of this method. If I only had the non-constant version, I wouldn't be able to use it on a const object or in a const method of DynArray. In fact, our program wouldn't compile for exactly that reason.

If I only had the const version, I wouldn't be able to modify the elements of the array using indexing—I couldn't use them as lvalues.

> There is a third possibility: you could say that by returning a reference, even though it's a non-const reference, you are not really changing the state of the object.
>
> ```
> T & operator [] (int i) const { return _arr[i]; }
> ```
>
> C++ follows this restricted definition of const-ness, which has its pluses and minuses. It's a plus that you can have a single overload of operator[] for both const and non-const objects. The minus is that it allows you to change the contents of a const object easily.

The implementation of the dynamic array is pretty straightforward. Here's the constructor and the destructor.

```
template <class T>
DynArray <T>::DynArray (T const valDefault)
  : _capacity (initDynArray), _valDefault (valDefault)
{
  _arr = new T [initDynArray]; // Allocate memory
  for (int i = 0; i < initDynArray; ++i)
    _arr[i] = _valDefault;
}

template <class T>
DynArray <T>::~DynArray ()
{
  delete []_arr;
}
```

The method Set has the potential of extending the array.

```
template <class T>
void DynArray <T>::Set (int i, T const val)
{
  if ( i >= _capacity )
    Grow(i);
  _arr [i] = val;
}
```

Here are the two versions of the array access operator. Notice that neither of them can be used to extend the array—the assertions are there to make sure that nobody even tries. We want array access to be very fast (at least in the non-debug version), and testing for overflow and trying to extend the array during each access would impose too much overhead. This is especially important when we want to access array elements one-by-one in a loop.

```
template <class T>
inline T DynArray<T>::operator [] (int i) const
{
  assert (i < _capacity);
  return _arr[i];
}
template <class T>
inline T & DynArray<T>::operator [] (int i)
{
  assert (i < _capacity);
  return _arr[i];
}
```

The Grow method works by doubling the size of the array. However, when asked to extend the array beyond doubling, it will oblige, too.

```
// Private non-inline method
template <class T>
void DynArray <T>::Grow (int idxMax)
{
  int newSize = 2 * _capacity;
  if (idxMax >= newSize)
    newSize = idxMax + 1;
  // Allocate new array
  T * arrNew = new T [newSize];
  // Copy all entries
  int i;
  for (i = 0; i < _capacity; ++i)
    arrNew [i] = _arr [i];
  for (; i < newSize; ++i)
    arrNew [i] = _valDefault;
  _capacity = newSize;
  // Free old memory
  delete []_arr;
  // Substitute new array for old array
  _arr = arrNew;
}
```

9.1.1   Dynamic `MultiNode`

Now it's time to use our dynamic array template to see how easy it really is. Let's start with the class `MultiNode`. In the old, limited implementation it had two arrays: an array of pointers to `Node` and an array of Boolean flags. Our first step is to change the types of these arrays to, respectively, `DynArray<Node*>` and `DynArray<bool>`. We have to pass default values to the constructors of these arrays in the preamble to the `MultiNode` constructor. Methods that simply access the arrays will work without any changes (due to our overloading of `operator []`), except for the places where we used to check for array bounds. Those are the places where we might have to extend the arrays, so we should use the `Set` method. It so happens that the only place we do it is inside the `AddChild` method, and that conversion is straightforward.

```cpp
class MultiNode: public Node
{
public:
  MultiNode (Node * pNode)
      : _aChild (0),
        _aIsPositive (false),
        _iCur (0)
  {
    AddChild (pNode, true);
  }
  ~MultiNode ();
  void AddChild (Node * pNode, bool isPositive)
  {
    _aChild.Set (_iCur, pNode);
    _aIsPositive.Set (_iCur, isPositive);
    ++_iCur;
  }
protected:
  int                 _iCur;
  DynArray<Node*>     _aChild;
  DynArray<bool>      _aIsPositive;
};
MultiNode::~MultiNode ( )
{
  for (int i = 0; i < _iCur; ++i)
    delete _aChild [i];
}
```

Let's have one more look at the `Calc` method of `SumNode`. Other than the removal of error checking (we have gotten rid of the unnecessary flag `_isError`), it works as if nothing has changed.

```cpp
double SumNode::Calc ( ) const
{
  double sum = 0.0;
  for (int i = 0; i < _iCur; ++i)
  {
```

```
        double val = _aChild [i]->Calc ();
        if (_aIsPositive[i])
          sum += val;
        else
          sum -= val;
      }
      return sum;
    }
```

The only difference is that when we access our arrays _aChild [i] and
_aIsPositive [i], we are really calling the overloaded operator [] of the respec-
tive dynamic arrays. And, since the method Calc is const, it is the const version of
the overload we're calling.

To test the dynamic array, try setting initDynArray to 1 (zero will not work in
our program).

9.1.2   Dynamic StringBuffer

Script 22   Using the same techniques we can make the string buffer dynamic. However, since
the string buffer patterns of growth are different, instead of using a general purpose dynamic array we'll do something more specialized. The only case when the
string buffer might have to be extended is when appending a new string to it.
Here's the new implementation:

```
class StringBuffer
{
public:
  StringBuffer ()
    : _buf (0), _bufSize (0), _curOffset (0)
  {}
  ~StringBuffer ()
  {
    delete []_buf;
  }
  int Add (char const * str);
  int GetOffset () const
  {
    return _curOffset;
  }
  bool IsEqual (int offStr, char const * str) const;
  char const * GetString (int offStr) const
  {
    assert (offStr < _curOffset);
    return &_buf [offStr];
  }
private:
  void Reallocate (int addLen);

  int     _bufSize;
  char  * _buf;
  int     _curOffset;
};
```

When the buffer runs out of space, the Add method reallocates the whole buffer.

```
int StringBuffer::Add (char const * str)
{
  int len = std::strlen (str);
  int offset = _curOffset;
  // Is there enough space?
  if (_curOffset + len + 1 > _bufSize)
  {
    Reallocate (len + 1);
  }
  // Copy the string there
  std::strncpy (&_buf [_curOffset], str, len);
  // Calculate new offset
  _curOffset += len;
  _buf [_curOffset] = 0;   // Null terminate
  ++_curOffset;
  return offset;
}
```

The reallocation follows the standard doubling pattern, but makes sure that the new string will fit even if the buffer doubling in size is not enough.

```
void StringBuffer::Reallocate (int addLen)
{
  int newSize = _bufSize * 2;
  if (newSize < _curOffset + addLen)
    newSize = _curOffset + addLen;
  char * newBuf = new char [newSize];
  for (int i = 0; i < _curOffset; ++i)
    newBuf [i] = _buf [i];
  delete []_buf;
  _buf = newBuf;
  _bufSize = newSize;
}
```

9.1.3 Dynamic SymbolTable

Another part of the SymbolTable class besides StringBuffer that needs to be dynamic is the array of offsets _aOffStr.

```
class SymbolTable
{
  enum { hTabSize = 65 };
public:
  enum { idNotFound = -1} ;
  SymbolTable ();
  int ForceAdd (char const * str);
  int Find (char const * str) const;
  char const * GetString (int id) const;
```

```
private:
  HTable          _htab;   // String -> ids
  DynArray<int>   _offStr; // id -> offset
  int             _curId;
  StringBuffer    _strBuf; // Offset -> string
};
```

Notice that we no longer need a destructor; the subobjects' destructors will take care of the cleanup.

Here's the new improved implementation of ForceAdd. We don't have to worry anymore about overflowing the offset table or the string buffer.

```
int SymbolTable::ForceAdd (char const * str)
{
  int offset = _strBuf.Add (str);
  _offStr.Set (_curId, offset);
  _htab.Add (str, _curId);
  return _curId++; // Post-increment
}
```

It's always a pleasure to be able to simplify some code—this is the part of programming that I like best. ForceAdd now reads almost like haiku.

This is how the constructor of the symbol table shrinks:

```
SymbolTable::SymbolTable ( )
  : _curId (0),
  _htab (htabSize),
  _offStr (0)
{}
```

And this is how simple the parsing of a symbolic variable becomes:

```
// Factor := Ident
if (id == SymbolTable::idNotFound)
    id = _symTab.ForceAdd (strSymbol);
assert (id != SymbolTable::idNotFound);
pNode = new VarNode (id, _store);
```

(I left the assertion as a protection against somebody changing the implementation of SymbolTable to use a nondynamic array.)

9.1.4 Dynamic Store

Script 23   The class Store needs two dynamic arrays and a few small changes where the bounds used to be checked.

```
class Store
{
private:
```

```
      enum { stNotInit, stInit };
public:
  explicit Store (SymbolTable & symTab);
  bool IsInit (int id) const
  {
    assert (id >= 0);
    return _status.InRange (id) &&
           _status [id] != stNotInit;
  }
  double Value (int id) const
  {
    assert (id >= 0);
    assert (IsInit (id));
    return _cell [id];
  }
  void SetValue (int id, double val)
  {
    assert (id >= 0);
    if (_cell.InRange (id))
    {
      _cell [id] = val;
      _status [id] = stInit;
    }
    else
    {
      AddValue (id, val);
    }
  }

  void AddValue (int id, double val)
  {
    assert (id >= 0);
    _cell.Set (id, val);
    _status.Set (id, stInit);
  }
private:
  DynArray<double>        _cell;
  DynArray<unsigned char> _status;
};
```

In the preamble to the constructor of Store we pass the arguments to the constructors of the dynamic arrays. The memory cells are initialized to zero and the
statuses to stNotInit.

```
Store::Store (SymbolTable & symTab)
  : _cell (0.0), _status (stNotInit)
{
  // Add predefined constants
  // Note: if more needed, do a more general job
  std::cerr << "e = " << std::exp (1) << std::endl;
  int id = symTab.ForceAdd ("e");
  AddValue (id, std::exp (1));
  std::cerr << "pi = " << 2*std::acos (0.0) << std::endl;
```

```
    id = symTab.ForceAdd ("pi");
    AddValue (id, 2.0 * std::acos (0.0));
}
```

Finally, our getting rid of built-in limitations is reflected in some nice simplifications in main. We no longer need to pass size arguments to the constructors.

```
int main ()
{
    ...
    SymbolTable symTab;
    Function::Table funTab (symTab);
    Store store (symTab);
    ...
}
```

9.2   **Standard Vector**

Script 24   Now that you know how a dynamic array works, it's time to introduce the most useful member of the C++ standard library, the vector. The vector is all that you might expect from a dynamic array and more. Without further ado, let's quickly substitute all the occurrences of DynArray with std::vector (yes, it's a member of the std namespace), making sure we include the appropriate header:

```
#include <vector>
```

Let's start with MultiNode and its two dynamic arrays.

```
std::vector<Node*> _aChild;
std::vector<bool>  _aIsPositive;
```

Before our code can compile, we have to make a few adjustments. For instance, std::vector doesn't have the Add method. We can, however, append new elements by calling push_back, which has the side effect of growing the array if necessary. (Notice, by the way, the particular naming convention of the C++ standard library. All names are lower case, with underscores for word separators. You'll have no problem distinguishing them from our own names.)

Another thing: there seems to be no simple way of providing the default values for the elements of a vector. Fortunately, the C++ standard library uses default constructors to fill empty spaces in vectors and other containers. It so happens that C++ provides default constructors for all built-in types. For instance, the default value for an int or a pointer is zero, for a bool, false, and so on. Try it!

```
int i = int ();
bool b = bool ();
```

```
typedef void * voidptr;
void * p = voidptr ();
std::cout << "int " << i << ", bool " << b
          << ", pointer " << p << std::endl;
```

It turns out that the introduction of std::vector further simplifies the implementation of class MultiNode:

```
class MultiNode: public Node
{
public:
  MultiNode (Node * pNode)
  {
    AddChild (pNode, true);
  }
  ~MultiNode ();
  void AddChild (Node * pNode, bool isPositive)
  {
    _aChild.push_back (pNode);
    _aIsPositive.push_back (isPositive);
  }
protected:
  std::vector<Node*> _aChild;
  std::vector<bool>  _aIsPositive;
};
```

I have eliminated the member variable _iCur because it's no longer needed. We can quickly find out how many children there are by calling the vector's size method. Knowing the size of the vector, we can loop over all its elements. However, if all we need is to iterate the elements of a vector, like we do in the destructor of MultiNode, there is a better, more "standard" way—we can use an *iterator*.

If you think of a vector as an array, an iterator is like a pointer to one of its elements. Remember when I said that it's better to use an index instead of a pointer to access elements of an array? With vectors it's sort of the opposite, at least as far as iteration goes.

You can get an iterator pointing to the beginning of a vector by calling the vector's begin method. Similarly, you can get the iterator pointing *one beyond the last element* of a vector by calling its end method. You can move the iterator to point to the next element of the vector by applying the increment operator, ++. You can test whether two iterators are equal (point to the same entry in the vector) using the equality or inequality operators. Finally, you can get the value of vector's element by dereferencing the iterator using the star (asterisk) operator.

This is what the new destructor of MultiNode looks like:

```
MultiNode::~MultiNode ()
{
  typedef std::vector<Node *>::iterator NodeIter;
  for (NodeIter it = _aChild.begin ();
       it != _aChild.end (); ++it)
```

```
    {
      delete *it;
    }
  }
```

The type `iterator` is internal to the template class `vector`. That makes for a very unwieldy type name, `std::vector<Node *>::iterator`. It is customary to declare local `typedef`s for such complex type names.

In case you're wondering, `vector<T>::iterator` is in all likelihood implemented as a pointer. And if, for some reason or another, it's not, you can still do with it virtually anything you can do with a pointer. What's even more important is that you get from it the same kind of performance as from a pointer. You can pass it around just like a pointer. You can return it from a function like a pointer. In fact, performancewise, there is no difference between the code above and the following:

```
Node * aChild [size];
typedef Node * NodeIter;
for (NodeIter it = aChild; it != aChild + size; ++it)
  delete *it;
```

I want to stress this point because some programmers might hesitate to use some of the features of the C++ standard library for fear of performance degradation. No need to worry—the creators of the C++ standard library made it their highest priority not to jeopardize performance. That's why, for instance, they selected the pointer-like approach to iteration, rather than the somewhat safer sequencer approach.

Pointer-like iteration requires two separate pieces of data—the current position and the end position. A sequencer has access to both. With a sequencer there is no danger that you might, by mistake, compare the current position in one vector against the end position that belongs to some other vector. In fact, if you are worried about this kind of error, you can easily create a sequencer out of two iterators.

```
class NodeSeq
{
public:
  NodeSeq (std::vector<Node *> & vec)
    : _cur (vec.begin ( )), _end (vec.end ())
  {}
  bool AtEnd () const { return _cur == _end; }
  void Advance () { ++_cur; }
  Node * Get () { return *_cur; }
private:
  std::vector<Node *>::iterator _cur;
  std::vector<Node *>::iterator _end;
};
```

The only drawback of the sequencer is that it's slightly more expensive to pass it by value—as you can see, a sequencer is usually twice as large as the corresponding iterator. And iterators are passed around a lot, once you start using standard algorithms.

Script 25   Next on our list of dynamic array substitutions is the symbol table with its _offStr array. We'll have to recode the ForceAdd method, incidentally getting rid of the _curId member.

```
std::size_t SymbolTable::ForceAdd (char const * str)
{
  int offset = _strBuf.Add (str);
  std::size_t id = _offStr.size ();
  _offStr.push_back (offset);
  _htab.Add (str, id);
  return id;
}
```

As you might remember, we use the current position in the array of offsets as our string ID. Again, the size method of the vector helps us locate the current end of the vector. There is one little problem, however. The method size returns an unsigned type (after all, size cannot be negative). So far we've been using an int (which is signed) for our IDs. Most compilers will issue a warning when you try to implicitly convert an unsigned type to a signed one because of the possible loss of precision. This is an extremely unlikely problem in our program, since it would require the insertion of more than two billion identifiers (it's the unsigned numbers between two billion and four billion that become negative when converted to a signed 32-bit integer). However remote the possibility of overflow is, we don't want *any* warnings when compiling our program.

This is why I decided to switch from using int type to the library-defined std::size_t type (it can be found, among other places, in the <cstdlib> header). This was a painful process—I had to find all occurrences of "int id" and change them to "std::size_t id". Moreover, the value idNotFound could no longer be defined as an enum (which is signed) equal to –1, but rather a static const member of SymbolTable:

```
class SymbolTable
{
public:
  static const std::size_t idNotFound = 0xffffffff;
  ...
};
```

Notice how static const members can be initialized inside the scope of the class. The value 0xffffffff is the largest 32-bit unsigned number. The standard doesn't require a separate definition (but this time without initialization) inside an implementation file, as long as you don't use its address anywhere in your code.

By the way, did you notice that the compiler didn't complain about our initializing the vector in the constructor of `SymbolTable`? Unlike `DynArray`, `std::vector` doesn't take a default element value. However, it has a one-argument constructor that accepts the initial size for the vector. Of course, that's not what we had in mind, so we better remove it.

Script 26   Finally, let's get rid of the two `DynArray`s in `Store`. Here the situation is a bit trickier. One of the arrays stores enumerated values for which the compiler doesn't know the default. Instead of coming up with a clever trick, why don't we simply replace this array with a vector of `bool`? All we ever ask this array is whether a given element has been initialized or not, and that has a yes or no answer. So here are the new data members of `Store`:

```
std::vector<double>  _cell;
std::vector<bool>    _isInit;
```

Next, we have to substitute all calls to `DynArray::InRange` with a test against `vector::size`. For instance,

```
bool IsInit (std::size_t id) const
{
  assert (id != idNotFound);
  return id < _isInit.size () && _isInit [id];
}
```

Notice one important change I had to make in order to avoid signed/unsigned mismatch warnings from the compiler.

The `AddValue` method has to be able to insert an item beyond the current end of each vector. The way to do this is to first resize them. The `resize` method increases the size of the vector and fills the new slots with default values.

```
void AddValue (std::size_t id, double val)
{
  assert (id >= 0);
  _cell.resize (id + 1);
  _isInit.resize (id + 1);
  _cell [id] = val;
  _isInit [id] = true;
}
```

Script 27   *To summarize: There is no reason for any program to have unreasonable limitations due to the use of fixed-size arrays. The C++ standard library vector should be used whenever a resizable array is needed.*

Chapter 10
Resource Management

I don't know if you've noticed, but there's one important flaw in our program: it assumes that memory allocation never fails. This assumption is blatantly false. Granted, in a virtual-memory system, allocation limits are rather high. In fact, the computer is not even limited by the size of its physical memory. The only way memory allocation can fail is if you run out of space in the swap file on your disk, which is not something unheard of in the world of huge applications and multimedia files. An industrial-strength program should protect itself from this possibility. The question is, how? What should a program do when the call to new fails? First of all, if we don't do anything about it (as indeed we haven't in this program), the system will terminate the application with extreme prejudice. That's totally unacceptable!

The next, slightly more acceptable thing would be to print a good-bye message and exit. For a program such as our calculator, that might actually be the right thing. It's not like the user runs the risk of losing hours of work when the calculator unexpectedly exits.

There are a few different ways to globally intercept a memory failure. One is to catch the std::bad_alloc exception (more about this in a moment); another is to create your own "new handler" and register it with the runtime at the beginning of your program. The function set_new_handler is defined in the header <new>. It accepts a pointer to a function that's to be called in case new fails. Here's an example of a user-defined new handler:

```
void NewHandler ()
{
  std::cerr << "Out of memory\n";
  exit (1);
}
```

It displays a message and exits by calling a special function, `exit` from `<cstdlib>`. This is how you register your handler—preferably at the beginning of `main`.

```
set_new_handler (&NewHandler);
```

> You might have to modify this code if you have a nonstandard-compliant compiler. For instance, in Microsoft VC++ 6.0 there is a function called `_set_new_handler` that serves a similar purpose. Its declaration is in `<new.h>`. You'll also have to change the signature of the function you pass to it—to `int NewHandler (size_t size)`.

Although in many cases such a solution is perfectly acceptable, most commercial programs require more sophisticated techniques. Just try to imagine a word processor or a compiler suddenly exiting without giving you a chance to save your work. (Sounds familiar?!)

What happens when memory allocation fails? In standard C++, the operator `new` generates an *exception*. So let's talk about exceptions.

10.1 Exceptions

In C++, we deal with exceptional failures using exceptions. Essentially it is up to the programmer to decide what is exceptional and what isn't. A memory allocation failure is considered exceptional, as is a failed disk read or write. On the other hand, "file not found" or "end of file" are considered normal events. When an exceptional condition occurs, the program can `throw` an exception. A `throw` bypasses the normal flow of control and lands us in the `catch` part of the nearest enclosing `try`/`catch` block. So `throw` really behaves like a *nonlocal* `goto` (nonlocal meaning that the control can jump across function calls). Using the `goto` control flow device is strongly discouraged because it's extremely error prone and creates a maintenance nightmare. We'll see an example of its use on page 229.

To better understand the use of exceptions, let's have a fresh look at our calculator. The only exceptional condition that we can anticipate is memory allocation failure. As I mentioned before, when `new` is not able to allocate the requested memory, it throws an exception of the type `std::bad_alloc`.

> At the time of this writing many compilers still haven't caught up with the standard. But don't despair; you can work around this problem by providing your own `new`-failure handler that throws an exception.

```
class bad_alloc {};
int NewHandler (size_t size)
{
  throw bad_alloc;
  return 0;
}
```

Then, if you're using the Microsoft 6.0 compiler, call _set_new_handler (&NewHandler) first thing in main. (Notice that the handler creates an object of the type bad_alloc by calling its default constructor, which does nothing. The type bad_alloc itself is a dummy—we define it only to be able to distinguish between different types of exceptions.)

Script 28   If you don't catch this exception, the program will terminate in a rather unpleasant way. So we better catch it. The program is prepared to catch an exception as soon as the flow of control enters a try/catch block. So let's open our try block in main. We have to do it before we construct the symbol table, whose constructor does the first memory allocations. At the end of the try block we have to start a catch block that does the actual catching of the exceptions.

```
int main ()
{
  try
  {
    char buf [maxBuf];
    Status status;
    SymbolTable symTab;
    Function::Table funTab (symTab);
    Store store (symTab);
    ...
  }
  catch (std::bad_alloc)
  {
    std::cerr << "Out of memory!\n";
  }
  catch (...)
  {
    std::cerr << "Internal error\n";
  }
}
```

Here we have two catch blocks, one after another. The first will catch only the bad_alloc type of exception; the second one, with the ellipsis, will catch all the rest. The "internal error" may be a general protection fault or division by zero in our program—not that we plan on allowing such bugs! But it's always better to display a message and exit than to let the system kill us and display its own message.

Always enclose the main body of your program within a `try`/`catch` block.

Figure 10.1 illustrates the flow of control after an exception is thrown during the allocation of SumNode inside Parser::Expr that was called by Parser::Parse, which was called from within the try block inside main.

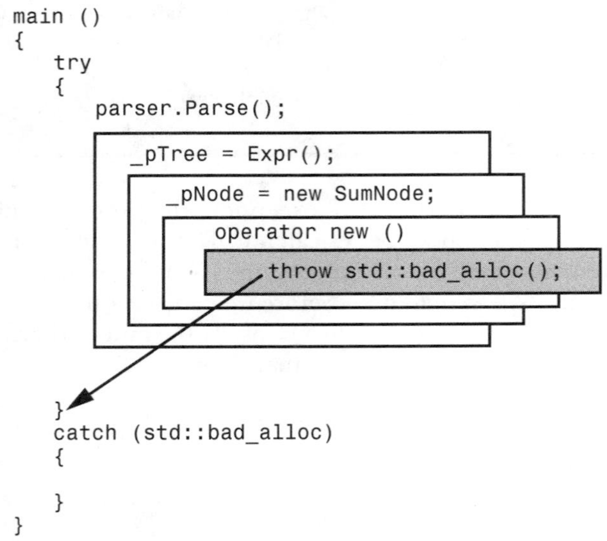

```
main ()
{
    try
    {
        parser.Parse();
        _pTree = Expr();
            _pNode = new SumNode;
                operator new ()
                    throw std::bad_alloc();


    }
    catch (std::bad_alloc)
    {

    }
}
```

Figure 10.1   Throw and catch across multiple function calls

The use of exceptions solves the problem of error propagation (see the box) by bypassing the normal flow of control.

In the old times, memory allocation failure used to be reported by new returning a null pointer. Programmers who wanted to protect their programs from catastrophic failures had to test the result of every allocation. Not only was it tedious and error-prone, but most of the time it wasn't immediately clear what to do when such a failure occurred. All a low-level routine could do is to stop executing and return an error code to the calling routine. That, of course, put the burden of checking for error returns on the caller. In most cases the caller had little choice but to pass the same error code to its caller, and so on. Eventually, at some higher level—maybe even in main—somebody had the right context to do something about the problem, e.g., report it to the user, try to salvage any work, and maybe exit. Not only was such methodology error-prone (forgetting to check for error returns), but it contributed dangerously to the obfuscation of the main flow of control.

10.2 Stack Unwinding

Many a scheme was invented to deal with the cleanup during traditional error propagation. Many procedures allocate and then free memory. When an error is discovered, whatever memory has already been allocated must be freed before an emergency error return is performed. Since in many cases memory resources are freed at the bottom of a procedure, one method is to use gotos to jump to the bottom whenever an error is detected. A typical procedure without error propagation might look like this:

```
void foo ()
{
  Type1 * p1 = new Type1;
  call1 (p1);
  Type2 * p2 = new Type2;
  call2 (p2);
  delete p2;
  delete p1;
}
```

With error propagation and cleanup it becomes this:

```
ERRCODE foo ()
{
  ERRCODE status = errNoError;
  Type1 * p1 = 0;
  Type2 * p2 = 0;
  p1 = new Type1;
  if (p1 == 0)
  {
    status = errOutOfMemory;
    goto Cleanup;
  }
  status = call1 (p1);
  if (status != errNoError)
    goto Cleanup;
  p2 = new Type2;
  if (p2 == 0)
  {
    status = errOutOfMemory;
    goto Cleanup;
  }
  status = call2 (p2);
  if (status != errNoError)
    goto Cleanup;
  // More of the same
Cleanup:
  delete p2;
  delete p1;
  return status;
}
```

Here `Cleanup` is a label that is used as a target of `goto`s. All this code is just to allocate and destroy two objects and make two function calls.

If you think I'm exaggerating, don't! I've seen file after file of commercial code written in this style. Incidentally, if somebody later adds a `return` statement in the middle of such a procedure, the whole cleanup logic will be totally invalidated.

Wait, it gets worse before it gets better! Using exceptions to propagate errors doesn't immediately solve this problem. You don't get a chance to clean up your allocations unless you put `try`/`catch` pairs in every procedure, or so it seems. The straightforward translation of the above example would look like this:

```cpp
void foo ()
{
  Type1 * p1 = 0;
  Type2 * p2 = 0;
  try
  {
    p1 = new Type1;
    call1 (p1);
    p2 = new Type2;
    call2 (p2);
    // More of the same
  }
  catch (...)
  {
    delete p2;
    delete p1;
    throw;
  }
  delete p2;
  delete p1;
}
```

The `throw` with no argument rethrows the same exception that was caught in the enclosing `catch` block.

This code looks a little cleaner, but it's still very error-prone. Pointers are zeroed in the beginning of the procedure, assigned to in the middle, and deallocated at the end (notice the ugly, but necessary, repetition of the two `delete` statements). There's plenty of room for mistakes. At this point you might feel desperate enough to start thinking of switching to Java or some other language that offers automatic garbage collection, but before you do, read on.

There is a mechanism in C++ that just begs to be used for cleanup: the pairing of constructors and destructors of automatic objects. Once an object is constructed in some local scope, it is always automatically destroyed when the flow of control exits that scope. The important thing is that it really doesn't matter how the scope is exited: the flow of control may naturally reach the closing bracket, or it may jump out of the scope through a `goto`, a `break`, or a `return` statement. Automatic objects are *always* destroyed. And yes—this is very important—when the scope is exited because of an exception, automatic objects are cleaned up too!

Look again at Figure 10.1—all the stack-based objects in all the nested scopes between the outer `try` block and the inner `throw` block are automatically destroyed, and their destructors are executed in the inverse order of construction.

I'll show you in a moment how to harness this powerful mechanism, called *stack unwinding,* to do all the cleanup for us. But first let's consider a few tricky situations.

For instance, what happens when an exception is thrown during construction? Imagine an object with two embeddings. In its constructor the two embedded objects are constructed, either implicitly or explicitly (through the preamble). Now suppose that the first embedding has been fully constructed, but the constructor of the second embedding throws an exception. What do you think should happen? Shouldn't the first embedding be destroyed in the process of unwinding? Right! That's exactly what happens—the destructors of all fully constructed subobjects are executed during unwinding.

What if the object is dynamically allocated using `new` and its constructor throws an exception? Shouldn't the memory allocated for this object be freed? Right again! The memory allocated by `new` is automatically freed if the constructor throws an exception.

What if the heap object has subobjects and the constructor of the nth embedding throws an exception? Shouldn't the $n-1$ subobjects be destroyed and the memory freed? That's right—that's what happens!

Remember the rules of object construction? First the base class is constructed, then all the embedded objects, and finally the body of the constructor is executed. If at any stage of the construction an exception is thrown, the whole process is reversed and all the *completely constructed* parts of the object are destroyed (in the reverse order of construction).

What if an exception is thrown during the construction of the nth element of an array? Shouldn't all the $n-1$ fully constructed elements be destroyed? Certainly! That's exactly what happens.

It all just works!

These rules apply whether the object (array) is allocated on the stack or on the heap. The only difference is that once a heap object is *fully constructed,* it (and its parts) will not take part in the process of stack unwinding.

There is only one situation when stack unwinding might not do the right thing—when an exception is thrown from within a destructor. So don't even think of allocating some scratch memory, saving a file to disk, or doing any of the many error-prone actions in a destructor. A destructor is supposed to quietly clean up.

> **Never perform any action that could throw an exception inside a destructor.**

Now to our symbol table.

```
class SymbolTable
{
```

```
...
private:
  HTable            _htab;
  std::vector<int>  _offStr;
  StringBuffer      _strBuf;
};
```

It has three embedded objects, all of which have nontrivial constructors. The hash table allocates an array of lists, the vector of offsets might allocate some initial storage, and the string buffer allocates a buffer for strings. Any one of these allocations could fail and throw an exception.

If the constructor of the hash table fails, there is no cleanup (unless the whole SymbolTable object was allocated using new—in that case the memory for it is automatically freed). If the hash table has been successfully constructed but the vector constructor fails, the destructor of the hash table is executed during stack unwinding. Finally, if the exception occurs in the constructor of the string buffer, the destructors of the vector and the hash table are called (in that order).

The constructor of the hash table itself could have some potentially interesting modes of failure.

```
HTable::HTable (int size)
  : _size (size)
{
  _aList = new List<int> [size];
}
```

Assume, for the sake of this argument, that the constructor of List<int> is nontrivial (for example, it allocates memory). The array of 65 (hTabSize) lists is constructed in the calculator. Imagine that the constructor of the eighth list throws an exception. This will trigger stack unwinding and the destructors of the first seven entries of the array will automatically be called, after which the memory for the whole array will be freed. If, on the other hand, all 65 constructors succeed, the construction of the hash table will be successful and the only way of getting rid of the array will be through the destructor of the hash table.

But since the hash table is an embedded object inside the symbol table, and the symbol table is an automatic object inside the try block in main, its destruction is guaranteed. Lucky accident? Not really. Let's have another look at main.

```
int main ()
{
  try
  {
    ...
    SymbolTable symTab;
    Function::Table funTab (symTab);
    Store store (symTab);
    ...
    {
```

```
            Scanner scanner (buf);
            Parser  parser (scanner, store, funTab, symTab);
            ...
        }
    }
    catch (...)
    {
        ...
    }
}
```

It looks like all the resources associated with the symbol table, the function table, the store, the scanner, and the parser are *by design* guaranteed to be released. We'll see in a moment that this is indeed the case.

10.3 Resources

So far we've been dealing with only one kind of resource—memory. Memory is acquired from the runtime system by calling new, and released by calling delete. There are many other kinds of resources: file handles, semaphores, reference counts, and so on (you'll see plenty of examples in the upcoming chapters on Windows programming). They all have one thing in common—they have to be acquired and released. Hence the definition:

> **A resource is something that can be acquired and released.**

The acquiring part is easy—it's the releasing that's a problem. An unreleased resource, or resource leak, can be anywhere from annoying (the program uses more memory than is necessary) to fatal (the program deadlocks because of an unreleased semaphore). We can guarantee the matching of the acquisition and the release of resources by following the simple *Rule of Acquisition:*

> **Acquire resources in constructors; release resources in matching destructors.**

> As far as I know, this idea was first introduced in 1990 in *The Annotated C++ Reference Manual* by Margaret Ellis and Bjarne Stroustrup. The authors described it in the context of (then experimental) exception handling. In subsequent books Stroustrup calls this technique "resource acquisition is initialization."

In particular, the acquisition of memory through new should only be done in a constructor of some object, with the matching delete in its destructor. You'll find such matching pairs in the constructors and destructors of FunctionTable and HTable (and in std::vector<T>, if you look it up in <vector>).

It so happens that, at some point, I had an implementation of SymbolTable that didn't use StringBuffer but rather dealt directly with an array of chars. Its constructor and destructor looked like this:

```
SymbolTable::SymbolTable (int size)
  : _size (size),_curId (0),_curStrOff (0),_htab (size+1)
{
  _offStr = new int [size];
  _bufSize = size * 10;
  _strBuf = new char [_bufSize];
}

SymbolTable::~SymbolTable ()
{
  delete []_offStr;
  delete []_strBuf;
}
```

The Rule of Acquisition was being followed, but the code was not exception-safe. Consider what would happen if the second allocation (of _strBuf) failed. The first allocation of _offStr would never be freed—its memory would leak.

To prevent such situations when programming with exceptions, we should keep in mind the following supplement to the Rule of Acquisition:

> **Allocation of resources should either be the last thing in the constructor or be followed by exception-safe code.**

If more than one resource needs to be allocated in a constructor, you should create subobjects to hold these resources. As embedded objects, they will be automatically destroyed even if the constructor fails before completion (see the discussion on page 231).

As you can see, there are many different arguments that lead to the same conclusion—it makes sense to separate subobjects! We can even enhance our rule of thumb that suggested the separation of subobjects when a class had too many data members: Create subobjects when more than one data member points to a resource. In our symbol table it was the introduction of the following two subobjects that did the job.

```
std::vector<int> _aOffStr;
StringBuffer     _bufStr;
```

10.4   Ownership of Resources

An object or a block of code owns a resource if it is responsible for its release. The concept of *ownership of resources* is central to the resource management paradigm. The owns-a relationship between objects parallels the more traditional is-a (inheritance) and has-a (embedding) relationships. There are several forms of ownership.

A block of code owns all the automatic objects defined in its scope. The job of releasing these resources (calling the destructors) is fully automated.

Another form of ownership is by embedding. An object owns all the objects embedded in it. The job of releasing these resources is automated as well (the destructor of the outer object calls the destructors of the inner objects).

In both cases, the lifetime of the resource is limited to the lifetime of the embedding entity: the activation of a given scope or the lifetime of an embedding object. Because of that, the compiler can fully automate destructor calls.

The same cannot be said of dynamically allocated objects, which are always accessed through pointers. During their lifetimes, pointers can point to a sequence of resources, and several pointers can point to the same resource. The release of dynamically allocated resources is not automated (in other words, there is no *garbage collection* in C++). If the object is being passed from pointer to pointer and the ownership relationships cannot be easily traced, the programmer is usually in for trouble. The symptoms may be various: uninitialized pointers, memory leaks, double deletions, and so on.

Imposing the Rule of Acquisition clarifies the ownership relationships and guarantees the absence of most errors of the types we have just listed. A block of code can only own its automatic objects—"no naked" (not embedded in objects) pointers should be allowed there. An object can own other objects by embedding as well as through pointers. In the latter case, though, the acquisition of the resources (initialization of pointers) has to take place in the object's constructor and their release in the destructor. Constructors are the only places where a naked pointer may appear, and then only for a very short time (see the supplement to the Rule of Acquisition).

Notice that if all resources have owners, they are guaranteed to be released. The objects that own resources are either defined in the global scope, in a local scope, or are owned by other objects—either through embeddings or through dynamic allocation in constructors. Global objects are destroyed after the exit from main, local objects are destroyed upon the exit from their scope, and embeddings are destroyed either when the enclosing object is destroyed or when the enclosing constructor is aborted because of an exception. Since all the owners are eventually destroyed, all the resources are eventually freed.

You have a formal guarantee that no resources will be leaked.

10.5   Access to Resources

A block of code or an object may operate on a resource without owning it, that is, without being responsible for its release. When granting or passing access, as opposed to ownership, one should, whenever possible, try to use references. We have already learned that the has-access-to relationship is best expressed using references. A reference cannot express ownership because an object cannot be deleted through a reference (at least not without some trickery).

There *are* cases when using a reference is awkward or impossible. It's only then that we should use a *weak pointer*—a pointer that doesn't express ownership. In C++ there is no syntactic difference between strong and weak pointers, so this distinction should be made by the appropriate commenting of the code.

The has-access-to relationship (either through a reference or through a weak pointer) is graphically represented by the dotted arrow in Figure 10.2.

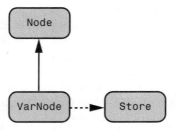

Figure 10.2   Graphical representation of the has-access-to relationship between VarNode and Store

10.6   Smart Pointers

Our calculator was implemented without any regard for resource management. There are naked pointers all over the place, especially in the parser. Consider this fragment.

```
do
{
  scanner.Accept();
  Node * pRight = Term ();
  if (pRight == 0)
     break;
  pMultiNode->AddChild (pRight, (token == tPlus));
  token = _scanner.Token();
} while (token == tPlus || token == tMinus);
```

The call to `Term` returns a node pointer that is temporarily stored in `pRight`. Then the `MultiNode`'s method `AddChild` is called, and we know very well that it might try to resize its array of children. If the reallocation fails and an exception is thrown, the tree pointed to by `pRight` will never be deallocated. We have a memory leak!

Script 29   Before I show you the systematic solution to this problem, let's try the obvious thing. Since our problem stems from the presence of a naked pointer, let's create a special purpose class to encapsulate it. This class should acquire the node in its constructor and release it in the destructor. In addition to that, we would like an object of this class to behave like a regular pointer. Here's how we can do it.

```cpp
class NodePtr
{
public:
    NodePtr (Node * pNode) : _p (pNode) {}
    ~NodePtr () { delete _p; }
    Node * operator->() const { return _p; }
    Node & operator * () const { return *_p; }
    bool IsNull () const { return _p == 0; }
private:
    Node * _p;
};
```

Such objects are called *safe* or *smart* pointers. The pointer-like behavior is implemented by overloading the pointer-access and pointer-dereference operators. This clever device makes an object behave like a pointer. In particular, one can call all the public methods (and access all public data members, if there were any) of `Node` by "dereferencing" an object of the type `NodePtr`.

```cpp
{
    Node * pNode = Expr ();
    NodePtr smartNode (pNode);
    double x = smartNode->Calc (); // Pointer-like behavior
    ...
    // Automatic destruction of pSmartNode.
    // pNode is deleted by its destructor.
}
```

We invoke the `Node`'s method `Calc` by applying a pointer access operator to `smartNode`. Since `smartNode` is not a pointer, the compiler picks up the overloaded `operator->` from the definition of `NodePtr` and dereferences its return value, which *is* a pointer.

Of course, a smart pointer by itself will not solve our problems in the parser. After all, we don't want the nodes created by calling `Term` or `Factor` to be automatically destroyed upon normal exit from the scope. We want to be able to build them into the parse tree whose lifetime extends well beyond the local scope of these methods. To do that we will have to relax our Rule of Acquisition.

10.7 Ownership Transfer: First Attempt

When the lifetime of a given resource can be mapped into the lifetime of some scope, we encapsulate this resource in a smart pointer and we're done. When this can't be done, we have to somehow pass the resource between scopes. There are two possible directions for such transfer: up or down. A resource may be passed up (returned) from a procedure to the caller, or it can be passed down (as an argument) from a caller to the procedure. We assume that before being passed, the resource is owned by some type of owner object (e.g., a smart pointer).

Passing a resource down to a procedure is relatively easy. We can simply pass a reference to the owner object (a smart pointer, in our case) and let the procedure acquire the ownership from it. We'll add a special method, Release, to our smart pointer, to release the ownership of the resource.

```
Node * NodePtr::Release ()
{
  Node * tmp = _p;
  _p = 0;
  return tmp;
}
```

Notice that Release zeros the internal pointer, so that the delete in the NodePtr's destructor will no longer destroy the node.

We will also need a way to pass the ownership of a resource to an existing NodePtr.

```
void Reset (Node * pNode)
{
  delete _p;
  _p = pNode;
}
```

Passing a resource up is a little trickier. Technically, there's no problem. We just have to call Release to acquire the resource from the owner and then return the naked resource. For instance, here's how we *could* return a node from Parser::Expr.

```
Node * Parser::Expr ()
{
  // Parse a term
  NodePtr pNode (Term ());
  ...
  return pNode.Release ();
}
```

What makes it tricky is that now the caller of Expr has a naked pointer. Of course, if the caller is smart, he or she will immediately find a new owner for this pointer—presumably a smart pointer—just like we did a moment ago with the result of Term. But it's one thing to expect programmers to take special care of the naked pointers returned by new and Release, and quite a different story to expect the same level of vigilance with every single procedure that happens to return a pointer, because it's not immediately obvious which ones are returning strong pointers (that are supposed to be deleted), and which return weak pointers (that must *not* be deleted).

Of course, you can study the code of every procedure you are calling and find out what's expected from you. You might hope that procedures that transfer ownership will be appropriately commented in their header files. Or you might rely on some special naming convention—for instance, start the names of all resource-returning procedures with the prefix "Query" (been there!).

Fortunately, you don't have to do any of these horrible things. There is a better way. Read on!

To summarize, even though there are some big holes in our methodology, we have accomplished no mean feat. We have encapsulated all the resources following the Rule of Acquisition. This will guarantee automatic cleanup in the face of exceptions. We have a crude method of transferring resources up and down between owners.

10.8 Ownership Transfer: Second Attempt

So far, our attempt at resource transfer through procedure boundaries has been to release the resource from its owner, pass it in its "naked" form, and then immediately encapsulate it again. The obvious danger is that although the passing happens within a few nanoseconds in a running program, the code that accepts the resource may be written months or even years after the code that releases it. The two sides of the procedure barrier don't necessarily talk to each other.

But who says that we have to "undress" the resource for the duration of the transfer? Can't we pass it together with its encapsulator? Let's see what can be done.

First of all, if we were to pass a smart pointer "as is" from a procedure to the caller, we'd end up with a dangling pointer. Look at this example:

```
NodePtr Parser::Expr ()
{
  // Parse a term
  NodePtr pNode = Term (); // <- Assignment
  ...
  return pNode; // <- By value
}
NodePtr Parser::Term ()
{
  NodePtr pNode = Factor (); // <- Assignment
  ...
  return pNode; // <- By value
}
```

Remember how objects are returned from procedures? First, a copy constructor is called to construct a temporary object, then the assignment operator is called to copy this temporary object into the caller's variable. If an object doesn't define its own copy constructor (or assignment operator), the compiler provides one for it. The default copy constructor/assignment operator makes a shallow copy of the object. The default copying of a smart pointer doesn't copy the object it points to.

That's fine—we don't want a copy of our resource. The problem is that we end up with two smart pointers pointing to the same resource. That's bad in itself. But to make things even worse, one of them is going out of scope—the smart pointer defined inside the procedure. It will delete the object it points to, not realizing that its clone sibling has a pointer to it, too. We've returned a smart pointer, all right, but it points to a deleted object—it's a *dangling* pointer.

We somehow need to enforce the rule that there can only be *one owner* of a given resource at any given time. If somebody tries to clone a smart pointer, we have to steal the resource from the original owner. We *can* do that if we define our own copy constructor and assignment operator.

```
NodePtr::NodePtr (NodePtr & pSource)
  : _p (pSource.Release ())
{}

NodePtr & NodePtr::operator= (NodePtr & pSource)
{
  if (_p != pSource._p)
  {
    delete _p;
    _p = pSource.Release ();
  }
}
```

Notice that these are *not* your usual copy constructor and assignment operator. For one, they don't take const references to their source objects. They can't, because they modify them. And modify they do, by zeroing their contents.

Since we can't really call it "copy semantics," we'll call it "transfer semantics." We can give a class *transfer semantics* by giving it a "transfer constructor" and an overloaded assignment operator, such that both these operations take away the ownership of a resource from their arguments.

Script 30   In order to generalize this idea to an arbitrary pointer type, we need a template class—a smart pointer with transfer semantics. But instead of creating it from scratch, we'll use the one that's already implemented in the C++ standard library. The template is called auto_ptr, and it's defined in the header file <memory>. So, for instance, instead of NodePtr we'll use std::auto_ptr<Node>.

> The C++ standards committee struggled with the definition of `auto_ptr` almost until the last moment before releasing the final document.[1] So don't be surprised if your compiler's library contains an older version of this template. For instance, you might discover that your `auto_ptr` contains an ownership flag besides the pointer. Such implementations are now obsolete.

Let's begin with `UniNode`, which has to accept the ownership of its child node in the constructor. But now the child node is passed in an `auto_ptr`. We could retrieve it from the `auto_ptr` by calling its `release` method. We could then store the pointer and delete it in the destructor of `UniNode`—all in the spirit of resource management. But there's a much better way. We can embed an `auto_ptr` inside `UniNode` and let *it* deal with ownership chores.

```
class UniNode: public Node
{
public:
   UniNode (std::auto_ptr<Node> & pChild)
      : _pChild (pChild) // <- "Transfer" constructor
   {}
protected:
   std::auto_ptr<Node> _pChild;
};
```

Look what happened—since embeddings are destroyed automatically, there no longer is a need for `UniNode` to have a destructor. Also, we don't have to call `release` on the argument to the constructor, because we can pass it directly to the "transfer" constructor of our embedded `auto_ptr`.

This change propagates easily down to `FunNode` and `UMinusNode`. For instance:

```
class UMinusNode: public UniNode
{
public:
   UMinusNode (std::auto_ptr<Node> & pNode)
      : UniNode (pNode)
   {}
   double Calc () const;
};
```

Internally, the implementation of `UMinusNode::Calc` remains unchanged, because the syntax for accessing a pointer and `auto_ptr` is identical.

We can immediately do the same conversion with `BinNode` and `AssignNode`. `BinNode` contains two `auto_ptrs`.

---

1. ISO/IEC 14882: 1998(E), *Programming Languages—C++*.

```cpp
class BinNode: public Node
{
public:
  BinNode (std::auto_ptr<Node> & pLeft,
           std::auto_ptr<Node> & pRight)
     : _pLeft (pLeft), _pRight (pRight)
  {}
protected:
  std::auto_ptr<Node> _pLeft;
  std::auto_ptr<Node> _pRight;
};

class AssignNode : public BinNode
{
public:
  AssignNode (std::auto_ptr<Node> & pLeft,
              std::auto_ptr<Node> & pRight)
    : BinNode (pLeft, pRight)
  {
    assert (_pLeft->IsLvalue ());
  }
  double Calc () const;
};
```

As before, we don't need an explicit destructor anymore.

We can continue our destructor derby with the Parser itself. It can own its parsing tree through auto_ptr, and gone is its explicit destructor.

And now let's look at the Parser::Expr method after it's been generously sprinkled with auto_ptrs. Notice how we access the pointer stored inside auto_ptr by calling the method get.

```cpp
std::auto_ptr<Node> Parser::Expr ()
{
  std::auto_ptr<Node> pNode = Term ();
  if (pNode.get () == 0)
      return pNode;

  EToken token = _scanner.Token ();
  if (token == tPlus || token == tMinus)
  {
    // Expr := Term { ('+' | '-') Term }
    std::auto_ptr<MultiNode> pMultiNode (
      new SumNode (pNode));
    do
    {
      _scanner.Accept ();
      std::auto_ptr<Node> pRight = Term ();
      if (pRight.get () == 0)
        return pNode;
      pMultiNode->AddChild (pRight, (token == tPlus));
      token = _scanner.Token ();
    } while (token == tPlus || token == tMinus);
```

```
      // With member template support
      pNode = pMultiNode; // <- Up-casting!
    }
    else if (token == tAssign)
    {
      // Expr := Term = Expr
      _scanner.Accept ();
      std::auto_ptr<Node> pRight = Expr ();
      if (pRight.get () == 0)
        return pNode;
      // Provided the Term is an lvalue
      if (pNode->IsLvalue ())
      {
        // Assignment node
        pNode = std::auto_ptr<Node> (
                new AssignNode (pNode, pRight));
      }
      else
      {
        _status = stError;
        pNode = Expr ();
      }
    }
    return pNode;
}
```

There is one tricky point in this code that requires some explaining. We are dealing with two types of auto_ptrs—one encapsulating Node and another encapsulating MultiNode (only MultiNode has the AddChild method). At some point, when we are done adding children, we must convert a pointer to MultiNode to a pointer to Node. With pointers it was no trouble, because MultiNode "is-a" Node (they are related through inheritance). But auto_ptr<Node> is a totally different class from auto_ptr<MultiNode>. These are two separate instantiations of the template auto_ptr. So this simple line of code,

```
    pNode = pMultiNode; // <- Up casting!
```

hides some pretty interesting stuff. In fact, there is a special mechanism called a *member template* that's used inside auto_ptr to make possible these types of conversions (it's called *up casting*, because it casts the pointer *up* the class hierarchy). Look at the following code—a new transfer constructor and a new assignment operator are added to auto_ptr template.[2]

---

2. The actual library implementation is even more complicated. Since transfer semantics requires non-const reference arguments, this simple-minded implementation would not work for temporary auto_ptr objects (you can't take a non-const reference to a temporary object). Such temporary objects are created, for instance, when returning auto_ptr from a procedure by value. The trick used in the C++ standard library is to introduce an intermediate class called auto_ptr_ref. But we are getting ahead of ourselves.

```
template<class T>
class auto_ptr
{
public:
   ...
   // "Transfer" from derived class
   template<class U>
   auto_ptr (auto_ptr<U> & pSrc)
   {
     _p = pSrc.release ();
   }
   // Assignment of derived class
   template<class U>
   auto_ptr & operator= (auto_ptr<U> & pSrc)
   {
     if (this != &pSrc)
       _p = pSrc.release ();
     return *this;
   }
};
```

These new methods are templates themselves. They are parameterized by another type, U, different from the type T that parameterizes auto_ptr.

The new transfer constructor can be used to construct auto_ptr of one type, parameterized by T, from auto_ptr of another type, parameterized by U. So, in fact, this constructor is a template parameterized by two types, T and U.

The new overload of the assignment operator can accept auto_ptr parameterized by an arbitrary type U. It's this override that's invoked in the statement

```
pNode = pMultiNode; // Up casting from MultiNode to Node
```

Here, pNode is of the type auto_ptr<Node> and pMultiNode is of the type auto_ptr<MultiNode>. The compiler will automatically try to instantiate the appropriate implementation of the method auto_ptr<Node>::operator= (auto_ptr<MultiNode> &). And here's where type safety kicks in. When the compiler generates the line from the template of operator=

```
_p = pSrc.release ();
```

it has to assign a pointer to MultiNode returned from pSrc.release, to a pointer to Node, _p. The pointer conversion works because of the is-a relationship between the two classes. Had we tried the opposite conversion,

```
pMultiNode = pNode; // <- Error! Down casting
```

the compiler would generate an error, because it would fail in the conversion of Node* to MultiNode* during the instantiation of the operator= template.

The bottom line is that the assignment of `auto_ptrs` will only work for those types for which the assignments of pointers works. Notice that the types don't have to be related by inheritance. Since you can, for instance, implicitly convert a pointer to `Node` to a `void` pointer, it follows, then, that you can convert `auto_ptr<Node>` to `auto_ptr<void*>`.

If your compiler doesn't support member templates, don't despair! I have a workaround for you. Since you won't be able to do implicit `auto_ptr` conversion, you'll have to do it explicitly.

```
pNode = up_cast<Node> (pMultiNode);
```

I created the `up_cast` function template, parameterized by two types, `To` and `From`.

```
template<class To, class From>
std::auto_ptr<To> up_cast (std::auto_ptr<From> & from)
{
  return std::auto_ptr<To> (from.release ());
}
```

Notice that when I invoke this template, I don't have to specify the second type, `From`. The compiler can figure it out by looking at the type of the argument (`pMultiNode`, in this case). As before, the type checking is done by the compiler when instantiating this template for the requested pair of types.

Now it's pretty straightforward to convert the rest of the `Parser` to use `auto_ptrs`. There are just a few things to look for.

You can't directly test `auto_ptr` against zero. You'll have to get the pointer from it using its `get` method.

You'll have to include `Tree.h` in `Parser.h` (you should get a compiler warning if you don't). The reason is that since there no longer is an explicit `Parser` destructor, the compiler will have to provide a default one. But since `Parser` contains `auto_ptr` to `Node`, the default destructor of `Parser` must call the destructor of `auto_ptr`, which in turn should delete the `Node`. At this point the compiler needs to find out what kind of a destructor is defined for `Node`. That information is only available in the header file where `Node` is defined—`Tree.h`. The crucial point is that the compiler will realize the need for a default `Parser` destructor while scanning the file `Parser.h`, and that's where the `include` statement of `Tree.h` must go.

Script 31   If it's important (and it often is!) not to include too many files in a header file, there is another workaround. Just provide the `Parser` with an empty non-inline destructor. The compiler will see the *declaration* of this destructor when scanning the file `Parser.h` and will conclude that there's no need to create a default one on the spot. Thus there will be no need to include Tree.h in Parser.h. When scanning the implementation file, Parser.cpp, the compiler will find the *definition* of the (empty) destructor and will embellish it with all the default destructor calls, including the one to auto_ptr::~auto_ptr. Only at that point will the compiler need to see the definition of Node. So instead of including Tree.h in the header file, we'll include it in the implementation file.

To summarize: Memory resources can be safely kept and transferred from one point to another using auto_ptr*s. You can easily transform an existing program to use resource management techniques. Just search your project for all calls to* new *and make sure that all the pointers returned by* new *are safely tucked inside* auto_ptr*s.*

10.9   Safe Containers

We are not done yet. There are still some parts of our program that are not 100% resource-safe. Let's go back to one such part, the class MultiNode.

```
class MultiNode: public Node
{
public:
  MultiNode (std::auto_ptr<Node> & pNode)
  {
    AddChild (pNode, true);
  }
  ~MultiNode ();
  void AddChild (std::auto_ptr<Node> & pNode,
                 bool isPositive)
  {
    _aChild.push_back (pNode.release ());
    _aIsPositive.push_back (isPositive);
  }
protected:
  std::vector<Node*> _aChild;
  std::vector<bool>  _aIsPositive;
};
```

Let's analyze what happens inside AddChild. We call release on pNode and then immediately call push_back on a vector. We know that push_back might reallocate the vector's internal array. A reallocation involves memory allocation which, as we know, might fail.

Do you see the problem? The pointer that we have just released from pNode will be caught naked in the middle of an allocation failure. This pointer will never get a chance to be properly deleted. We have a memory leak.

What is needed here is for the vector to be reallocated before the pointer is released. We could force a potential reallocation by first calling

```
_aChild.reserve (_aChild.size () + 1);
```

But that's an awkward solution (besides, it puts the burden on the programmer). So let's rethink the problem.

The culprit here is the vector of pointers, which has no notion of ownership. Notice that the deallocation of nodes is done not in the vector's destructor but is done explicitly in the MultiNode's destructor. What we need is some type of a vector of pointers that really *owns* the objects stored in it.

Could we use a vector of auto_ptrs?

```
std::vector<auto_ptr<Node> > _aChild;
```

(Notice the space between the two greater than signs. If we remove this space, the compiler will confuse it with the right-shift operator. It's just another quirk of C++ syntax.) Let's see, when we push_back auto_ptr on such a vector, the reallocation will definitely happen *before* the "transfer" assignment. Moreover, we would get rid of the explicit MultiNode destructor, because the vector's destructor would destroy all its auto_ptrs which, in turn, would destroy all the nodes.

Although in principle this is a valid solution to our problem, in practice it's hardly acceptable. The trouble is that the vector's interface is totally unsuitable for storing objects with transfer semantics. The implementation of a vector assumes that it's okay to pass or return items by value. This is fine, except that returning auto_ptr by value involves a resource transfer. Similarly, if you try to iterate over such a vector, you will get a resource transfer every time you dereference an iterator. So, unless you are very careful, you're bound to get some nasty surprises from a vector of auto_ptrs.

Script 32   At this point you might expect me to come up with some clever data structure from the C++ standard library that does exactly what we want. Unfortunately, there are no ownership-aware containers in the C++ standard library. We'll have to build one ourselves. Luckily, we have all the necessary tools. So let's start with the interface.

```
template <class T>
class auto_vector
{
public:
  typedef std::size_t size_t;
public:
  explicit auto_vector (size_t capacity = 0);
  ~auto_vector ();
  size_t size () const;
  T const * operator [] (size_t i) const;
  T * operator [] (size_t i);
  void assign (size_t i, std::auto_ptr<T> & p);
  void assign_direct (size_t i, T * p);
  void push_back (std::auto_ptr<T> & p);
  std::auto_ptr<T> pop_back ();
};
```

Notice my rather defensive design. I could have provided an array-access operator that would return an lvalue, but I decided against it. Instead, if we want to set a value, we have to use one of the `assign` or `assign_direct` methods. My philosophy is that resource transfer shouldn't be taken lightly and, besides, it isn't needed all that often—`auto_vector` is usually filled using the `push_back` method anyway.

As far as implementation goes, we can simply use a dynamic array of `auto_ptrs`.

```
template <class T>
class auto_vector
{
  ~auto_vector () { delete []_arr; }
private:
  void grow (size_t reqCapacity);
  std::auto_ptr<T> *_arr;
  size_t           _capacity;
  size_t           _end;
};
```

The `grow` method allocates a larger array of `auto_ptr<T>`, transfers all the items from the old array, swaps it in, and deletes the old array.

```
template <class T>
void auto_vector<T>::grow (size_t reqCapacity)
{
  size_t newCapacity = 2 * _capacity;
  if (reqCapacity > newCapacity)
      newCapacity = reqCapacity;
  // Allocate new array
  std::auto_ptr<T> * arrNew =
          new std::auto_ptr<T> [newCapacity];
  // Transfer all entries
  for (size_t i = 0; i < _end; ++i)
      arrNew [i] = _arr [i];
  _capacity = newCapacity;
  // Free old memory
  delete []_arr;
  // Substitute new array for old array
  _arr = arrNew;
}
```

The only method that might call `grow` is `push_back`:

```
void push_back (std::auto_ptr<T> & p)
{
  assert (_end <= _capacity);
  if (_end == _capacity)
    grow (_end + 1);
  _arr [_end] = p; // Transfer
  _end++;
}
```

The rest of the implementation of auto_vector is pretty straightforward, since all the complexity of resource management is built into auto_ptr. For instance, the assign method simply utilizes the overloaded assignment operator to both deallocate the old object and transfer the new object in one simple statement.

```
void assign (size_t i, std::auto_ptr<T> & p)
{
  assert (i < _end);
  _arr [i] = p;
}
```

The method assign_direct takes advantage of the reset method of auto_ptr:

```
void assign_direct (size_t i, T * p)
{
  assert (i < _end);
  _arr [i].reset (ptr);
}
```

The pop_back method returns auto_ptr by value, because it transfers the ownership away from auto_vector.

```
std::auto_ptr<T> pop_back ()
{
  assert (_end != 0);
  return _arr [--_end];
}
```

Indexed access to auto_vector is implemented in terms of the get method of auto_ptr, which returns a weak pointer.

```
T * operator [] (size_t i)
{
  return _arr [i].get ();
}
```

With the new auto_vector, the implementation of MultiNode is not only 100% resource-safe, but it's also simpler. One more explicit destructor bites the dust!

```
class MultiNode: public Node
{
public:
  MultiNode (std::auto_ptr<Node> & pNode)
  {
    AddChild (pNode, true);
  }
  void AddChild (std::auto_ptr<Node> & pNode,
                              bool isPositive)
  {
    _aChild.push_back (pNode);
```

```
        _aIsPositive.push_back (isPositive);
    }
protected:
    auto_vector<Node>  _aChild;
    std::vector<bool>  _aIsPositive;
};
```

How do we know when we're done? How do we know when our code is completely resource-safe? There is a simple set of tests—at least as far as memory resources are concerned—that will answer this question. We have to search our code for all occurrences of new and release and go through the following series of tests:

- Is this a direct transfer to auto_ptr?
- Are we inside a constructor of an object? Is the result of the call immediately stored within the object, with no exception-prone code following it in the constructor? If so, is there a corresponding delete in the destructor of the object?
- Are we inside a method that immediately assigns the result of new to a pointer owned by the object? If so, is the previous value deleted?

If none of these conditions are true, our code is not resource-safe. Notice that all these tests are *local*. We don't have to follow all possible execution paths, just the close vicinity of the calls (except for the occasional look at some destructors). It can't get any easier than that!

10.10   Iterators

Like any other standard container, our auto_vector needs iterators. I will not attempt to provide the full set of iterators—it's a tedious chore best left to library implementors. All we'll ever need in our calculator is a forward-only constant iterator, so that's what I'll define.

Script 33   An *iterator* is an abstraction of a pointer to an array's element. It is also usually implemented as a pointer, so that it can be cheaply passed around and copied. Our auto_vector is implemented as an array of auto_ptr, so it's only natural that we should implement its iterator as a pointer to auto_ptr. It will be cheap to create, pass around, and copy. Moreover, incrementing such an iterator is as easy as incrementing a pointer. The only thing that prevents us from just typedefing an auto_vector iterator to a pointer to auto_ptr is its dereferencing behavior. When you dereference a pointer to an auto_ptr, you get an auto_ptr with all its resource-transfer semantics. What we need is an iterator that produces a regular weak pointer upon dereferencing (and in the case of a constant iterator, a weak pointer to const). Operator overloading to the rescue!

```
template<class T>
class const_auto_iterator: public
    std::iterator<std::forward_iterator_tag, T const *>
```

```
{
public:
  const_auto_iterator () : _pp (0) {}
  const_auto_iterator (std::auto_ptr<T> const * p)
    : _pp (p) {}
  bool operator != (const_auto_iterator<T> const & it) const
    { return it._pp != _pp; }
  bool operator == (const_auto_iterator<T> const & it) const
    { return it._pp == _pp; }
  const_auto_iterator operator++ (int) { return _pp++; }
  const_auto_iterator operator++ () { return ++_pp; }
  T const * operator * () { return _pp->get (); }
  T const * operator-> () { return _pp->get (); }
private:
  std::auto_ptr<T> const * _pp;
};
```

First of all, a well-behaved iterator should inherit from the `std::iterator` template so it can be passed to various standard algorithms that might inquire about its capabilities. This template is parameterized by an iterator tag (`forward_iterator_tag` in our case), which specifies the iterator's capabilities and its value type (pointer to const `T`, in our case). (Strictly speaking, there are even more parameters: for instance, the difference type—the type that you get when you subtract one iterator from another—but this one correctly defaults to `ptrdiff_t`.)

We have two constructors—one default and one taking a pointer to const `auto_ptr`. We have two comparison operators. We have two increment operators: one overloads the post-increment and the other the pre-increment operator. To distinguish between the declarations of these two, you provide a dummy `int` argument to your declaration of the post-increment operator (yet another quirk of C++ syntax).

In many cases, the implementation of the pre-increment operator is simpler and more efficient then the corresponding implementation of the post-increment operator. It's easy to first increment something and then return it. Post-increment, on the other hand, may be tricky. In principle, you have to somehow remember the original state of the iterator, increment its internal variables, and return an iterator that's created using the remembered state.

Fortunately, when you're dealing with pointers, the compiler does all the work for you, so the statement `return p++;` does just the right thing. But try implementing a post-increment operator for a linked list iterator and you'll see what I mean. By the way, this is the reason why I'm biased towards using the pre-increment operator in my code, in particular in all the `for` loops.

Our iterator has two dereference operators, both returning a weak pointer to const. The second one lets you call methods implemented by class T.

Inside the class auto_vector, we provide a traditional typedef and two methods, begin and end, to support iteration. Notice again that the end iterator points one beyond the last element of the array. Notice also how in both methods a pointer to auto_ptr is automatically converted to a const_iterator. That's because we haven't restricted the constructor of const_auto_iterator to be explicit.

```
typedef const_auto_iterator<T> const_iterator;
const_iterator begin () const { return _arr; }
const_iterator end () const { return _arr + _end; }
```

Finally, let's look at an example of how our iterator might be used in the Calc method of SumNode.

```
double SumNode::Calc () const
{
  double sum = 0.0;
  auto_vector<Node>::const_iterator childIt =
    _aChild.begin ();
  std::vector<bool>::const_iterator isPosIt =
    _aIsPositive.begin ();
  for (; childIt != _aChild.end (); ++childIt, ++isPosIt)
  {
    assert (isPosIt != _aIsPositive.end ());
    double val = childIt->Calc ();
    if (*isPosIt)
      sum += val;
    else
      sum -= val;
  }
  assert (isPosIt == _aIsPositive.end ());
  return sum;
}
```

I said "might," because it's not immediately obvious that this style of coding, using iterators, is more advantageous than the traditional array-index iteration, especially when two parallel arrays are involved. I had to use the comma sequencing operator to squeeze two increment operations into one slot in the for-loop header. (If you remember, expressions separated by commas are evaluated in sequence. The value of the sequence is equal to the value of its last expression.)

On the other hand, it would be easier to convert this code if we were to reimplement MultiNode to use linked lists instead of vectors. That, however, seems rather unlikely.

10.11 **Error Propagation**

Script 34 Now that our code is exception-safe, we should reconsider our error-handling policy. Consider what we are doing now when we detect a syntax error. We set the parser's status to stError and return a null pointer from whatever parsing method we're in. It so happens that all syntax errors are detected at the lowest level, inside Parser::Factor. However, both Parser::Term and Parser::Expr have to deal with the possibility of a null node coming from a lower-level parsing method. In fact, Parser::Factor itself has to deal with the possibility that the recursive call to Expr might return a null. Our code is thus sprinkled with error-propagation artifacts like this one:

```
if (pNode.get () == 0)
    return pNode;
```

Whenever there is a situation where an error has to be propagated straight through a set of nested calls, we should consider using exceptions instead. If we let Parser::Factor throw an exception whenever it detects a syntax error, we won't have to worry about detecting and propagating null pointers through other parsing methods. All we'll need is to catch this exception at the highest level—say, in Parser::Parse.

```
class Syntax {};
Status Parser::Parse ()
{
  try
  {
    // Everything is an expression
    _pTree = Expr ();
    if (!_scanner.IsDone ())
        _status = stError;
  }
  catch (Syntax)
  {
    _status = stError;
  }
  return _status;
}
```

I defined a separate class of exceptions, Syntax, for propagating syntax errors. For now this class is empty, but its distinct type lets the compiler separate it from other types of exceptions. In particular, we don't want to catch bad_alloc exceptions in Parser::Parse, since we don't know what to do with them. They will be caught and dealt with in main.

Here's an example of code from Parser::Factor converted to use exceptions for syntax error reporting. Notice that we no longer test for null return from Expr (in fact, we can assert that it's not null!).

```
        if (_scanner.Token () == tLParen) // Function call
        {
            _scanner.Accept (); // Accept '('
            pNode = Expr ();
            assert (pNode.get () != 0);
            if (_scanner.Token () == tRParen)
                _scanner.Accept (); // Accept ')'
            else
                throw Syntax ();
            if (id != SymbolTable::idNotFound
                && id < _funTab.Size ())
            {
                pNode = std::auto_ptr<Node> (
                    new FunNode (_funTab.GetFun (id), pNode));
            }
            else
            {
                std::cerr << "Unknown function \"";
                std::cerr << strSymbol << "\"\n";
                throw Syntax ();
            }
        }
    }
```

10.12 Conversion to Resource Management

By now you should be convinced that any program that doesn't follow the principles of resource management described in this chapter has little chance of ever
getting anywhere near the state of being bug-free. So what should you do if you
already have a project that's ridden with resource bugs? Do you have to convert
the whole project all at once, just like we did in our little program? Fortunately
not! You can do the conversion one step at a time.

Start by finding all occurrences of new in the project. If this is too much, divide
your project into smaller areas and work on each of them in turn.

- For calls to new that occur in constructors, make sure there is a corresponding
  delete in the destructor. Consider embedding auto_ptr in your class to hold
  the result of such a new.

- For calls outside of constructors, make sure the result of new is either
  - Immediately stored in a member variable that accepts the ownership, i.e.,
    there is a matching delete in the destructor and the previous value is re-
    leased prior to assignment
  - Immediately stored in an auto_ptr

- If you had to create a local auto_ptr in the previous step, call its release
  method before passing it down or up the chain of ownership. This is a temporary solution that will allow you to work in small increments.

- Once you're done with `new`, search for all occurrences of `release` that you have introduced in previous steps. Then mark those spots where the resource transfer takes place.

    - If a resource is being passed down, change the signature of the called procedure to accept an `auto_ptr` (by reference). If that procedure has to pass the ownership of the pointer still further, call `release`. You'll get back to this `release` during the next iteration.

    - If a resource is being passed up, return `auto_ptr` by value. Fix all the callers to accept the returned `auto_ptr`. If they have to pass the ownership of the pointer still further, call `release`.

    - If the ownership of a resource is being passed down to a container, consider converting that container to `auto_vector`.

- Whenever a pointer is converted to `auto_ptr`, the compiler will detect all the calls to `delete` that are no longer needed. Remove them.

This conversion procedure is recursive. At each step you might create some calls to `release` that will have to be fixed later. You will be finished converting when you can convince yourself that all the remaining calls to `new` and `release` are absolutely necessary and they pass the ownership directly into the member variables that know how to deal with them.

There are many other types of resources besides memory. They are usually obtained from the operating system and have to be returned back to it. They, too, should be encapsulated in smart objects. We'll see some examples later.

10.13   Conclusion

Script 35   We started with a simple question: "What should a program do when memory allocation fails?" The answer turned out to be much more complex than anticipated. We had to go though exceptions, stack unwinding, error propagation, resource management, resource transfer, smart pointers, auto pointers, smart containers, auto iterators, and a lot of really advanced features of C++. As you can see, each of these features is essential to our ability to write robust programs.

It's one thing to write a program that works most of the time and another to write a program that guarantees a certain degree of reliability. When an internet browser fails, users get annoyed but they can always restart it and try again. When a word processor or a spreadsheet program fails and wipes out a document, that's a much more serious problem.

If you want to learn more about writing reliable programs, you can read about transactions in Appendix B.

Chapter 11
Using the Standard
Template Library

Programming in C++ is so much easier once you start using the C++ standard library. If I were to start the whole calculator project from scratch, with the full use of the library, it would look a lot different. I didn't, though, for a couple of reasons. First of all, the C++ standard library is based on templates—especially the part called the standard template library (STL), which has all of the containers (vectors, lists, queues, maps, and so on) and algorithms (iterating, sorting, searching, and so on)—so I had to first explain what templates are and what kind of problems they solve. Second, you wouldn't know how much work they could save you unless you tried programming without them.

So what would the calculator have looked like if I had had a free run of the STL from the very beginning? First off, I wouldn't have bothered implementing the hash table. No, there isn't a ready-made implementation of a hash table in the STL—although many compiler vendors will undoubtedly add one to their version of the C++ standard library. There is, however, another useful data structure that fulfills the same role. It's an associative array, known in the STL as std::map. An *associative array* is like an array, except that it can be indexed using variables whose type doesn't have to be an integer.

You already know how to define an array of strings. You can index it with an (unsigned, in our case) integer and it gives you a string. An associative array can do the inverse—you can index it, for instance, with a string, and it can give you an integer, like this:

```
std::size_t id = assoc ["foo"];
```

This looks very much like what we need in our symbol table. Given the name of an identifier, we want to get its integer ID.

You implement an associative array using the STL's map template. A *map* is parameterized by two types—the type used to index it, called the *key*, and the *value* type. There is only one requirement for the key type—there must be a way to compare keys. Actually, it's not even necessary to provide a method to compare keys for equality or inequality. What is important for the map is to be able to tell if one key is *less* than the other. By default, a map expects the key type to either be directly comparable (like int or double) or have the overloaded *less than* operator.

The naive, and for most purposes incorrect, approach to implementing an associative array of strings would be to use char const * as the key type, like this:

```
std::map<char const *, std::size_t> dictionary;
```

The first problem is that there indeed *is* an operator "<" defined for this key type, but it's totally inappropriate. Consider this:

```
char const * str1 = "sin";
char const * str2 = "sin";
if (str1 < str2) // <- Not what you'd expect!
    cout << str1 << " is less than " << str2 << endl;
```

The result of this comparison is meaningless, because it's comparing two pointers—in other words, numerically comparing two memory addresses. This has nothing to do with what we normally consider "string comparison."

There is, however, a special function strcmp defined in <cstring> that can compare strings that are represented as pointers to characters. It returns zero when two strings are equal, character-by-character and lengthwise. When the first string precedes the second lexicographically, strcmp returns a number that is less than zero. Similarly, it returns a number greater than zero when the first string follows the other. (Think of it as subtracting two strings and it will make sense.) Lexicographical comparison is the one used in dictionaries (let's forget about localization issues—here the characters are simply treated as numbers).

Script 36   The C++ standard library provides a version of map that takes a third template argument—a functor type. A *functor* (or *function object*) is a class that defines a *function-call* operator. Here's an example of a functor that's suitable for our purposes:

```
class LessThan
  : public std::binary_function<char const *,
                                char const *, bool>
{
public:
  bool operator () (char const * str1,
                    char const * str2) const
  {
    return std::strcmp (str1, str2) < 0;
  }
```

```
};
std::map<char const *, int, LessThan> dictionary;
```

The way you could use a functor object, other than in a map, would be to treat it just like a function (or function pointer—the syntax is the same).

```
char const * str1 = "cos";
char const * str2 = "sin";
LessThan lessThan;
if (lessThan (str1, str2))
    cout << str1 << " is less than " << str2 << endl;
```

In fact, a functor is even more efficient than a function pointer, because it may be inlined. In the example above, the implicit call to `lessThan.operator ()` will be inlined, according to its declaration in `LessThan`.

If you think this is too complicated—having to define a predicate to do such a simple thing as a string comparison in a map—you're right! In fact, not only is it complicated but also incorrect. This is because we are trying to fit a square peg into a round hole. The equivalent of a square peg is the low-level data structure that we are insisting on using to represent strings. The C++ standard library has a perfectly round peg for this purpose—it's called a `string`.

And that brings us to the second problem with the naive implementation of the symbol table: the keys could disappear from under the map. When you enter a new association—a pair (key, value)—in the map, the map has to remember both the key and the value. If you use a pointer to a character as a key, the map will store the pointer, but you'll have no idea where the actual characters are stored and for how long. Somebody could call the map with a character string that's allocated on the stack and that will disappear as soon as the caller returns.

We want the map to *own* the keys! And no, we can't use `auto_ptrs` as keys. C++ standard library containers use value semantics for all their data—they get confused by objects that exhibit transfer semantics. And that's the second reason to use `strings`.

Script 37   The standard `string` not only has value semantics, but it also comes with a lot of useful methods—one of them being the less than operator. That makes string and map a perfect match. Implementing an associative array of strings is a no-brainer. So let's do it first and ask the questions later. Here's the declaration of the new symbol table:

```
#include <map>
#include <string>

class SymbolTable
{
public:
  static const std::size_t idNotfound = 0 x ffffffff;
  SymbolTable () : _id (0) {}
```

```
    std::size_t ForceAdd (char const * str);
    std::size_t Find (char const * str) const;
private:
    std::map<std::string, std::size_t> _dictionary;
    std::size_t _id;
};
```

Notice that since the map now owns the strings, we no longer have any use for StringBuffer.

We are still clinging to the old char const * C-style strings in the symbol table interface. That's because I want to show you how you can start converting old legacy code without having to rewrite everything all at once. The two representations of strings can co-exist quite peacefully. Of course, we'll have to make some conversions at the boundaries of the two worlds. For instance, the method ForceAdd starts by creating a standard string from the C-string argument. It then stores the corresponding integer ID under this string in the associative array.

```
std::size_t SymbolTable::ForceAdd (char const * str)
{
    std::string s (str);
    _dictionary [s] = _id;
    return _id++;
}
```

Here, the mere act of accessing a map by indexing it with a key will create an entry in the map (if one wasn't there already).

> Don't get fooled by the syntactic simplicity of accessing a map. The time it takes to index an associative array that's implemented as an STL map is not constant (as it is with regular arrays or hash tables), but it depends on its size (the number of elements). The good news is that it's not linear—the array is not searched element-by-element. The recommended implementation of an STL map is in terms of a balanced tree that can be searched in logarithmic time. Logarithmic access is reasonably good for most applications.

There is also a more explicit way of adding entries to a map by calling its insert method. You insert a pair (key, value) using an STL pair template. For instance, ForceAdd can be implemented this way:

```
std::size_t SymbolTable::ForceAdd (char const * str)
{
    std::string s (str);
    std::pair<std::string, std::size_t> p (s, _id);
    _dictionary.insert (p);
    return _id++;
}
```

The `Find` method of the symbol table could have been simply implemented by returning `_dictionary [str]`, if it weren't for the fact that we sometimes *do* want to know if the name was already there. We have to use a more explicit approach:

```
std::size_t SymbolTable::Find (char const * str) const
{
  std::map<std::string, std::size_t>::const_iterator it;
  it = _dictionary.find (str);
  if (it != _dictionary.end ())
      return it->second;
  return idNotFound;
}
```

The `find` method of `map` returns an iterator. This iterator could either point to the end of the dictionary or to a pair (key, value). A pair has two public data members, `first` and `second`, with obvious meanings.

Notice also that I called `find` with a C-style string. It was possible, because the standard string (`std::string`) has a constructor that accepts a C-string. This constructor can be used for implicit conversions.

There is no implicit inverse conversion from `string` to `char const *`; however, there is a method `c_str` that retrieves a C-string from a `string`.

Script 38   We can take advantage of implicit conversions to further simplify the implementation of the symbol table. We can change the signature of its methods to accept strings rather than C-strings.

```
int ForceAdd (std::string const & str);
int Find (std::string const & str) const;
```

This will work without any changes to the callers because of the implicit conversions. The trick is that both methods take const references to strings. The compiler will have no trouble creating temporary strings at the point of call and passing out const references. This would not work, however, if symbol table methods required non-const references (we already talked about it, but this point is worth repeating: the compiler will refuse to create a non-const reference to a temporary object).

There's an interesting twist on the topic of passing strings—we can pass them by value.

```
int ForceAdd (std::string str);
int Find (std::string str) const;
```

This will work because, as I mentioned, strings have value semantics. They behave as if every copy were a deep copy. However, since memory allocation and copying is rather expensive, a good implementation of a standard string uses all kinds of clever tricks to avoid, or at least postpone, these operations. Let's talk about this in some more detail.

11.1   Reference Counting and Copy-On-Write

string 1   Remember our discussion of value strings in the section Value Semantics in
Chapter 5? Here's a slight variation on this topic.

```cpp
class StringVal
{
public:
  StringVal (char const * cstr = 0)
    : _buf (0)
  {
    if (cstr != 0)
       Init (cstr);
  }
  StringVal (StringVal const & str)
    : _buf (0)
  {
    if (str.c_str () != 0)
       Init (str.c_str ());
  }
  ~StringVal ()
  {
    delete _buf;
  }
  StringVal & operator= (StringVal const & str);
  char const * c_str () const { return _buf; }
  void Upcase ();
private:
  void Init (char const * cstr)
  {
    assert (cstr != 0);
    _buf = new char [std::strlen (cstr) + 1];
    std::strcpy (_buf, cstr);
  }
private:
  char * _buf;
};
```

When overloading the assignment operator, we have to take care of a few special cases, like source equal to this or empty source.

```cpp
StringVal & StringVal::operator= (StringVal const & str)
{
  if (this != &str)
  {
    char const * cstr = str.c_str ();
    if (cstr == 0)
    {
      delete _buf;
      _buf = 0;
    }
    else
```

```
      {
        std::size_t len = std::strlen (cstr);
        if (_buf == 0 || std::strlen (_buf) < len)
        {
          delete _buf;
          Init (cstr);
        }
        else
          std::strcpy (_buf, cstr);
      }
    }
    return *this;
  }
```

I added the `Upcase` method to demonstrate what happens when a string is modified.

```
  void StringVal::Upcase ()
  {
    if (_buf)
    {
      int len = std::strlen (_buf);
      for (int i = 0; i < len; ++i)
          _buf [i] = std::toupper (_buf [i]);
    }
  }
```

In particular, we can create two copies of the same string and, when we `Upcase` one of them, the other will remain unchanged.

```
  StringVal str1 ("foo");
  StringVal str2 (str1); // Copy
  str2.Upcase ();
  std::cout << str1.c_str () << std::endl;
  std::cout << str2.c_str () << std::endl;
```

Semantically, this is how we want our string to behave. Performancewise, we might not be too happy with this implementation. Consider, as an exercise, how many memory allocations and string copies are made when, for instance, `StringVal` is returned by value:

```
  StringVal ByValue ()
  {
    StringVal ret ("foo");
    return ret;
  }
  StringVal str;
  str = ByValue ();
```

To save on allocating and copying, we might consider a scheme where multiple copies of the same string would internally share the same representation object—they'd have a pointer to the same buffer. But then the question of ownership arises. Who's supposed to delete the buffer? We have to somehow keep track of how many shared owners of the buffer there are at any point in time. Then, when the last owner disappears, we should delete the buffer.

The best way to implement this scheme is to divide the responsibilities between two classes. One class encapsulates the reference-counted shared object—in our case this object will also hold the string buffer. The other class deals with the ownership issues—it increments and decrements the shared object's reference count—in our case this will be the "string" object (see Figure 11.1). When the string object discovers that the reference count of the shared object has gone down to zero (nobody else references this object), it deletes it.

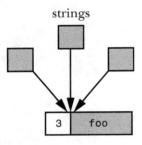

strings

Figure 11.1 Multiple objects can share the same reference-counted representation. Here, three "strings" are sharing the same reference-counted buffer

string2

You may think of a reference count as a type of resource—it is acquired by incrementing and it must subsequently be released by decrementing. Like any other resource, it has to be encapsulated. Our "string" object will be such an encapsulator. In fact, since reference count is a common type of resource, we might want to build the equivalent of a smart pointer to deal with reference-counted objects.

```
template <class T>
class RefPtr
{
public:
  RefPtr (RefPtr<T> const & p)
  {
    _p = p._p;
    _p->IncRefCount ();
  }
  ~RefPtr ()
  {
```

```
             Release ();
        }
        RefPtr<T> const & operator= (RefPtr<T> const & p)
        {
          if (this != &p)
          {
              Release ();
              _p = p._p;
              _p->IncRefCount ();
          }
          return *this;
        }
     protected:
        RefPtr (T * p) : _p (p) {}
        void Release ()
        {
          if (_p->DecRefCount () == 0)
              delete _p;
        }

        T * _p;
     };
```

Notice that the reference-counted type T must provide at least two methods,
IncRefCount and DecRefCount. We also tacitly assume that type T is created with a
reference count of one before being passed to the protected constructor of
RefPtr.

Although it's not absolutely necessary, we might want the type T to be a descendant of a base class that implements a reference-counting interface.

```
        class RefCounted
        {
        public:
          RefCounted () : _count (1) {}
          int GetRefCount () const { return _count; }
          void IncRefCount () const { _count++; }
          int DecRefCount () const { return --_count; }
        private:
          mutable int _count;
        };
```

Notice one interesting detail: the methods IncRefCount and DecRefCount are declared const, even though they modify the object's data. You can do that without
the compiler raising an eyebrow (metaphorically speaking) if you declare the relevant data member mutable. We *do* want these methods to be const (or at least one
of them, IncRefCount), because they will be called on const objects inside RefPtr.
Both the copy constructor and the assignment operator take const references to
their arguments, but they modify their reference counts. So we decided not to
consider the updating of the reference count a "modification" of the object even

though, strictly speaking, it is. It will make even more sense when we get to the copy-on-write implementation.

Just for demonstration purposes, let's create a reference-counted string using our original StringVal encapsulated inside class StringRep (string representation). Normally, one would do it more efficiently by combining the reference count with the string buffer.

```
class StringRep: public RefCounted
{
public:
  StringRep (char const * cstr)
    :_string (cstr)
  {}
  char const * c_str () const { return _string.c_str (); }
  void Upcase ()
  {
    _string.Upcase ();
  }
private:
  StringVal _string;
};
```

Our actual string class is built on the base of RefPtr. Internally, it represents string data using StringRep.

```
class StringRef: public RefPtr<StringRep>
{
public:
  StringRef (char const * cstr)
    : RefPtr<StringRep> (new StringRep (cstr))
  {}
  StringRef (StringRef const & str)
    : RefPtr<StringRep> (str)
  {}
  char const * c_str () const { return _p->c_str (); }
  void Upcase ()
  {
    _p->Upcase ();
  }
};
```

We now have so many classes that we might get lost without a diagram (see Figure 11.2).

Other than in the special C-string-taking constructor, there is no copying of data. The copy constructor just increments the reference count of the string-representation object. So does the assignment operator. Consequently, "copying" and passing StringRef by value is relatively cheap. There is only one tiny problem with this implementation. After you call Upcase on one of the copies of StringRef, all other copies change to uppercase.

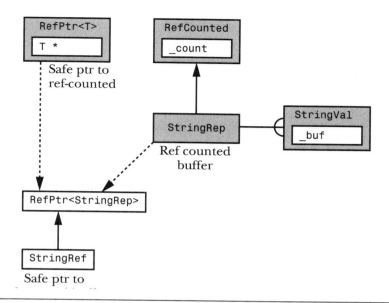

Figure 11.2 Templates and classes involved in the implementation of a reference-counted string

```
StringRef strOriginal ("text");
StringRef strCopy (strOriginal);
strCopy.Upcase ();
// The original will be uppercased!
std::cout << "The original: " << strOriginal.c_str ()
          << std::endl;
```

That's not very intuitive behavior.

string 3   There is, however, a way to have your cake and eat it too. It's called *copy-on-write,* or *COW* for short. The idea is to share a single representation between multiple copies, as long as they don't need to make any modifications. Every modifying method has to make sure that its modifications are not shared. It checks the reference count of its representation and, if it's greater than one, makes a private copy. This way, the copying is delayed as long as possible. Passing by value is as cheap as shared representation, but modifications are no longer shared between copies.

```
class StringCow: public RefPtr<StringRep>
{
public:
  StringCow (char const * cstr)
    : RefPtr<StringRep> (new StringRep (cstr))
  {}
  StringCow (StringCow const & str)
```

```
        : RefPtr<StringRep> (str)
    {}
    char const * c_str () const { return _p->c_str (); }
    void Upcase ()
    {
      Cow ();
      _p->Upcase ();
    }
  private:
    void Cow ()
    {
      if (_p->GetRefCount () > 1)
      {
        // Clone it
        StringRep * rep = new StringRep (_p->c_str ());
        Release ();
        _p = rep;
      }
    }
};
```

The beauty of this implementation is that, from the user's point of view,
StringCow behaves exactly like StringVal, down to the const-reference-taking copy
constructor and assignment operator. Except that, when it comes to passing
around by value, its performance is superior.

There is a good chance that your C++ standard library implements string
using some version of copy-on-write.

11.2 End of Restrictions

Script 39   Now that we are no longer afraid to pass strings by value, we might try some more
code improvements. For instance, we can replace this awkward piece of code:

```
void Scanner::GetSymbolName (char * strOut, int lenBuf)
{
  assert (lenBuf > maxSymLen);
  assert (_lenSymbol < lenBuf);
  std::strncpy (strOut, &_buf [_iSymbol], _lenSymbol);
  strOut [_lenSymbol] = '\0';
}
```

When you use strings, you don't have to worry about sending appropriately
sized buffers. You let the callee create a string of the correct size and return it by
value. Here's one way to do it:

```
std::string Scanner::GetSymbolName ()
{
  return std::string (&_buf [_iSymbol], _lenSymbol);
}
```

And here's what it looks like on the receiving side.

```
std::string strSymbol = _scanner.GetSymbolName ();
std::size_t id = _symTab.Find (strSymbol);
...
std::cerr << "Unknown function \"";
std::cerr << strSymbol << "\"\n";
```

Notice that the string `strSymbol` is a local variable with limited scope. It will disappear when the flow of control leaves the scope, and it will deallocate whatever resources it owns (or at least it will decrement their reference count).

As you can also see, a string can be sent to the standard output (or standard error) and it will be printed just like a C-string.

Actually, it gets even better. You can read text from the standard input directly into a string. The beauty of it is that, because a string can dynamically resize itself, there is practically no restriction on the size of acceptable text. The string will accommodate as much text as the user wants to type into it. So when does the input operation return? There has to be a way to terminate a string. Normally, the standard input will stop filling a string once it encounters any whitespace character. It means you can, for instance, read one word at a time with simple code like this:

```
std::string str;
std::cin >> str;
```

In our program we have a slightly different requirement. We want to be able to read one line at a time. The C++ standard library has an appropriate function to do that, so let's just use it directly in `main`.

```
std::cerr << "> "; // Prompt
std::string str;
std::getline (std::cin, str);
Scanner scanner (str.c_str ());
```

> Bug alert! The C++ standard library that comes with VC++ 6.0 has a bug that makes `getline` expect two new lines rather than one as the line terminator. A fix for this and many other bugs is available on the Internet at www.dinkumware.com.

Let's stop here for a moment. We have just removed the last built-in limitation from our program. There is no longer any restriction on the length of the input line or on the length of an identifier. The file `params.h` is gone!

How did that happen? Well, we started using dynamic data structures. Is our program more complex because of that? No, it's not! In fact it's simpler now. Is there any reason to introduce limitations into programs? Hardly!

11.3 Getting Rid of C-Strings

Script 40   Now let's follow the fate of the input string from main into the scanner. It makes little sense to store a naked C-string in the scanner. So let's rewrite it to use a standard string instead.

```
class Scanner
{
public:
    Scanner (std::string const & buf);
    EToken  Token () const { return _token; }
    EToken  Accept ();
    bool IsDone () const
    {
        return _iLook == std::string::npos;
    }
    bool IsEmpty () const { return _buf.length () == 0; }
    double Number ()
    {
        assert (_token == tNumber);
        return _number;
    }
    std::string GetSymbolName ();
private:
    void EatWhite ();
    typedef std::string::size_type size_type;

    std::string const & _buf;
    size_type           _iLook;
    EToken              _token;
    double              _number;
    size_type           _lenSymbol;
    size_type           _iSymbol;
    static char         _whiteChars [];
};
```

The natural way of marking that the Scanner reached the end of the string is to use a special index value, string::npos. This is the value that is returned by the string's various "find" methods when the end of the string is reached. For instance, we can use one such method, find_first_not_of, to skip whitespace in our buffer.

```
char Scanner::_whiteChars [] = " \t\n\r";
void Scanner::EatWhite ()
{
    _iLook = _buf.find_first_not_of (_whiteChars, _iLook);
}
```

The method find_first_not_of takes a null-terminated array of characters to be skipped (in our case the array contains a space, a tab, a newline and a carriage return) and the optional starting index, which defaults to zero. It returns the index of the first occurrence of a character that is not in the skip list. If no such character is found, it returns `string::npos`.

By the way, the value `string::npos` is guaranteed to be greater than any valid index as long as you are comparing the same integral types. That's why we made sure we used the same type, `size_type`, for our index as the one used internally by the string itself.

This is an alternative implementation of `GetSymbolName`, which returns a substring of the buffer.

```
std::string Scanner::GetSymbolName ()
{
    return _buf.substr (_iSymbol, _lenSymbol);
}
```

The rest of the scanner's implementation works with almost no changes. We only have to make sure that, at the end of `Accept`, we set the position to `string::npos` if the buffer has been consumed.

```
if (_iLook == _buf.length ())
    _iLook = std::string::npos;
```

Also, code like this, although not the most elegant, will work with strings as well as with straight character arrays:

```
char * p;
_number = strtod (&_buf [_iLook], &p);
_iLook = p - &_buf [0];
```

This is not the preferred way of writing a program if you've decided to use the C++ standard library from the onset of the project. But I wanted to show you that it's quite possible to start the conversion in a legacy program and not have to go all the way at once.

11.4 Exploring Streams

So what is the preferred way of parsing the input using the C++ standard library? First of all, we shouldn't bother reading a line from the standard input into a string. We should just pass the stream directly to the scanner. After all, we don't need random access to the input line—we are parsing it more or less one character at a time. Except in rare cases, we don't have to go back in the string to reparse it (there are some grammars that require it, but ours doesn't). In the rare cases when we have to backtrack, it's only by one character.

Script 41   Let's start from the top. We can create the scanner and pass it the standard input stream as an argument.

```
cerr << "> ";   // Prompt
Scanner scanner (std::cin);
```

Here's the new definition of the Scanner class. Notice that, from the point of view of the Scanner, cin is just an example (subclass) of std::istream.

```
class Scanner
{
public:
  explicit Scanner (std::istream & in);
  bool IsDone () const { return _token == tEnd; }
  bool IsEmpty () const { return _isEmpty; }
  EToken   Token () const { return _token; }
  void    Accept ();
  std::string GetSymbolName () const { return _symbol; }
  double Number () const { return _number; }
private:
  void ReadChar ();

  std::istream & _in;
  int            _look;    // Lookahead character
  bool           _isEmpty;
  EToken         _token;
  double         _number;
  std::string    _symbol;
};
```

I did a little reorganizing here. I'm keeping a lookahead character in _look. I also decided to have a Boolean flag, _isEmpty, to keep the information that the stream was empty when the scanner was constructed (I can no longer look back at the beginning of the input once Accept has been called). I changed the test for IsDone to simply compare the current token with tEnd. Finally, I needed a string to keep the name of the last symbolic variable read from the input.

Here's the constructor of the Scanner:

```
Scanner::Scanner (std::istream & in)
  : _in (in)
{
  Accept ();
  _isEmpty = (Token () == tEnd);
}
```

The Accept method needs a little rewriting. Where we used to call EatWhite, we now call ReadChar. It skips whitespace as before, but it also initializes the lookahead character to the first nonwhitespace character. Since the lookahead has been consumed from the input stream by ReadChar, we don't have to do any incrementing after we've recognized it in Accept.

```
void Scanner::Accept ()
{
  ReadChar ();
```

```
    switch (_look)
    {
    case '+':
      _token = tPlus;
      // No incrementing
    break;
    ...
    }
}
```

This is the implementation of ReadChar:

```
void Scanner::ReadChar ()
{
  _look = _in.get ();
  while (_look == ' ' || _look == '\t')
    _look = _in.get ();
}
```

I had to rethink the handling of the end of input. Before, when we used getline to read input, we actually never had to deal with a newline. By definition, getline eats the newline and terminates the string appropriately (i.e., the C-string version appends a null; the std::string version updates the internal length). The get method, on the other hand, reads every character as is, including the newline. So I let the scanner recognize a newline as the end of input.

```
case '\n': // End of input
case '\r':
case EOF: // End of file
_token = tEnd;
  break;
```

Incidentally, I did some thinking ahead and decided to let the scanner recognize the end of the file. The special EOF value is returned by the get method when it encounters the end of the file. This value is not even a character (that's why get is defined to return an int rather than char).

How can a standard input stream encounter the end of a file? There's actually more than one way it can happen. First, you can enter it from the keyboard—in DOS it's the combination Ctrl+Z. Second, the program might be called from the command line with redirected input. You can create a text file, say calc.txt, filled with commands for the calculator and then call it like this:

```
calc < calc.txt
```

The operating system will plug the contents of this file into the program's standard input and execute it. You'll see the results of calculations flashing on your standard output. That is, unless you redirect it too, like this:

```
calc < calc.txt > results.txt
```

In the latter case, you'll see only the standard error (including the prompts) flashing before your eyes, and the file results.txt will be filled with the results of your calculations.

Let's continue with our rewriting of the scanner. Here's what we do when we recognize a number:

```
case '0': case '1': case '2': case '3': case '4':
case '5': case '6': case '7': case '8': case '9':
case '.':
  _token = tNumber;
  _in.putback (_look);
  _in >> _number; // Read the whole number
  break;
```

Reading a floating-point number from the standard input is easy. The only complication arises from the fact that we've already read the first character of the number—our lookahead. So before we read the whole number, we have to put our lookahead back into the stream. Don't worry, this is a simple operation. After all, the input stream is buffered. When you call get, the character is simply read from a buffer (unless the buffer is empty—in that case the system replenishes it by actually reading the input). To putback a character means putting it back into that buffer. Input streams are implemented in such a way that it's *always* possible to put back one character.

When reading an identifier, we do a slight variation of the same trick.

```
default:
  if (std::isalpha (_look) || _look == '_')
  {
    _token = tIdent;
    _symbol.erase (); // Erase string contents
    do {
      _symbol += _look;
      _look = _in.get ();
    } while (std::isalnum (_look));
    _in.putback (_look);
  }
  else
    _token = tError;
  break;
```

We don't have to putback a lookahead at the beginning of reading an identifier. Instead, we have to putback the last character, the one that is not part of the identifier, so that the next call to ReadChar can see it.

Haven't we lost some generality by switching from a string to a stream? After all, you can always convert a stream to a string (e.g., using getline). Is the opposite possible? Not to worry! Converting a string into a stream is as easy. The appropriate class is called istringstream and is defined in the header <sstream>. Since istringstream inherits from istream, our scanner won't notice the difference. For instance, we can do this:

```
std::istringstream in ("sin (2 * pi / 3)");
Scanner scanner (in);
```

Script 42   *We have just skimmed the surface of the standard library and we've already found a lot of useful stuff. It really pays to study it, rather than implement your own solutions from scratch.*

Chapter 12
Persistence

Most programs have a mechanism for storing data persistently between sessions. Data is commonly stored in disk files, but other options are also available (a database, Windows registry, CD-ROM, and so on). There are also different approaches to structuring data on disk. Some programs use text files, others prefer binary format.

A text file is easy to handle, debug, or fix if necessary. The drawback is that it can also be easily corrupted by a user with a text editor. A binary file, whose contents is not human-readable, is safer in this respect and it usually takes less disk space. But when storing the state of your program in a binary file, you have to come up with a well-designed binary format. This is where an object-oriented approach pays benefits.

In preparation for adding persistence and as an exercise in program modification, we'll first simplify the top-level structure of the calculator.

12.1 The Calculator Object

Script 43 Look at main: there are too many objects in it—the symbol table, the function table, and the store. All three objects have the same life span—the duration of the program execution. They have to be initialized in a particular order and all three of them are passed to the constructor of the parser. They just scream to be combined into a single object called—what else?—the Calculator. Embedding them in the right order inside this class will take care of the correct order of initialization.

```
class Calculator
{
```

```
        friend class Parser;
    public:
      Calculator ()
        : _funTab (_symTab),
          _store (_symTab)
      { }
    private:
      Store & GetStore () { return _store; }
      PtrFun GetFun (std::size_t id) const
      {
        return _funTab.GetFun (id);
      }
      bool IsFunction (std::size_t id) const
      {
        return id < _funTab.Size ();
      }
      int AddSymbol (std::string const & str)
      {
        return _symTab.ForceAdd (str);
      }
      int FindSymbol (std::string const & str) const
      {
        return _symTab.Find (str);
      }

      SymbolTable      _symTab;
      Function::Table _funTab;
      Store            _store;
    };
```

Of course, now we have to make appropriate changes (read: simplifications) in main and in the parser. Here are just a few examples in the declaration of the parser

```
    class Parser
    {
    public:
      Parser (Scanner & scanner, Calculator & calc);
      ...
    private:
      ...
      Scanner              & _scanner;
      std::auto_ptr<Node> _pTree;
      Status               _status;
      Calculator           & _calc;
    };
```

and in its implementation.

```
    // Factor := Ident
    if (id == SymbolTable::idNotFound)
    {
      id = _calc.AddSymbol (strSymbol);
    }
```

```
pNode = std::auto_ptr<Node>
            (new VarNode (id, _calc.GetStore ()));
```

Have you noticed something? We have just made another major top-level change in our project, just like that! In fact, it was almost trivial to do, with a little help from the compiler. Let me describe the step-by-step process that leads to it.

Start in the spot in main where the symbol table, function table, and store are defined (constructed). Replace them with the new object, calculator. Declare the class for Calculator and write a constructor for it. Now, if you are really lazy and tired of thinking, fire off the compiler. It will immediately tell you what to do next: You have to modify the constructor of the parser. You have to pass it the calculator rather than its three separate parts. At this point you might notice that it will be necessary to change the class declaration of the Parser to let it store a reference to the Calculator. Or, you could run the compiler again and let it remind you.

Next, you will notice all the compilation errors in the implementation of the Parser. You can fix them one-by-one, adding new methods to the Calculator as the need arises. The whole procedure is so simple that you might ask an intern who has just started working on the project to do it with minimal supervision.

Script 44   We should also take this opportunity to move main out of the file Calc.cpp now that we have a header file, Calc.h. Where should main go? How about creating a separate file, Main.cpp, for that purpose? When a new person joins your development, he or she will know immediately where to start reading your code.

The moral of this story is that it's never too late to work on improving the high-level structure of the project. The truth is that you rarely get it right the first time.

By the way, you have just seen the method of top-down program modification in action. You start from the top and let the compiler lead you all the way down to the nitty-gritty details of the implementation. That's the third part of the top-down methodology, which consists of

- Top-down design
- Top-down implementation
- Top-down modification

I can't stress enough the importance of the top-down methodology. I have yet to see a clean, well-written piece of code that was created bottom-up. You'll hear people saying that some things are better done top-down, others bottom-up. Some people will say that starting from the middle and expanding in both directions is the best way to go. Don't listen to them!

It is a fact that bottom-up development is more natural when you have no idea what you're doing—when your goal is not to write a specific program, but rather to play around with some "neat stuff." It's an easy way, for instance, to learn the interface of some obscure subsystem that you might want to use. Bottom-up development is also preferable if you're not very good at design or if you dislike just sitting there and thinking instead of coding. It is a definite plus if you enjoy long hours of debugging or have somebody else (hopefully not the end user!) to debug your code.

Finally, if you embrace the bottom-up philosophy, you'll have to resign yourself to never being able to write a professional-looking piece of code. Your programs will always look to the trained eye like those electronics projects created with Radio Shack parts on breadboards with bent wires sticking out in all directions and batteries held together with rubber bands.

The real reason I decided to finally get rid of the top-level mess and introduce the `Calculator` object was to simplify the job of adding a new piece of functionality. Every time management asks you to add new features, take the opportunity to sneak in a little rewrite of the existing code. The code isn't good enough if it hasn't been rewritten at least three times. I'm not kidding!

By rewriting I don't mean throwing it away and starting from scratch. Just take your time every now and then to improve the structure of each part of the project. It will pay off tremendously. It will actually shorten the development cycle. Of course, if you have stress-puppy managers, you'll have a hard time convincing them of this. They will keep running around shouting nonsense like "If it ain't broken, don't fix it" or "If we don't ship it tomorrow, we're all dead." The moment you buy into that, you're doomed! You'll never be able to do anything right and you'll be spending more and more time fixing the scaffolding and chasing bugs in some low-quality temporary code pronounced to be of the "ain't broken" quality. Welcome to the maintenance nightmare!

So here we are, almost at the end of our project, when we are told by the imaginary management that if we don't provide a command to save and restore the state of the calculator we're dead. Fortunately, we can add this feature to the program without much trouble and, as a bonus, do some more cleanup.

12.2   Command Parser

We'll go about adding new functionality in an orderly fashion. We must provide the user with a way to input commands. So far we've had a hack for inputting the *quit* command—an empty line was interpreted as "quit." Now that we want to add two more commands, *save* and *restore,* we may as well find a more general solution. I probably don't have to tell you this, but . . .

> **Whenever there are more than two special cases, you should generalize them.**

Script 45   Currently, the calculator expects expressions from the user. Let's distinguish commands from expressions by prefixing the former with an exclamation sign. The exclamation sign has the natural connotation of commanding somebody to do something. We'll use it as a prefix rather than a suffix to simplify our parsing. We'll also make *quit* a regular command to be input as !q. We'll even remind the user of this command when the calculator starts.

```
        std::cerr << "\n!q to quit\n";
```

The new Scanner method, IsCommand, will simply check for the leading exclamation sign (we can add a new token, tCommand, to the Scanner). Once we've established that a line of text is a command, we'll create a simple CommandParser to parse and execute it.

```
if (!scanner.IsEmpty ())
{
  if (scanner.IsCommand())
  {
    CommandParser parser (scanner, calc);
    status = parser.Execute ();
  }
  else
  {
    Parser  parser (scanner, calc);
    status = parser.Parse ();
    if (status == stOk)
    {
      double result = parser.Calculate ();
      std::cout << result << std::endl;
    }
    else
    {
      std::cerr << "Syntax error\n";
    }
  }
}
```

Here's the new class, CommandParser.

```
class CommandParser
{
  enum ECommand
  {
    comSave,
    comLoad,
    comQuit,
    comError
  };
public:
  CommandParser (Scanner & scanner, Calculator & calc);
  Status Execute ();
private:
  Status Load (std::string const & fileName);
  Status Save (std::string const & fileName);
  Scanner &    _scanner;
  Calculator & _calc;
  ECommand     _command;
};
```

This is how it parses a command.

```
CommandParser::CommandParser (Scanner & scanner,
                              Calculator & calc)
  : _scanner (scanner), _calc (calc)
{
  assert (_scanner.IsCommand());
  _scanner.Accept ();
  std::string name = _scanner.GetSymbolName ();
  switch (name [0])
  {
    case 'q':
    case 'Q':
      _command = comQuit;
      break;
    case 's':
    case 'S':
      _command = comSave;
      break;
    case 'l':
    case 'L':
      _command = comLoad;
      break;
    default:
      _command = comError;
      break;
  }
}
```

Notice that we reuse the Scanner method GetSymbolName to retrieve the command string.

In name[0] we access the first character of a string using array indexing. You can index a standard string the same way you can index a C-string—it defines its own operator[]. The load and save commands require an argument, the file name. We retrieve it from the scanner using, again, the method GetSymbolName.

```
Status CommandParser::Execute ()
{
  _scanner.AcceptCommand ();
  std::string nameFile;
  switch (_command)
  {
  case comSave:
    nameFile = _scanner.GetSymbolName ();
    return Save (nameFile);
  case comLoad:
    nameFile = _scanner.GetSymbolName ();
    return Load (nameFile);
  case comQuit:
    std::cerr << "Good-bye!" << std::endl;
    return stQuit;
  case comError:
```

```
            std::cerr << "Error" << std::endl;
            return stError;
        }
        return stOk;
    }
```

We use the new method `AcceptCommand` to accept the command and read the string following it. The string, presumably a file name, must be terminated by a whitespace. Notice that we can't use the regular `Accept` method of the `Scanner`, because it will only read strings that have the form of C++ identifiers. It would stop, for instance, after reading a dot, which is considered a perfectly valid part of a file name. (If we were stricter, we would even make provisions for filenames with embedded spaces. We'd require them to be enclosed in quotation marks, though.)

```
void Scanner::AcceptCommand ()
{
  ReadChar ();
  _symbol.erase ();
  while (!std::isspace (_look))
  {
    _symbol += _look;
    _look = _in.get ();
  }
}
```

As usual, we should provide simple stubs for `Load` and `Save` and test our program before proceeding any further.

12.3 Serialization and Deserialization

We often imagine data structures as two- or even three-dimensional creatures (just think of a parsing tree, a hash table, or a multi-dimensional array). A disk file, on the other hand, has a one-dimensional structure—it's linear. When you write to a file, you write one thing after another—serially. Hence the name *serialization*. Saving a data structure means transforming a multidimensional idea into its one-dimensional representation. Of course, in reality computer memory is also one-dimensional. Our data structures are already, in some manner, serialized in memory. Some of them, like multidimensional arrays, are serialized by the compiler; others are fit into linear memory with the use of pointers. Unfortunately, pointers have no meaning outside of the context of the currently running instance of the program. You can't save pointers to a file, close the program, start it again, read the file, and expect the newly read pointers to point to the same data structures as before.

In order to serialize a data structure, you have to come up with a well-defined procedure for walking it, i.e., visiting its every element, one after another. For instance, you can walk a simple linked list by following the *next* pointers until you hit the end of the list. If the list is circular, you have to remember the initial pointer and, with every step, compare it to the *next* pointer. A binary tree can be walked by walking the left child first and the right child next (notice that it's a recursive prescription). For every data structure there is at least one deterministic procedure for walking it, but the procedure might be arbitrarily complicated.

Once you know how to walk a data structure, you know how to serialize it. You have a prescription for how to visit every element of the structure, one after another—a serial way of scanning it. At the bottom level of every data structure you always find simple, built-in types, like int, char, long, and so on. They can be written into a file following a set of simple rules—we'll come back to this point in a moment. If you know how to serialize each basic element, you're done.

Serializing a data structure makes sense only if we know how to restore it—*deserialize* it from file to memory. Knowing the original serialization procedure helps—we can follow the same steps when deserializing it, only now we'll *read* from file and *write* to memory, rather than the other way around. We have to make sure, however, that the procedure is unambiguous. For instance, we have to know when to stop reading elements of a given data structure. We must know where the end of a data structure is. The clues that were present during serialization might not be present on disk. For instance, a linked list had a null pointer as *next* in its last element. But if we decide not to store pointers, how are we to know when we have reached the end of the list? Of course, we may decide to store the pointers anyway, just to have a clue when to stop. Or, even better, we could store the count of elements in front of the list.

The need to know sizes of data structures before we can deserialize them imposes additional constraints on the order of serialization. When we serialize one part of the program's data, all other parts are present in memory. We can often infer the size of a given data structure by looking into other data structures. When deserializing, we don't have this comfort. We either have to make sure that these other data structures are deserialized first, or add some redundancy to the serialized image, e.g., store the counts multiple times. A good example is a class that contains a pointer to a dynamically allocated array and the current size of the array. It really doesn't matter which member comes first, the pointer or the count. However, when serializing this object we must store the count first and the contents of the array next. Otherwise we won't be able to allocate the appropriate amount of memory or read the correct number of entries.

Another kind of ambiguity might arise when storing polymorphic data structures. For instance, a binary node contains two pointers to Node. That's not a problem when we serialize it—we can tell the two children to serialize themselves by calling the appropriate virtual functions. But when the time comes to deserialize the node, how do we know what the real type of each child is? We have to know that before we can even start deserializing them. That's why the serialized image of any polymorphic data structure has to start with some kind of code that identifies the class of the data structure. Based on this code, the deserializer will be able to call the appropriate constructor.

Let's now go back to our project and implement the serialization and deserialization of the `Calculator`'s data structures. First we have to create an output file. We'll encapsulate a file inside a *serial stream* object. A serial stream can accept a number of basic data types—e.g., long, short, and double—as well as some simple aggregates like strings and write them to a file.

Notice that I didn't mention the most common type—the integer. That's because the size of the integer is system-dependent. Suppose you serialize a data structure that contains integers and send it on a diskette or through e-mail to somebody who has a version of the same program running on a different processor. Your program might write an integer as two bytes and their program might expect a four-byte or even an eight-byte integer. That's why, when serializing, we usually convert the system-dependent types, like integers, to system-independent types like longs. In fact, it's not only the size that matters—the order of bytes is important as well.

> There are essentially two kinds of processors: ones that use big-endian and ones that use little-endian order (some can use either). For instance, a `short` or a `long` can be stored most-significant-byte-first or least-significant-byte-first. The Intel family of processors store the least significant byte first—the little-endian style—whereas the Motorola family does the opposite. So if you want your program to interoperate between Wintel (Windows running on Intel) and Macintosh, you'll have to take the order of bytes into account when you serialize simple data types. Of course, if you're *not* planning on porting your program between the two camps, you can safely ignore one of them.
>
> Having said that, I still believe that in most cases you *should* take precautions against variable size types and convert integers or enumerations to fixed-size types.

It would be great to be able to assume that, once you come up with the on-disk format for your program, it would never change. Unfortunately, that would be very naive. Formats change and the least you can do to acknowledge it is to refuse to load a format you don't understand.

> **Always store a version number as part of your on-disk data structures.**

Script 46   In order to implement serialization, all we have to do is to create a stream, write the version number into it, and tell the calculator to serialize itself. By the way, we are now reaping the benefits of our earlier combining of several objects into the `Calculator` object.

```
const long Version = 1;
Status CommandParser::Save (std::string const & nameFile)
```

```
{
  std::cerr << "Save to: \"" << nameFile << "\"\n";
  Status status = stOk;
  try
  {
    Serializer out (nameFile);
    out.PutLong (Version );
    _calc.Serialize (out);
  }
  catch (char const * msg)
  {
    std::cerr << "Error: Save failed: "
              << msg << std::endl;
    status = stError;
  }
  catch (...)
  {
    std::cerr << "Error: Save failed\n";
    status = stError;
  }
  return status;
}
```

When deserializing, we follow exactly the same steps, except that now we *read* instead of writing, and *de*-serialize instead of serializing. And, if the version number doesn't match, we refuse to load.

```
Status CommandParser::Load (std::string const & nameFile)
{
  std::cerr << "Load from: \"" << nameFile << "\"\n";
  Status status = stOk;
  try
  {
    DeSerializer in (nameFile);
    long ver = in.GetLong ();
    if (ver != Version)
        throw "Version number mismatch";
    _calc.DeSerialize (in);
  }
  catch (char const * msg)
  {
    std::cerr << "Error: Load failed:"
              << msg << std::endl;
    status = stError;
  }
  catch (...)
  {
    std::cerr << "Error: Load failed\n";
    // Data structures may be corrupt
    throw;
  }
  return status;
}
```

Script 47   There are two objects inside the Calculator that we'd like to save to the disk—the symbol table and the store—one storing the names of the variables and the other their values. So that's what we'll do.

```
void Calculator::Serialize (Serializer & out)const
{
  _symTab.Serialize (out);
  _store.Serialize (out);
}
void Calculator::DeSerialize (DeSerializer & in)
{
  _symTab.DeSerialize (in);
  _store.DeSerialize (in);
}
```

Script 48   The symbol table consists of a dictionary that maps strings to integers, plus a variable that contains the current ID. And the simplest way to walk the symbol table is indeed in this order. To walk the standard map, we will use its iterator. First we have to store the count of elements, so that we know how many to read during deserialization. Then we will iterate over the whole map and store pairs (string, id). Notice that the iterator for `std::map` points to `std::pair`, which has `first` and `second` data members. According to our previous discussion, we store the ID as a `long`.

```
void SymbolTable::Serialize (Serializer & out) const
{
  out.PutLong (_dictionary.size ());
  std::map<std::string, std::size_t>::const_iterator it;
  for (it = _dictionary.begin ();
       it != _dictionary.end (); ++it)
  {
    out.PutString (it->first);
    out.PutLong (it->second);
  }
  out.PutLong (_id);
}
```

The deserializer must read the data in the same order as they were serialized: first the dictionary, then the current ID. When deserializing the map, we first read its size. Then we simply read pairs of strings and longs and add them to the map. Here we treat the map as an associative array. Notice that we first clear the existing dictionary—we have to do this, or else we could get into conflicts with the same ID corresponding to different strings.

```
void SymbolTable::DeSerialize (DeSerializer & in)
{
  _dictionary.clear ();
  int len = in.GetLong ();
  for (int i = 0; i < len; ++i)
  {
```

```
        std::string str = in.GetString ();
        std::size_t id = in.GetLong ();
        _dictionary [str] = id;
    }
    _id = in.GetLong ();
}
```

Notice that for every serialization procedure we immediately write its counterpart—the deserialization procedure. This way we make sure that the two match.

Script 49   The serialization of the store is also very simple: first the size, and then the series of pairs (`double, bool`).

```
void Store::Serialize (Serializer & out) const
{
    std::size_t len = _cell.size ();
    out.PutLong (len);
    for (std::size_t i = 0; i < len; ++i)
    {
        out.PutDouble (_cell [i]);
        out.PutBool (_isInit [i]);
    }
}
```

When deserializing the store, we first clear the previous values, read the size, and then read the pairs (`double, bool`) one by one. We have a few options when filling the two vectors with new values. One would be to push them back, one by one. Since we know the number of entries up front, we could reserve space in the vectors by calling the method `reserve`. Here I decided to `resize` the vectors instead, and then treat them as arrays. The resizing fills the vector of doubles with zeros and the vector of `bool` with `false` (these are the default values for these types).

There is an important difference between `reserve` and `resize`. Most standard containers have either one or both of these methods. `reserve` makes sure that there will be no reallocation when elements are added, e.g., using `push_back`, up to the reserved *capacity*. This is a good optimization when we know the required capacity up front. In the case of a vector, the absence of reallocation also means that iterators, pointers, or references to the elements of the vector won't be suddenly invalidated by internal reallocation.

`reserve`, however, does not change the `size` of the container; `resize` does. When you `resize` a container, new elements are added to it. (Consequently, you can't `resize` containers that store objects with no default constructors or default values.)

- `reserve`—changes capacity but not size
- `resize`—changes size

You can inquire about the current capacity of the container by calling its `capacity` method. And, of course, you get its size by calling `size`.

```
      void Store::DeSerialize (DeSerializer & in)
      {
        _cell.clear ();
        _isInit.clear ();
        std::size_t len = in.GetLong ();
        _cell.resize (len);
        _isInit.resize (len);
        for (std::size_t i = 0; i < len; ++i)
        {
          _cell [i] = in.GetDouble ();
          _isInit [i] = in.GetBool ();
        }
      }
```

Script 50   Finally, let's look at the implementation of the deserializer stream. It is a pretty
thin layer on top of the output stream.

```
      #include <fstream>
      using std::ios_base;

      const long TruePattern = 0xfab1fab2;
      const long FalsePattern = 0xbad1bad2;

      class DeSerializer
      {
      public:
        DeSerializer (std::string const & nameFile)
          : _stream (nameFile.c_str (),
                     ios_base::in | ios_base::binary)
        {
          if (!_stream.is_open ())
              throw "couldn't open file";
        }
        long GetLong ()
        {
          if (_stream.eof ())
              throw "unexpected end of file";
          long l;
          _stream.read (reinterpret_cast<char *> (&l),
                        sizeof (long));
          if (_stream.bad ())
              throw "file read failed";
          return l;
        }
        double GetDouble ()
        {
          double d;
          if (_stream.eof ())
             throw "unexpected end of file";
          _stream.read (reinterpret_cast<char *> (&d),
                        sizeof (double));
          if (_stream.bad ())
             throw "file read failed";
```

```
        return d;
    }
    std::string GetString ()
    {
      long len = GetLong ();
      std::string str;
      str.resize (len);
      _stream.read (&str [0], len);
      if (_stream. bad ())
          throw "file read failed";
      return str;
    }
    bool GetBool ()
    {
      long b = GetLong ();
      if (_stream.bad ())
          throw "file read failed";
      if (b == TruePattern)
          return true;
      else if (b == FalsePattern)
          return false;
      else .
          throw "data corruption";
      return false; // To avoid compiler warning
    }
  private:
    std::ifstream _stream;
};
```

Several interesting things are happening here. First of all, what are these strange flags that we pass to ifstream::open? The first one, ios_base::in, means that we are opening the file for input. The second one, ios_base::binary, tells the operating system that we don't want any carriage return linefeed translations.

What is this carriage return linefeed nonsense? It's one of the biggest blunders of the DOS file system, and was unfortunately inherited by all flavors of Windows. The creators of DOS decided that the system should convert the single character '\n' into a pair '\r', '\n'. The reasoning was that when you print a file, the printer interprets the carriage return, '\r', as the command to go back to the beginning of the current line, and the linefeed, '\n', as the command to move down to the next line (not necessarily to its beginning). So a printer requires two characters to go to the beginning of the next line. Nowadays, when we use laser printers that understand PostScript and print WYSIWYG documents, this whole idea seems rather odd, and even more so if you consider that an older operating system, UNIX, found a way of dealing with this problem without involving low-level file system services.

Anyway, if all you want is to store bytes of data in a file, you have to remember to open it in "binary" mode, or else you might get unexpected results. By the way, the default mode is `ios_base::text`, which does the unfortunate character translation.

Another interesting point is that the method `ifstream::read` reads data to a character buffer—it expects `char *` as its first argument. When we want to read a long, we can't just pass the address of a long to it—the compiler doesn't know how to convert a `long *` to a `char *`. This is one of those cases when we *have* to force the compiler to trust us. We want to split the long into its constituent bytes (we're ignoring here the big-endian/little-endian problem). A reasonably clean way to do it is to use `reinterpret_cast`. We are essentially telling the compiler to "reinterpret" a chunk of memory occupied by the long as a series of chars. We can tell how many chars a long contains by applying to it the operator `sizeof`.

This is a good place to explain the various types of casts (see Table 12.1).

Use this type of cast:	To:
`const_cast`	Remove the const attribute.
`static_cast`	Convert related types.
`reinterpret_cast`	Convert pointers (references) to unrelated types.

Table 12.1   Casts

(There is also a `dynamic_cast`, which we won't discuss here.)

Here's an example of `const_cast`:

```
char const * str = "No modify!";
char * tmp = const_cast<char *> (str);
tmp [0] = 'D';
```

To understand `static_cast`, think of it as the inverse of implicit conversion. Whenever type T can be implicitly converted to type U (in other words, T is-a U), you can use `static_cast` to perform the conversion the other way. For instance, a char can be implicitly converted to an int:

```
char c = '\n';
int i = c; // Implicit conversion
```

Therefore, when you need to convert an int into a char, you should use
static_cast:

```
int i = 0x0d;
char c = static_cast<char> (i);
```

Or, if you have two classes, Base and Derived: public Base, you can implicitly
convert a pointer to Derived to a pointer to Base (Derived is-a Base). Therefore,
you can use static_cast to go the other way:

```
Base * bp = new Derived; // Implicit conversion
Derived * = static_cast<Base *> (bp);
```

You should realize that casts are dangerous and should be used very
judiciously. A cast shifts the responsibility of error checking from the compiler to
the programmer. Try to avoid casting at all costs. Serialization and deserialization
are special in this respect, since they require low-level manipulation of types.

Finally, notice the strange way we store Boolean values. A Boolean value really
requires only one bit for its storage. But, since we don't want to split bytes (or even
longs, for that matter), we'll use some redundancy here. We could, in principle,
store the value true as one and false as zero. However, it costs the same to write a
zero as it does to write an arbitrary value. The difference is that zeros are much
more common in files than, say, 0xbad1bad2. So when I read back the value
0xbad1bad2 and I expect a Boolean, I feel reassured that I'm reading sensible data
and not some random garbage. This is only one of the ways of using redundancy
for consistency checking.

The output serializing stream is the mirror image of DeSerializer.

```
class Serializer
{
public:
  Serializer (std::string const & nameFile)
    : _stream (nameFile.c_str (),
               ios_base::out | ios_base::binary)
  {
    if (!_stream.is_open ())
        throw "couldn't open file";
  }
  void PutLong (long x)
  {
    _stream.write (reinterpret_cast<char *> (&x),
                   sizeof (long));
    if (_stream.bad ())
        throw "file write failed";
  }
  void PutDouble (double x)
  {
    _stream.write (reinterpret_cast<char *> (&x),
                   sizeof (double));
```

```
      if (_stream.bad ())
          throw "file write failed";
    }
    void PutString (std::string const & str)
    {
      std::size_t len = str.length ();
      PutLong (len);
      _stream.write (str.data (), len);
      if (_stream.bad ())
          throw "file write failed";
    }
    void PutBool (bool x)
    {
      long l = x? TruePattern: FalsePattern;
      PutLong (l);
      if (_stream.bad ())
          throw "file write failed";
    }
private:
  std::ofstream _stream;
};
```

There is a shortcut notation combining assignment with a conditional. The following code:

```
long l = x? TruePattern: FalsePattern;
```

is equivalent to:

```
long l;
if (x)
  l = TruePattern;
else
  l = FalsePattern;
```

The ternary (meaning, three-argument) operator **A? B: C** first evaluates A. If A is true, it evaluates and returns B, otherwise it evaluates and returns C. A piece of trivia: unlike in C, in C++ the ternary operator returns an lvalue, so it can be used on the left side of the assignment. Not that I would recommend this style!

There is an even more obscure operator in C++, the comma sequencing operator (we've encountered it once before). The expression

```
A, B
```

first evaluates A, then evaluates and returns B. The evaluation of A is therefore a side effect of the whole operation. Most often the comma operator is used to combine two expressions where only one is expected, like in this double loop:

```
for (int i = 0, j = 0; i < maxI && j < maxJ; ++i, ++j)
```

> By the way, the first comma separates the declarations (complete with ini-
> tialization) of two variables of the same type. It's the second comma, between
> ++i and ++j, that is the sequencing operator.

Notice how careful we are when reading from or writing to a file. That's because our program doesn't have full control of the disk. A write may fail because
we run out of disk space. This can happen at any time, because we might not be
the only client of the file system—there may be other applications and system services that keep allocating (and presumably freeing) disk space.

Reading is worse, because we're not even sure what to expect in the file. Not
only may a read fail because of a hardware problem (unreadable disk sector), but
we must be prepared for all kinds of sabotage. Other applications could get hold
of our precious file and truncate, edit, or write over it. We can't even be sure that
the file we are trying to parse has been created by our program. The user could
have mistakenly or maliciously passed to our program the name of some executable, a spreadsheet or autoexec.bat.

We already have the first line of defense against such cases of mistaken identity
or downright corruption—the version number. The first four bytes Command Parser
reads from the file must match our current version number or it will refuse to load
it. However, the error message we display in such a case, "Version number mismatch" is a bit misleading. A much better solution would be to spare a few additional bytes and stamp all our files with a magic number. Some people use their
initials for the magic number in the hope that one day they'll be able to say to
their children or grandchildren, "Do you see these bytes at the beginning of each
file of this type? These are your mom's (dad's, gramma's, grampa's) initials."
(Provided the application or the system survives that long and is not widely considered an example of bad software engineering.)

12.4 In-Memory Serialization and Deserialization

The serialization of data structures is not necessarily related to their storage in
files. Sometimes you just want to store some data structure in a chunk of memory,
especially if you want to pass it to another application. Programs can talk to each
other and pass data through shared memory or other channels (the Windows
clipboard comes to mind). You might also want to send data in packets across the
network. These are all situations in which you can't simply pass pointers embedded in your data. You have to change the format of the data.

The serialization procedure is the same whether the output goes to a file or to
memory. In fact, if your data structure is serializable (if it has the Serialize and
DeSerialize methods), all you need to do to serialize it to memory is to change
the implementation of Serializer and DeSerializer. Even better, you might make
these classes abstract—turn methods PutLong, PutDouble, PutBool, and PutString

to pure virtual—and provide two different implementations, one writing to a file and one writing to memory. Of course, you'd do the same with the deserializer.

There is one big difference between a file and a chunk of memory—the file grows as you write to it, but a chunk of memory has a fixed size. You have two choices—you can either grow your buffer as needed, or you can calculate the required amount of memory up front and preallocate the whole buffer. As it turns out, calculating the size of a serializable data structure is surprisingly easy. All you need is yet another implementation of the `Serializer` interface called the counting serializer. The *counting serializer* doesn't write anything, it just adds up the sizes of the various data types it is asked to write.

```
class CountingSerializer: public Serializer
{
public:
  CountingSerializer ()
    : _size (0) {}
  std::size_t GetSize () const { return _size; }
  void PutLong (long l)
  {
    _size += sizeof (long);
  }
  void PutDouble (double d)
  {
    _size += sizeof (double);
  }
  void PutString (std::string const & str)
  {
    _size += sizeof (long); // Count
    _size += str.length ();
  }
  void PutBool (bool b)
  {
    _size += sizeof (long);
  }
private:
  std::size_t _size;
};
```

For instance, if you want to calculate the size of the file or memory buffer required for the serialization of a calculator, you can call its `Serialize` method with a counting serializer.

```
CountingSerializer counter;
calc.Serialize (counter);
std::size_t size = counter.GetSize ();
```

Remember that in order for this to work, all methods of `Serializer` *must* be virtual.

12.5 Multiple Inheritance

In order to make a class serializable, you have to add two methods to it, `Serialize` and `DeSerialize`, and implement them. It makes sense, then, to create a separate abstract class—a pure interface—in order to abstract this behavior.

```
class Serializable
{
public:
  virtual void Serialize (Serializer & out) const = 0;
  virtual void DeSerialize (DeSerializer & in) = 0;
};
```

All classes that are serializable should inherit from the `Serializable` interface.

```
class Calculator: public Serializable
class SymbolTable: public Serializable
class Store: public Serializable
```

What's the advantage of doing that? After all, even when you inherit from `Serializable` you still have to add the declaration of the two methods to your class and provide their implementations.

Suppose that a new programmer joins your group and he or she has to add a new class to the project. One day this person sends you an e-mail asking, "How do I make this class serializable?" If this functionality is abstracted into a class, your answer could simply be "Derive your class from `Serializable`." That's it! No further explanation is necessary.

There is, however, a catch. What if your class is already derived from some other class? It will have to inherit from that class *and* from `Serializable`. This is exactly the case in which multiple inheritance can be put to work. In C++, a class can have more than one base class. The syntax for multiple inheritance is pretty straightforward:

```
class MultiDerived: public Base1, public Base2
```

Suppose, for instance, that you were not satisfied with treating `std::string` as a simple type known to `Serializer`. Instead, you'd like to create a separate type, a serializable string. Here's how you could do it using multiple inheritance:

```
using std::string;
class SerialString: public string, public Serializable
{
public:
  SerialString (string const & str)
    : string (str) {}
  void Serialize (Serializer & out) const;
  void DeSerialize (DeSerializer & in);
};
```

Script 52   Multiple inheritance is particularly useful when deriving from abstract classes. This kind of inheritance deals with the interface rather than implementation. In fact, this is exactly the restriction on multiple inheritance that's built into Java and C#. In these languages you can inherit only from one full-blown class, but you can add multiple inheritance from any number of interfaces to it (the equivalent of C++ abstract classes). In most cases this is indeed a very reasonable restriction.

Chapter 13
Overloading Operator new

Both `new` and `delete` are considered operators in C++. What this means, in particular, is that they can be overloaded like almost any other operator. And just as you can define a class-specific `operator=`, you can also define class-specific operators `new` and `delete`. They will be automatically called by the compiler to allocate and deallocate objects of that particular class. Moreover, you can overload and override global versions of `new` and `delete`.

13.1 Class-Specific new

Dynamic memory allocation and deallocation is not cheap. A lot of programs spend the bulk of their time inside the free store, searching for free blocks, recycling deleted blocks, and merging them to prevent fragmentation. If memory management is a performance bottleneck in your program, there are several optimization techniques you can use.

Overloading `new` and `delete` on a per-class basis is usually used to speed up the allocation and deallocation of objects of that particular class. There are two main techniques—caching and bulk allocation.

13.1.1 Caching

The idea behind caching is that recycling is cheaper than manufacturing. Suppose that we wanted to speed up additions to a hash table. Every time an addition is performed, a new link is allocated.

In our program, these links are only deallocated when the whole hash table is destroyed, which happens at the end of the program, so that's not a very good example of actual performance enhancement. Imagine, however, using our hash table in a different program, where it's possible to selectively remove items from the hash table, or where many hash tables can be created and destroyed during the lifetime of the program. In both cases we might speed up the average link allocation time by keeping the links that are currently not in use.

new1
We'll use a `List::Free` object as storage for unused links. To get a new link we'll call its `NewLink` method. To return a link back to the pool, we'll call its `Recycle` method. There is also a `Purge` method that frees the whole pool. The pool of links is implemented as a linked list.

```cpp
class Link;

class Free
{
public:
  Free () : _p (0) {}
  ~Free ();
  void Purge ();
  void * NewLink ();
  void Recycle (void * link);
private:
  Link * _p;
};
```

The class `Link` has a static member, `_freeList`, which is used by the overloaded class-specific operators `new` and `delete` (remember, a static member is shared by all instances of the class).

```cpp
class Link
{
  friend class Free;
public:
  Link (Link * pNext, int value)
    : _pNext (pNext), _value (value) {}

  Link *  Next () const { return _pNext; }
  int     GetValue () const { return _value; }
  // Allocator
  void * operator new (std::size_t size)
  {
    assert (size == sizeof (Link));
    return _freeList.NewLink ();
  }
  void operator delete (void * mem)
  {
    if (mem)
      _freeList.Recycle (mem);
  }
  static void Purge () { _freeList.Purge (); }
```

```
private:
  static   Free _freeList;

  int    _value;
  Link * _pNext;
};
```

Notice that the assertion in operator new protects us from somebody calling this particular operator for a different class. How could that happen? Operators new and delete are inherited. If a class derived from Link didn't override these operators, new called for the derived class would return an object of the wrong size (base-class size).

The creation of a new Link inside List::Add is now translated by the compiler into the call to the class-specific operator new, followed by the call to its constructor (if any). The beauty of this method is that no changes to the implementation of List are needed.

```
List::~List ()
{
  while (_pHead != 0)
  {
    Link * pLink = _pHead;
    _pHead = _pHead->Next (); // Unlink pLink
    delete pLink;
  }
}

void List::Add (int value)
{
  Link * pLink = new Link (_pHead, value);
  _pHead = pLink;
}
```

A hash table contains an array of Lists that will all internally use the special-purpose allocator for its links (see Figure 13.1).

After we finish using the hash table, we might want to purge the memory stored in the private allocator. That would make sense, for instance, if there was only one hash table in our program, and it allowed deletion as well as addition of entries. Conversely, if we wanted our pool of links to be shared between multiple hash tables, we wouldn't want to purge it every time a hash table is destroyed.

```
class HTable
{
public:
  explicit HTable (int size): _size(size)
  {
    _aList = new List [size];
  }
```

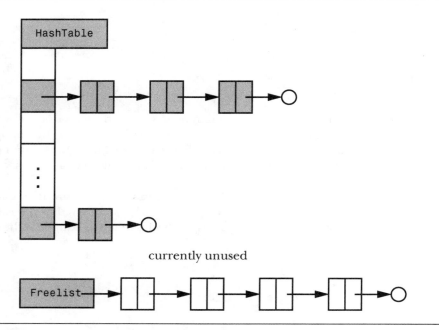

Figure 13.1 Links used in a hash table and links stored in a free list

```
    ~HTable ()
    {
      delete [] _aList;
      // Release memory in free list
      List::Link::Purge (); // Optional
    }

    // ...
private:
    List * _aList;
    int    _size;
};
```

Notice that Purge is a *static* method of Link, so we don't need an instance of Link to call it.

In the implementation file, we first have to define the static member _freeList of the class Link. Static data is automatically initialized to zero.

```
    List::Free List::Link::_freeList;
```

The implementation of List::Free is pretty straightforward. We try to reuse Links from the free list, if possible; otherwise we call the global operator new. Since we are allocating raw memory, we ask for sizeof (Link) bytes (chars). When we delete this storage, we cast Links back to their raw form. Deleting a Link as a Link would result in a (second!) call to its destructor. We don't want to do it here, since destructors for these Links have already been called when the class-specific `delete` was called. Here we are already below the level of objects and their destructors; we are now concerned with the deallocation of raw storage.

```
void * List::Free::NewLink ()
{
  if (_p != 0)
  {
    void * mem = _p;
    _p = _p->_pNext;
    return mem;
  }
  else
  {
    // Use global operator new
    return ::new char [sizeof (Link)];
  }
}

void List::Free::Recycle (void * mem)
{
  Link * link = static_cast<Link *> (mem);
  link->_pNext = _p;
  _p = link;
}

List::Free::~Free ()
{
  Purge ();
}

void List::Free::Purge ()
{
  while (_p != 0)
  {
    // It was allocated as an array of char
    char * mem = reinterpret_cast<char *> (_p);
    _p = _p->Next();
    ::delete [] mem;
  }
}
```

Notice all the casting we have to do. When our overloaded new is called, it is expected to return a void pointer. Internally, however, we either recycle a Link from a linked-list pool or allocate a raw chunk of memory of the appropriate size. We don't want to call ::new Link, because that would have an unwanted side effect of calling Link's constructor (it will be called anyway after we return from operator new).

Our delete, on the other hand, is called with a void pointer, so we have to cast it to a Link in order to store it in the list. Purge deletes all Links as if they were arrays of chars, since that is how they were allocated. Again, we don't want to delete them as Links, because Link destructors have already been called.

. As usual, calls to the global operators new and delete can be disambiguated by prepending double colons. Here they are not strictly necessary, but they enhance readability.

13.1.2 Bulk Allocation

new2   Another approach to speeding up allocation is to allocate in bulk and thus amortize the cost of memory allocation across many calls to operator new. The implementation of Links, Lists, and HashTables is the same as before, except that a new class, LinkAllocator, is used in the place of List::Free. It has the same interface as List::Free, but its implementation is more involved. Besides keeping a list of recycled Links, it also has a separate list of blocks of links. Each block consists of a header of class Block and a block of 16 consecutive raw pieces of memory each the size of a Link (see Figure 13.2).

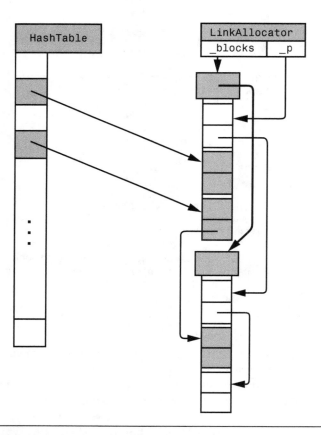

Figure 13.2 Blocks of memory are partitioned into links. Some links are in a free list and some are used by a hash table

```
class LinkAllocator
{
  enum { BlockLinks = 16 };
  class Block
  {
  public:
    Block * Next () { return _next; }
    void SetNext (Block * next) { _next = next; }
  private:
    Block * _next;
  };
public:
  LinkAllocator () : _p (0), _blocks (0) {}
  ~LinkAllocator ();
  void Purge ();
  void * NewLink () ;
  void Recycle (void * link);
private:
  List::Link  * _p;
  Block * _blocks;
};
```

This is how a new Link is created:

```
void * LinkAllocator::NewLink ()
{
  if (_p == 0)
  {
    // Use global operator new to allocate a block of links
    char * p = ::new char [sizeof (Block)
                    + BlockLinks * sizeof (List::Link)];
    // Add it to the list of blocks
    Block * block = reinterpret_cast<Block *> (p);
    block->SetNext (_blocks);
    _blocks = block;
    // Add it to the list of links
    p += sizeof (Block);
    for (int i = 0; i < BlockLinks; ++i)
    {
      List::Link * link =
                    reinterpret_cast<List::Link *> (p);
      link->SetNext (_p);
      _p = link;
      p += sizeof (List::Link);
    }
  }
  void * mem = _p;
  p = _p->Next ();
  return mem;
}
```

The first chunk of code deals with the situation when there are no unused links in the Link list. A whole block of 16 (BlockLinks) Link-sized chunks of memory is allocated all at once, together with some room for the Block header. Block is immediately linked into the list of blocks and then chopped up into separate Links, which are added to the Link list. Once the Link list is replenished, we can pick a Link from it and pass it out. The implementation of Recycle is the same as before—links are returned to the Link list. Purge, on the other hand, does bulk deallocations of whole blocks.

```
void LinkAllocator::Purge ()
{
  while (_blocks != 0)
  {
    // It was allocated as an array of char
    char * mem = reinterpret_cast<char *> (_blocks);
    _blocks = _blocks->Next();
    ::delete [] mem;
  }
}
```

Only one call in sixteen to new Link results in actual memory allocation; all the others are dealt with very quickly by picking a ready-made Link from a list.

13.1.3   Array new

Even though class Link has overloaded its operators new and delete, if you were to allocate a whole *array* of Links, as in new Link [10], the compiler would call global new to allocate memory for it. It would *not* call the class-specific overload. This is done for two main reasons, one of them being efficiency. The other reason has to do with the fact that an *array* of Links is a different type than a Link. An array of Links *is not* a Link; therefore, a Link-specific operator new doesn't apply to an array of Links.

Conversely, deleting such an array will result in the call to the global operator delete—not its class-specific overload. Since in our program we never allocate arrays of Links, we have nothing to worry about. And even if we did, global new and delete would do the right thing anyway.

However, in the rare case when you actually *want* to have control over array allocations, C++ provides a way. It lets you overload operators new[] and delete[]. The syntax and the signatures are analogous to the overloads of straight new and delete.

```
void * operator new [] (size_t size);
void operator delete [] (void * p);
```

The only difference is that the size passed by the compiler to new[] takes into account the total size of the array plus some additional data used by the compiler to distinguish between pointers to objects and arrays of objects. (For instance, the compiler has to know the number of elements in the array to be able to call destructors on all of them when delete [] is called.)

All four operators—new, delete, new[], and delete[]—are treated as static members of the class that overloads them (i.e., they don't have access to this).

13.2 Global new

Unlike class-specific new, global new is usually being overloaded for debugging purposes—when NDEBUG is not defined. In some cases, however, you might want to overload global new and delete permanently, because you have a better allocation strategy or you want more control over it.

In any case, you have a choice of either overriding global new and delete or adding your own special versions that follow a slightly different syntax. The standard operator new takes one argument of type size_t; standard delete takes one argument of type void *. You can define your own versions of new and delete to take additional arguments of arbitrary types. For instance, you can define

```
void * operator new (size_t size, char * name);
void operator delete (void * p, char * name);
```

and call the special new using this syntax:

```
Foo * p = new ("special") Foo;
```

Unfortunately, there is no way to call the special delete explicitly, so you have to be sure that the standard delete will correctly handle memory allocated using your special new (or that delete is never called for such objects).

So what's the use of the overloaded delete with special arguments? There is actually one case in which it will be called—when an exception is thrown during object construction. As you might recall, there is a contract, implicit in the language, that if an exception happens during the construction of an object, the memory for this object will be automatically deallocated. It so happens that during an object's construction the compiler is still aware of which version of operator new was called to allocate memory. It is therefore able to generate a call to the corresponding version of delete in case an exception is thrown.

After the successful completion of construction, this information is no longer available and the compiler has no means to guess which version of global delete is appropriate for a given object.

Once you have defined an overloaded version of new, you can call it explicitly by specifying its additional argument(s). Or you can substitute all calls to new in your code with the overloaded version using macro substitution.

13.2.1   Macros

We haven't really talked about macros in this book—they are part of standard C++, but their use is strongly discouraged. In the old days they were used in place of the more sophisticated C++ features, such as inline functions and templates. Now that there are better ways of getting the same functionality, macros are fast becoming obsolete. But just for completeness, let me explain how they work.

> "Macros are obnoxious, smelly, sheet-hogging bedfellows for several reasons, most of which are related to the fact that they are a glorified text-substitution facility whose effects are applied during preprocessing, before any C++ syntax and semantic rules can even begin to apply."
> —*Herb Sutter,* from a post in the comp.lang.c++.moderated newsgroup

A macro works through literal substitution. You can think of macro expansion as a separate process performed by the compiler before even getting to the main task of parsing C++ syntax. In fact, in older compilers, macro expansion was done by a separate program, the (macro) preprocessor.

There are two major types of macros. The first type simply substitutes one string with another in the code that logically follows it (by *logically* I mean that if the macro is defined in an include file, it will also work in the file that includes it, and so on).

Let me give you an example that might actually be useful. Let's define the following macro in the file DebugNnew.h

```
#define new new (__FILE__, __LINE__)
```

This macro will substitute all occurrences of new that logically follow this definition with the string new (__FILE__, __LINE__). Moreover, the macro preprocessor will then substitute all occurrences of the special predefined symbol __FILE__ with the full name of the source file in which it finds it, and all occurrences of __LINE__ with the appropriate line number. So if you have a file c:\test\main.cpp with the contents

```
#include "DebugNew.h"
int main ()
{
   int * p = new int;
}
```

it will be preprocessed to produce the following code:

```
int main ()
{
   int * p = new ("c:\test\main.cpp", 4) int;
}
```

Now you can use your own overloaded operator new, for instance, to trace all memory allocations. Here's a simple example of such implementation.

```
void * operator new (size_t size,
                     char const * file,
                     int line)
{
  std::cout << file << ":" << line << std::endl;
  return ::new char [size];
}
```

Notice that we have to make sure that our macro is *not* included in the file that defines this particular overload. Otherwise both occurrences of "new" would be substituted by "new(__FILE__, __LINE)," and would result in incorrect code.

The second type of macro also works through textual substitution, but it behaves more like an inline function—it takes arguments. And again, since macro expansion works outside of the C++ compiler, there is no type checking and there is a possibility of unexpected side effects. A classic example is the max macro:

```
#define max(a, b) (((a) > (b))? (a): (b))
```

Notice the parentheses paranoia, a characteristic feature of macros. Programmers learned to put parentheses around macro parameters, because they might be substituted by expressions containing low-precedence operators. Consider, for instance, what happens when you call

```
c = max (a & mask, b & mask)
```

Without the parentheses around parameters in the definition of max, the preprocessor would expand it into

```
c = a & mask >  b & mask? a & mask: b & mask;
```

which, because of operator precedence rules, would be interpreted as:

```
c = (a & (mask > b) & mask)? (a & mask): (b & mask);
```

(The operator > binds its operands stronger than the bitwise "and.") The result of this calculation would most likely be erroneous.

Things get even worse when you call a macro with expressions that have side effects. Consider, for instance, the expansion of max (a++, b++):

```
(((a++) > (b++))? (a++): (b++))
```

One of the variables will be incremented twice, the other once. This is probably not what the programmer expected.

By the way, there is one more gotcha—notice that I didn't put a space between max and the parenthesis that opens the argument list in the macro definition:

```
#define max(a, b)...
```

This is one of these rare occasions in C++ where the presence or absence of whitespace between an identifier and a punctuation changes the meaning of a construct. Without a space, this is a macro with arguments a and b. With a space, it would be a no-argument macro, and (a, b) would become part of the macro body.

13.3 Tracing Memory Leaks

Script 53

A more interesting application of this technique lets you trace unreleased allocations, a.k.a. memory leaks. The idea is to store information about each allocation in a global data structure and dump its contents at the end of the program. The overloaded operator new would add entries to it and delete would remove entries from this data structure.

Since operator delete only has access to a pointer to previously allocated memory, we have to be able to reasonably quickly find the entry based on this pointer. A map keyed by a pointer comes to mind immediately. We'll call this global data structure a Tracer.

```
class Tracer
{
private:
  class Entry
  {
  public:
    Entry (char const * file, int line)
      : _file (file), _line (line)
    {}
    Entry ()
      : _file (0), _line (0)
    {}
    char const * File () const { return _file; }
    int Line () const { return _line; }
  private:
    char const * _file;
    int _line;
  };
  class Lock
  {
  public:
    Lock (Tracer & tracer)
      : _tracer (tracer)
    {
      _tracer.lock ();
```

```
      }
      ~Lock ()
      {
        _tracer.unlock ();
      }
    private:
      Tracer & _tracer;
    };
    typedef std::map<void *, Entry>::iterator iterator;
    friend class Lock;
public:
    Tracer ();
    ~Tracer ();
    void Add (void * p, char const * file, int line);
    void Remove (void * p);
    void Dump ();

    static bool Ready;
private:
    void lock () { ++_lockCount; }
    void unlock () { --_lockCount; }
private:
    std::map<void *, Entry> _map;
    int _lockCount;
};
```

We have defined two auxiliary classes: Tracer::Entry, which is used as the value for the map, and Tracer::Lock, which is used to temporarily disable tracing. They are used in the implementation of Tracer::Add and Tracer::Remove.

The method Add adds a new entry to the map, but only when tracing is active. Notice that it disables tracing when accessing the map—we don't want to trace the allocations inside the map code.

```
void Tracer::Add (void * p, char const * file, int line)
{
  if (_lockCount > 0)
    return; // Don't trace it
  Tracer::Lock lock (*this);
  _map [p] = Entry (file, line);
}
```

The method Remove makes the same preparations as Add and then searches the map for the pointer to be removed. If it's found, the whole entry is erased.

```
void Tracer::Remove (void * p)
{
  if (_lockCount > 0)
    return;

  Tracer::Lock lock (*this);
  iterator it = _map.find (p);
```

```
      if (it != _map.end ())
      {
        _map.erase (it);
      }
}
```

Finally, at the end of the program, the method `Dump` is called from the destructor of `Tracer` to display all the leaks.

```
void Tracer::Dump ()
{
  if (_map.size () != 0)
  {
    std::cerr << "*** Memory leak(s):\n";
    for (iterator it = _map.begin ();
         it != _map.end (); ++it)
    {
      char const * file = it->second.File ();
      int line = it->second.Line ();
      unsigned int addr = reinterpret_cast<unsigned int> (it->first);
      std::cerr << "0x" << std::hex << addr << ": "
        << file << ", line " << std::dec << line
        << std::endl;
    }
    std::cerr << std::endl;
  }
}
```

> If your implementation of the C++ standard library cannot deal correctly with standard output after the termination of `main`, read the next section, Debug Output.

Since we are overloading the global operators `new` and `delete`, the `Tracer` has to be a global object too.

```
extern Tracer NewTrace;
```

Notice that this might lead to some problems if there are other global objects that allocate memory in their constructors. The order of construction of global objects residing in different files is undefined. If a memory-allocating global object is constructed before the construction of `NewTracer`, we could be in trouble. That's why I introduced a static Boolean flag, `Tracer::Ready`, which is originally set to `false`.

```
bool Tracer::Ready = false;
```

The constructor of Tracer sets this flag to true and the destructor sets it back to false.

```
Tracer::Tracer ()
  : _lockCount (0)
{
  Ready = true;
}

Tracer::~Tracer ()
{
  Ready = false;
  Dump ();
}
```

The implementation of the overloaded new is straightforward.

```
void * operator new (std::size_t size,
                     char const * file,
                     int line)
{
  void * p = std::malloc (size);
  if (Tracer::Ready)
    NewTrace.Add (p, file, line);
  return p;
}
```

Notice that we use the low-level memory allocating function malloc rather than calling operator ::new. That's because we are going to overload the regular, argument-less new as well.

There must be a corresponding overload of delete to be used during aborted constructions.

```
void operator delete (void * p,
                      char const * ,
                      int )
{
  if (Tracer::Ready)
    NewTrace.Remove (p);
  std::free (p);
}
```

Since we used malloc for memory allocation, we have to use free for deallocation. Notice that I haven't *named* the last two arguments to delete. This trick lets you eliminate the compiler warning, "Argument not used in function."

For completeness, we also override the regular global new, in case there are parts of our code outside of the reach of macro substitution (for instance, parts of the C++ standard library).

```
void * operator new (std::size_t size)
{
  void * p = std::malloc (size);
  if (Tracer::Ready)
    NewTrace.Add (p, "?", 0);
  return p;
}
```

Finally, we have to override the global delete in order to trace all deallocations.

```
void operator delete (void * p)
{
  if (Tracer::Ready)
    NewTrace.Remove (p);
  std::free (p);
}
```

Since we only want the tracing to be enabled in the debug version of our program, we'll enclose the definition of the macro in conditional compilation directives. The contents of the header DebugNew.h is below. Include this file in all those source files that you want to test for memory leaks. For now, don't try to include it in files that call new to allocate arrays, unless you overload the *array* new and delete as well. (Similarly, this macro will interfere with calls to placement new—see Section 13.3.2)

```
#if !defined NDEBUG
#include "Tracer.h"

#define new new(__FILE__, __LINE__)
#endif
```

Most compilers define the flag NDEBUG (no debug) when building the release (non-debugging) version of the program. The file Tracer.h contains, among others, the declaration of the overloaded operators new and delete.

Similarly, we have to make sure that the implementation of the *overloaded* new and delete is compiled conditionally. That's because the decision as to which version of new and delete will be called from your program is done by the linker after all the source files are already compiled. If the linker doesn't find an implementation of these operators in your code, it will use the ones provided by the runtime library. If it does, it will call your overrides throughout the program.

Finally, we add the definition of the global object NewTrace to main.cpp. The destructor of this object will dump memory leaks after the end of main.

```
#if !defined NDEBUG
Tracer NewTrace;
#endif
```

A word of caution: I haven't talked about *thread safety*, because it is outside the scope of this book. You should be aware, however, that in a multithreaded application your global operator new might be called from several places at once, so you usually have to think of some kind of synchronization (a critical section or a mutex). The standard operator new (as well as delete) is thread-safe, as is indeed most of the C++ standard library.

13.3.1 Debug Output

An even better idea is to redirect the dump to the debugger. (An additional advantage of doing this is to bypass potential library bugs that prevent standard output after main). If your program is supposed to run under Windows, you can use the function OutputDebugString, declared in <windows.h>. It will output strings to the debug window when you run the program under the debugger. You can format the strings using std::stringstream.

```
if (_map.size () != 0)
{
  OutputDebugString ("*** Memory leak(s):\n");
  for (iterator it = _map.begin ( );
       it != _map.end (); ++it)
  {
    char const * file = it->second.File ();
    int line = it->second.Line ();
    int addr = reinterpret_cast (it->first);
    std::ostringstream out;
    out << "0x" << std::hex << addr << ": "
    << file << ", line " << std::dec << line << std::endl;
    OutputDebugString (out.str ().c_str ());
  }
  OutputDebugString ("\n");
}
```

If your C++ standard library doesn't handle even that, try bypassing integer output by using a low-level conversion routine, itoa (integer-to-ASCII).

```
char buffer1 [10];
char buffer2 [8];
out << "0x" << itoa (addr, buffer1, 16) << ": "
    << file << ", line " << itoa (line, buffer2, 10) << std::endl;
```

13.3.2 Placement new

There is one particular overload of new that is part of the C++ standard library. It's called *placement* new (note that sometimes all overrides of new that take extra arguments are called *placement* new). This overload takes one additional argument, a void pointer. It can be used whenever the memory for the object has already been allocated or reserved by other means, and all you really need is to execute the constructor(s) in an orderly manner. The void pointer argument could be a pointer to some static memory or to a chunk of preallocated raw dynamic memory. Placement new does *not* allocate memory—it uses the memory passed to it through

the void pointer (it is your responsibility to make sure the chunk is big enough)
and calls the appropriate constructor. It is declared in the standard header <new>.

new3   For instance, in our earlier example with bulk allocation, we could have used
placement new to create a Block object using the memory that's been allocated as
an array of bytes. With this change, it would also make sense to have a constructor
of Block initialize the pointer to next.

```
LinkAllocator::Block::Block (Block * next)
  : _next (next) { }
```

That would eliminate the need for the method SetNext.

```
char * p = ::new char [sizeof (Block)
                    + BlockLinks * sizeof (List::Link)];
Block * block = ::new (p) Block (_blocks);
_blocks = block;
```

The C++ standard library defines a corresponding placement delete, which
does absolutely nothing but is required in case the constructor throws an exception. Since placement new doesn't allocate any memory, it is an error to delete the
object created by it. Of course, the *raw* memory that's been passed to placement
new has to be dealt with appropriately. In our example, it's the Purge method that
frees raw memory.

By the way, there is also an *array* placement operator new[] and the corresponding delete[]. It is left as an exercise for you to use it for converting memory following the Block header into an array of Links (what kind of a constructor would
you add to Link for that purpose?).

13.4 Conclusion

Script 54   Congratulations! You have now officially advanced from the level of weekend programming to the new level of industrial-strength programming. You've learned
some of the important techniques that will allow you to build robust applications
in the future. You also became familiar with the process of working on a software
project. This is what the work of a programmer looks like most of the time.

If you compare the original version of the calculator with the current one,
you'll notice that hardly a line of code has remained unchanged. And yet we were
able to accomplish this change in small incremental steps, each step producing a
working version of the program. This is the essence of good software engineering.

There is still one fundamental problem with our calculator. There is virtually
no market for command-line applications. Gone are the days when a programmer
could make a living creating DOS programs. It's time for us to explore the land of
GUI.

Part 3

Windows

No serious programmer can ignore Windows—or, more generally, a window-based programming environment. I knew from the beginning that this book would have to include a section on Windows. At some point I had several chapters written, complete with a multithreaded application that painted a three-dimensional animated polygon mesh. Then I tossed it all.

The problem is that teaching Windows programming is a huge undertaking. It calls for a separate book, maybe even a multivolume compendium. So if I wanted to include an introduction to Windows in this book, I had to be very selective. I had to focus on a few important issues and give the foundations on which the reader could build his or her understanding of Windows programming.

Chapter 14
Libraries

From the point of view of C++ programming methodologies, Windows programming is essentially virgin territory. There are a few books that use a limited subset of C++ to demonstrate the Windows API (application programming interface—the name given to the set of library functions that give the programmer access to the Windows operating system). There are a few commercial libraries that develop their own dialects—again, based on a subset of C++. But the attempts at providing a comprehensive strategy of dealing with a window-based environment using modern C++ are essentially nonexistent.

A few years ago I started posting little Windows tutorials and snippets of code at my company's web site. Nothing sophisticated, just a few tips on how to encapsulate some basic Windows functionality. I was amazed at the positive response I got from the programming community. Judging from the number of visits and the tenor of e-mail messages, both from beginning and experienced Windows programmers, my tutorials must have fulfilled a significant demand.

So here's the plan. I'll start with a small diatribe against some existing solutions, then I'll introduce the Windows programming paradigm. I'll show you how to write some simple programs to get you started programming Windows. Then I'll get to the main topic—how to best encapsulate Windows API using the object-oriented paradigm in C++. Even though it's not my ambition to write a complete Windows library, I'll try to explain a lot of the techniques that could be used in writing one.

14.1 Of Macros and Wizards

Let's start by talking about how *not* to write a library. First of all, do not try to create an obscure dialect of C++. By a dialect I mean a system of macros that generate C++ code. For instance, would you recognize this as a fragment of a C++ program?

```
IMPLEMENT_DYNAMIC(CMyThing, CMyObject)
BEGIN_MESSAGE_MAP(CMyThing, CMyObject)
    ON_WM_PAINT()
    ON_WM_LBUTTONDOWN()
END_MESSAGE_MAP()
```

If this were the only way to write Windows programs in C++, I'd say C++ is just not the right language for the task. Instead of creating a new dialect using a C++ macro preprocessor, let's invent a new language altogether—a language that is more suitable for Windows and has a semblance of a half-decent programming language. In fact, I toyed with this idea but decided to first give C++ a chance.

Another language escape mechanism used by library writers are "wizards"— little programmer-friendly gadgets that generate C++ code. In principle, generating code using GUI (graphical user interface) controls is not such a bad idea. If well thought out, it is equivalent to introducing some sort of a higher-level programming language, in which programming might involve the manipulation of UI gadgets. There is some research into "visual" languages, and this might be just the thing for visually intensive Windows applications.

However, if you want to invent a new language—visual or otherwise—you better be a pretty good language designer. Throwing together a few ad hoc wizards is no substitute for a programming paradigm. It might in fact do more damage than good. One major unspoken requirement of any programming language is that your programming environment doesn't discard your source code.

> **Imagine a C++ compiler that deletes your source files after producing machine code.**

This is exactly what happens when you use wizards! Once they generate the target C++ code, your input is lost, because *input* in this case consists of the strings you entered in edit controls, the check boxes you checked, the buttons you pushed, and so on. These actions are all part of the "visual" language that the wizard implements. If they are not saved, there is no way you (or, for that matter, anybody else) can make incremental modifications. You either have to redo the whole procedure from scratch, or abandon the visual language altogether and modify the generated code by hand. At this point the whole advantage of the wizard is lost. No matter how good the wizard is, the code it generates is *not* human-friendly.

So as long as we don't have two-way wizards that can reverse-engineer C++ code into its visual form and let you not only create, but also *maintain* visual code, we have little choice but to use the programming language at hand—in our case, C++.

Chapter 15
Programming Paradigm

A Windows program, like any other interactive program, is for the most part input-driven. However, the input of a Windows program is conveniently predigested by the operating system. When a user presses a key or moves the mouse, Windows intercepts the event, preprocesses it, and dispatches it to the appropriate user program. The program gets all its messages from Windows. It may do something about them or not—in the latter case it lets Windows do the "right" thing (the default processing).

When a Windows program starts, it registers a *window class* with the system (it's not a C++ class). Through this "class data structure" it gives the system, among other things, a pointer to a callback function called the *window procedure*. Windows will call this procedure whenever it wants to pass a message to the program and to notify it of interesting events. The name "callback" means just this: don't call Windows, Windows will call you back.

The program also gets a peek at every message in the *message loop* before it gets dispatched to the appropriate window procedure. In most cases, the message loop just forwards the message back to Windows to do the dispatching (see Figure 15.1).

Windows is a multitasking operating system—there may be many programs running at the same time. So how does Windows know which program should get a particular message? Mouse messages, for instance, are usually dispatched to the application that created the window over which the mouse cursor is positioned at a given moment (unless an application "captures" the mouse).

Most Windows programs create one or more *windows* on the screen. At any given time, one of these windows has the *focus* and is considered *active* (its title bar is usually highlighted). Keyboard messages are sent to the window that has the focus.

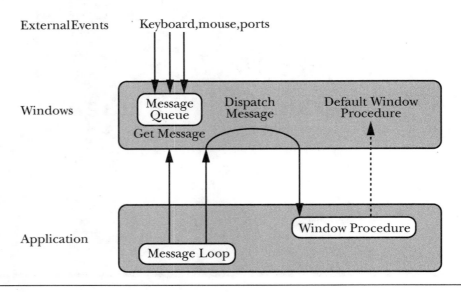

Figure 15.1 Input-driven Windows paradigm

Events such as resizing, maximizing, minimizing, covering, or uncovering a window are handled by Windows, although the concerned program that owns the window also gets a chance to process messages for these events. There are dozens and dozens of types of messages that can be sent to a Windows program. Each program handles the ones that it's interested in and lets Windows deal with the others.

Windows programs use Windows services to output text or graphics to the screen. Windows not only provides a high-level graphical interface, but it separates the program from the actual graphical hardware. In this sense Windows graphics are, to a large extent, device independent.

It is very easy for a Windows program to use standard Windows controls. Menus are easy to create; so are message boxes. Dialog boxes are more general— they can be designed by a programmer using a *dialog editor,* and icons can be created using an *icon editor.* List boxes, edit controls, scroll bars, buttons, radio buttons, check boxes, and so on, are all examples of built-in, ready-to-use controls that make Windows programs so attractive and usable.

All this functionality is available to the programmer through the Windows API. It is a (very large) set of C functions, typedefs, structures, and macros whose declarations are included (directly or indirectly) in <windows.h>, and whose code is linked to the program through a set of libraries and DLLs (dynamic-link libraries).

In this chapter we will be using the Code Co-op project named *windows*. Margin notes give the script numbers to unpack.

15.1 Hello Windows!

Start project
windows
Our first Windows program will do nothing more than create a window with the title bar "Hello Windows!" However, it is definitely more complicated than Kernighan and Ritchie's "Hello World!" and our first "Hello!" C++ program. What we are getting here is much more than the simple old-fashioned teletype output. We are creating a window that can be moved around, resized, minimized, maximized, overlapped by other windows, and so on. It also has a standard system menu in the upper left corner. So let's not complain too much!

In Windows, the main procedure is called `WinMain`. It must use the `WINAPI` calling convention and the system calls it with the following parameters:

- `HINSTANCE hInst`—The handle to the current instance of the program.
- `HINSTANCE hPrevInst`—Obsolete in Win32, this is kept for compatibility with Win16.
- `LPSTR cmdParam`—A string with the command-line arguments.
- `int cmdShow`—A flag that says whether to show the main window or not.

Notice the strange type names. You'll have to get used to them—Windows is full of typedefs. In fact, you will rarely see an `int` or a `char` in the description of the Windows API. For now, it's enough to know that `LPSTR` is in fact a typedef for a `char *` (the abbreviation stands for Long Pointer to STRing, where string is a null-terminated array, and "long pointer" is a fossil left over from the times of 16-bit Windows).

In what follows, I will prefix all Windows API functions with a double colon. A double colon simply means that it's a globally defined function (not a member of any class or namespace). It is somehow redundant, but it makes the code more readable. The classes `WinClassMaker`, `WinMaker`, and `Window` will be defined in a moment.

```
int WINAPI WinMain
  (HINSTANCE hInst, HINSTANCE hPrevInst, LPSTR cmdParam, int cmdShow)
{
  char className [] = "Winnie";
  WinClassMaker winClass (WinProcedure, className, hInst);
  winClass.Register ();
  WinMaker maker (className, hInst);
  Window win = maker.Create ("Hello Windows!");
  win.Display (cmdShow);
```

```
    // Message loop
    MSG  msg;
    int status;
    while ((status = ::GetMessage (& msg, 0, 0, 0)) != 0)
    {
        if (status == -1)
            return -1;
        ::DispatchMessage (& msg);
    }
    return msg.wParam;
}
```

First, the program creates a window class and registers it. Then it creates a window with the caption "Hello Windows!" and displays it (or not, depending on the flag it is given). Finally, it enters the message loop that waits for a message from Windows (the ::GetMessage API) and then lets the system dispatch it. The message will come back to our program when Windows calls the Window procedure, WinProcedure. For the time being we don't have to worry about the details of the message loop. The program normally terminates when ::GetMessage returns zero. The wParam of the last message contains the return code of our program.

The ::GetMessage function is an interesting example of three-state logic. It is defined to return the type BOOL, which is a typedef for int, not bool (in fact, there was no bool in C++, not to mention C, when Windows was first released). The documentation, however, specifies three types of returns: nonzero, zero, and –1 (I am not making this up!). Here's the actual excerpt from the Help file:
  If the function retrieves a message other than WM_QUIT, the return value is **nonzero**.
  If the function retrieves the WM_QUIT message, the return value is **zero**.
  If there is an error, the return value is **–1**.

We introduce the class WinClassMaker to encapsulate the WNDCLASSEX data structure and the ::RegisterClass API.

```
    class WinClassMaker
    {
    public:
      WinClassMaker (WNDPROC WinProcedure,
                     char const * className,
                     HINSTANCE hInst);
      void Register ()
      {
       if (::RegisterClassEx (&_class) == 0)
         throw "RegisterClass failed";
      }
```

```
    private:
      WNDCLASSEX _class;
    };
```

In the constructor of `WinClassMaker` we initialize all parameters to some sensible default values. For instance, we set the default for the mouse cursor to an arrow, and the brush (used by Windows to paint the window's background) to the default window color. We will translate most Windows errors into exceptions. For the time being I will use literal strings as exception objects—they can be caught by the following catch clause:

```
    catch (char const * msg)
```

Later we'll switch to a more sophisticated mechanism (see page 397).

When registering a class, we have to provide the pointer to the window procedure, the name of the class, and the handle to the instance that owns the class.

```
    WinClassMaker::WinClassMaker
      (WNDPROC WinProcedure,
       char const * className,
       HINSTANCE hInst)
    {
      _class.lpfnWndProc = WinProcedure;// Mandatory
      _class.hInstance = hInst;         // Mandatory
      _class.lpszClassName = className; // Mandatory
      _class.cbSize = sizeof (WNDCLASSEX);
      _class.hCursor = ::LoadCursor (0, IDC_ARROW);
      _class.hbrBackground = reinterpret_cast<HBRUSH>
                             (COLOR_WINDOW + 1);
      _class.style = 0;
      _class.cbClsExtra = 0;
      _class.cbWndExtra = 0;
      _class.hIcon = 0;
      _class.hIconSm = 0;
      _class.lpszMenuName = 0;
    }
```

Notice some of the ugly tricks we have to do. The `hbrBackground` data member of `WNDCLASSEX` is defined as `HBRUSH`. However, you can initialize it using one of the standard color constants defined by Windows, `COLOR_WINDOW` in our case. That requires an explicit type cast. Unfortunately, one of the color constants, `COLOR_SCROLLBAR`, is defined to be zero, so it would be confused by Windows with a null brush. That's why you are required to add the spurious one to the color constant when passing it to `WNDCLASSEX`. Windows is full of such "clever hacks."

The class `WinMaker` initializes and stores all the parameters describing a particular window.

```
    class WinMaker
    {
```

```
public:
    WinMaker (char const * className, HINSTANCE hInst);
    HWND Create (char const * title);
private:
    HINSTANCE      _hInst;       // Program instance
    char const * _className;     // Name of Window class
    DWORD          _style;       // Window style
    DWORD          _exStyle;     // Window extended style
    int            _x;           // Horizontal position
    int            _y;           // Vertical position
    int            _width;       // Window width
    int            _height;      // Window height
    HWND           _hWndParent;  // Parent or owner
    HMENU          _hMenu;       // Menu or child-window ID
    void         * _data;        // window-creation data
};
```

The constructor of WinMaker takes the name of its window class and the handle
to program instance. The class name is necessary for Windows to find the window
procedure for this window. The rest of the parameters are given some reasonable
default values. For instance, we let the system decide the initial position and size of
our window. The style, WS_OVERLAPPEDWINDOW, is the most common style for top-
level windows. It includes a title bar with a system menu on the left and the minimize, maximize, and close buttons on the right. It also provides for a "thick"
border that can be dragged with the mouse to resize the window.

```
WinMaker::WinMaker (char const * className,
                    HINSTANCE hInst)
    : _style (WS_OVERLAPPEDWINDOW),
      _exStyle (0),
      _className (className),
      _x (CW_USEDEFAULT),       // Horizontal position
      _y (0),                   // Vertical position
      _width (CW_USEDEFAULT),   // Window width
      _height (0),              // Window height
      _hWndParent (0),          // Parent or owner window
      _hMenu (0),               // Menu or child-window identifier
      _data (0),                // Window-creation data
      _hInst (hInst)
{}
```

All these parameters are passed to the ::CreateWindowEx API that creates the
window (but doesn't display it yet).

```
HWND WinMaker::Create (char const * title)
{
    HWND hwnd = ::CreateWindowEx (
        _exStyle,
        _className,
        title,
        _style,
```

```
                        _x,
                        _y,
                        _width,
                        _height,
                        _hWndParent,
                        _hMenu,
                        _hInst,
                        _data);

        if (hwnd == 0)
            throw "Window Creation Failed";
        return hwnd;
    }
```

Create takes a window title which will appear in the title bar and returns a handle to the successfully created window. We will conveniently encapsulate this handle in a class called Window. Other than storing a handle to a particular window, this class will later provide an interface to a multitude of Windows APIs that operate on that window.

```
    class Window
    {
    public:
        Window (HWND h = 0) : _h (h) { }
        void Display (int cmdShow)
        {
            assert (_h != 0);
            ::ShowWindow (_h, cmdShow);
            ::UpdateWindow (_h);
        }
    private:
        HWND _h;
    };
```

To make the window visible, we have to call ::ShowWindow with the appropriate parameter, which specifies whether the window should be initially minimized, maximized, or the default size. ::UpdateWindow causes the contents of the window to be refreshed.

The window procedure must have the following signature, which is hard-coded into Windows:

```
    LRESULT CALLBACK WinProcedure
        (HWND hwnd, UINT message, WPARAM wParam, LPARAM lParam);
```

Notice the calling convention and the types of parameters and the return value. These are all typedefs defined in windows.h. CALLBACK is a predefined language-independent calling convention (what order the parameters are pushed on the stack, and so on). LRESULT is a type of return value. HWND is a handle to a window,

UINT is an unsigned integer that identifies the message, and WPARAM and LPARAM are
the types of the two parameters that are passed with every message.

WinProcedure is called by Windows every time it wants to pass a message to our
program (see Figure 15.2). The window handle identifies the window that is supposed to respond to this message. Remember that the same window procedure may
service several instances of the same window class. Each instance will have its own
window with a different handle, but they will all go through the same procedure.

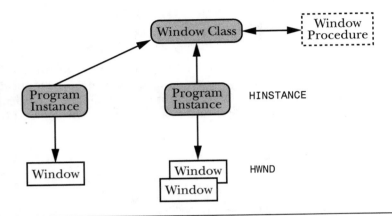

Figure 15.2 The relationship between instances of the same program, their windows, and
the program's window class and procedure

The message is just a number. Symbolic names for these numbers are defined
in windows.h. For instance, the message that tells the window to repaint itself is
defined as

```
#define WM_PAINT          0x000F
```

Every message is accompanied by two parameters whose meaning depends on the
kind of message. (In the case of WM_PAINT, the parameters are meaningless.)

To learn more about window procedures and various messages, study the Help
files that come with your compiler.

Here's our minimalist implementation of the window procedure.

```
LRESULT CALLBACK WinProcedure
  (HWND hwnd, UINT message, WPARAM wParam, LPARAM lParam)
{
  switch (message)
  {
  case WM_DESTROY:
    ::PostQuitMessage (0);
    return 0;
```

```
        }
        return ::DefWindowProc (hwnd, message, wParam, lParam );
    }
```

It doesn't do much in this particular program. It only handles one message, WM_DESTROY, that is sent to the window when it is being destroyed. At that point the window has already been closed—all we have to do is terminate WinMain. We do it by posting the final *quit* message. We also pass the return code through it—zero in our case. This message will terminate the message loop and control will be returned to WinMain.

Figure 15.3 shows the window created by our little application—complete with sizing borders; minimize, maximize, and close buttons; a Windows default icon, and a system menu that can be opened by clicking on the icon.

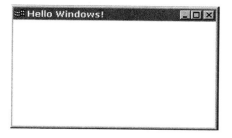

Figure 15.3 The output of Hello Windows!

Script 1   To make the project more structured, we will distribute the source code between multiple files.

15.2 Encapsulation

A lot of Windows APIs take a large number of arguments. For instance, when you create a window, you have to be able to specify its position, size, style, title, and so on. That's why CreateWindowEx takes 12 arguments. RegisterClassEx also requires 12 parameters, but they are combined into a single structure, WNDCLASSEX. As you can see, there is no consistency in the design of Windows API.

Our approach to encapsulating this type of API is to create a C++ class that combines all the arguments in one place. Since most of these arguments have sensible defaults, the constructor should initialize them appropriately. Those parameters that don't have natural defaults are passed as arguments to the constructor. The idea is that once an object of such a class is constructed, it should be usable without further modification. However, if modifications are desired, they can be done by calling appropriate methods. For instance, if we are to develop the class `WinMaker` into a more useful form, we should add methods such as `SetPosition` and `SetSize` that override the default settings for `_x`, `_y`, `_width`, and `_height`.

Let's analyze the classes `WinClassMaker` and `WinMaker` in this context. `WinClassMaker` encapsulates the API `RegisterClassEx`. The argument to this API is a structure that we can embed directly into our class. Three of the ten parameters— window procedure, class name, and program instance—cannot use the defaults so they are passed in the constructor. The window background color normally defaults to whatever the current system setting is—that's the `COLOR_WINDOW` constant. The mouse cursor in most cases defaults to whatever the system considers an arrow—that's the `IDC_ARROW` constant. The size of the structure must be set to `sizeof(WNDCLASSEX)`. The rest of the parameters can be safely set to zero. We don't have to do anything else before calling `WinClassMaker::Register`. Of course, in a more sophisticated program we might want to modify some of these settings, and we would most certainly add methods to do that. We'll talk about it later.

In a similar way, the API `CreateWindowEx` is encapsulated in the class `WinMaker`. The nondefaultable parameters are the class name, the program instance, and the title of the window. This time, however, we might want to call `WinMaker::Create` multiple times in order to create more than one window. Most likely these windows would have different titles, so we pass the title as an argument to `Create`.

To summarize, in the main procedure your program creates a window of a particular class and enters the message processing loop. In this loop, the program waits idly for a message from Windows. Once the message arrives, the program dispatches it back to Windows. The system then calls back the program's window procedure with the same message. It is either processed manually or by the default processing. The window procedure must be implemented in your program, and its address is passed to the system during window class registration. After returning from the window procedure, control goes back to the message loop and the whole process repeats itself. Eventually a "quit" message is posted and the loop ends.

Chapter 16
Controlling Windows
through C++

Before we can develop our Windows library any further, we need to make an important naming decision. As you might have noticed, I employed a convention to use the prefix `Win` for all classes related to Windows. Such naming conventions used to make sense in the old days. Now we have better mechanisms not only to introduce but also to enforce naming conventions. I'm talking about namespaces.

Script 2   It's easy to enclose all definitions of Windows-related classes, templates, and functions in one namespace, which we will conveniently call `Win`. The net result, for the user of our library, will be to type `Win::Maker` instead of `WinMaker`, `Win::Dow` instead of `Window`[1], etc. It also frees the prefix `Win` for use in user-defined names (e.g., our library clients will still be able to define their own class called `WinMaker`, without worrying about a name collision with our library).

Script 3   The classes `Win::ClassMaker` and `Win::Maker` will each get a pair of header/ implementation files. The `Win::Procedure` function will also get its own pair, since the plan is to make it part of our library.

---

1. The naming of the `Win::Dow` class might seem a little odd. The runner-ups were `Win::H` and `Win::Handle`, but they reflect more the implementation (it's a handle) than the functionality. Naming can be difficult, especially when encapsulating existing interfaces.

16.1   Model-View-Controller

The biggest challenge in Windows programming is to hide the ugliness of the big switch statement that forms the core of a window procedure. We'll approach this problem gradually.

> You have to understand that the basic structure of the Windows API was established in prehistoric times, when computers were many orders of magnitude slower than they are now, and when using C instead of an assembly language was a risk not many software companies were willing to take. C++ didn't even exist, and strong typing was a fringe idea. A switch statement was the fastest way to dispatch a message to the appropriate chunk of code crammed under the corresponding case: label. It didn't matter that programs were unreliable and buggy, as long as they were reasonably fast. The feedback loop between user input and screen output had to be as tight as possible, or else the computer would seem sluggish and unresponsive.
>
> Things are different now. Processors are breaking the 1GHz barrier—a billion clock ticks per second. This means that a computer may easily execute hundreds of thousands of instructions in the time between when the user pushes the mouse and the cursor moves on the screen. The mere act of processing user input—deciding what to do with it—is no longer a bottleneck.

The first step is to distinguish the program's user interface from the engine that does the actual work. Traditionally, the UI-independent part is called the *model*. The UI-dependent part is split into two main components: the *view* and the *controller*.

The view's responsibility is to display the data to the user. This is the part of the program that draws pictures or displays text in the program's window(s). It obtains the data to be displayed by querying the model.

The controller's responsibility is to accept and interpret user input. When the user types text, clicks a mouse button, or selects a menu item, the controller is the first to be informed about it. The controller converts raw input into something intelligible to the model. After notifying the model, the controller also calls the view to update the display (in a more sophisticated implementation, the model might selectively notify the view about the changes).

The model-view-controller paradigm is very powerful and we'll definitely use it in our encapsulation of Windows. The technical problem is deciding how to notify the appropriate controller when a *global* window procedure is notified of user input. The first temptation is to make the Controller object global too, so that a window procedure can access it. Remember, however, that there may be several windows and several window procedures in one program. Some window procedures may be shared by multiple windows. What we need is a mapping between window handles and controllers. Each window message comes with a window handle, HWND, which uniquely identifies the window for which it was destined.

Script 4
The window-to-controller mapping can be done in many ways. For instance, one can have a global map that does the translation. There is, however, a much simpler way—we can let Windows store the pointer to a controller in its internal data structures. Windows keeps a separate data structure for each window, and each data structure has storage for a user-defined long. Whenever we create a new window, we can create a new Controller object, and let Windows store the pointer to it. Every time our window procedure gets a message, we can retrieve this pointer from the window handle that's passed along with the message.

The APIs to set and retrieve an item stored in the internal Windows data structure are SetWindowLong and GetWindowLong. You have to specify the window whose internals you want to access. You also have to specify *which* long you want to access—there are several predefined longs, as well as some that you can add to a window when you create it. To store the pointer to a controller, we'll use the long called GWL_USERDATA. Every window has this long, even a button or a scroll bar (which, by the way, are also windows). As the name suggests, the purpose of this long is to store user-defined data. Using this long takes advantage of the fact that a pointer is the same size as a long—at least in 32-bit Windows. I don't know if this will be true in 64-bit Windows, but I strongly suspect so. If not, the Windows 64 API will have to deviate even more from the Windows 32 API.

There is a minor problem with the Get/SetWindowLong API: it is typeless. It accepts or returns a long, which is not exactly what we want. We'd like to make it type-safe. To this end, let's encapsulate both functions in templates, parameterized by the type of the stored data.

```
namespace Win
{
  template <class T>
  inline T GetLong (HWND hwnd, int which = GWL_USERDATA)
  {
    return reinterpret_cast<T>
           (::GetWindowLong (hwnd, which));
  }

  template <class T>
  inline void SetLong (HWND hwnd, T value,
                       int which = GWL_USERDATA)
  {
    ::SetWindowLong (hwnd, which,
                     reinterpret_cast<long> (value));
  }
}
```

In fact, if your compiler supports member templates, you can make GetLong and SetLong methods of Win::Dow. A member template is a method that is parameterized by a type. The class itself may also be a template on its own, parameterized by other types. (The template auto_ptr has such member templates. See page 244 for more information.)

```
namespace Win
{
  class Dow
  {
  public:
    Dow (HWND h = 0) : _h (h) {}
    template <class T>
    inline T GetLong (int which = GWL_USERDATA)
    {
        return reinterpret_cast<T> (
                    ::GetWindowLong (_h, which));
    }
    template <class T>
    inline void SetLong (T value, int which = GWL_USERDATA)
    {
      ::SetWindowLong (_h, which,
                  reinterpret_cast<long> (value));
    }
    void Display (int cmdShow)
    {
      assert (_h != 0);
      ::ShowWindow (_h, cmdShow);
      ::UpdateWindow (_h);
    }
  private:
    HWND _h;
  };
}
```

Notice the use of the default value for the which argument. If the caller calls any of these functions without the last argument, the value defaults to GWL_USERDATA.

We are now ready to create a stub implementation of the window procedure. We always start by retrieving the pointer to our controller object from the window handle.

```
LRESULT CALLBACK Win::Procedure (
            HWND hwnd,
            UINT message,
            WPARAM wParam,
            LPARAM lParam)
{
  Win::Dow win (hwnd);
  Win::Controller * pCtrl = win.GetLong<Win::Controller *> ();
  switch (message)
  {
    case WM_NCCREATE:
    {
```

```
          Win::CreateData const * create =
            reinterpret_cast<Win::CreateData const *> (lParam);
          pCtrl = static_cast<Controller *> (
            create->GetCreationData());
          pCtrl->SetWindowHandle (hwnd);
          win.SetLong<Win::Controller *> (pCtrl);
          break;
        }
        case WM_DESTROY:
          // We're no longer on screen
          pCtrl->OnDestroy ();
          return 0;
        case WM_MOUSEMOVE:
        {
          POINTS p = MAKEPOINTS (lParam);
          Win::KeyState kState (wParam);
          if (pCtrl->OnMouseMove (p.x, p.y, kState))
            return 0;
        }
      }
      return ::DefWindowProc (hwnd, message, wParam, lParam);
    }
```

We initialize the GWL_USERDATA slot of win in one of the first messages sent to
our window. The message is WM_NCCREATE (Non-Client Create), and it's sent before
the creation of the non-client part of the window (the border, the title bar, the
system menu, etc.). (There is another message before that one, WM_GETMINMAXINFO,
which might require special handling beyond the scope of this book.)

The pointer we store in GWL_USERDATA is passed to WM_NCCREATE as *window creation data*. We use the class Win::CreateData, a thin encapsulation of the Windows
data structure CREATESTRUCT. Since we want to be able to cast a pointer from
CREATESTRUCT, which is passed to us by Windows, to Win::CreateData, we must use
inheritance rather than embedding (you can inherit from a struct, as well as from
a class).

```
    namespace Win
    {
      class CreateData: public CREATESTRUCT
      {
      public:
        void * GetCreationData () const
          { return lpCreateParams; }
        int GetHeight () const { return cy; }
        int GetWidth () const { return cx; }
        int GetX () const { return x; }
        int GetY () const { return y; }
        char const * GetWndName () const { return lpszName; }
      };
    }
```

Here's the play-by-play analysis of what happens when a window is created. The API `CreateWindowEx` (called from `Win::Maker::Create`) initializes Windows internal data structures and then calls our window procedure: first with the `WM_GETMINMAXINFO` message, which we ignore, then with the `WM_NCCREATE` message. At that point the `GWL_USERDATA` value is still zero, but we initialize it during the processing of `WM_NCCREATE`. All subsequent calls to the window procedure will be able to obtain the pointer to the controller from `GWL_USERDATA`.

The message `WM_DESTROY` is important for the top-level window. That's where the "quit" message is usually posted. There are other messages that might be sent to a window after `WM_DESTROY`, most notably `WM_NCDESTROY`, but we'll ignore them for now.

I also added the processing of `WM_MOUSEMOVE` to illustrate the idea of message handlers. This message is sent to a window whenever a mouse moves over it. In the generic window procedure we always unpack message parameters and pass them to the appropriate handler—a method of the controller.

Three parameters are associated with `WM_MOUSEMOVE`: the x coordinate, the y coordinate, and the state of control keys and buttons. Two of these parameters, the x and y coordinates, are packed into one `LPARAM`, and Windows conveniently provides a macro to unpack them. The macro, `MAKEPOINTS`, turns `lParam` into a structure called `POINTS`. We retrieve the values of x and y from `POINTS` and pass them to the handler.

The state of control keys and buttons is passed inside `WPARAM` as a set of bits. Access to these bits is given through special bitmasks like `MK_CONTROL`, `MK_SHIFT`, etc., which are defined by Windows. We will encapsulate these bitwise operations inside the class `Win::KeyState`.

```
namespace Win
{
  class KeyState
  {
  public:
    KeyState (WPARAM wParam): _data (wParam) {}
    bool IsCtrl ( ) const
      { return (_data & MK_CONTROL) != 0;}
    bool IsShift ( ) const
      { return (_data & MK_SHIFT) != 0; }
    bool IsLButton ( ) const
      { return (_data & MK_LBUTTON) != 0; }
    bool IsMButton ( ) const
      { return (_data & MK_MBUTTON) != 0; }
    bool IsRButton ( ) const
      { return (_data & MK_RBUTTON) != 0; }
  private:
    WPARAM     _data;
  };
}
```

The `Win::KeyState` methods return the state of the control and shift keys and of the left, middle, and right mouse buttons. For instance, if you move the mouse while pressing both the left button and the shift key, both `IsLButton` and `IsShift` will return `true`.

In `WinMain`, where the window is created, we initialize our controller and pass it, along with the window's title, to `Win::Maker::Create`. `TopController` is our very simplified implementation of `Win::Controller` for the top-level window.

```
TopController ctrl;
win.Create (ctrl, "Simpleton");
```

This is the modified `Create`. It passes a pointer to `Controller` as the user-defined part of window creation data—the last argument to `CreateWindowEx`.

```
HWND Win::Maker::Create (Win::Controller & controller,
                         char const * title)
{
    HWND hwnd = ::CreateWindowEx (
      _exStyle,
      _className,
      title,
      _style,
      _x,
      _y,
      _width,
      _height,
      _hWndParent,
      _hMenu,
      _hInst,
      &controller);

    if (hwnd == 0)
      throw "Internal error: Window Creation Failed.";
    return hwnd;
}
```

To summarize, the client creates the controller and passes it to the `Create` method of `Win::Maker`. There, the pointer to the controller is added to the creation data, which Windows passes as a parameter of the `WM_NCREATE` message. The window procedure unpacks creation data and stores the pointer to the controller under `GWL_USERDATA` in the window's internal data structure. During the processing of each subsequent message, the window procedure retrieves the controller from this data structure and calls its appropriate method to handle the message. Finally, in response to `WM_DESTROY`, the window procedure calls the controller one last time.

16.1.1 Controller

Now that the mechanics of passing the controller around are figured out, let's talk about the implementation of Controller. Our goal is to concentrate the logic of a window in this one class. We want to have a *generic* window procedure that takes care of the ugly stuff—the big switch statement, the unpacking and repacking of message parameters, and the forwarding of messages to the default window procedure. Once the message is routed through the switch statement, the appropriate Controller method should be called with the correct (strongly-typed) arguments.

For now, we'll just create a stub of a controller. Eventually we'll add a lot of methods to it—as many as there are different Windows messages.

The controller keeps a handle for the window it services. This handle is initialized inside the window procedure during the processing of WM_NCCREATE. This is why we made Win::Procedure a friend of Win::Controller. The handle itself is protected, not private—derived classes will need access to it. There are only two message-handler methods at this point, OnDestroy and OnMouseMove.

```cpp
namespace Win
{
  class Controller
  {
    friend LRESULT CALLBACK Procedure (HWND hwnd,
                      UINT message, WPARAM wParam, LPARAM lParam);
    void SetWindowHandle (HWND hwnd) { _h = hwnd; }
  public:
    virtual ~Controller () {}
    virtual bool OnDestroy ()
      { return false; }
    virtual bool OnMouseMove (int x, int y, KeyState kStat)
      { return false; }
  protected:
    HWND  _h;
  };
}
```

You should keep in mind that Win::Controller will become part of our Windows library—it will be used as a base class for all user-defined controllers. That's why all message handlers are declared virtual. The meaning of the Boolean return value is "I have handled the message, so there is no need to call DefWindowProc." Since our default implementation doesn't handle any messages, it always returns false.

The client of our Windows library is supposed to define his or her own controller that inherits from Win::Controller and overrides some of the message handlers. In our case, the only message handler that has to be overridden is OnDestroy—it must close the application by sending the "quit" message. It returns true so the default window procedure is not called.

```
class TopController: public Win::Controller
{
public:
  bool OnDestroy ()
  {
    ::PostQuitMessage (0);
    return true;
  }
};
```

To summarize, our library is designed so users only have to do minimal work and are protected from making trivial mistakes. For each Windows class, the user has to create a customized controller class that inherits from our library class Win::Controller. *The user implements (overrides) only those methods that require nondefault implementation. Since the user has prototypes of all these methods, there is no danger of misinterpreting message parameters. This part—the interpretation and unpacking—is done in our generic* Win::Procedure. *It is written only once and is thoroughly tested.*

16.1.2   Client Code

This part of the program is written by our library's clients. As straightforward as it is, we will simplify it even more later (see Script 14).

```
#include "Class.h"
#include "Maker.h"
#include "Procedure.h"
#include "Control.h"
#include "Window.h"

class TopController: public Win::Controller
{
public:
  bool OnDestroy ()
  {
    ::PostQuitMessage (0);
    return true;
  }
};
int WINAPI WinMain
  (HINSTANCE hInst, HINSTANCE hPrevInst,
    LPSTR cmdParam, int cmdShow)
{
  char className [] = "Simpleton";
  Win::ClassMaker winClass (className, hInst);
  winClass.Register ();
  Win::Maker maker (className, hInst);
  TopController ctrl;
  Win::Dow win = maker.Create (ctrl, "Simpleton");
```

```
        win.Display (cmdShow);

        MSG  msg;
        int status;
        while ((status = ::GetMessage (& msg, 0, 0, 0)) != 0)
        {
          if (status == -1)
            return -1;
          ::DispatchMessage (& msg);
        }
        return msg.wParam;
    }
```

Notice that we no longer have to pass a window procedure to a class maker. The class maker can use our generic Win::Procedure, which is implemented entirely in terms of our generic Win::Controller interface.

```
    Win::ClassMaker::ClassMaker (char const * className,
                                 HINSTANCE hInst)
    {
      _class.lpfnWndProc = Win::Procedure;
      ...
    }
```

What really distinguishes the behavior of different windows is the implementation of a *particular* controller that is passed to Win::Maker::Create. Figure 16.1

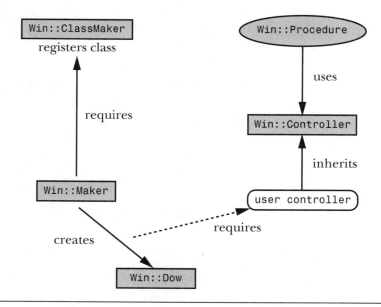

Figure 16.1 Some relationships between classes and procedures in our Windows library

graphically summarizes the interactions and dependencies between various components of our small library.

The cost of this simplicity is mostly in program size and some minimal speed deterioration.

Let's start with speed. Each message has to go through parameter unpacking and a virtual method call, even if it's not processed by the application. Is this a big deal? I don't think so. An average window doesn't get many messages per second. In fact, some messages are queued in such a way that if the window doesn't process them, they are overwritten by new messages. For example, this is the case with mouse-move messages: No matter how fast you move the mouse over the window, your window procedure will not choke on these messages. And it shouldn't matter if a few of them are dropped, as long as the last one ends up in the queue. The frequency with which a mouse sends messages when it slides across the pad is quite arbitrary. With the current processor speeds, the processing of window messages takes a minimal amount of time.

Program size could be a consideration, even though modern computers have so much memory that a megabyte here and there doesn't really matter (although this isn't necessarily true if you want to be able to download an application over the Internet). A full blown `Win::Controller` will have as many virtual methods as there are window messages. How many are there? About 200. The full vtable will be 800 bytes. That's less than a kilobyte! For comparison, a single icon is 2K. You can have a dozen controllers in your program and the total size of their vtables won't exceed 10K. There is also the code for the default implementation of each `Win::Controller` method. The code's size depends on how aggressively your compiler optimizes it, but it adds up to at most a few K.

The worst case—let's say a program with a dozen types of windows—is already pretty complex (read: intrinsically large), and it will probably include many icons and bitmaps. Seen from that perspective, the price we have to pay for the simplicity and convenience of using generic controllers is minimal.

16.2 Exception Specification

What would happen if a `Controller` method threw an exception? It would pass through our `Win::Procedure`, then through several layers of Windows code, and finally emerge from the message loop. We could, in principle, catch it in `WinMain`. Then the best we could do would be to display a polite error message and quit. Not only that, it's not certain how Windows would react to an exception rushing through its code. It might, for instance, fail to deallocate some resources or even get into some unstable state. The bottom line is that Windows doesn't expect an exception to be thrown from a window procedure. We have to live with this fact.

We have two choices: either we put a `try/catch` block around the switch statement in `Win::Procedure`, or we solemnly promise not to throw any exceptions from any `Controller` methods. A `try/catch` block might (depending on your compiler) add time to the processing of every single message, whether it's overridden by the client or not, but that's not a big problem. However, we would again be faced with the problem of what to do with such an exception. Terminate the program? That seems pretty harsh!

So how about not throwing exceptions from message handlers? But a contract like this is impossible to enforce. Or is it?!

Script 5   Enter exception specifications. In C++ it's possible to declare what kind of exceptions can be thrown by a function or method. In fact, we can specify that *no exceptions* can be thrown by a certain method. The declaration:

```
virtual bool OnDestroy () throw ();
```

promises that `OnDestroy` (and all its overrides in derived classes) will not throw any exceptions. The general syntax of an exception specification lists the types of exceptions a procedure can throw like this:

```
void Foo () throw (bad_alloc, char *);
```

How strong is this contract? Unfortunately, the standard doesn't promise much as far as compile time is concerned. The compiler is only obliged to detect exception specification mismatches between base class methods and their derived-class overrides. In particular, the specification can be only made stronger (that is, fewer exceptions allowed) in the derived class. There is no stipulation that the compiler should detect even the most blatant violations of this contract—for instance, an explicit `throw` inside a method defined as `throw()` (throw nothing). The hope, however, is that compiler writers will give in to the demands of programmers and at least make the compiler issue a warning when an exception specification is violated. Just as it is possible for the compiler to report violations of const-ness, so it should be possible to track down violations of exception specifications.

All an exception specification can accomplish in a standard-compliant compiler is to guarantee that all unspecified exceptions will get converted to a call to the library function `unexpected`, which by default terminates the program. That's good enough for now. Declaring all methods of `Win::Controller` as "throw nothing" will at least force the client who overrides them to think twice before allowing any exception to be thrown.

Notice that you can still use exceptions for error reporting. However, you have to be careful not to let any exception pass to the level of a message handler, or put a `try/catch` inside it.

16.3   Cleanup

Script 6   It's time to separate our Windows library files from the application files. For now, we'll create a subdirectory `Lib` and copy all the library files into it. As part of the cleanup, we'll also move the definition of `TopController` to a separate file, `Ctrl.h`.

Some compilers require a little help from the user to find the include files that are stored in a separate directory. You might, for instance, have to add the directory `Lib` to your compiler's "include" path.

Script 7

Chapter 17
Painting

One of the major strengths of a window-based environment is that it makes it relatively easy for programs to display data in the form that is most suitable for viewing and manipulation. This is accomplished by seamlessly combining graphics with text. This chapter introduces the basics of graphics programming in Windows.

17.1 Application Icon

Script 8   Every Windows program must have an icon, if only for the sake of the Windows shell. When you browse in the directory where your executable is stored, the Windows browser will try to display this executable's icon. When the executable is running, this icon shows in the Windows taskbar, as well as in the upper left corner of the program's window. If you don't provide an icon for your executable, Windows will provide a default.

The obvious place to specify an icon for your application's title bar is in the window class of the top-level window. Actually, it's best to provide two icons at once, the large one and the small one, or else Windows will try to stretch or shrink the one icon you gave it, often with unesthetic results.

Let's add a `SetIcons` method to `Win::ClassMaker` and embed two icon objects in this class.

```
namespace Win
{
  class ClassMaker
  {
```

```
public:
    ...
    void SetIcons (int id);
protected:
    WNDCLASSEX    _class;
    StdIcon       _stdIcon;
    SmallIcon     _smallIcon;
};
}
```

We'll get to the implementation of StdIcon and SmallIcon soon. First, let's look at the implementation of SetIcons. Icon images are usually loaded from program resources.

```
void Win::ClassMaker::SetIcons (int id)
{
    _stdIcon.Load (_class.hInstance, id);
    _smallIcon.Load (_class.hInstance, id);
    _class.hIcon = _stdIcon;
    _class.hIconSm = _smallIcon;
}
```

Program resources are things like icons, bitmaps, strings, mouse cursors, dialog templates, and so on, that you can tack on to your executable. Your program, instead of having to search the disk for files containing such resources, simply loads them from its own executable.

How do you identify resources when you want to load them? The whole set of your program's resources is identified by the instance handle that is passed to WinMain. You can give individual resources names or integer IDs. For simplicity (and efficiency), we will use IDs.

Let's start with the base class, Win::Icon. When you load an icon, you have to specify the resources where it can be found (the instance handle), the unique ID of the particular icon, its dimensions in pixels (if the actual icon has different dimensions, Windows will stretch or shrink it), and some random flags.

```
namespace Win
{
    class Icon
    {
    public:
        Icon (HINSTANCE res,
            int id,
            int dx = 0,
            int dy = 0,
            unsigned flag = LR_DEFAULTCOLOR)
        {
            Load (res, id, dx, dy, flag);
        }
        ~Icon ();
        operator HICON () const { return _h; }
    protected:
```

```
      Icon () : _h (0) {}
      void Load (HINSTANCE res,
                 int id,
                 int dx = 0,
                 int dy = 0,
                 unsigned flag = LR_DEFAULTCOLOR);
   protected:
     HICON _h;
   };
}
```

Using the *conversion operator,* operator HICON, the compiler will be able to make an implicit conversion from an object (or a reference to an object) of the type Icon directly to the Windows-defined type HICON. This is handy when you want to make a call to a Windows API that accepts HICON but you want to pass it an Icon object. You might even say that an Icon is-a HICON, even though it doesn't inherit from HICON (which might not even be a class or a struct, for all we know).

The API to load an icon is called LoadImage, and can also be used to load other types of images. Its return type is ambiguous, so it has to be cast to HICON. Once the icon is no longer used, DestroyIcon should be called.

```
void Icon::Load (HINSTANCE res, int id,
                 int dx, int dy, unsigned flag)
{
  _h = reinterpret_cast<HICON> (
     ::LoadImage (res,
                  MAKEINTRESOURCE (id),
                  IMAGE_ICON,
           dx, dy,
           flag));
  if (_h == 0)
    throw "Icon load image failed";
}

Icon::~Icon ()
{
  ::DestroyIcon (_h);
}
```

Notice that we can't pass the icon ID directly to the API. We have to use a macro, MAKEINTRESOURCE, which does some cheating behind the scenes.

> LoadImage and several other APIs that deal with resources have to guess whether you are passing them a string name or an integer ID. Since all the APIs are C functions, they can't be overloaded. Instead, you have to trick them into accepting both types and then let them guess their real identity. MAKEINTRESOURCE mucks with the bits of the integer to make it look different than a pointer to char. (This is the kind of programming that was popular when the Windows API was first designed.)

We can immediately subclass Icon to SmallIcon and StdIcon. Their constructors and Load methods are simpler—they don't require dimensions or flags.

```
namespace Win
{
  class SmallIcon: public Icon
  {
  public:
    SmallIcon () {}
    SmallIcon (HINSTANCE res, int id);
    void Load (HINSTANCE res, int id);
  };

  class StdIcon: public Icon
  {
  public:
    StdIcon () {}
    StdIcon (HINSTANCE res, int id);
    void Load (HINSTANCE res, int id);
  };
}
```

The Load methods are implemented using the parent class' Icon::Load
method (you have to use the parent's class name followed by double colon to disambiguate—without it, the compiler would interpret it as a recursive call and the
program would go into an infinite loop).

To find out what the correct sizes for small and standard icons are, we use the
universal API GetSystemMetrics that knows a lot about the current system's defaults.

```
void SmallIcon::Load (HINSTANCE res, int id)
{
  Icon::Load (res, id,
         ::GetSystemMetrics (SM_CXSMICON),
         ::GetSystemMetrics (SM_CYSMICON));
}

void StdIcon::Load (HINSTANCE res, int id)
{
  Icon::Load (res, id,
         ::GetSystemMetrics (SM_CXICON),
         ::GetSystemMetrics (SM_CYICON));
}
```

There's one more thing: how do we create icons? There is a hard way and an
easy way. The hard way is to have some kind of separate icon editor, write your own
resource script that names the icon files and, using a special tool, compile it and
link to the executable.

Just to give you an idea of what's involved, here are some details. Your
resource script file, let's call it script.rc, must contain these two lines:

```
#include "Resource.h"
IDI_MAIN    ICON    "main.ico"
```

IDI_MAIN is a constant you define in Resource.h. The keyword ICON means that it corresponds to an icon. What follows it is the name of the icon file, in our case, main.ico.

The header file, Resource.h, contains the definitions of constants, for instance,

```
#define IDI_MAIN    101
```

(The number 101 is arbitrary.)
Unfortunately, you can't use the safer, C++ version of it,

```
const int IDI_MAIN = 101;
```

The script file has to be compiled using a program called rc.exe (resource compiler) to produce the file script.res. The linker will then link script.res with the rest of the object files into one executable.

The easy way to create icons is to use an IDE (integrated development environment), with a resource editor—you can create an icon in it, add it to your resources under an appropriate symbolic ID, and let the environment do the work for you. (A graphical resource editor becomes really indispensable for designing dialog boxes.)

Notice that I'm using the same ID for both icons. It's possible, because you can have two (or more) images of different sizes in the same icon file. When you call LoadImage, the one with the closest dimensions is picked. Normally, you'd create at least 32x32 and 16x16 icons (the sizes are in pixels).

I have created a set of two icons and given them the integer ID IDI_MAIN (defined in Resource.h, which has to be included in main.cpp). All I need now is to make one additional call in WinMain.

```
Win::ClassMaker winClass (className, hInst);
winClass.SetIcons (IDI_MAIN);
winClass.Register ();
```

Once you have an icon in your program's resources, the Windows shell will find it and use it for its own display purposes. If you have several icons in your resources, Windows will pick the one with the lowest numerical ID.

17.2 Window Painting and the View Object

Just like with any other action in Windows, window painting is done in response to external actions. For instance, your program may paint something whenever a user moves a mouse or clicks a mouse button; it may draw characters in response to key presses, and so on. The part of the window that you normally paint is called the client area. This *doesn't* include the window borders, the title bar, the menu, and so on—these are part of the nonclient area.

There is one more situation when Windows may ask your program to redraw some part or the whole of the client area of your window. That might happen because Windows is lazy (or short of resources). Whenever another application overlaps your program's window, the system simply throws away the part of the image that's occluded. Eventually, when your program's window is uncovered, somebody has to redraw the discarded part. Guess who! Your program! The same thing happens when a window is minimized and then maximized again, or when the user resizes the window.

Since, from the point of view of your application, these actions happen more or less randomly, your program has to be prepared at any time to paint the whole client area from scratch. There is a special message, WM_PAINT, that Windows sends to your program when it needs assistance in repainting the window. This message is also sent the first time the window is displayed.

Script 9   To illustrate the principles of painting, let's extend our Windows program to trace mouse movements. Whenever the mouse moves, the program will draw a line connecting the new cursor position with the previous one. But before we do that, we'll want to add the second object from the triad Model-View-Controller to our program. The View will take care of all painting operations. It will also store the last recorded position of the mouse.

```
class TopController: public Win::Controller
{
    ...
private:
    View _view;
};
```

17.3 The Canvas

All display operations are done in the context of a particular device, be it the screen, a printer, a plotter, or something else. To draw in a window, the program has to obtain a *device context* (DC) for this window's client area. Windows can internally create a DC for us and give us a handle to it. We use this handle for all window output operations. When done with the output, we must release the handle.

A DC is a resource, and the best way to deal with it is to apply resource management methods to it. We'll call the generic owner of a DC, Canvas. We will have many different types of Canvas, depending on how the DC is created and disposed of. They will all, however, share the same functionality. For instance, we can call any Canvas object to draw a line or print some text. Let's make these two operations the starting point of our implementation.

```
namespace Win
{
  class Canvas
  {
  public:
    operator HDC ()
    {
      return _hdc;
    }
    void Line (int x1, int y1, int x2, int y2)
    {
      ::MoveToEx (_hdc, x1, y1, 0);
      ::LineTo (_hdc, x2, y2);
    }
    void Text (int x, int y, char const * buf, int count)
    {
      ::TextOut (_hdc, x, y, buf, count);
    }
  protected:
    Canvas (HDC hdc) :_hdc (hdc) {}

    HDC  _hdc;
  };
}
```

HDC is a Windows data structure, a Handle to a Device Context.

Our generic class, Canvas, doesn't provide any public way to initialize this handle—that responsibility is left to derived classes. The member operator HDC provides implicit conversion from Canvas to HDC. It comes in handy when passing a Canvas object to an API that requires HDC (again, think of it as an expression of the relationship Canvas is-a HDC).

In order to draw a line from one point to another, we have to make two API calls. The first one, MoveToEx, sets the "current position." The second, LineTo, draws a line from the current position to the point specified as its argument (it also moves the current position to that point). Point positions are specified by two coordinates, x and y. In the default coordinate system, both are in units of screen pixels. The origin, corresponding to $x = 0$ and $y = 0$, is in the upper left corner of the client area of the window. The x coordinate increases from left to right; the y coordinate grows from top to bottom.

To print text, you have to specify where in the window you want it to appear. The x, y coordinates passed to TextOut tell Windows where to position the upper left corner of the string. This is different than printing to standard output, where the only control over placement was by means of newline characters. For a Windows DC, newlines have no meaning (they are blocked out like all other nonprintable characters). In fact, the string-terminating null character is also meaningless to Windows. The string to be printed using TextOut doesn't have to be null-terminated. Instead, you are supposed to specify the count of characters you want printed.

So how and where should we obtain the DC? Since we want to do the drawing in response to every mouse move, we have to do it in the handler of the WM_MOUSEMOVE message. That means our Controller has to override the OnMouseMove virtual method of Win::Controller.

The type of Canvas that gets the DC from Windows *outside* of the processing of WM_PAINT will be called UpdateCanvas. The pair of APIs to get and release a DC are GetDC and ReleaseDC, respectively.

```cpp
namespace Win
{
  class UpdateCanvas: public Canvas
  {
  public:
    UpdateCanvas (HWND hwnd)
        :  Canvas (::GetDC(hwnd)),
           _hwnd (hwnd)
    {}
    ~UpdateCanvas ()
    {
      ::ReleaseDC (_hwnd, _hdc);
    }
  protected:
    HWND _hwnd;
  };
}
```

We create the Canvas, or an object derived from Canvas, in the appropriate Controller method—in this case OnMouseMove. This way the methods of View will work independently of the actual type of Canvas passed to them.

```cpp
bool TopController::OnMouseMove
    (int x, int y, Win::KeyState kState) throw ()
{
  Win::UpdateCanvas canvas (_h);
  _view.MoveTo (canvas, x, y);
  return true;
}
```

We are now ready to implement the View object.

```cpp
class View
{
public:
  View () : _x (0), _y (0) {}
  void MoveTo (Win::Canvas & canvas, int x, int y)
  {
    canvas.Line (_x, _y, x, y);
    _x = x;
    _y = y;
    PrintPos (canvas);
  }
```

```
private:
  void PrintPos (Win::Canvas & canvas)
  {
    std::string str ("Mouse at: ");
    str += ToString (_x);
    str += ", ";
    str += ToString (_y);
    canvas.Text (0, 0, &str [0], str.length ());
  }
private:
  int _x, _y;
};
```

The PrintPos method is interesting. The purpose of this method is to print
"Mouse at:" followed by the *x* and *y* coordinates of the mouse position, for
instance, "Mouse at: 124, 211." We want the string to appear in the upper left corner of the client area, at coordinates (0, 0).

First, we have to format the string. In particular, we have to convert two numbers to their string representations. The formatting of numbers for printing is
built into standard streams, so we'll just use the capabilities of a string-based
stream. In fact, any type that is accepted by a stream can be converted to a string
using this simple template function:

```
#include <sstream>

template<class T>
std::string ToString (T const & val)
{
  std::ostringstream out;
  out << val;
  return out.str ();
}
```

We use the operator += to concatenate the various strings. Finally, converting a
string to a pointer-to-character, as required by the API, is done by taking the address of the first character in the string.

You can now run this simple program, move the mouse cursor over the client
area, and see for yourself that it indeed leaves a trail and that the mouse coordinates
are printed in the upper left corner. You will also discover several shortcomings. For
instance, try minimizing the window. After you maximize it again, all the previous
traces disappear and so does the mouse-position indicator. Also, if you cover part of
the window with some other application window and then uncover, the restored area
will be empty—the mouse traces will be erased. The same happens after resizing.

Other minor annoyances are related to the fact that when the cursor leaves
the window its position is not updated, and when it enters the window again, a
spurious line is drawn from the last remembered position to the new entry point.

To round out the list of complaints, try moving the mouse towards the lower
right corner and back to the upper left corner. The string showing mouse

coordinates becomes shorter (fewer digits), but the trailing digits from previous strings are not erased.

Let's try to address these problems one by one.

17.4   The `WM_PAINT` Message

Script 10
First of all, every well-behaved Windows application must be able to respond to the `WM_PAINT` message. Ours didn't, so after its window was occluded or minimized and then restored, it didn't repaint its client area. So what should we do when Windows asks us to restore the client area? Obviously, the best solution would be to redraw the mouse tracing and redisplay the mouse coordinates. The trouble is that we don't remember the trace. So let's start with a simple fix—redisplaying the coordinates.

A new case has to be added to our generic window procedure:

```
case WM_PAINT:
  if (pCtrl->OnPaint ())
      return 0;
  break;
```

Strictly speaking, `WM_PAINT` comes with a `WPARAM` that, in some special cases having to do with common controls, might be set to a DC. For now, let's ignore this parameter and concentrate on the common case. We also have to update our Windows library by adding a dummy virtual method `OnPaint` to the generic `WinController`.

```
virtual bool OnPaint () throw () { return false; }
```

The standard way to obtain a DC in response to `WM_PAINT` is to call the API `BeginPaint`. This DC has to be released by a matching call to `EndPaint`. The ownership functionality is nicely encapsulated into the `PaintCanvas` object:

```
namespace Win
{
  class PaintCanvas: public Canvas
  {
  public:
    PaintCanvas (HWND hwnd)
      : Canvas (::BeginPaint (hwnd, &_paint)),
        _hwnd (hwnd)
    {}
    ~PaintCanvas ()
    {
      ::EndPaint(_hwnd, &_paint);
    }
    int Top () const    { return _paint.rcPaint.top; }
    int Bottom () const { return _paint.rcPaint.bottom; }
```

```
        int Left () const    { return _paint.rcPaint.left; }
        int Right () const   { return _paint.rcPaint.right; }
      protected:
        PAINTSTRUCT _paint;
        HWND        _hwnd;
    };
}
```

Notice that BeginPaint gives the caller access to some additional useful information by filling the PAINTSTRUCT structure. In particular, it is possible to retrieve the
coordinates of the rectangular area that has to be repainted. In many cases this
area is only a small subset of the client area (for instance, after uncovering a small
portion of the window or resizing the window by a small increment). In our unso-
phisticated application we won't use this additional info—we'll just repaint the
whole window from scratch.

Here's our own override of the OnPaint method of the controller. It creates a
PaintCanvas and calls the appropriate View method.

```
bool TopController::OnPaint () throw ()
{
  Win::PaintCanvas canvas (_h);
  _view.Paint (canvas);
  return true;
}
```

View simply calls its private method PrintPos. Notice that View doesn't distinguish
between UpdateCanvas and PaintCanvas. For all it knows, it is being given a generic
Win::Canvas.

```
void View::Paint (Win::Canvas & canvas)
{
  PrintPos (canvas);
}
```

What can we do about the varying sizes of the strings being printed? We need
more control over formatting. The following code will make sure that each of the
two coordinates is printed using a fixed field with a width of 4. We do this by passing the std::setw (4) manipulator to the output stream. If the next number to be
printed contains fewer than four digits, it will be padded with spaces. This and
other stream manipulators are defined in <iomanip>.

```
void View::PrintPos (Win::Canvas & canvas)
{
  std::stringstream out;
  out << "Mouse at: " << std::setw (4) << _x;
  out << ", " << std::setw (4) << _y;
  out << "    ";
  std::string s = out.str ();
  canvas.Text (0, 0, &s [0], s.length ());
}
```

You may notice that, in a fit of defensive programming, I appended *four* spaces to the string. Actually, without these spaces, we could still have a problem of a shrinking string. The fact that the number of characters in the string is now fixed to 24 doesn't guarantee that the displayed string will always occupy the same area. That's because Windows uses *proportional* fonts, in which some characters are wider than others. In particular, a space is usually narrower than a nonspace character. Hence the fudge factor.

The WM_PAINT message is also sent to our program in response to the user re-sizing the window. This is one of the cases when it would make sense to repaint only the newly added area (if any). The coordinates of the fresh rectangle are, after all, available through PaintCanvas.

This is not always as simple as it sounds. For instance, for some applications, any resizing of a window should call for a total repaint. Think of a window that stretches the picture to fill the whole client area.

Yet even for such an application, outside of resizing, it might make sense to limit the repainting only to freshly uncovered areas. So is it possible to have our cake and eat it too? The answer lies in two style bits that can be set when register-ing a window class. These bits are CS_HREDRAW and CS_VREDRAW. The first one tells Windows to ask for the complete redraw (i.e., invalidate the whole client area) whenever the horizontal size (width) of the window changes. The second one does the same for height. You can set both by combining them using the binary or:
CS_HREDRAW | CS_VREDRAW.

Invalidating an area not only sends a WM_PAINT message with the appropriate bounding rectangle to our window, but it also erases the area by overpainting it with the background brush. The background brush is set in the window class defi-nition—our default has been the standard brush with COLOR_WINDOW. (If instead the background brush is set to 0, no erasing will be done by Windows—try it!)

17.5 The Model

Script 11 If we want to be able to do a meaningful redraw, we must store the history of mouse moves. This can mean only one thing: we are finally ready to introduce the Model part of the triad Model-View-Controller. In general, you don't want to put too much intelligence or history into the view or the controller. Mouse trace is our program's data, its I/O-independent part. You could even imagine a command-line version of the program. It wouldn't be able to display the line visually, and you'd have to input each point by typing in its coordinates—but the model would be the same.

I decided to use a new data structure from the C++ standard library, the *deque* (pronounced "deck"). It works like a double-ended vector. You can push and pop items from both ends, and the methods push_front and pop_front work as effi-ciently as push_back and pop_back.

We don't want the history to grow beyond MAX_SIZE points. So when we add a new point to it, if it would cause the deque to exceed this count, we will pop the oldest point. In fact, this is the gist of the traditional queue, or LIFO (last in, first out), data structure.

```cpp
#include <deque>
#include <utility> // Pair

class Model
{
  enum { MAX_SIZE = 200 };
public:
  typedef
  std::deque< std::pair<int, int> >::const_iterator iter;

  Model ()
  {
    AddPoint (0, 0);
  }
  void AddPoint (int x, int y)
  {
    if (_queue.size () >= MAX_SIZE)
      _queue.pop_front ();
    _queue.push_back (std::make_pair (x, y));
  }
  iter begin () const { return _queue.begin (); }
  iter end () const { return _queue.end (); }
private:
  std::deque< std::pair<int, int> > _queue;
};
```

As you can see, points are stored as `std::pairs` of integers. I didn't bother to create a special data structure for a two-dimensional point. The function `make_pair` comes in handy when you don't want to explicitly specify the types of the members of the pair. You simply let the compiler deduce them from the types of arguments—in this case, both are integers. Were we to store x and y as a pair of shorts instead, we would have to use the more explicit construct:

```cpp
_queue.push_back (std::pair<short, short> (x, y));
```

The controller must have access to both the model and the view. In response to a mouse move, it adds a new point to the model and, as before, tells the view to move to a new position.

```cpp
bool TopController::OnMouseMove
  (int x, int y, Win::KeyState kState) throw ()
{
  _model.AddPoint (x, y);
  Win::UpdateCanvas canvas (_h);
  _view.MoveTo (canvas, x, y);
  return true;
}
```

The repainting can now be done more intelligently (albeit wastefully—we still repaint the whole client area instead of just the rectangle passed to us in `PaintCanvas`). We obtain the iterator from the model and pass it to the view. The iterator gives the view access to the part of the trace that is still remembered.

```cpp
bool TopController::OnPaint () throw ()
{
  Win::PaintCanvas canvas (_h);
  _view.Paint (canvas, _model.begin (), _model.end ());
  return true;
}
```

All the view has to do now is to connect the dots. We'll use a little trick from the `<algorithm>` section of the C++ standard library. The `for_each` algorithm takes the starting iterator, the ending iterator, and a functor.

We've already seen the use of a functor as a predicate for sorting. Here we'll use a type of functor that can operate on objects "pointed to" by iterators. In our case, the iterator "points to" a pair of coordinates—that is, when it's dereferenced, it returns a reference to a `std::pair<int, int>`.

Our functor, called `DrawLine`, draws a line from the last remembered position to the position passed to it in a pair. We have to initialize the functor with the starting position and let the `std::for_each` template call it for each value from the iterator.

```cpp
void View::Paint (Win::Canvas & canvas,
                  Model::iter beg,
                  Model::iter end)
{
  PrintPos (canvas);
  if (beg != end)
  {
    DrawLine draw (canvas, *beg);
    ++beg;
    std::for_each (beg, end, draw);
  }
}
```

If you're curious to know how `for_each` is implemented, it's really simple:

```cpp
template<class Iter, class Op>
inline Op for_each (Iter it, Iter end, Op operation)
{
  for (; it != end; ++it)
    operation (*it);
  return (operation);
}
```

`Op` here could be a pointer to a global function or an object of a class that overloads the function-call operator. This is the implementation of our functor:

```
class DrawLine
{
public:
  DrawLine (Win::Canvas & canvas,
            std::pair<int, int> const & p)
    : _canvas (canvas)
  {
    _canvas.MoveTo (p.first, p.second);
  }
  void operator () (std::pair<int, int> const & p)
  {
    _canvas.LineTo (p.first, p.second);
  }
private:
  Win::Canvas & _canvas;
};
```

The two new methods of Canvas, MoveTo, and LineTo are easy to implement:

```
void Canvas::LineTo (int x, int y)
{
  ::LineTo (_hdc, x, y);
}
void Canvas::MoveTo (int x, int y)
{
  ::MoveToEx (_hdc, x, y, 0);
}
```

17.6 Capturing the Mouse

It doesn't make much sense to unconditionally draw the trace of the mouse. If you have ever used any Windows graphical editor, you know that you're supposed to press and hold a mouse button while drawing. Otherwise there would be no way to "lift the pen" in order to access some controls or start drawing in a different place.

We could in principle use the Win::KeyState argument to OnMouseMove and check if a button is pressed. But we can do better than that and solve one more problem at the same time. I'm talking about being able to follow the mouse outside of the window.

Normally, mouse messages are sent only to the window over which the mouse cursor hovers. But if your window "captures" the mouse, Windows will redirect *all* mouse messages to it—even when the cursor is outside of its area. Obviously, capturing a mouse requires some caution. As long as the mouse is captured, the user will not be able to click any controls or interact with any other application (e.g., to activate it). That's why it is customary only to capture the mouse while it's being dragged—and the drag has to originate in the capturing window. (Dragging is done by pressing and holding a mouse button while moving the mouse).

There are three APIs related to mouse capture: SetCapture, ReleaseCapture, and GetCapture. SetCapture takes the handle to the window that wants to capture the mouse. ReleaseCapture ends the capture and sends the WM_CAPTURECHANGED message to the captor. GetCapture returns the handle to the window in the current application that currently has the capture (strictly speaking, in the current thread).

Script 12 We will add these APIs to our class Win::Dow, which represents a window handle (due to the presence of operator HWND (), Win::Dow is-a HWND).

```cpp
namespace Win
{
  class Dow
  {
  public:
    Dow (HWND h = 0) : _h (h) {}
    void Init (HWND h) { _h = h; }
    operator HWND () const { return _h; }
    template <class T>
    inline T GetLong (int which = GWL_USERDATA)
    {
      return reinterpret_cast<T> (
                          ::GetWindowLong (_h, which));
    }
    template <class T>
    inline void SetLong (T value, int which = GWL_USERDATA)
    {
      ::SetWindowLong (_h, which,
                          reinterpret_cast<long> (value));
    }
    void CaptureMouse ()
    {
      ::SetCapture (_h);
    }
    void ReleaseMouse ()
    {
      if (HasCapture ())
        ::ReleaseCapture ();
    }
    bool HasCapture () const
    {
      return ::GetCapture () == _h;
    }
    // Window visibility
    void Show (int cmdShow = SW_SHOW)
    {
      ::ShowWindow (_h, cmdShow);
    }
    void Hide ()
    {
      ::ShowWindow (_h, SW_HIDE);
    }
    void Update ()
    {
      ::UpdateWindow (_h);
    }
```

```
      void Display (int cmdShow)
      {
        Show (cmdShow);
        Update ();
      }
    private:
      HWND _h;
    };
  }
```

The typical procedure for capturing a mouse goes like this:

1. Capture the mouse when the user presses the appropriate mouse button.

2. While processing mouse-move messages, check if you have the capture. If so, implement dragging behavior.

3. Release capture when the user releases the mouse button.

4. Finish dragging in response to WM_CAPTURECHANGED message.

It's important to finish dragging inside the WM_CAPTURECHANGED handler, rather than directly in response to the button release, because your window may lose capture for unrelated reasons and it's important to clean up also in that case. (An example of externally initiated mouse capture change is when the system displays an alert message.)

We will apply this procedure by overriding the handlers for WM_LBUTTONDOWN, WM_LBUTTONUP, and WM_CAPTURECHANGED. The corresponding changes to Win::Controller from our Windows library also include replacing HWND with Win::Dow for easier window manipulation.

```
      class Controller
      {
      public:
        ...
        virtual bool OnLButtonDown
                (int x, int y, Win::KeyState kState) throw ()
          { return false; }
        virtual bool OnLButtonUp
                (int x, int y, Win::KeyState kState) throw ()
          { return false; }
        virtual bool OnCaptureChanged
                (HWND hwndNewCapture) throw ()
          { return false; }
      protected:
        Win::Dow  _h;
      };
```

Here are the implementations of the new methods in the client-defined TopController. (Notice that after all this talk, we are leaving the implementation of OnCaptureChange empty. That's because we don't have to do any dragging wrap-up.)

```
bool TopController::OnLButtonDown
  (int x, int y, Win::KeyState kState) throw ()
{
  _h.CaptureMouse ();
  _model.AddPoint (x, y, true); // Starting point
  Win::UpdateCanvas canvas (_h);
  _view.MoveTo (canvas, x, y, false); // Don't draw
  return true;
}

bool TopController::OnLButtonUp
  (int x, int y, Win::KeyState kState) throw ()
{
  // ReleaseMouse will send WM_CAPTURECHANGED
  _h.ReleaseMouse ();
  return true;
}

bool TopController::OnCaptureChanged
  (HWND hwndNewCapture) throw ()
{
  return true;
}
```

The implementation of OnLButtonDown (that's *Left Button Down*) has some interesting points. Since the user now has the option to "lift the pen," we must be able to draw (and redraw) noncontinuous lines. The MoveTo method of View must be able to shift the current position without drawing a line, and Model has to somehow mark the starting point of a new line. That's the meaning of the two Boolean flags inside OnLButtonDown. We'll come back to that. Now let's examine the new implementation of the OnMouseMove method.

```
bool TopController::OnMouseMove
    (int x, int y, Win::KeyState kState) throw ()
{
  Win::UpdateCanvas canvas (_h);
  if (_h.HasCapture ())
  {
    _model.AddPoint (x, y);
    _view.MoveTo (canvas, x, y);
  }
  else
    _view.PrintPos (canvas, x, y);
  return true;
}
```

Notice that we're recording the mouse position only if we have capture; otherwise, we only update the mouse coordinates display (and, since we don't have the mouse capture, we stop recording when the mouse leaves the window boundaries).

Repainting the window gets slightly more complicated because there might be multiple disconnected lines. I chose to store a Boolean flag with each remembered point, and set it to true only for points that are starting a new line (see the OnLButtonDown implementation, above). We have now outgrown our simple representation of a point as a std::pair. In fact, to save space, I decided to store coordinates as shorts (obviously, we'll have to rewrite this program when screen resolutions overcome the 32K pixels-per-line barrier).

```
class Model
{
  enum { MAX_SIZE = 1000 };
public:
  class Point
  {
  public:
  Point (int x = 0, int y = 0, bool isStart = false)
        : _x (static_cast<short> (x)),
          _y (static_cast<short> (y)),
          _isStart (isStart)
    {}
    int X () const { return _x; }
    int Y () const { return _y; }
    bool IsStart () const { return _isStart; }
  private:
    short _x;
    short _y;
    bool  _isStart;
  };

  typedef std::deque<Point>::const_iterator iter;

  void AddPoint (int x, int y, bool isStart = false)
  {
    if (_queue.size () >= MAX_SIZE)
      _queue.pop_front ();
    _queue.push_back (Point (x, y, isStart));
  }
  iter begin () const { return _queue.begin (); }
  iter end () const { return _queue.end (); }
private:
  std::deque<Point> _queue;
};
```

Notice the default values for all arguments of the Point contructor. It turns out that Point needs a default (no-arguments) constructor if we want to store it in a deque. The deque must be able to allocate and initialize new blocks of Points when it grows internally. It does this by calling the default constructors.

The implementation of View::Paint doesn't really change much, except that PrintPos now takes the values of coordinates to be displayed (and also updates the remembered position).

```
void View::Paint (Win::Canvas & canvas,
                  Model::iter beg,
                  Model::iter end)
{
  PrintPos (canvas, _x, _y);
  if (beg != end)
  {
    DrawLine draw (canvas, *beg);
    ++beg;
    std::for_each (beg, end, draw);
  }
}
```

The relevant change is in the implementation of the DrawLine functor: it doesn't draw lines that lead to starting points of line segments, it just quietly moves the current position.

```
class DrawLine
{
public:
  DrawLine (Win::Canvas & canvas, Model::Point const & p)
    : _canvas (canvas)
  {
    _canvas.MoveTo (p.X (), p.Y ());
  }
  void operator () (Model::Point const & p)
  {
    if (!p.IsStart ())
      _canvas.LineTo (p.X (), p.Y ());
    else
      _canvas.MoveTo (p.X (), p.Y ());
  }
private:
  Win::Canvas & _canvas;
};
```

17.7 Adding Colors and Frills

Script 13   Let's have some fun with our program. For instance, how do we draw colored lines? The LineTo API doesn't have any arguments that could be used to specify color.

It's the device context, encapsulated in our Canvas object, that stores all the parameters used for drawing. We have to instruct the canvas to change the drawing color. And, like good citizens, we should change it back after we're done with our drawing.

Various drawing and printing modes are conveniently grouped in GDI (graphics device interface) objects. The one that controls the drawing of lines is called a *pen*. You change the properties of the DC by *selecting* an object into it. Again, if you're a good citizen, you deselect it afterwards, usually by selecting the one you displaced.

This object selection mechanism is best encapsulated in various resource management objects. Let's start with the most common type of object, the *stock object*. Windows conveniently provides a whole bunch of the most commonly used device context settings in the form of predefined objects. We'll see in a moment how well-stocked the Windows storeroom is. Right now we want to have a nice encapsulator for such objects.

```
namespace Win
{
  class StockObject
  {
  public:
    StockObject (int type)
      : _obj (::GetStockObject (type))
    {}
    operator HGDIOBJ () const { return _obj; }
  protected:
    HGDIOBJ _obj;
  };

  class StockObjectHolder
  {
  public:
    StockObjectHolder (HDC hdc, int type)
      : _hdc (hdc)
    {
      _hObjOld = ::SelectObject (_hdc, StockObject (type));
    }

    ~StockObjectHolder ()
    {
      ::SelectObject (_hdc, _hObjOld);
    }
  private:
    HGDIOBJ  _hObjOld;
    HDC      _hdc;
  };
}
```

The constructor of Win::StockObjectHolder takes a handle to the device context (which means we can pass it any Canvas object) and selects a particular stock object into it. The SelectObject API returns the previous object of that type, which we diligently remember for later. We also remember the DC, so that, in the destructor, we can restore the previous object into its proper place in that DC.

That's the resource management part. The various types of stock objects are identified by predefined integer IDs. Given such an ID, we use GetStockObject to retrieve the proper object from the Windows storeroom. We'll mostly use Win::StockObjectHolder as a base class for specific stock object holders.

There are several stock pens that might be useful. For instance, there is a black pen and a white pen. We'll enclose these in the new namespace Pen as embedded classes of the more general class Pen::Holder. This class, for the moment, will be empty—but that will change soon.

This kind of class embedding gives rise to a rather convenient naming convention. Not only do we have classes like Pen::Holder::White and Pen::Holder::Black, but also a more general class Pen::Holder that will soon make sense.

```cpp
namespace Pen
{
  class Holder
  {
  public:
    class White : public Win::StockObjectHolder
    {
    public:
      White (HDC hdc)
        : Win::StockObjectHolder (hdc, WHITE_PEN)
      {}
    };

    class Black : public Win::StockObjectHolder
    {
    public:
      Black (HDC hdc)
        : Win::StockObjectHolder (hdc, BLACK_PEN)
      {}
    };
  }
}
```

For simplicity, I didn't nest the Pen namespace inside Win, so instead of Win::Pen::Holder::Black, you simply call it Pen::Holder::Black. If I were to design a commercial library, I'd probably nest the namespaces to avoid naming conflicts.

The way to use a stock pen is to define a holder in a given scope. For instance, to draw white lines you'd write code like this:

```cpp
{
  Pen::Holder::White wp (canvas);
  // Do the drawing
}
```

Don't forget to *name* your pen holder (wp in our case). The following code

```cpp
{
  Pen::Holder::White (canvas);
  // Do the drawing
}
```

is also valid, although it doesn't produce the desired result. The compiler will create an anonymous temporary object and then immediately destroy it, without waiting for the end of the scope (temporary objects have a lifetime limited to the duration of the current statement).

If you want to use *real* colors, not just black and white, you have to create your own GDI objects. A color pen is created by calling CreatePen and destroyed using DeleteObject. You specify the color by splitting it into three components: red, green, and blue. Each of them takes values between 0 and 255. This doesn't necessarily mean that your computer can display different colors for all 256x256x256 combinations. Unless you set your display mode to at least 24-bit color ("True Color", in Winspeak), the system will attempt to find the closest available match. Windows provides a macro, RGB, that is used to combine the three color components into one data structure called COLORREF.

```
namespace Pen
{
  class Color
  {
  public:
    Color (int r, int g, int b, int style = PS_SOLID)
    {
      _hPen = ::CreatePen (style, 0, RGB (r, g, b));
    }
    ~Color ()
    {
      ::DeleteObject (_hPen);
    }
    operator HPEN () { return _hPen; }
  private:
    HPEN     _hPen;
  };
}
```

Creating a colored pen doesn't, by itself, change the color of the lines being drawn. You still have to select your pen into the device context. According to the principles of resource management, we will encapsulate such a selection in an object called Pen::Holder—yes, that's the same class we used for embedding the classes White and Black. Defining a *named* object of the type Pen::Holder will temporarily change the color of all subsequent line drawings.

```
namespace Pen
{
  class Holder
  {
  public:
    Holder (HDC hdc, HPEN hPen)
      : _hdc (hdc)
    {
      _hPenOld = reinterpret_cast<HPEN> (
```

```
                ::SelectObject (_hdc, hPen));
        }
        ~Holder ()
        {
            ::SelectObject (_hdc, _hPenOld);
        }
    private:
        HDC      _hdc;
        HPEN     _hPenOld;
    public:
        class White : public Win::StockObjectHolder
        ...
        class Black : public Win::StockObjectHolder
        ...
    };
}
```

Notice that since Win::Canvas can be implicitly converted to HDC, and Pen::Color
to HPEN, the holder's constructor can be (and usually is) called with Win::Canvas
and Pen::Color.

The standard way to use pens and holders is to define and store your pens in
the View object and then "hold" them for the duration of a particular drawing
operation. Let's define two pen colors, dark red and light blue, for our drawings.

```
class View
{
public:
    View ()
        : _x (0), _y (0),
          _redPen (128, 0, 0),
          _bluePen (0, 0, 255)
    {}
    ...
private:
    int _x, _y;
    Pen::Color _redPen;
    Pen::Color _bluePen;
};
```

We'll use the blue pen for our regular drawing:

```
void View::MoveTo (Win::Canvas & canvas,
                   int x, int y, bool visible)
{
    if (visible)
    {
        Pen::Holder ph (canvas, _bluePen);
        canvas.Line (_x, _y, x, y);
    }
    PrintPos (canvas, x, y);
}
```

We'll use the red pen for repainting.

```
void View::Paint (Win::Canvas & canvas,
                  Model::iter beg,
                  Model::iter end)
{
  PrintPos (canvas, _x, _y);
  if (beg != end)
  {
    Pen::Holder ph (canvas, _redPen);
    DrawLine draw (canvas, *beg);
    ++beg;
    std::for_each (beg, end, draw);
  }
}
```

This is not what you would normally do—visually distinguish between active drawing and passive redrawing—but here we are trying to learn something. Play with this program and observe what areas are being redrawn when you uncover parts of your window or resize it. You'll notice that the red lines appear only in the freshly uncovered areas, even though our algorithm seems to be repainting the whole client area in response to WM_PAINT messages.

Well, the thing is, not everything your program draws is displayed by Windows. For instance, you should be aware that parts of the lines that fall outside of the boundaries of the client area are never displayed (they would overwrite other windows!). Windows *clips* all drawings down to the client area. In fact, during the processing of WM_PAINT, Windows clips your drawings even further—down to the invalidated area. And even though in PaintCanvas Windows sends us a single bounding rectangle for our convenience, the invalidated area may be more complicated (e.g., multiple rectangles), and PaintCanvas will clip all subsequent drawings down to this area. If you really want to draw outside of this area, you have to create an additional UpdateCanvas and work with it.

Script 14   But what should you do if, every time you draw, you want to use a different color? You can't possibly prepare all possible pens in View's constructor! In that case, you are stuck with creating a pen on the spot, selecting it into the DC, and discarding it immediately after deselecting it. This use is common enough to call for a separate encapsulator, Pen::Holder::Instant.

```
namespace Pen
{
  class Holder
  {
    ...
  public:
    ...
    class Instant
    {
```

```
    public:
      Instant (HDC hdc, int r, int g, int b)
            : _hdc (hdc)
      {
        _hPen = ::CreatePen (PS_SOLID, 0, RGB (r, g, b));
        _hPenOld = reinterpret_cast<HPEN> (
                      ::SelectObject (_hdc, _hPen));
      }
      ~Instant ()
      {
        ::SelectObject (_hdc, _hPenOld);
        ::DeleteObject (_hPen);
      }
    private:
      HDC      _hdc;
      HPEN     _hPen;
      HPEN     _hPenOld;
    };
  };
}
```

You can do with brushes the same thing we've done with pens. A brush is used for filling areas—for instance, a solid rectangle or ellipse. If you substitute the word "brush" for "pen," you can almost directly copy the above code and use it for brushes. The only real difference is the use of the API CreateSolidBrush in place of CreatePen. There are other types of brushes besides solid—hatched and patterned—that you can use as well. Just provide the appropriate overloaded constructors for Brush::Color.

There is one special place where a brush is used—in the definition of a window class. This is the brush used for painting the window background. For instance, Windows automatically paints a fresh background over all the invalidated areas in response to BeginPaint (called in the constructor of our PaintCanvas). By the way, EndPaint does the *validation* of this area, so if you forget to call it, Windows will keep sending WM_PAINT messages forever.

To choose a nondefault background color for the windows of a particular class, you have to create a brush and pass it to the WNDCLASSEX structure. The brush will automatically be destroyed when the application exits (or the class is discarded).

```
    void Win::ClassMaker::SetBkColor (int r, int g, int b)
    {
      _class.hbrBackground = ::CreateSolidBrush (RGB (r, g, b));
    }
```

We call this method in WinMain, setting the window background to very light blue.

```
    Win::ClassMaker winClass (className, hInst);
    winClass.SetIcons (IDI_MAIN);
    winClass.SetBkColor (128, 128, 255);
    winClass.Register ();
```

Script 15   Finally, we can play similar games with text. We can change the color of the
                   printed text, the color of its background, and even the typeface (font). This last
                   option, in particular, might help us with our incredible shrinking string. Changing
                   the font from *proportional* to *fixed* does the trick. In a fixed-pitch font, all charac-
                   ters, including spaces, are the same size. We'll be able to get rid of the spurious
                   spaces at the end of our string.

```cpp
namespace Font
{
  class Stock: public Win::StockObject
  {
  public:
    Stock (int type) : Win::StockObject (type) {}
    operator HFONT () const
    {
      return reinterpret_cast<HFONT> (_obj);
    }
  };

  class SysFixed: public Stock
  {
  public:
      SysFixed () : Stock (SYSTEM_FIXED_FONT) {}
  };

  class Holder
  {
  public:
    class Color
    {
    public:
      Color (HDC hdc, int r, int g, int b)
        : _hdc (hdc),
          _oldColor (::SetTextColor (_hdc, RGB (r, g, b)))
      {}
      ~Color ()
      {
        ::SetTextColor (_hdc, _oldColor);
      }
    private:
      HDC             _hdc;
      COLORREF     _oldColor;
    };

    class Background
    {
    public:
      Background (HDC hdc, int r, int g, int b)
          : _hdc (hdc),
            _oldColor (::SetBkColor (_hdc, RGB (r, g, b)))
      {}
```

```
    ~Background ()
    {
        ::SetBkColor (_hdc, _oldColor);
    }
private:
    HDC          _hdc;
    COLORREF     _oldColor;
};

class SysFixed : public Win::StockObjectHolder
{
public:
    SysFixed (HDC hdc)
        : Win::StockObjectHolder (hdc, SYSTEM_FIXED_FONT)
    {}
};
};
}
```

Equipped with all these tools, we can now print the position of the mouse in yellow on dark blue, using a fixed-pitch system font.

```
void View::PrintPos (Win::Canvas & canvas, int x, int y)
{
    ...
    Font::Holder::Color fc (canvas, 255, 255, 0); // Yellow
    Font::Holder::Background bk (canvas, 0, 64, 128); //Blue
    Font::Holder::SysFixed fix (canvas); // Fixed pitch
    canvas.Text (0, 0, &s [0], s.length ());
}
```

Of course, there is much more to Windows graphics than what I was able to present here. But it's a good starting point for further exploration. As always, study the Windows API and try to fit its various functions and data types into the object-oriented framework we started building.

Chapter 18
A Windows Application

Since I can't possibly cover Windows programming in any depth within the confines of this book, I will now switch to a bird's-eye view of how one could approach the task of writing a Windows application. I will concentrate on the two main challenges of Windows programming: how the program should work and look like, and how to encapsulate and categorize various APIs. The mere number of Windows APIs is so overwhelming that some kind of classification (with C++ classes and namespaces) is a must.

After (and during) the reading of this chapter, I strongly suggest browsing the source code and studying the details of the implementation.

18.1 Porting the Calculator to Windows

Project WinCalc Taking a command-line application, like our symbolic calculator, and making a minimal port to Windows can be quite easy. We have to find a way, other than `std::cin`, to get user input and to display the results in a window. Error reporting could be dealt with using message boxes. In principle, a single dialog box with two edit fields—one for input and one for output—would suffice.

But this kind of port is not only primitive, it doesn't even cover the whole functionality of our original application. In the command-line calculator, the user was at least able to see some of his or her previous inputs—the history of the interaction—in the command window. Also, in Windows, program commands like *load*, *save*, and *quit* are usually disengaged from text-based input and are available through menus, buttons, toolbars, or accelerator keys. Finally, there are certain possibilities specific to Windows that can enhance the functionality of our program and are expected by the user. An obvious example would be to display the contents of the calculator's memory.

Some of these features don't require substantial changes to the calculator engine. Disengaging commands from text input will actually make the parsing simpler—the Scanner will have to recognize fewer tokens and the CommandParser object will become unnecessary. Other features, such as the display of memory, will require deeper changes inside the Calculator object (which, by the way, will play the role of a model in our MVC triad).

18.2　User Interface

Whether you are porting an application or designing one from scratch, the first step is to envision the user interface.

In our case, we obviously need an input field, where the user will type the expressions to be evaluated. We also need an output field, where the results of the calculations will appear. We'd also like to have one window for the (scrollable) history of user input, and another to display the contents of the calculator's memory.

The design of the menu is a nontrivial problem. We know, more or less, what we would like there: Load, Save, as well as the traditional About and Exit. We can also add one more command—clear memory. The big problem is how to organize these commands.

The traditional approach, which often leads to barely usable menu systems, is to follow the historical pattern. Menu commands are grouped under File, Edit, View, Tools, Window, Help, and so on. Notice that these words are a mix of nouns and verbs. Tradition also dictates arbitrarily that, for instance, Exit goes under File, About under Help, Search under Edit, Options under Tools, and so on.

The more modern approach is to group commands mostly under noun headings that describe objects upon which these commands act. The headings are, as far as possible, ordered from general to specific. The first most general menu item is Program. This is where you should put the commands About and Exit. The About command displays information about the Program (not the Help, as its traditional placing would suggest). Similarly, you Exit a Program, not a File.

The Program item is usually followed by such groups as Project, Document (or File); then View or Window, Edit and Search; then the elements of the particular display, such as All or Selection; and finally Help. Even if the user is accustomed to traditional groupings, he or she is likely to find this new arrangement more logical and easier to use. For more insight into the design of menus and other elements of user interface, I recommend reading Alan Cooper's excellent book *About Face: The Essentials of User Interface Design*.

In our calculator we'll have the Program menu with About and Exit followed by the Memory menu. The operations we can apply to Memory are Clear, Save, and Load. (A more complete version would also have a separate Help menu.)

Finally, it's nice to have a status bar at the bottom of the window to show the readiness of the calculator to accept user input, as well as little command-specific Help snippets when the user selects menu items.

Instead of showing you various sketches I made before starting the port, I'll present the final result—the actual screenshot of the calculator's user interface (see Figure 18.1).

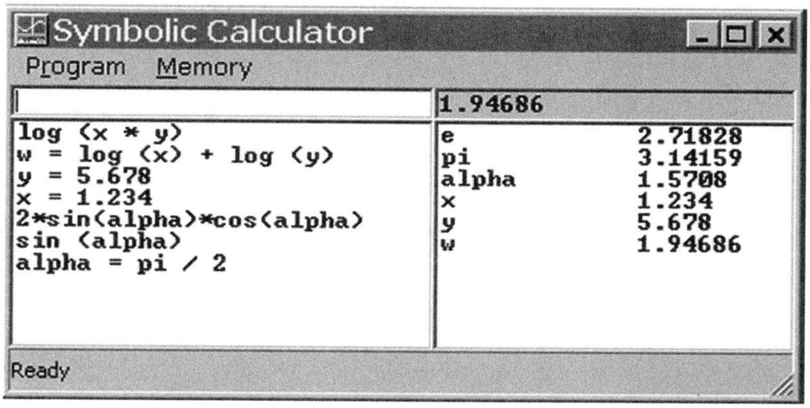

Figure 18.1 The user interface of the symbolic calculator

18.3 Child Windows

The calculator's main window is tiled with various subwindows, or child windows. Some of these children—like the title bar, the menu bar, the minimize and maximize buttons, and so on—are created and managed by Windows. Others are the programmer's responsibility. Figure 18.2 shows some of the windows that are part of our calculator's user interface.

A *child* window is owned by its parent window. Since there is often some confusion between the meaning of a "child" window versus an "owned" window, here's a short summary.

- A child window lives in the coordinate system of its parent and is clipped to its boundaries. A child cannot have a menu, but it can have an integer ID (that's why the *menu* member of the CREATESTRUCT doubles as a child ID). To create a child window, specify WS_CHILD as window style and initialize the hwndParent member of CREATESTRUCT to its parent's window handle.

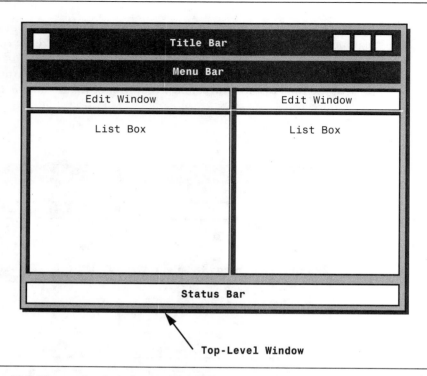

Figure 18.2 The top-level window and its child windows

- An owned window always appears in front (on top) of its owner, is hidden when the owner is minimized, and is destroyed when the owner is destroyed. The handle to the owner window is passed in the hwndParent member of CREATESTRUCT. An owned window doesn't have to be a child window—when it's not, it doesn't use the owner's coordinate system and is not clipped to its boundaries.

You will probably want all windows in your applications to be owned by the top-level window. Furthermore, if you'd like them to be constrained to the client area of the top-level (or some other) window, you should create them as children of their owners. (Examples of owned but *nonchild* windows are dialog boxes and message boxes, which I'll talk about later.)

Script1-2   I introduced a separate class, Win::ChildMaker, derived from Win::Maker, to encapsulate the creation of child windows. You can have a child window based on any window class, as long as you know the class' name. For our purposes, however, we'll be creating windows based on classes that are predefined (and preregistered) by Windows.

There are several useful window classes corresponding to standard controls. Instead of writing and testing new window procedures, we can get a lot of standard

functionality by reusing these controls. That's why I created a subclass of
`Win::ChildMaker` called `Win::ControlMaker` that can be used as base for specialized
control makers such as `Win::EditMaker`, `Win::ListBoxMaker`, and
`Win::StatusBarMaker`.

Before going into any more detail about controls, let's talk some more about
the management of child windows. I made them part of the `View` object, whose
constructor uses various control makers to create them. There are two edit controls, one of which is read-only. There are two list boxes that are particularly suited
for displaying lists. Finally, there is a status bar control.

The first thing our program has to take care of is the proper positioning of
these child windows. This is usually done in response to the `WM_SIZE` message sent
to the top-level window. The first such message arrives just before the child windows are displayed, so that's a great time to size and position them for the first
time. Then every time the user resizes the top-level window, the `WM_SIZE` message is
sent again. The parameters of `WM_SIZE` are the width and the height of the client
area. All we have to do is partition that rectangle among all the children. After
doing some simple arithmetic, we tell the children to move to their new positions.

Next, we have to take care of the focus. Whenever the calculator is active, we
would like the keyboard input to go directly to the input edit control. Since this
doesn't happen automatically, we have to explicitly pass the keyboard focus to this
child window whenever the calculator gets the focus. Fortunately, the top-level
window is notified every time this happens. The `WM_SETFOCUS` message is sent to the
top-level window whenever the child window becomes active, including when it is
created.

18.4 Windows Controls

A *Windows control* is a window whose class and procedure—the major elements of
behavior—are implemented by the system. Controls vary from extremely simple,
like static text, to very complex, like ListView or TreeView. They are ubiquitous in
dialog boxes (about which we'll talk soon), but they can also be created as stand-
alone child windows. The application communicates with a control by sending it
messages. Conversely, a control communicates with its parent window by sending
messages to it. In addition to common messages, each type of control has its own
distinct set of messages it understands.

I defined the class `Win::SimpleCtrl` so it combines the attributes common to
all controls. Since a control is a window, `Win::SimpleCtrl` inherits from `Win::Dow`.
Like all child windows, controls can be assigned numerical IDs so their parent
window can distinguish between them (although it may also tell them apart by
their window handles). If a control is created as a standalone using an appropriate
maker, we can initialize the corresponding `SimpleCtrl` object directly with its window handle. Otherwise, we initialize it with the parent's window handle and the
child ID (this pair is immediately translated to the window handle using the
`GetDlgItem` API).

18.4.1   Static Text

The simplest control, called *static text,* displays text in a simple frame. The corresponding object, `Win::StaticText`, is the simplest descendant of `Win::SimpleCtrl`. The program can modify the text displayed in it by calling the `SetText` method that `Win::StaticText` inherits from `Win::Dow`.

18.4.2   Edit Control

A little more interesting is the *edit control.* Its read-only version behaves just like static text, except that you can copy text from it to the clipboard (by selecting the text and pressing Ctrl+C). The full-blown edit control can be used not only to display text, but also to read user input. It also supports several editing functions, like delete, copy, cut, paste, and so on. In fact, a multiline edit control is the engine behind the Windows Notepad.

The most important thing an application may want to get from an edit control is the text that's been input there by the user. The class `Win::Edit`, another descendant of `Win::SimpleCtrl`, provides two different ways of doing that. The low-level method `GetText` takes a buffer and a count (you can use the `GetLen` method to inquire about the length first). The high-level method `GetText` takes no arguments and returns a `std::string`.

Controls keep sending messages to their parent windows. The interesting ones are `WM_COMMAND` and, for the newer generation of controls, `WM_NOTIFY`. It so happens that, for some historical reason, `WM_COMMAND` is not only used by controls, but also by menus and accelerators. Our generic window procedure sorts them out and calls, respectively, `OnControl` or `OnCommand`. `OnControl` is passed the control's window handle, its numerical ID, and the ID of the command. For instance, every time the user changes the text in an edit control, a command message is set to the parent window with the command ID `EN_CHANGE` (applications usually ignore this message).

In order for the controls to work correctly, we have to add one more call, `TranslateMessage`, to the main message loop.

```
MSG  msg;
int status;
while ((status = ::GetMessage (& msg, 0, 0, 0)) != 0)
{
  if (status == −1)
    return −1;
  ::TranslateMessage (& msg);
  ::DispatchMessage (& msg);
}
return msg.wParam;
```

This API translates raw keyboard input into commands and characters. Without it, our edit control wouldn't be able to display characters typed on the keyboard.

18.4.3 Window Subclassing

The main question with edit controls is: When is it a good time to retrieve their text? The user must have some way of telling the program that the input is ready—in our case, that the whole expression has been entered. We could have added a special button "Evaluate" for the user to click on. But that's not what the user expects. He or she will most likely press the Enter key on the keyboard and expect the program to take it as a cue that the input is ready. Surprisingly, this very basic feature is not so easy to implement. There is no simple way to tell the edit control to notify the parent window when the Enter key is pressed.

So what are we to do? We'll have to use the backdoor approach called *window subclassing*. We have to write our own window procedure and plug it into the edit control. Fortunately, our window procedure doesn't have to implement all the editing functionality from scratch. All it has to do is intercept the few messages we're interested in, and pass the rest to the original Windows-defined procedure (see Figure 18.3).

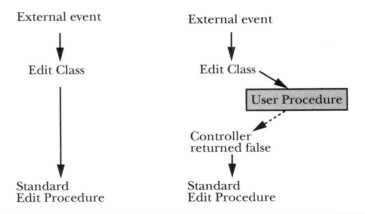

Figure 18.3 Subclassing the Windows edit control by plugging in a user-defined procedure

Script 3-4   I have conveniently encapsulated window subclassing in two `Win::Dow` methods, `SubClass` and `UnSubClass`. The `SubClass` method takes a pointer to the `SubController` object. It substitutes a generic `SubProcedure` in place of the old window procedure. The `SubProcedure` first calls the `SubController` to process every message. If the `SubController` doesn't process the message (i.e., returns `false`), it calls the old window procedure. Notice how the procedures are chained together. Each of them either processes a message or calls the next, until the last one calls the default window procedure.

The subclassing of the edit control proceeds as follows. We define a subclass of `Win::SubController` and call it `EditController`. It overrides only one method, `OnKeyDown`, and processes keyboard input only if the key code corresponds to the

Enter key (VK_RETURN). On intercepting the Enter key EditController sends a message to the parent window. I decided to use a standard control message, WM_CONTROL, which could be processed by the OnControl method of the parent window. I had to pack the wParam and lParam arguments to mimic the control messages sent by Windows. I chose the predefined constant IDOK as the control ID (thus imitating the pressing of the OK button in dialog boxes—see the section Dialog Boxes later in this chapter).

To actually perform the subclassing, we call the SubClass method of the edit window and pass it the EditController.

> You might be curious about the use of this apparently object-oriented terminology in Windows. Even though the Windows API seems to be anything but object-oriented, it uses terms like window class, subclassing, and so on. You have to realize that the windowing system was not invented by Microsoft or even Apple—it was conceived at Xerox PARC. The original implementation of a windowing system was written in Smalltalk—a paragon of object-oriented languages. So a window class was indeed implemented as a Smalltalk class. It had its data members and methods. In Windows, the window procedure plays the role of a "method." The Get/SetWindowLong APIs give access to "data members." Subclassing means overriding virtual functions—in the case of Windows, it's the overriding of the window procedure.

18.4.4 Plugging in the Calculator

Script 5   We now have to override the OnControl method of our main controller to intercept the IDOK message and react appropriately. In fact, that's where all the code from our old main goes. We retrieve the string from the edit control, encapsulate it in a stream, create the scanner and the parser, and evaluate the result. At this point we display the result and update the history display.

The most natural place to embed the Calculator object is inside the TopController object. This is the model part of our Model-View-Controller triad.

Now is a good time to do some Calculator cleanup. First of all, we have to get rid of cerr and <iostream> (we still need <istream> in our implementation of the scanner). Some errors in the calculator are converted to exceptions—we'll make the Syntax exception more descriptive by embedding a string in it. Other errors, the ones that don't invalidate the calculation, will be redirected to a global object, TheOutput, that will turn them into message boxes.

Also, in anticipation of a menu system, we can now get rid of command parsing.

18.4.5 List Box Control

Displaying history is very simple. We just tell the list box to add a line to its window containing the string that was input by the user. The list box will then take care of storing the string, displaying it, as well as scrolling and repainting when necessary. We don't have to do anything else. That's the power of Windows controls.

Displaying memory, on the other hand, is not so simple. That's because, in this case, the display has to reflect the state of a data structure that constantly changes. New variables are added and the values of old variables are modified as a result of user actions. Only the parser has any understanding of these actions. It decides whether an expression entered in the input window modifies the calculator's memory or not. Thus the display has to change in response to some internal change in the model. The view needs feedback from the model.

18.4.6 Model-View Feedback Loop

There are two ways to deal with the model-view feedback loop. The shotgun approach assumes that every user action that may change the state of the model requires refreshing that part of the view. In this scheme, display changes are controller-driven. The controller tells the view to refresh itself, and the view queries the model for the changes to be displayed. The model has no dependency on the view.

The notification approach, on the other hand, assumes that the model will notify the view directly. A notification might simply tell the view to refresh itself, or it might provide the exact information about what and how it should change. The problem with this scheme is that it introduces a circular dependency. The view depends on the model, because it has to know how to query for data to be displayed. The model depends on the view, because it has to know how to notify it about changes. If you look back at our definition of the model, you'll find that it was supposed to be unaware of the details of the user interface. It seems like we'll have to abandon this nice subdivision of responsibilities and break the simple hierarchy of dependencies in favor of a more entangled (and complex) system.

But don't despair yet! I'll show how you can have your cake of hierarchies and eat it too with notifications. The trick is to give the model only a very minimal glimpse of the view. All the model needs is a *notification sink*, an object that expresses interest in being notified about certain events. The model won't have a clue how these notifications are used. Furthermore, it won't have any knowledge of the existence of the class View.

Script 6   A notification sink is a separate class that encapsulates only the notification interface. The model has to know about this class' interface, have access to an object of this class, and call its methods. The view simply inherits from the notification sink and implements its virtual methods. When the model sends a notification to its notification sink object, it really sends it to the view. But it still lives in a state of ignorance about the details of the UI (see Figure 18.4).

The absence of the dependency loop in this scheme is best illustrated by the hierarchy of includes. The header file that defines the notification sink is at the top of the hierarchy. It has to be included in View.h, because the class View inherits from the class NotificationSink. Some of the files that constitute the implementation of the model (the Calculator object) will also have to include it, because they call methods of NotificationSink. View.cpp will have to include Calc.h, because it needs data from the model. The important thing is that *no model file* will have to

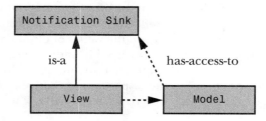

Figure 18.4 Breaking the dependency loop by introducing a notification sink

include `View.h`. The graph of dependencies is a DAG—a *directed acyclic graph*—a sign of good design.

The `NotificationSink` interface is an abstract class:

```
class NotificationSink
{
public:
  virtual void AddItem (int id) = 0;
  virtual void UpdateItem (int id) = 0;
};
```

`NotificationSink` talks about memory items (variables) using their numerical IDs. The recipient of notifications (the implementor of the actual sink) must have a way to retrieve memory data (the name and the current value of the variable) using these IDs.

Script 7

This is how `View` implements these two methods. `AddItem` simply appends a new line (formatted by `FormatMemoryString`) to the list box.

```
void View::AddItem (int id)
{
  std::string varStr = FormatMemoryString (id);
  int i = _memoryView.AddString (varStr);
  _memoryView.SetData (i, id);
}
```

Notice that we use the feature of the list box that lets us add a hidden item of data to each line. We attach the ID of the variable to the line that displays its name and value. This makes the implementation of `UpdateItem` easy.

```
void View::UpdateItem (int id)
{
  int count = _memoryView.GetCount ();
  int i;
  for (i = 0; i < count; ++i)
  {
```

```
      int idDisp = _memoryView.GetData (i);
      if (id == idDisp)
      {
        std::string varStr = FormatMemoryString (id);
        _memoryView.ReplaceString (i, varStr);
        _memoryView.SetData (i, id);
        break;
      }
    }
    assert (i != count); // Found it!
  }
```

Each line of the memory list box has to display the name and value of a variable.
We format each line to appear as consisting of two columns.

```
  std::string View::FormatMemoryString (int id)
  {
    std::string varStr = _calc.GetVariableName (id);
    varStr.resize (_varNameChars, ' ');
    varStr += ' ';
    double x;
    if (_calc.GetVariableValue (id, x))
      varStr.append (ToString (x));
    else
      varStr.append ("?");
    return varStr;
  }
```

Notice the two new Calculator methods required by this implementation.
      The side effect of this kind of formatting is that we have to change it every
time the list box is resized—the widths of the two columns change. We do this by
adding two calls to the Size method.

```
  void View::Size (int width, int height)
  {
    _memoryView.Clear ();
    ...do the resizing work
    _calc.RefreshMemory ();
  }
```

The hard work is actually delegated to the Calculator object. Its RefreshMemory
method tells Store to go through all the variables and send AddItem notifications
to NotificationSink. This clever trick not only simplifies refreshing the memory
display, but it also takes care of its initialization when the application starts. The
WM_SIZE message is one of the first ones sent to the top-level window after
WM_CREATE. The OnCreate method makes sure that everything is ready for it.

```
  bool TopController::OnCreate (
    Win::CreateData const * create, bool & success) throw ()
  {
```

```
    try
    {
      _view.reset(new View (_h, _calc));
      _calc.SetNotificationSink (_view.get ());
      success = true;
    }
    catch (...)
    {
      TheOutput.Error (
          "Internal Error:\nFailure to initialize.");
    }
    return true;
}
```

Finally, here's an example of how the notification sink is used by the calculator:

```
int SymbolTable::ForceAdd (std::string const & str)
{
  _dictionary [str] = _id;
  // Notify of new item
  if (_sink)
    _sink->AddItem (_id);
  return _id++;
}
```

18.5   Commands and Menus

Pointers to members.

Script 8   In the command-line version of our program we had to use a special parser to decipher user commands. In Windows it is much simpler. Commands are entered mainly by making menu selections. The obvious advantage of this approach is that the user doesn't have to remember the exact name and syntax of each command. They are listed and nicely organized in a system of menus. Even if a program offers other means to enter commands, like keyboard shortcuts or toolbars, menus still play an important role in teaching a newcomer what functionality is available.

It's relatively easy to equip a Windows program with a menu. You can define it in the resource script—the task which can be made really easy by using a resource editor. For instance, the calculator's menu can be described in the script.rc file like this:

```
ID_MENU MENU DISCARDABLE
BEGIN
POPUP "&Program"
BEGIN
MENUITEM "&About...",      ID_PROGRAM_ABOUT
MENUITEM SEPARATOR
MENUITEM "E&xit",          ID_PROGRAM_EXIT
END
```

```
POPUP "&Memory"
BEGIN
MENUITEM "&Clear",              ID_MEMORY_CLEAR
MENUITEM SEPARATOR
MENUITEM "&Save...",            ID_MEMORY_SAVE
MENUITEM "&Load...",            ID_MEMORY_LOAD
END
END
```

Note that each display name has an embedded ampersand. This ampersand is translated by Windows into a keyboard shortcut (not to be confused with a keyboard accelerator). The ampersand itself is not displayed, but the letter following it will be underlined. The user will then be able to select a given menu item by pressing the key corresponding to that letter while holding down the Alt key.

You give the menu a name or a numeric ID (ID_MENU, in this case), which you then pass to Win::ClassMaker or to each individual Win::Maker.

Each menu item is given a unique ID, called *command ID* (for example ID_PROGRAM_ABOUT). This ID becomes one of the arguments to the WM_COMMAND message, which is sent by Windows whenever the user selects a menu item. All you have to do is implement the OnCommand method of the top-level controller to respond to these commands.

The obvious implementation of OnCommand would be to write a big switch statement with a case for each command. Did I hear "switch?" Can't we come up with something better? Can we hide the switch in the library, just like we did with the window procedure? Not really—unlike Windows messages, which are defined up front by Windows and are not supposed to change, each user-defined menu comes with its own completely different set of commands and command IDs.

On the other hand, a menu command doesn't come with variable numbers and types of arguments. In fact, a menu command doesn't have any arguments—the arguments, if needed, are later picked up by dialog boxes. So why not organize all commands into an array of pointers to functions that take no arguments, the way we organized our built-in functions in the calculator?

There is only one problem with this approach—in order to use pointers to functions, commands would have to be implemented as *free functions*. But we know that most of them need to have access to the model (the Calculator). We don't want to make the calculator a global object and give commands the knowledge of its name. Such implicit dependency through global objects is a sign of bad design and will cause maintenance nightmares in more complex programs.

How about creating a separate object, Commander, whose methods would be our commands? Such an object could be made a member of TopController and be initialized in the controller's OnCreate method. We could easily give it access to the Calculator without making it global. We could create a vector of pointers to Commander methods, and use it for dispatching menu commands (see Figure 18.5). This is the same scheme we used for dispatching function calls in the calculator.

But what is a *pointer to method*? Unlike a free function, a (nonstatic) method can only be called in the context of an object, which becomes the provider of the

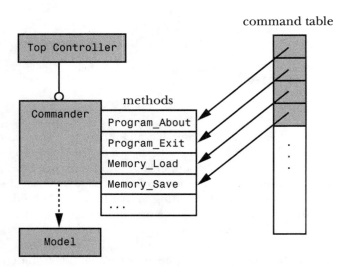

Figure 18.5 The Commander object and a vector of pointers to its methods

this pointer. Also, a definition of a pointer to method must specify the class whose method it might point to. A pointer to a Controller method is a different beast altogether than a pointer to a Commander method. This requirement is reflected in the declaration of a pointer to member. For instance, a pointer to the Commander method pCmdMethod that takes no arguments and has no return value will be declared like this:

```
void (Commander::*pCmdMethod) ();
```

Such a pointer can be initialized to point to a particular method, e.g., Program_About, of a Commander object.

```
pCmdMethod = &Commander::Program_About;
```

Given an object, _commander, of the class Commander, we can call its method through the pointer to member.

```
(_commander.*pCmdMethod) ();
```

Alternatively, if _commander were a pointer rather than an object (or reference), the syntax would change to:

```
(_commander->*pCmdMethod) ();
```

We'll define all the commands as members of `Commander` and give them names corresponding to their positions in the menu. The definition and initialization of the command vector looks like this:

```
*typedef void (Commander::*CmdMethod) ();

const CmdMethod CmdTable [] =
{
  &Commander::Program_About,
  &Commander::Program_Exit,
  &Commander::Memory_Clear,
  &Commander::Memory_Save,
  &Commander::Memory_Load,
  0 // Sentinel
};
```

So how does our `CmdTable` work with a menu system? What happens when the user selects a menu item? First, the message `WM_COMMAND` is sent to the generic window procedure, which calls the `OnCommand` method of our `TopController`. This method should somehow translate the command ID (defined in the resource script together with the menu) to the appropriate index in the `CmdTable`, and execute the corresponding method.

```
(_commander->*CmdTable [idx]) ();
```

The translation from command ID to an index is the weakest point of this scheme. In fact, the whole idea of defining your menu in the resource file is not as convenient as you might think.

Script 9   A reasonably complex application will require dynamic changes to the menu depending on the current state of the program. The simplest example is the Memory>Save item in the calculator. It would make sense for it to be inactive (grayed out) until the user adds a new variable to memory. We could try to somehow reactivate this menu item when a variable is added. But that would require the model to know something about the user interface—the menu. We could still save the day by using our notification sink. However, there is a better and more general approach—dynamic menus.

18.6 Dynamic Menus

First, let's generalize and extend the idea of a command table. We already know that we need an array of pointers to member functions. Nothing prevents us from adding more data (and functionality) to each command item. Besides a pointer to a member through which we can execute a given command, let's add another pointer to a member through which we can quickly test the *availability* of this command. The availability information might, for instance, be used to dynamically gray out some menu items or other controls. A short Help string for each command would be nice, too. We could display it in the status bar.

I also decided that it's more general to associate string names with commands rather than integer identifiers. Granted, searching through strings is slower than finding an item by ID, but usually there aren't that many command items to make a perceptible difference. Moreover, when the program grows to include not only menus but also accelerators and toolbars, being able to specify commands by name rather than by offset is a great maintainability win.

Script 10   So here's the new definition of a (reusable) command item—the building block of a command table.

```
namespace Cmd
{
  template <class T>
  class Item
  {
  public:
    char const * _name;           // Official name
    void (T::*_exec)();            // Execute command
    Status (T::*_test)() const;    // Test command status
    char const * _help;            // Help string
  };
}
```

If we want to reuse Cmd::Item, we have to make it a template. The template's parameter is the class of the particular commander whose methods we want to access.

Here's how the client of our Windows library creates a static command table and initializes it with appropriate strings and pointers to members.

```
namespace Cmd
{
  const Cmd::Item<Commander> Table [] =
  {
    { "Program_About",    &Commander::Program_About,
                          &Commander::can_Program_About,
                          "About this program"},
    { "Program_Exit",     &Commander::Program_Exit,
                          &Commander::can_Program_Exit,
                          "Exit program"},
    { "Memory_Clear",     &Commander::Memory_Clear,
                          &Commander::can_Memory_Clear,
                          "Clear memory"},
    { "Memory_Save",      &Commander::Memory_Save,
                          &Commander::can_Memory_Save,
                          "Save memory to file"},
    { "Memory_Load",      &Commander::Memory_Load,
                          &Commander::can_Memory_Load,
                          "Load memory from file"},
    { 0, 0, 0, 0}
  };
}
```

Here, `Commander` is the name of the commander class used by the calculator.

The command table is used to initialize the actual command vector, `Cmd::VectorExec`, which adds functionality to this data structure. The relationship between `Cmd::Table` and `Cmd::VectorExec` is analogous to the relationship between `Function::Array` and `Function::Table` inside the calculator. As before, this scheme makes it very easy to add new items to the table—new commands to our program.

```
namespace Cmd
{
  template <class T>
  class VectorExec: public Vector
  {
  public:
    VectorExec (Cmd::Item<T> const * cmdTable,
                T * commander);
    void Execute (int cmdId) const;
    Status Test (char const * cmdName) const;
    char const * GetHelp (int cmdId) const;
  protected:
    T *                     _commander;
    Cmd::Item<T> const *  _cmd;
  };
}
```

`Cmd::VectorExec` has to be a template for the same reasons `Cmd::Item` is. However, in order *not* to have to templatize everything else that uses this vector (in particular, the menu system), I derived it from a nontemplate class, `Cmd::Vector`. This class defines a few pure virtual functions and some generic functionality, like searching commands by name using a map.

```
namespace Cmd
{
  class Vector
  {
  public:
    virtual ~Vector () {}
    int CmdToId (char const * cmdName) const;
    virtual void Execute (int cmdId) const = 0;
    virtual Status Test (char const * cmdName) const = 0;
  protected:
    typedef map<char const *, int, NocaseCmp> CmdMap;
    CmdMap _cmdMap; // Name to ID
  };
}
```

Figure 18.6 shows the relationships between various classes and objects involved in the derivation and initialization of a command vector. Let's go through it again. `Cmd::Vector` is a base class from which the `Cmd::VectorExec` template is derived. The client of the library instantiates this template using his or her own `Commander` class. Once an object of the type `Cmd::VectorExec` is initialized, the

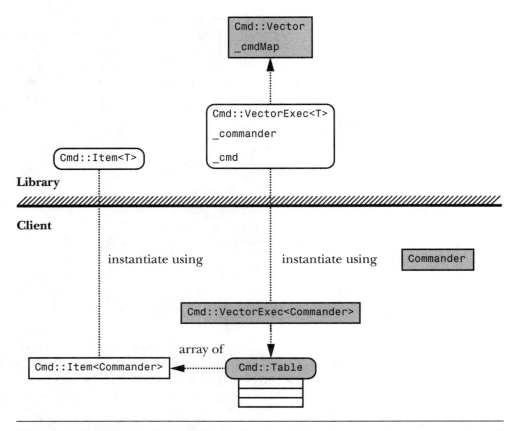

Figure 18.6 Relationships between library classes and client classes in the implementation of a command vector

client treats it as a `Cmd::Vector`. As we'll see in a moment, other components of the library are also written in terms of the `Cmd::Vector` interface (this way, they don't have to be templatized with respect to some `Controller` class). The initialization of the client's `Cmd::VectorExec` object is done using a static `Cmd::Table`, which is an array of `Cmd::Items`.

Script 11   The menu provides access to the command vector. In a dynamic menu system, we initialize the menu from a static table. The table is organized hierarchically: menu bar items point to pop-up menus that contain commands. For instance, this is what the initialization table for our calculator menu looks like:

```
namespace Menu
{
  const Item programItems [] =
  {
```

```
            {CMD,        "&About...",  "Program_About"},
            {SEPARATOR,  0,            0},
            {CMD,        "E&xit",      "Program_Exit"},
            {END,        0,            0}
        };
        const Item memoryItems [] =
        {
            {CMD,        "&Clear",     "Memory_Clear"},
            {SEPARATOR,  0,            0},
            {CMD,        "&Save...",   "Memory_Save"},
            {CMD,        "&Load...",   "Memory_Load"},
            {END,        0,            0}
        };
        //--- /---- Menu bar ---- / ----
        const BarItem barItems [] =
        {
            {POP,    "P&rogram", "Program",   programItems},
            {POP,    "&Memory",  "Memory",    memoryItems},
            {END,    0,          0,           0}
        };
    }
```

Notice that commands requiring further user input—e.g, from a dialog box—have names followed by an elipsis (three dots). All items also specify command names—for pop-up items, these are the same strings that were used in the naming of commands. Menu bar items are also named, but they don't have commands associated with them. Finally, menu bar items have pointers to the corresponding pop-up tables. By the way, similar tables can be used for the initialization of accelerators and toolbars.

Notice that the class `Menu::Item` has nothing to do with `Cmd::Item` introduced earlier. We treat the namespace qualifier as part of the name of the class. Before the advent of namespaces, these two classes would probably be called `MenuItem` and `CmdItem`.

The actual menu object of the class `Menu::DropDown` is created in the constructor of `View`. It is initialized with the table of menu bar items, `Menu::barItems`, shown above, and a `Cmd::Vector` object (initialized using `Cmd::Table`) (see Figure 18.7). The rest is conveniently encapsulated in our Windows library.

You might be interested to know that since a menu is a resource (released using `DestroyMenu` API), the class `Menu::Maker` has transfer semantics. For instance, when we create a menu bar, all the pop-up menus are transferred to `Menu::BarMaker`, one by one.

Script 12   But that's not the end of the story. We want to be able to dynamically activate or deactivate particular menu items. We already have `Commander` methods for testing the availability of particular commands—these methods are, in fact, accessible through the command vector. The question remains, though: What is the best time to call these methods? It turns out that Windows sends a message, WM_INIT-MENUPOPUP, right before opening a pop-up menu. The handler for this message is called `OnInitPopup`. We can use that opportunity to manipulate the menu while

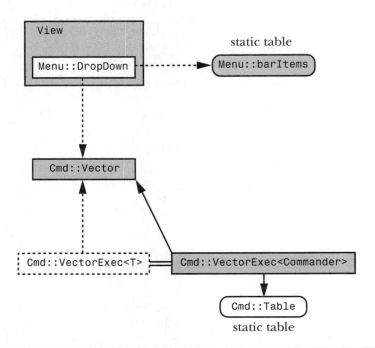

Figure 18.7 The initialization of the drop-down menu and related classes

testing for the availability of particular commands. In fact, since the library class
`Menu::DropDown` has access to the command vector, it can implement the
`RefreshPopup` method. Library clients do not need to write any additional code.

Displaying short Help for each selected menu item is also very simple. When
the user moves the mouse cursor to a pop-up menu item, Windows sends us the
message, `WM_MENUSELECT`, which we can process in the controller's method
`OnMenuSelect`. We just call the `GetHelp` method of the command vector and send
the Help string to the status bar.

Let's now review the whole task from the point of view of the client of our
Windows library. What code must the client write to use our dynamic menu system? To begin with, he or she has to implement the commander, which is just a
repository of all commands available in the particular program. Two methods
must be implemented for each command: one to execute it and one to test for its
availability.

The role of the commander is:

- Get data from the user (if required), usually by means of a dialog box
- Dispatch the request to the model for execution

Once the commander is in place, the client has to create and statically initialize a static table of commands. In this table, all the commands are given names and assigned short Help strings. This table is then used in the initialization of the command vector.

The menu system is likewise initialized by a static table. This table contains command names, display names for menu items, and markers to differentiate between commands, separators, and bar items. Once the menu bar is ready, it has to be attached to the top-level window. However, don't try to attach the menu inside the constructor of `View`. Both `View` and `Controller` must be fully constructed before adding the menu. Menu attachment results in a series of messages sent to the top-level window (most notably, to resize its client area), so the whole controller has to be ready to process them in an orderly manner.

Finally, the client must provide simple implementations of `OnInitPopup` and, if needed, `OnMenuSelect`, to refresh a pop-up menu and to display short Help, respectively.

Because major data structures in the menu system are initialized by tables, it is very easy to change them. For instance, reorganizing the menu or renaming menu items requires changes only to a single file—the one that contains the menu table. Modifying the behavior of commands requires only changes to the commander object. Finally, adding a new command can be done in three independent stages: adding the appropriate methods to the commander, adding an entry to the command table, and adding an item to the menu table. It can hardly be made simpler and less error-prone.

Figure 18.8 shows the relationships and dependencies between various elements of the controller.

Script 13   Because `Commander` doesn't (and shouldn't) have direct access to `View`, it has no simple way to force the refreshing of the display after commands such as `Memory_Clear` and `Memory_Load`. Again, we can only solve this problem by brute force (refresh the memory display after every command) or using notifications. I decided to use the most generic notification mechanism—sending a Windows message. In

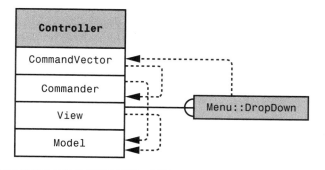

Figure 18.8 The relationships between various elements of the controller

order to force the clearing of the calculator's memory display, the Commander sends a special user-defined message, UM_MEMCLEAR, to the top-level window.

Remember, a message is just a number. You are free to define your own messages, as long as you assign them numbers that won't conflict with any messages used by Windows. There is a special identifier, WM_USER, that defines a number that is guaranteed to be larger than that of any Windows-specific message.

To process user-defined messages, I added a new handler, OnUserMessage, to the generic Win::Controller. This handler is called whenever the message number is larger than or equal to WM_USER.

One more thing is necessary to make the menus work correctly. The message loop must contain the call to TranslateMessage before DispatchMessage. We have already made this change to the message loop in order for embedded controls to work correctly. This time we rely on the fact that TranslateMessage filters out those keyboard messages that have to be translated into menu shortcuts and turns them into WM_COMMAND messages.

If you are also planning on adding keyboard accelerators (not to be confused with keyboard shortcuts, which are processed directly by the menu system)—for instance, Ctrl+L to load memory—you'll have to further expand the message loop to call TranslateAccelerator.

Script 14   Although we won't discuss modeless dialog boxes here, you might be interested to know that they also require a preprocessing step, a call to IsDialogMessage in the message loop. It makes sense to stick all these accelerators and modeless dialog box handles in a separate preprocessor object of the class Win::MessagePrepro. Its method Pump enters the message loop and returns only when the top-level window is destroyed. One usually passes the preprocessor object to the top-level controller to make it possible to dynamically switch accelerator tables or to create and destroy modeless dialog boxes.

18.7   Dialog Boxes

Script 15   The other, and indeed more common, application of Windows controls is in the construction of dialog boxes. A *dialog box* is a prefabricated window that provides a frame for various controls specified by the programmer. The type of controls and their positions are usually described in the resource script (the same in which we described the icon). Here's an example of such a description:

```
#include <winres.h>
IDD_ABOUT DIALOG DISCARDABLE  0, 0, 142, 70
STYLE DS_MODALFRAME | WS_POPUP | WS_CAPTION
CAPTION "About Symbolic Calculator"
FONT 8, "MS Sans Serif"
BEGIN
    DEFPUSHBUTTON     "OK",IDOK,46,49,50,14
    CTEXT             "Bartosz Milewski © 2000",
                      IDC_STATIC,10,33,121,14
    ICON              IDI_MAIN,IDC_STATIC,60,7,20,20
END
```

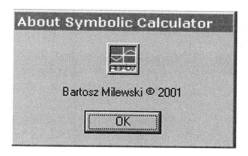

Figure 18.9 The Symbolic Calculator "About" dialog box

You don't really have to learn the language of resource scripts, because their creation is normally handled by the resource editor. The above script corresponds to the dialog box shown in Figure 18.9.

This dialog box contains three controls: a default push button, static text, and a static icon. The button's ID is IDOK, and the two static controls both have the same ID, IDC_STATIC. These particular IDs are predefined, but in general you are free to assign your own IDs to controls, as long as you define symbols for them in the resource header file (Resource.h, in our case).

The Load and Save dialog boxes (displayed after selecting Load or Save from the Memory menu—to be implemented soon) are a little more involved. They both have an OK button and a Cancel button. The Save dialog box, moreover, contains an edit control, and the Load dialog box has a list box. These are the same controls we used in the main window, but here it's up to the dialog box to create and position them according to the script. Not only that, the dialog box responds the same way whether the user presses the Enter key or clicks on the OK button. There is no need for us to subclass the edit control in a dialog box. You can also understand now why I chose the constant IDOK as the command identifier for the subclassed edit control in the main window.

The dialog box takes care of one more thing—the focus. In our main window we had a very simple rule—the focus always went to the input edit control. It's not so simple when you can have more than one potentially active control. Suppose that you, as the user, have activated one of the controls (i.e., one of several edit boxes in the same dialog box, for instance, by typing something into it). You may want to temporarily switch the focus to a different application, and then go back to finish the typing. You'd expect the focus to return to the same edit control you left activated. The dialog box is supposed to *remember* which control had been active before losing focus, and give the focus back to it upon being reactivated. A dialog box takes care of it, transparently. In contrast, if you arrange a few controls in an arbitrary (nondialog box) window, you'd have to add special logic to its controller to take care of the correct focus restoration.

There's more! A dialog box provides means of navigating between various controls using the keyboard. You can move the focus from one group to another by pressing the Tab key, and you can move within one group (e.g., of radio buttons) by pressing the arrow keys.

So why, you might ask, didn't I make the top-level window of the calculator a dialog box? It would have solved several problems all at once. Indeed, there are some applications that use a dialog box as their main window—the Windows built-in calculator applet comes to mind. But I wanted to write a more mainline Windows program, with a menu, a status bar, and a resizable main window. Taking all of this into account, it was simpler to just put together a few controls and stick them into a resizable parent window.

A dialog box provides a generic way of handling all the controls it owns. But if you want the dialog box to do something useful, you have to intercept some of the communications between the controls and the dialog box. The least you can do is to close the dialog box when the user clicks the OK (or CANCEL) button. If there is some data the user has input through the dialog box, you might want to retrieve it from one (or more) of its controls and pass it on to the caller. You might also want to mediate between some of the controls. All of this is possible through the use of a *dialog box procedure*.

A dialog box procedure is a simplified version of a window procedure. All messages that the dialog box receives from its controls are first filtered by this user-defined procedure. The main difference between a dialog box procedure and a window procedure is that a dialog box procedure doesn't call `DefWindowProc`, but instead returns `FALSE` when it doesn't care about a particular message. If, on the other hand, it *does* process a message, it is supposed to return `TRUE`. Notice that these are Windows-defined Boolean values, not the C++ `true` and `false`.

> The Windows `BOOL` is just a typedef for an integer. `FALSE` is defined (using the `#define` macro) to be zero and `TRUE` is defined to be one. It's the latter definition that leads to conflicts with the C++ understanding of Boolean. The C++ `true`, when converted to an integer, can yield any value other than zero. Unfortunately, Windows will often test a `BOOL` directly against `TRUE`, and if your `bool` return is nonzero but not equal to one, you lose.

That's the theory behind dialog boxes: Now we have to come up with a way to encapsulate them into something easier to use and less error-prone.

A dialog box is like a function that uses the UI to get its data. You "call" a dialog box with some initial data (the arguments), and it returns a result, presumably obtained from the user.

> What we are talking about now is the so-called *modal* dialog box. During the execution of a modal dialog box, the parent window is temporarily suspended—it doesn't react to any user input (it can still repaint itself, though). Only after the user closes a modal dialog box, can he or she continue interacting with the parent window (usually the top-level application window).

We can always encapsulate the input and output data into some user-defined data structure. But we also have to define the active part, some kind of a *controller* that can be plugged into the generic dialog box procedure. We can even combine the input/output data with this controller, so that it can operate on the data in response to control messages.

Here's the simplest example of how to use this abstraction in order to display the About dialog box (we are designing it top-down).

```
AboutCtrl ctrl;
Dialog::Modal dialog (_h, IDD_ABOUT, ctrl);
```

The dialog box object takes three arguments: the owner window (here, it's the top-level window), the dialog box ID (to identify the appropriate script in the resources), and the controller object.

The controller is derived from the library class `Dialog::ModalController`. In this absolutely minimal implementation of the About box, it only overrides the `OnCommand` method to intercept the OK button action.

```
bool AboutCtrl::OnCommand (int ctrlId, int notifyCode)
                        throw (Win::Exception)
{
  if (ctrlId == IDOK)
  {
    EndOk ();
    return true;
  }
  return false;
}
```

The `EndOk` method terminates the dialog box and returns success code to the caller.

I have also introduced a new Windows-specific exception class, `Win::Exception`. Most Windows APIs don't return a detailed error code. Instead, the caller is supposed to retrieve the error code immediately after a failure by calling `GetLastError`. This is what the constructor of `Win::Exception` does. The error code can then be translated into a text message by calling the `FormatMessage` API.

Script 16 The Save dialog box has some more functionality. It contains a string, _path, that can store the path to be returned by the dialog box. It has a Win::Edit object that it uses to communicate with the edit control present in the dialog box. The OK handler retrieves the string from the edit control and copies it to _path. The CANCEL handler just terminates the dialog box by calling the method Dialog::ModalController::EndCancel.

```
bool SaveCtrl::OnCommand (int ctrlId, int notifyCode)
                    throw (Win::Exception)
{
  if (ctrlId == IDOK)
  {
    SetPath (_edit.GetText ());
    EndOk ();
    return true;
  }
  else if (ctrlId == IDCANCEL)
  {
    EndCancel ();
    return true;
  }
  return false;
}
```

The caller can distinguish between a successful input (OK was activated) and an aborted input (Cancel was activated) by calling the method IsOk. So here's the top level:

```
SaveCtrl ctrl;
Dialog::Modal dialog (_h, IDD_SAVE, ctrl);
if (dialog.IsOk ())
{
  std::string const & path = ctrl.GetPath ();
  Serializer out (path);
  _calc.Serialize (out);
}
```

The controller must also initialize the _edit object by providing it with the dialog box window handle (the dialog box is the parent window of the edit control) and a control ID. This is done inside the OnInitDialog method.

```
void SaveCtrl::OnInitDialog () throw (Win::Exception)
{
  _edit.Init (GetWindow (), IDC_EDIT);
}
```

Notice that we are using the same Win::Edit class that we used in the top-level window to encapsulate its own edit control. The only difference is that here we don't use a *maker* to create the edit control—the dialog box itself creates the con-

trol based on the resource script. We can retrieve the control's window handle by
calling ::GetDlgItem inside Win::Edit::Init.

Script 17   The Load dialog box is even more advanced. It has a list box control that we
use to display the list of files in the current directory. It also has a static text control that the list box uses to display the path to the current directory. The
ListDirectory method of Win::ListBox takes care of the listing of the directory
and the initialization of the static text.

```
void LoadCtrl::OnInitDialog () throw (Win::Exception)
{
  _listBox.Init (GetWindow (), IDC_LIST);
  _listBox.ListDirectory (GetWindow (),
                          GetBuffer (), IDC_STATICPATH);
}
```

When a user clicks the OK button or double-clicks on an item, the dialog box
retrieves the full path of the selection from the list box. The method
GetSelectedPath fills the buffer with data and returns true if the selection was a
directory (not a file). If it's a directory, we change the current directory and reinitialize the list box. If it's a file, we close the dialog box and let the caller retrieve
the file path from the buffer.

```
bool LoadCtrl::OnCommand (int ctrlId, int notifyCode)
                         throw (Win::Exception)
{
  if (ctrlId == IDOK
   || ctrlId == IDC_LIST && notifyCode == LBN_DBLCLK)
  {
    if (_listBox.GetSelectedPath (GetWindow (),
                                  GetBuffer (), GetBufLen ()))
    {
      // Directory selected
      ChangeDirectory ();
    }
    else if (_listBox.IsSelection ())
      EndOk ();
    else
      EndCancel ();
    return true;
  }
  else if (ctrlId == IDCANCEL)
  {
    EndCancel ();
    return true;
  }
  return false;
}
```

This is how ChangeDirectory is implemented:

```
void LoadCtrl::ChangeDirectory ()
{
  ::SetCurrentDirectory (GetBuffer ());
  ResetBuf ();
  _listBox.ListDirectory (GetWindow (), GetBuffer (),
                          IDC_STATICPATH);
}
```

I must admit that this type of user interface for retrieving files is somewhat obsolete. For one, it doesn't display long file names (in fact, it doesn't even list files on NTFS—the Windows NT File System). Also, navigation between directories is not very intuitive. There is a Windows API called GetOpenFileName that has all the functionality of our Load dialog box and a much better user interface (see Exercise 5 below). I chose the old-fashioned way (still used in some applications) only to illustrate the use of dialog boxes with nontrivial controls.

Script 18   The final (cosmetic) modification is to start the calculator in a smaller window. This is done using a new Win::Maker method, SetSize.

Exercises

1. In response to the user's double-clicking on an item in the history pane, copy the selected string into the edit control so the user can edit and re-execute it.

2. A truly dynamic menu system should also provide the possibility of removing certain menu items, depending on the state of the application. Change the menu system so that a pop-up menu is cleared and then created from scratch every time the user clicks on any of the menu bar items.

    Hint: Add the methods AddItem, AddSeparator, and Clear to Menu::Manip. The "can" methods of the Commander should return Cmd::Invisible if they shouldn't appear in the pop-up.

3. Add the item "Function" to the menu bar. The corresponding pop-up menu should display the list of available built-in functions. When the user selects one, its name and the opening parenthesis should be appended to the string in the edit control.

    Hint: This pop-up menu should not be initialized statically. It should use the function table from the calculator for its initialization.

4. Add keyboard accelerators for Ctrl+L and Ctrl+S for invoking the Load and Save commands, respectively. Use a statically initialized accelerator table. Pass this table, together with the command vector (for command name to command ID translation), to the accelerator maker. The API to create an accelerator table is called CreateAcceleratorTable. Since an accelerator table is a resource (released via DestroyAcceleratorTable), you'll have to apply resource management in the design of your classes.

To attach the accelerator, pass a reference to the message preprocessor from `WinMain` to `TopController`. After creating the accelerator, use the `MsgPrepro::SetKbdAccelerator` method to activate it.

Hint: Remember to change the display string in menu items to include the accelerator key. For instance, the Load item should read, "`&Load...\tCtrl+L`" (the tab marker `\t` right-aligns the accelerator string).

5. Convert the Load command to use `GetOpenFileName` for browsing directories.

6. You probably think that the shotgun approach to notifications is easier to implement than the notification sink approach. You should try it!

Make the controller call `View::RefreshMemory` every time a new expression is processed by the parser. As you might recall, this processing is done in response to the `IDOK` command sent by the edit control after detecting the Enter key.

In order not to be really crude (and not to cause too much screen flicker), update the memory display line-by-line and modify only those entries that have *really* changed since the last refresh. This means you'll have to implement some mechanism to mark (and unmark) individual memory entries. Use the following snippet of code in your implementation:

```cpp
void View::UpdateMemory ()
{
  int count = _memoryView.GetCount ();
  for (int i = 0; i < count; ++i)
  {
    int id = _memoryView.GetData (i);
    if (_calc.HasValueChanged (id))
    {
      _calc.ResetChange (id);
      std::string varStr = FormatMemoryString (id);
      _memoryView.ReplaceString (i, varStr);
      _memoryView.SetData (i, id);
    }
  }
  int iNew;
  while ((iNew = _calc.FindNewVariable ()) !=
                            SymbolTable::idNotFound)
  {
    _calc.ResetChange (iNew);
    std::string varStr = FormatMemoryString (iNew);
    int i = _memoryView.AddString (varStr);
    _memoryView.SetData (i, iNew);
  }
}
```

Part 4

Scaling Up

The symbolic calculator is an example of a small software project that can be created by a single person in a reasonable amount of time. The real challenge of software engineering is building programs that are orders of magnitude more complex. The techniques I've described so far are as applicable to a large software project as they are to a small one. But there is much more to software engineering than just the techniques.

Programming is a struggle with complexity. If a problem is too complex to be solved by one person, a team has to take over. But a team of n programmers doesn't work like one programmer with a brain that's n times larger. Designing the program by splitting it into manageable pieces that can be implemented by individual team members is a task that requires both the knowledge of how our brains work and how people interact in a group.

Chapter 19
About Software

It's time now to rise above the nitty-gritty details of programming and have a birds-eye view of the process of software development.

19.1 Complexity

Dealing with complexity, the finite capacity of the human mind, divide and conquer, abstraction.

Dealing with complexity is the essence of software engineering. It is also the most demanding part of it, requiring both discipline and creativity. Why do we need special methodologies to deal with complexity? The answer is in our brains. In our immediate memory we can deal only with a finite and rather small number of objects—whatever type they are, ideas, images, or words. The ballpark figure is seven plus or minus two, depending on the complexity of the objects themselves. I am not making this up. In a seminal paper published in *The Psychological Review* in 1953 entitled "The Magical Number Seven Plus or Minus Two," George Miller argues that there are inherent limitations in the way we can comprehend things.

There are essentially two ways in which we, human beings, can deal with complexity: the divide-and-conquer method and the abstraction method. The divide-and-conquer method is based on imposing a tree-like structure on top of a complex problem. The idea is that at every node of the tree we have to deal with only a small number of branches, which are within the limits of our immediate memory. The traversal of the tree leaf-to-root or root-to-leaf requires only a logarithmic number of steps—again, presumably within the limits of our immediate memory. For instance, the body of academic knowledge is divided into humanities and sciences (a branching factor of two). Sciences are subdivided into various areas, one of them being computer science, and so on.

To understand Kernighan and Ritchie's book *The C Programming Language,* the computer science student needs only a very limited education in the humanities. On the other hand, a poet is not required to be able to program in C to write a poem. The tree-like subdivision of human knowledge not only facilitates in-depth traversal and search, it also enables division of work between various teams. We can think of the whole of humanity as one large team taking part in the enormous project of trying to understand the world.

Another very powerful tool developed by all living organisms and perfected by humans is abstraction. The word "abstraction" has the same root as "subtraction." Abstracting means subtracting nonessential features. Think of how many features you can safely subtract from the description of your car before it stops being recognizable as a car. You can skip the color of the paint, the license plates, the windshield wipers, the capacity of the trunk, and so on. The same process is applied unconsciously by a bird when it creates its definition of a "predator." Abstraction is not 100% accurate: a crow may get scared by a scarecrow, which somehow matches its abstract notion of a "predator."

Division and abstraction go hand-in-hand in what we can call the divide-and-abstract paradigm. A complex system can be visualized as a very large network of interconnected nodes (see Figure 19.1). We divide this network into a few "objects"—subsets of nodes. A good division has the property that there are as few interobject connections as possible (see Figure 19.2). To describe the objects resulting from such a division we use abstraction. In particular, we can describe the objects by the way they connect to other objects (the interfaces). We can simplify their inner structure by subtracting as many inessential features as possible (see Figure 19.3). At every stage of division it should be possible to understand the

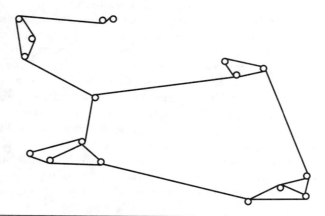

Figure 19.1 A complex system

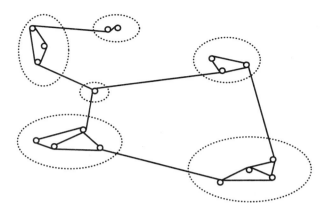

Figure 19.2 Abstracting objects out of a complex system

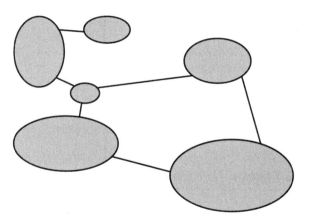

Figure 19.3 The high-level view of the complex system after abstracting objects

whole system in terms of interactions between a few well-abstracted objects. If there is no such way, we give up. The real miracle of our world is that large portions of it (maybe even everything) can be approached using this paradigm.

This divide-and-abstract process is repeated recursively by dividing objects into subobjects, and so on. To go a level deeper, we first undo the abstraction for a given object by adding back all the features we have subtracted, divide it into subobjects, and use new abstractions to define them (see Figure 19.4). An object should become understandable in terms of a few well-abstracted subobjects. In some way this recursive process creates a self-similar, fractal-like structure.

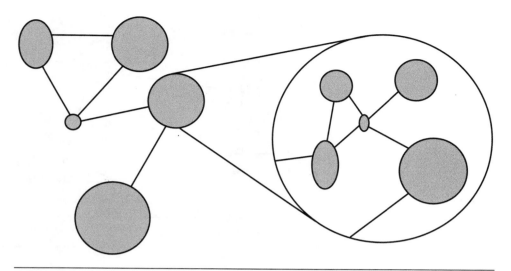

Figure 19.4 The fractal structure of a complex systems

In software engineering we divide a large project into manageable pieces. In order to define, name, and describe these pieces we use abstraction. We can talk about symbol tables, parsers, indexes, storage layers, and so on. They are all abstractions. And they let us divide a bigger problem into smaller pieces.

19.2 The Fractal Nature of Software

Let me illustrate these ideas with the familiar example of the software project that we've been developing in this book—the calculator. The top-level of the project is structured into a set of interrelated objects (see Figure 19.5).

This system is closed in the sense that we can explain how the program works (what the function main does) using only these objects—their public interfaces and their functionality. It is not necessary to know *how* these objects perform their functions; it is enough to know *what* they do.

So how does the program work? First, the Calculator is created inside main. The Calculator is Serializable, which means that its state can be saved and restored. Notice that, at this level, we don't need to know anything about streams— they are black boxes with no visible interface (that's why I didn't include them in this picture).

Once the Calculator is created, we enter the loop in which we get a stream of text from the user and create a Scanner from it. The Scanner can tell us whether the user input is a command or not. If it is a command, we create a CommandParser;

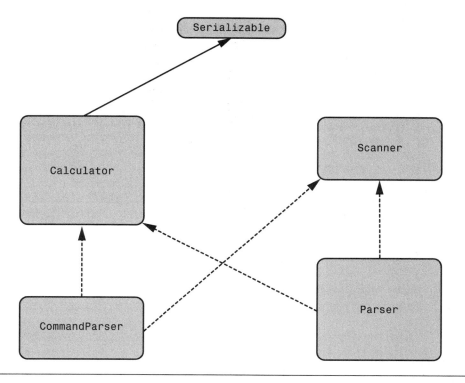

Figure 19.5 The top-level view of the calculator project

otherwise we create a `Parser`. Either of them requires access to both the
`Calculator` and the `Scanner`. `CommandParser` can `Execute` a command, whereas the
`Parser` can `Parse` the input and `Calculate` the result. We then display the result
and go back to the beginning of the loop. The loop terminates when
`CommandParser` returns status `stQuit` from the `Execute` method.

That's it! It could hardly be simpler than that. It's not easy, though, to come
up with such a nice set of abstractions on the first try. In fact we didn't! We had to
go through a series of rewrites in order to arrive at this simple structure. All the
techniques and little rules of thumb described in the second part of the book had
this goal in mind.

But let's continue the journey. Let's zoom in on one of the top-level components—the Calculator. Again, it can be described in terms of a set of interrelated
objects (see Figure 19.6).

And again, we could explain the implementation of all Calculator methods
using only these objects (and a few from the level above).

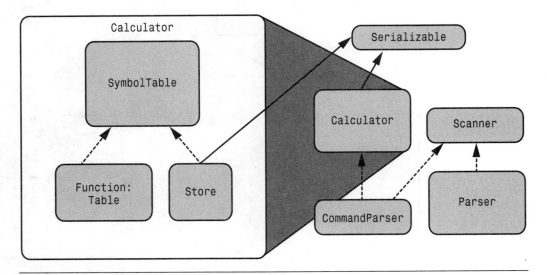

Figure 19.6 The result of zooming in on the Calculator

Next, we could zoom in on the Store object and see a very similar picture (see Figure 19.7).

We could go on like this, just like in one of those Mandelbrot set programs, where you can zoom in on any part of the picture and see something that is different and yet similar. With a mathematical fractal, you can keep zooming in indefinitely and keep seeing the same infinite level of detail. With a software project you will eventually get to the level of plain built-in types and commands. (Of course, you may continue zooming in into assembly language, microcode, gates, transistors, atoms, quarks, superstrings, and further, but that's beyond the scope of this book.)

19.3 The Living Project

The lifetime of the project, cyclic nature of programming, the phases, open-ended design, the program as a living organism.

Every software project has a beginning. Very few have an end (unless they are cancelled by the management). You should get used to this kind of open-ended development. You will save yourself and your coworkers a lot of grief. Assume from the very beginning that

- New features will be added
- Parts of the program will be rewritten
- Other people will have to read, understand, and modify your code
- There will be a version 2.0 (and further)

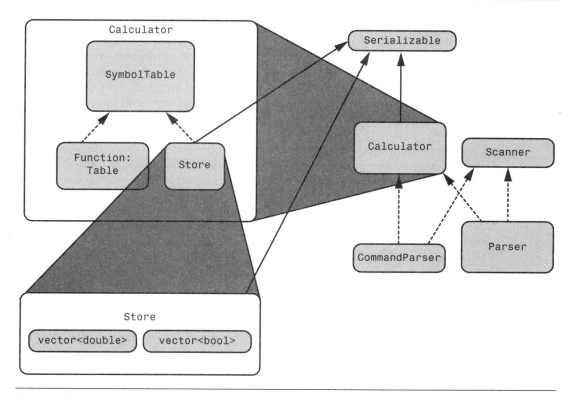

Figure 19.7 The result of zooming in on the Store object

Design for version 2; implement for version 1. Some of the functionality expected in v.2 should be stubbed out in v.1 using dummy components.

The development of a software project consists of cycles of different magnitude. The longest scale cycle is the major version cycle. Within it we usually have one or more minor version cycles. The creation of a major version goes through the following stages:

- Requirement (or external) specification
- Architectural design (or redesign)
- Implementation
- Testing and bug fixing

Timewise, these phases are interlaced. Architectural design feeds back into the requirements spec. Some features turn out to be too expensive; the need for others arises during the design.

Implementation feeds back into the design in a major way. Some even suggest that the development should go through the cycles of implementation of throwaway prototypes and phases of redesign. Throwing away a prototype is usually too big a waste of development time. It means that too little time was spent designing and studying the problem, and that the implementation methodology was inadequate.

One is *not* supposed to use a different methodology when designing and implementing prototypes, scaffolding, or stubs—as opposed to designing and implementing the final product. Not following this rule is a sign of hypocrisy. Not only is it demoralizing, but it doesn't save any development time. Quite the opposite! My fellow programmers and I were bitten by bugs or omissions in the scaffolding code so many times, and wasted so much time chasing such bugs, that we have finally learned to write scaffolding the same way we write production code. As a side effect, whenever the scaffolding survives the implementation cycle and gets into the final product (you'd be surprised how often that happens!), it doesn't lead to any major disasters.

Going back to the implementation cycle: Implementing or rewriting any major component has to be preceded by careful and detailed design or redesign. The documentation is usually updated in the process, and little essays are added to the architectural spec. In general, the design should be treated as an open-ended process. It is almost always strongly influenced by implementation decisions. This is why it's so important to have the discipline to constantly update the documentation. Documentation that is out-of-sync with the project is useless (or worse than useless—it creates misinformation).

The implementation proper is also done in little cycles. These are the fundamental edit-compile-run cycles, well known to every programmer. Notice how testing is again interlaced with the development. The *run* part of the cycle serves as a simple sanity test.

At this level, the work of a programmer resembles that of a physician. The first principle—*primum non nocere* (first, do no harm [to the patient])—applies equally well in programming as in medicine. In programming it's called "don't break the code." The program should be treated like a living organism. You have to keep it alive at all times. Killing the program and then resuscitating it is not the right approach. So make all changes in little steps that are self-contained and do as much testing as possible. Some functionality may be temporarily disabled when doing a big "organ transplant," but in general the program should be functional at all times.

Finally, a word of caution: How *not* to develop a project (and how it is still done in many places). Don't jump into implementation too quickly. Be patient. Resist the pressure from managers to have something for a demo as soon as possible. Think before you code. Don't sit in front of the computer with only a vague idea of what you want to do, with the hope that you'll figure it out by trial and error. Don't write sloppy code "to be cleaned up later." There is a big difference between stubbing out some functionality and writing sloppy code.

19.4 The Living Programmer

Humility, simplicity, team spirit, dedication.

A programmer is a human being. Failing to recognize that is a source of many misunderstandings. The fact that the programmer interacts a lot with a computer doesn't mean that he or she is any less human. Since it is the computer that is supposed to serve the humans and not the other way around, programming as an activity should be organized around the humans. It sounds like a truism, but you'd be surprised how often this simple rule is violated in real life. Forcing people to program in assembly (or C for that matter) is just one example of such abuse. Structuring the design around low-level data structures like hash tables, linked lists, and so on is another.

The fact that programming jobs haven't been eliminated by computers (quite the opposite!) tells us that being human has its advantages. The fact that some human jobs have been eliminated by computers means that being a computer has its advantages too. The fundamental equation of software engineering is thus

> **Human Creativity + Computer Speed and Reliability = Program**

Trying to write programs combining human speed and reliability with computer creativity is a big mistake! So let's face it: we humans are slow and unreliable. Computers are supposed to be fast, so when a programmer has to wait for the computer to finish compiling, something is wrong. When the programmer is supposed to write error-free code without any help from the compiler, linker, or debugger, something is wrong. If the programmer, instead of solving a problem with paper and pencil, tries to find the combination of parameters that doesn't lead to a general protection fault by trial and error, something is very wrong.

The character traits that make a good programmer are (maybe not so surprisingly) similar to those of a martial art disciple. Humility, patience, and simplicity on the one hand; dedication and team spirit on the other hand. And most of all, mistrust towards everybody including oneself.

- Humility: Recognize your shortcomings. It is virtually impossible for a human to write error-free code. We all make mistakes. You should write code in anticipation of mistakes. Use any means available to men and women to guard your code against your own mistakes. Don't be stingy with assertions. Use heap checking. Take time to add debugging output to your program.

- Patience: Don't rush towards the goal. Have patience to build solid foundations. Design before you code. Write solid code for future generations.

- Simplicity: Get rid of unnecessary code. If you find a simpler solution, rewrite the relevant parts of the program to make use of it. Every program can be simplified. Try to avoid special cases.

- Dedication: Programming is not a nine-to-five job. I am not saying that you should work nights and weekends. If you are, it is usually a sign of bad management. But you should expect a lifetime of learning. You have to grow in order to keep up with the tremendous pace of progress. If you don't grow, you'll be left behind by the progress of technology.

- Team spirit: Long gone are the times of a Lone Programmer. You'll have to work in a team. You'll have to work on your communication skills. You'll have to accept certain standards, coding conventions, commenting conventions, and so on. Be ready to discuss and change some of the conventions if they stop making sense. Some people preach the idea that "A stupid convention is better than no convention." Avoid such people.

- Paranoia: Don't trust anybody's code, not even your own.

Chapter 20
Design Strategies

Work on a software project should start long before the first line of code is written. It's impossible to create a commercial-grade software application without a good design. And unlike in other industries, in software development implementors are expected to take active part in the design of a product.

20.1 Top-Down Object-Oriented Design

Top-level objects, abstractions and metaphors, components.

It is all too easy to start the design by coming up with such objects as hash tables, linked lists, queues, and trees and trying to put them together. Such a bottom-up, implementation driven approach should be avoided. A program that is built bottom-up ends up with a structure of a soup of objects. There are pieces of vegetables, chunks of meat, and various kinds of noodles all floating in some kind of broth. It sort of looks object-oriented—there are "classes" of noodles, vegetables, meat, and so on. However, since you rarely change the implementation of linked lists, queues, trees, and so forth, you don't gain much from their object-orientedness. Most of the time you have to maintain and modify the shapeless soup.

When using the top-down approach, on the other hand, you divide your program into a small number of interacting high-level objects. The idea is to deal with only a few types of objects—classes (on the order of seven plus or minus two—the capacity of our short-term memory!). The top-level objects are divided into two groups: the main actors of the program, and the communication objects that are exchanged between the actors. If the program is interactive, you should start with the user interface and the objects that deal with user input and screen (or tele-type) output.

Once the top-level objects are specified, you should go through the exercise of rehearsing the interactions between the objects (this is sometimes called going through use-case scenarios). Go through the initialization process, decide which objects have to be constructed first, and in what state they should start. You should avoid using global objects at any level other than possibly the top level. After every-thing has been initialized, pretend that you are the user and see how the objects react to user input, how they change their state, and what kind of communication objects they exchange. You should be able to describe the interaction at the top without having to resort to the details of the lower-level implementations.

After this exercise you should have a pretty good idea about the interfaces of your top-level objects and the contracts they have to fulfill (that is, what the results of a given call with particular arguments should be). Every object should be clearly defined in as few words as possible, and its functionality should form a coherent and well-rounded abstraction. Try to use common language, rather than code, in your documentation to describe objects and their interactions. Remember, center the project around humans, not computers. If something can be easily described in common language, it usually is a good abstraction.

For things that are not easily abstracted use a *metaphor*. You might use an edi-tor as a metaphor for a sheet of paper; a calendar for a scheduler, pencils, brushes, erasers, and palettes for a drawing program, and so on. The user interface design revolves around metaphors, but they also come in handy at other levels of design. Files, streams, semaphores, ports, pages of virtual memory, trees, and stacks—these are all examples of very useful low-level metaphors.

The right choice of abstractions is always important, but it becomes absolutely crucial in the case of a large software project, where top-level objects are imple-mented by separate teams. Such objects are called *components*. Any change to the component's interface or its contract, once the development has started going full steam ahead, is a disaster. Depending on the number of components that use this particular interface, it can be a minor or a major disaster. The magnitude of such a disaster can only be measured by the Richter scale. Every project goes through a few such "earthquakes"—that's just life!

Now repeat the same design procedure with each of the top-level objects. Split them into subobjects with well-defined purposes and interfaces. If necessary, re-peat the procedure for the subobjects, and so on, until you have a pretty detailed (but not too detailed) design. Use this procedure again and again during the im-plementation of various pieces. The goal is to superimpose some sort of a self-similar, fractal structure on the project. The top-level description of the whole program should be similar to the description of each of the components, its sub-components, objects, subobjects, and so on. Every time you zoom in or zoom out, you should see more or less the same type of picture, with a few self-contained objects collaborating towards implementing some well-defined functionality.

20.2 User Interface

Designing user interface, input driven programs, Model-View-Controller paradigm.

Even the simplest modern-day programs offer some kind of interactivity. Of course, one can still see a few remnants of the grand UNIX paradigm, where every program was written to accept a one-dimensional stream of characters from its standard input and spit out another stream as its standard output. But with the advent of the graphical user interface (GUI), the so-called "command-line interface" is quickly becoming extinct. For the user, this means friendlier, more natural interfaces; for the programmer, this means more work and a change of philosophy.

With all the help available from the operating system and with the appropriate tools at hand, it isn't difficult to design and implement user interfaces, at least for graphically nondemanding programs. What is needed, however, is a change of perspective. An interactive program is, for the most part, *input-driven*. Actions in the program happen in response to user input. At the highest level, an interactive program can be seen as a series of event handlers for externally generated events. Every pressed key and every mouse click has to be handled appropriately.

The object-oriented response to the interactive challenge is the Model-View-Controller paradigm used in Chapter 16. The *controller* object is the focus of all external (and sometimes internal as well) events. Its role is to interpret these events as much as is necessary to decide which of the program objects will have to handle them. Appropriate messages are then sent to such objects (in Smalltalk parlance; in C++ we just call appropriate methods).

The *view* takes care of the program's visual output. It translates requests from other objects into graphical representations and displays them. In other words, it abstracts the output. Drawing lines, filling areas, writing text, and showing the cursor are some of the many responsibilities of the view.

Centralizing input in the controller and output in the view leaves the rest of the program independent from the intricacies of the input/output system (and also makes the program easy to port to other environments with slightly different graphical capabilities and interfaces). The part of the program that is independent of the details of input and output is called the *model*. It is the hard worker and the brains of the program. In simple programs, the model corresponds to a single object, but quite often it is a collection of top-level objects. Various parts of the model are activated by the controller in response to external events. As a result of changes of state, the model updates the view whenever it deem it appropriate.

As a rule, you should start the top-down design of an interactive program by establishing the functionality of the controller and the view. Whatever happens prior to any user action is considered initialization of these components and the Model itself. The M-V-C triad may also reappear at lower levels of the program to handle a particular type of control, a dialog box, an edit control, and so on.

20.3   Requirement Specification

Statement of purpose, functionality, user interface, input, output, size limitations and performance goals, features, compatibility.

The first document to be written before any other work on a project can begin is the *Requirement Specification* (also called an *External Specification*). In large projects the requirement spec might be prepared by a dedicated group of people with access to market research, user feedback, user tests, and so on. When a program is written for an external client, the requirement spec should be prepared by the client. However, no matter who does it, there has to be a feedback loop going back from the architects and implementers to the group responsible for the requirement spec.

The crucial part of the spec is the *statement of purpose*—what the purpose of the particular software system is. Sometimes restating the purpose of the program might bring some new insights or change the focus of the design. For instance, describing a compiler as a program that checks the source file for errors, and only occasionally creates an object file (when there are no errors), might result in a competitively superior product.

The statement of purpose might also contain a discussion of the key metaphor(s) to use in the program. An editor, for instance, may be described as a tool to manipulate lines of text. Experience, however, has shown that editors that use the metaphor of a sheet of paper are often more natural. Spreadsheet programs owe their popularity to another well-chosen metaphor.

Then, a detailed description of the *functionality* of the program follows. In a word processor requirement spec one would describe text input, ways of formatting paragraphs, creating styles, and so on. In a symbolic manipulation program one would specify the kinds of symbolic objects and expressions that are to be handled, the various transformations that could be applied to them, and so forth. This part of the spec is supposed to tell the designers and the implementers what functionality to implement. Some of it is described as mandatory; some of it goes into the wish list.

The *user interface* and the visual metaphors come next. This part usually undergoes the most extensive changes. When the first prototype of the interface is created, it goes through more or less (mostly less) rigorous testing, first by developers and then by potential users. Sometimes a manager doesn't like the feel of it and sends programmers back to the drawing board. It is definitely more art than science, yet a user interface may make or break a product.

What compounds the problems of user interface design is the fact that everybody feels competent enough to criticize it. No special training is required. And everybody has different tastes. The programmers who implement it are probably the least qualified people to judge it. They are often used to the terse and cryptic interfaces of their programming tools, like *grep, make, link, Emacs,* or *vi.* In any case, designing the user interface is the most frustrating and ungrateful job.

After the user interface is the *input/output* specification. It describes what kind of input is accepted by the program, and what output is generated by the program in response to this input. For instance, what is supposed to happen when the user clicks on the format-brush button and then clicks on a word or a paragraph in a document? Or what happens when the program reads a file that contains comma-separated lists of numbers? Or what happens when a picture is pasted from the clipboard?

Speed and size requirements can also be specified. The kind of processor, minimum memory configuration, and disk size are often given. Of course there is always conflict between the ever-growing list of desired features and the always conservative hardware requirements and breathtaking performance requirements. (In my experience, features win! But when the project enters its critical phase, features get decimated.)

Finally, there may be some *compatibility* requirements. The product has to understand (or convert) files that were produced by its earlier versions, by competitors' products, or both. It is wise to include some compatibility features that will make future versions of the product easier to implement (version stamps are a must).

20.4 Architectural Specification

Top-level view, crucial data structures and algorithms. Major implementation choices.

The architectural specification describes how things work and why they work the way they work. This is the document that gives the top-level view of the product as a program, as seen by the developers. All top-level components and their interactions are described in some detail—pictures and diagrams are invaluable here. The document should show clearly that if the top-level components implement their functionality according to their specifications, the system will work correctly. That will take the burden off the shoulders of developers—they won't have to think about too many dependencies. It's always a good idea to also describe theoretical foundations of the system, or at least give pointers to some literature.

The architectural spec defines the major data structures, especially the persistent ones. The document then proceeds with the description of major event scenarios and various states of the system. For example, the program may start in an empty slate, or it may load some history (documents, logs, and persistent data structures). It may have to finish some transactions that were interrupted during the previous session. It has to go through the initialization process and presumably get into some quiescent state.

External or internal events may cause some activity that transforms data structures and leads to state transitions. New states have to be described. In some cases the algorithms to be used during such activity are described as well. Too detailed a description of the implementation should be avoided, because it becomes obsolete so quickly that it makes little sense to try to maintain it.

Once more we should remind ourselves that the documentation is a living thing. It should be written in such a way that it is easy to update. It has to have a sensible structure of its own, because we know that it will be changed many times during the implementation cycle. In fact, it *should* be changed, and it is very important to keep it up-to-date and encourage fellow developers to look at it on a regular basis.

In the implementation cycle there are times when it is necessary to put some flesh into the design of some important object that has only been sketched in the architectural spec. This is the time to either expand the spec or write short essays on selected topics in the form of separate documents. In such essays we can describe nontrivial implementations, algorithms, data structures, programming notes, conventions, and so on.

Chapter 21
Team Work

The main challenge in large-scale software development is organizing the collaboration of large numbers of programmers. Far from being only an organizational problem, the need to collaborate must be reflected in the high-level design of the software project itself.

21.1 Productivity

Communication explosion, vicious circle.

The life of a large-team programmer is spent

- Communicating with other programmers, attending meetings, reading documents, reading e-mail, and responding to e-mail
- Waiting for others to finish their jobs, fix a bug, implement some vital functionality, and finish building their components
- Fighting fires, fixing build breaks, and chasing somebody else's bugs
- Staring at the computer screen while the machine is compiling, loading a huge program, running test suites, and rebooting

And finally, when time permits

- Developing new code

It's a well-known fact that there are $n(n-1)/2$ possible connections between n elements. That's of the order of $O(n^2)$. By the same token, the number of possible *interactions* within a group of n programmers is of the order of $O(n^2)$. The number of hours they can put out is of the order of $O(n)$. It is thus inevitable that at some point, as the size of the group increases, its members will start spending all their time communicating. In real life, people come up with various communication-overload defense mechanisms. One defense is to ignore incoming messages; another is to work odd hours (nights and/or weekends) when there aren't that many people around to disturb you (wishful thinking!).

As a programmer you are constantly bombarded with information from every possible direction. They will broadcast messages by e-mail, they will drop printed documents in your mailbox, they will invite you to meetings, they will call you on the phone, and in really urgent cases they will drop by your office or cubicle and talk to you directly.

If programmers were only to write and test code (and it used to be like this not so long ago), the market would be flooded with new operating systems, applications, tools, games, educational programs, and so on, all at ridiculously low prices. As a matter of fact, almost all public domain and shareware programs are written by people with very little communication overhead.

Figure 21.1 shows the results of a very simple simulation. I assumed that every programmer spends ten minutes a day communicating with every other programmer in the group. The rest of the time he or she does some real programming. The time spent programming, multiplied by the number of programmers in the group, measures team productivity— the effective work done by the group every day. Notice that, under these assumptions, the effective work peaks at about 25 people and then starts decreasing.

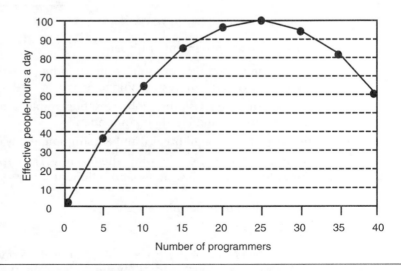

Figure 21.1 Simulation of team productivity as a function of team size

But that's not all! The more people you have in the group, the more complicated the dependency graph. Component A cannot be tested until component B works correctly. Component B needs some new functionality from component C, but C is blocked waiting for a bug fix in component D. People are waiting, they get frustrated, they send more e-mail messages, they drop by each other's offices.

Not enough yet? Consider the reliability of a system with n components. The more components, the more likely it is that one of them will break. When one component is broken, the testing of the other components is either impossible or at least impaired. That in turn leads to more buggy code being added to the project, causing even more breakages. It seems like all these mechanisms feed on each other in one vicious circle.

In view of all this, the team's productivity curve in Figure 21.1 is much too optimistic. It could be argued, and indeed some do, that the optimal size of a team is determined more by our hunter-gatherer ancestry than the requirements of the modern industry.

The other side of the coin is that if you can raise the productivity of a programmer, either by providing better tools, a better programming language, a better computer, or more help in nonessential tasks, you will create a positive feedback loop that will nonlinearly amplify the productivity of the team. If we can raise the productivity of every programmer in a fixed-size project, we can reduce the size of the team— that in turn will lead to decreased communication overhead, further increasing the effective productivity of every programmer.

> **Every dollar invested in a programmer's productivity saves several dollars that would otherwise be spent hiring other programmers.**

Continuing with our simple simulation, suppose that the goal is to produce 100,000 lines of code in 500 days. I assumed the starting productivity of 16 lines of code per day per programmer, if there was no communication overhead. Figure 21.2 shows how the required size of the team shrinks with the increase in productivity.

Notice that when the curve turns more or less linear (let's say at about 15 programmers), every 3% increase in productivity saves us one programmer, who can then be used in another project.

Several things influence productivity:

- The choice of a programming language and methodology. So far, in general programming tasks, it is hard to beat C++ and object-oriented methodology. If size or speed is not an issue, other specialized higher-level languages may be appropriate (Smalltalk, Prolog, BASIC, and so on). The trade-off is also in the initial investment in the education of the team.

- The choice of project-wide conventions. Decisions such as whether to use exceptions, how to propagate errors, what the code-sharing strategy is, how to deal with project-wide header files, and so on, are all very difficult to correct

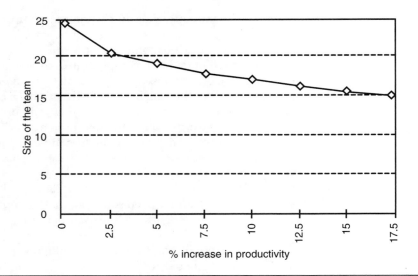

Figure 21.2 Simulated dependence of the size of the team required to perform a given task as a function of programmer productivity

during the development process. It is much better to think about them up front.

- The choice of a programming environment and tools.
- The choice of hardware for the development. RAM and disk space are of crucial importance. A local area network with shared printers and e-mail are a necessity. Also, the need for large monitors is often underestimated.

21.2 Team Strategies

In the ideal world we would divide work between small teams and let each team provide a clear and immutable interface to which other teams would write their code. We would couple each interface with a well-defined, comprehensive, and detailed contract. The interaction between teams would be reduced to the exchange of interface specifications and periodic updates as to which part of the contract had already been implemented.

This ideal situation is, to some extent, realized when the team uses externally created components, such as libraries, operating system APIs (application programming interfaces), and so on. Everything whose interface and contract can be easily described is a good candidate for a library. For instance, the string manipulation library, the library of container objects, iostreams, and so on are all well described either in online Help, in compiler manuals, or in other books. Some APIs are not that easily described, so using them is often a matter of trial and error (or customer support calls).

In the real world, things are more complicated than that. Yes, we do divide work between small teams and they do try to come up with some interfaces and contracts. However, the interfaces are far from immutable, the contracts are far from comprehensive, and they are being constantly renegotiated between teams. All we can do in practice is to try to smooth out this process as much as possible.

You have to start with a good design. Spend as much time as necessary on designing a good hierarchical structure of the product. This structure will be translated into the hierarchical structure of the teams. The better the design, the clearer the interfaces and contracts between all parts of the product. That means fewer changes and less negotiating at the later implementation stages.

Divide the work between teams in clear correspondence to the structure of the design, taking communication needs into account. As soon as the structure crystallizes during the design, assign team leaders to all the top-level components. Let them negotiate the contracts among themselves. Each team leader in turn should repeat this procedure with his or her team, designing the structure of the component and, if necessary, assigning subcomponents to leaders of smaller teams.

The whole design should go through several passes. The results of the lower-level design should serve as feedback to the design of the higher-level components, and eventually contribute to the design of the whole product. Each team writes its own part of the specification. These specifications are reviewed by other teams responsible for other parts of the same higher-level component.

The more negotiating that is done up front during the design, the better the chances of a smooth implementation. The negotiations should be structured in such a way that there are only a few people involved at a time. A plenary meeting is useful to describe the top-level design of the product to all members of all teams, so that everybody knows what the big picture is. Such meetings are also useful during the implementation phase to monitor the progress of the product. They are *not* a good forum for design discussions.

> Contract negotiations during implementation might look like this: Some member of team A is using one of team B's interfaces according to his or her understanding of the contract. The code behind the interface unexpectedly returns an error, hits an assertion, raises an exception, or goes haywire. The member of team A either goes to team B's leader to ask who is responsible for the implementation of the interface in question, or directly to the implementor of this interface to ask what caused the strange behavior. The implementor either clarifies the contract, changes it according to the needs of team A, fixes the implementation to fulfill the contract, or takes over tracking the bug. If a change is made to component B, it has to be thoroughly tested to see that it doesn't cause any unexpected problems for other users of B.

During the implementation of some major new functionality, it may be necessary to ask other teams to change or extend their interfaces and/or contracts. This is considered a *redesign*. A redesign, like any other disturbance in the system, produces concentric waves. The feedback process, described previously in the course of the original design, should be repeated again. The interface and contract disturbance are propagated first within the teams that are immediately involved (so that they make sure that the changes are indeed necessary, and to try to describe these changes in some detail), then up towards the top. Somewhere on the way to the top the disturbances of the design may get absorbed completely by internal changes to some components. Or they may reach the very top and change the way top-level objects interact. At that point the changes will be propagated downwards to all the involved teams. Their feedback is then bounced back towards the top, and the process is repeated as many times as is necessary for the changes to stabilize themselves. This "annealing" process ends when the project reaches a new state of equilibrium.

Chapter 22
Implementation Strategies

Once the design is in place, where do you start program development? In what order should various parts of the project be implemented? What's the best methodology for introducing changes? Although the answers to these questions depend on the specifics of the project, there are some general rules to be followed in preparation for and during the implementation of the project.

22.1 Global Decisions

Error handling, exceptions, common headers, code reuse, debug output.

The biggest global decision to be made, before the implementation can even begin, is how to handle errors and exceptions. There are a few major sources of errors:

- Bugs within components
- Incorrect parameters passed from other (trusted) components
- Incorrect user input
- Corruption of persistent data structures
- The system running out of resources

Bugs are not supposed to get through to the final retail version of the program, so we have to deal with them only during development. (Of course, in practice most retail programs still have some residual bugs.) Since during the development process we mostly deal with debug builds, we can protect ourselves from bugs by sprinkling our code with assertions. Assertions can also be used to enforce contracts between components.

User input, and in general input from other less-trusted parts of the system, must be thoroughly tested for correctness before proceeding any further. "Typing monkeys" tests have to be done to ensure that no input can break our program. If our program provides some service to another program, it should test the validity of externally passed arguments. For instance, operating system API functions always check the parameters passed to them from applications. This type of parameter error should be dealt with on the spot. If it's direct user input, we should provide immediate feedback; if it's the input from an untrusted component, we should return the appropriate error code or raise the appropriate exception.

Any kind of persistent data structures that are not totally under our control (and that is always true, unless we are the file system) can always get corrupted by other applications or tools, not to mention hardware failures and user errors. We should therefore always test for their consistency. A common programming error is to use assertions to enforce the consistency of data structures read from disk. Data on disk should *never* be trusted; therefore, all the checks must also be present in the retail version of the program.

> **Don't use assertions to validate the consistency of persistent data structures.**

Running out of resources—memory, disk space, handles, and so on—is the prime candidate for exceptions. Consider the case of memory. Suppose that all programmers are trained to always check the return value of the nonthrowing operator new (that's already unrealistic). But what are they supposed to do when the returned pointer is null? It depends on the situation. For every case of calling new, the programmer is supposed to come up with some sensible recovery. Now consider that the recovery path is rarely tested (unless the test team has a way of simulating all types of failures). We take up a lot of programmers' time to design something that is as likely to fail as the original thing whose failure they were handling.

The simplest way to deal with out-of-memory situations is to print a message "Out of memory" and exit. This can be easily accomplished by setting our own out-of-memory handler (the set_new_handler function in C++). This is, however, very rarely the desired solution. In most cases we at least want to do some cleanup, save some user data to disk, and maybe even get back to some higher level of our program and try to continue. Using the exceptions and resource management techniques (described earlier) seem most appropriate.

If C++ exception handling is not available or prohibited by managers, one is left with conventional techniques of testing the results of new, cleaning up, and propagating the error higher up. Of course, the program must be thoroughly tested using simulated failures. It is this kind of philosophy that leads to project-wide conventions such as "every function should return a status code." Normal return values then have to be passed by reference or a pointer. Very soon the system of status codes develops into a Byzantine structure. Essentially, in such a scheme, every error code should not only point at the culprit, but also contain the whole history of the error, since the interpretation of the error is enriched at each stage through which it passes. The use of constructors is then highly restricted, since these are the only functions that cannot return a value. Very quickly C++ degenerates to "better C," with its limited capabilities of handling complexity. Fortunately, most modern C++ compilers provide exception support and hopefully soon enough this discussion will only be of historical interest.

Another important decision to be made up front is the choice of project-wide debugging conventions. It is extremely handy to have progress and status messages printed to some kind of a debug output or log.

The choice of directory structure and build procedures comes next. The structure of the project and its components should be reflected in the directory structure of source code. There is also a need for a place where project-wide header files and code can be deposited. This is where one puts the debugging harness, definitions of common types, project-wide parameters, shared utility code, useful templates, and so on.

Some degree of code reuse within the project is necessary and should be well organized. What is usually quite neglected is the need for propagating the information about the availability of reusable code and its documentation. The information about what is available in the reusability department should be broadcast on a regular basis and the up-to-date documentation should be readily available.

One more observation: in C++ there is a very tight coupling between header files and implementation files—we rarely make modifications to one without inspecting or modifying the other. This is why in most cases it makes sense to keep them together in the same directory rather than in some special include directory. We make an exception for headers that are *shared* between directories.

It is also a good idea to separate platform-dependent layers into separate directories. We'll talk about this later in Chapter 23, Porting.

22.2 Top-Down Object-Oriented Implementation

The implementation process should be modeled on the design process as closely as possible. This is why implementation should start with the top-level components. The earlier we find that the top-level interfaces need modification, the better. Besides, we need a working program for testing as soon as possible.

The goal of the original implementation effort is to test the flow of control, lifetimes, and accessibility of top-level objects as well the as the initialization and shutdown processes. At this stage the program is not supposed to do anything useful, it cannot be demo'ed, and it is not a prototype.

If management needs a prototype, it should be implemented by a separate group, possibly using a different language (BASIC, Smalltalk, and so on). Trying to reuse code written for the prototype in the main project is usually a big mistake.

Only basic functionality that's necessary for the program to make progress is implemented at this point; everything else is stubbed out. Stubs of class methods should only print debugging messages and display their arguments if they make sense. The debugging and error handling harness should be put in place and tested.

If the program is interactive, we implement as much of the view and the controller as is necessary to get the information flowing towards the model and showing some minimal view. The model can be stubbed out completely.

Once the working skeleton of the program is in place, we can start implementing lower-level objects. At every stage we repeat the same basic procedure. We first create stubs of all objects at that level, then test their interfaces and interactions. We continue the descent until we hit the bottom of the project, at which point we start implementing some "real" functionality. The goal is for the lowest-level components to fit right into the whole structure. They should snap into place, get control when appropriate, get called with the right arguments, and return the right stuff.

This strategy produces professional programs of uniform quality, with components that fit together very tightly and efficiently like in a well-designed sports car. Conversely, the bottom-up implementation creates programs whose parts are of widely varying quality, put together using scotch tape and string. A lot of a programmer's time is spent trying to fit square pegs into round holes. The result resembles anything but a well-designed sports car.

22.3 Program Modifications

Modifications of existing code range from cosmetic changes, such as renaming a single variable, to sweeping global changes and major rewrites. Small changes are often suggested during code reviews. The rule of thumb is that when you see too many local variables or objects within a single function, or too many parameters being passed back and forth, the code is ripe for a new abstraction.

It is interesting to notice how the object-oriented paradigm gets distorted at the highest and lowest levels. It is often difficult to come up with a good set of top-level objects, and all too often the main function ends up being a very large procedure. Conversely, at the bottom of the hierarchy there is no good tradition of using a lot of short-lived lightweight local objects. The top-level situation is a matter of good or poor design; the bottom level situation depends a lot on the quality of code reviews. The above rule of thumb is of great help there. You should also be on the lookout for too much cut-and-paste code. If the same set of actions with only small modifications happens in many places, it may be time to look for a new abstraction.

Rewrites of small parts of the program happen, and they are a good sign of healthy development. Sometimes the rewrites are more serious. They could be related to abstracting a layer, in which case all the clients of a given service have to be modified, or to changing the high-level structure of the program, in which case a lot of lower-level structures are influenced. Fortunately, the top-down object-oriented design makes such sweeping changes much easier to make. It is quite possible to split a top-level object into more independent parts, or change the containment or access structure at the highest level (for example, move a subobject from one object to another). How is it done? The key is to make the changes incrementally, top-down.

During the first pass, you change the *interfaces* and pass different sets of arguments, for instance, pass reference variables to those places that used to have direct access to some objects but are about to lose it. Make as few changes to the implementation as possible. Compile and test.

In the second pass, *move objects* around and see if they have access to all the data they need. Compile and test.

In the third pass, once you have all the objects in place and all the arguments at your disposal, start making the necessary *implementation* changes, step by step.

Testing starts at the same time as the implementation. At all times you must have a working program. You need it for your testing; your teammates need it for their testing. The functionality might not be there, but the program will run and will at least print some debugging output. As soon as there is some functionality, start regression testing.

For regression testing, develop a test suite to test the basic functionality of your system. After every change, run it to see that you haven't broken any functionality. Expand the test suite to include basic tests of all new functionality. Running the regression suite should not take a long time.

Stress testing should start as soon as some functionality starts approaching its final form. Unlike regression testing, stress testing is there to test the limits of the system. For instance, a comprehensive test of all possible failure scenarios, like out-of-memory errors in various places, disk failures, unexpected power-downs, and so on should be made.

The scalability under heavy loads should be tested too. Depending on the type of program, the stress can be achieved by processing lots of small files, one extremely large file, lots of requests, and so on.

22.4 Inheriting Legacy Code

In the ideal world (from the programmer's point of view), every project would start from scratch and have no external dependencies. Once in a while such situations happen and this is when real progress is made. New languages, new programming methodologies, and new team structures can be applied and tested.

In the real world most projects inherit some source code, usually written using obsolete programming techniques, with its own model for error handling, debugging, use or misuse of global objects, gotos, spaghetti code, functions that go on for pages and pages, and so forth. Most projects have external dependencies—some code, tools, or libraries that are being developed by external groups. Worst of all, those groups have different goals, they have to ship their own product, compete in the marketplace, and so on. In most cases they are always enthusiastic about having their code or tool used by another group and they promise continuing support. Unfortunately, they usually have different priorities. Make sure your manager has some leverage over their manager.

If you have full control over inherited code, plan on rewriting it step by step. Go through a series of code reviews to find out which parts will cause the most problems and rewrite them first. Then do parallel development, interlacing rewrites with the development of new code. The effort will pay back in terms of debugging time and overall code quality.

22.5 Multi-Platform Development

A lot of programs are developed for multiple platforms at once, e.g., different hardware or a different set of APIs. Operating systems and computers evolve—at any point in time there is an obsolete platform, the most popular platform, and the platform of the future. Sometimes the target platform is different than the development platform. In any case, the platform-dependent things should be abstracted and separated into layers or libraries.

The operating system is supposed to provide an abstraction layer that separates applications from the hardware. Except for very specialized applications, access to the disk is very well abstracted into the file system. In windowing systems, graphics and user input is abstracted into windowing APIs. Our program should do the same with the platform-dependent services—abstract them into layers. A layer is a set of services through which our application can access some lower-level functionality. The advantage of layering is that we can tweak the layer's implementation without having to modify the code that uses it. Moreover, we can add new implementations or switch from one to another using a compile-time variable. Sometimes a platform doesn't provide or even need the functionality provided by other platforms. For instance, a non-multitasking system doesn't need semaphores. Still, we can provide a locking system whose implementation can be switched on and off, depending on the platform.

We can construct a layer by creating a set of classes that abstract some functionality. For instance, memory-mapped files can be combined with buffered files under one abstraction. It is advisable that the implementation choices be made in such a way that the platform-of-the-future implementation be the most efficient one.

It is worth noticing that if the platforms differ by the sizes of basic data types, such as 16-bit versus 32-bit integers, we should be extremely careful with the design of persistent data structures and data types that can be transmitted over the wire. The foolproof method would be to convert all fundamental data types into strings of bytes of a well-defined length.

In this way we could even resolve the big endian versus little endian differences. This solution is not always acceptable because of the runtime overhead. A trade-off is made to either support only those platforms where the sizes of shorts and longs are compatible (and the endians are the same), or provide conversion programs that can translate persistent data from one format to another.

Chapter 23
Porting

Writing a fresh chunk of code is an opportunity that doesn't come too often in the life of a software engineer. That's why it should be savored and stretched to the maximum. More often a programmer is faced with the task of maintenance, rewriting of existing code, or porting a program to a new platform. The complexity of a port may vary between making a program run on different hardware, a different operating system, or a different set of APIs. In fact, porting is such a common programming task that I decided to end this part of the book with a porting example.

23.1 Creating an Abstraction Layer

Project
PortCalc

Porting is an excellent opportunity to restructure your code. When porting, your primary goal should be to try to separate the part of the implementation that is platform-dependent and hide it inside an abstraction layer. The bulk of your program should just call into this layer without knowing how it is implemented. Switching to a new platform will then consist of rewriting the layer itself, without touching the rest of the code.

An abstraction layer in general is defined by a set of interfaces providing access to a subsystem. It serves as a firewall between the client and the lower-level implementation code. The client of the abstraction layer can only access the subsystem through these public interfaces. As long as the interfaces remain intact and both sides follow the contracts, the code on either side of the firewall can evolve freely.

After a well-performed port, the development of the system can continue in a platform-independent manner. If new platform-dependent functionality has to be added, its implementation should go inside the porting layer. In most cases, this kind of layering has a side effect of actually making the code more understandable and maintainable.

As usual, one thing to avoid is premature optimization. It might seem that putting a bunch of `ifdefs` (compilation directives) here and there is more optimal than going through an abstraction layer. Do it *only* as a last resort, when you have undeniable proof that the code in question is a major bottleneck in your program. Otherwise you'll be creating a maintenance nightmare for yourself and for those who follow you.

23.2   Porting the Calculator

We have already done some sort of a port when transforming our calculator from command-line interface to GUI. However, we did a one-way rewrite—the program could no longer be compiled to run as a command-line utility. This time we would like to do something more general.

Since I don't want to introduce yet another set of APIs in this book, we won't be targeting any particular system. We'll satisfy ourselves with completing the first phase of a port—the separation of Windows-specific functionality into a separate layer. The rewriting of this layer in terms of the Linux or Mac API is a separate problem that requires some knowledge of these systems and is left as an exercise to an ambitious reader.

So far we've done a pretty good job of encapsulating the Windows API. The interfaces to our Windows library already form a reasonably good abstraction layer, so our task should be relatively easy. To begin with, none of our nonlibrary files include `<windows.h>` or call any Windows API directly. We arrived at this situation not so much in anticipation of a port, but mostly because we decided that the old-fashioned low-level Windows API is not compatible with the modern style of programming.

To continue in this direction, we now have to make sure that none of the data types defined in `<windows.h>` is used directly in the application code. We'll be eliminating these step by step. And then, to prove that the rest of the code is totally Windows-independent, we'll create a stub library that doesn't include any of the Windows headers and we'll compile our program with it. This stub may be subsequently developed for different platforms, as the need arises.

23.2.1   Eliminating Simple Windows Dependencies

Script 1   In our first sweep we'll concentrate on such Windows-specific data types as UINT, WPARAM, LPARAM, various handles, and bitflags.

Most of the Windows message processing is thoroughly encapsulated inside our generic window procedure, except when it comes to user-defined messages. Not only does the `Win::Controller::OnUserMessage` method take raw Windows data types as arguments, but the client is also forced to define such application-specific messages as UM_MEMCLEAR in terms of Windows-defined WM_USER.

We can remedy this by creating a library class `Win::UserMessage` that knows how to deal with low-level details of message numbering and parameter packing. In particular, the library class can accept zero-based message IDs and internally add to them the Windows-specific constant `WM_USER`. The sending of a user message is done through an overloading of `Win::Dow::SendMsg` that takes a `Win::UserMessage` and does the necessary type conversions.

```
void Win::Dow::SendMsg (Win::UserMessage & msg) const
{
    LRESULT result = ::SendMessage (_h,
                                    msg.GetMsg () + WM_USER,
                                    msg.GetWParam (),
                                    msg.GetLParam ());
    msg.SetResult (result);
}
```

Consequently, the `Win::Controller`'s method `OnUserMessage` can now be defined in terms of `Win::UserMessage` as well.

There's another place where we are explicitly sending a Windows message—when we subclass the edit control to intercept the Enter key and turn it into a command message. Again, we can hide the mechanics of packing the parameters to a command message in a library class, `Win::CommandMessage`. At this point it becomes obvious that a more general class `Win::Message` should be created. It will serve as a parent to `Win::UserMessage`, `Win::ControlMessage`, or any other messages that we might want to use explicitly in our code.

Script 2   Our menu subsystem has several explicit Windows dependencies. For instance, methods like `OnInitPopup` take `HMENU` as an argument. That can be easily remedied by replacing `HMENU` with our class `Menu::Manip`.

Script 3   The method `TopController::OnMenuSelect` uses a whole set of Windows-specific constants, like `MF_SEPARATOR`, `MF_POPUP`, and so on. We can not only hide these constants inside a bitflag `Menu::State`, but we can also split the two cases of menu-select and menu-dismiss into two separate `Win::Controller` methods. Take note: the effort of porting paid an unexpected dividend of suggesting a better abstraction.

Script 4   The `PostQuitMessage` API may be encapsulated into a free function `Win::Quit`.

Script 5–9   Our `OnSize` handler also uses some Windows-specific flags. We'll encapsulate them in an enumeration, `Win::SizeType`. Similarly, we'll enumerate list box notification codes, virtual key codes, as well as several sundry Windows constants.

Script 10–14   It's not entirely clear what should be done with `HINSTANCE`. It's a Windows-specific data type—a handle to a program instance. Unfortunately, "program instance" doesn't seem to represent a general enough abstraction, and consequently it's not easy to port it to other systems. It is mostly used to identify the place from where program resources, such as icons, bitmaps, and so forth can be loaded. In our limited usage it was always the currently running executable, the handle that was passed to us in `WinMain` and that served as such a source. For the lack of a better idea I decided to replace `HINSTANCE` with a more neutral type, `Win::Instance`. In our Windows library it is simply a typedef for `HINSTANCE`. In a port, it could be turned into any other appropriate type.

Obviously, `WinMain` must remain in our code as a Windows-specific entry point. A ported version will have to provide its own entry point. To simplify things, I have also created a platform-independent entry point called `Main` that can be called from any of the platform-dependent entry points—in particular, from `WinMain`.

Script 15 The final step in eliminating simple Windows dependencies is the creation of a stubbed library. This is done by simply removing all Windows-specific includes (in particular `<windows.h>`) from the library and stubbing out the implementation of all library methods. If after this transformation the program still compiles (although it won't run!), we know that we have successfully de-Windowized our program.

This test assures us that the library interfaces that are used in our program are indeed Windows-independent. These interfaces can now be implemented—the stubs filled out—using a different set of APIs and, as long as the new implementation is functionally equivalent to the old one, our program should run in a new environment.

23.2.2 Nontrivial Windows Dependencies

Now that we have eliminated the more obvious Windows dependencies from our code, let's discuss the less obvious ones.

To begin with, there is no guarantee that a different set of windowing APIs could even be abstracted into classes and methods that were designed by us specifically for Windows. Fortunately, commercially available window-based GUI systems all have one common ancestor, the Xerox PARC (Palo Alto Research Center) Smalltalk system called Alto from the late 1970s. Because of that, we can rather safely assume that any windowing API set we come across will have abstractions for windows, window classes, message handlers, menus, dialog boxes, mouse cursors, and so on. Most likely you will also find the implementations of many standard Windows controls, like buttons, edit boxes, list boxes, and so forth. And the ones that are not available can always be implemented using the primitives that are available.

The way dialog boxes are defined in Windows is not very portable. Not only do resource scripts use a proprietary language, but the very way elements are positioned within a dialog box is nonportable. A Windows resource script specifies all the positions and sizes of various controls. The measurements, however, are specified not in pixels but in special *dialog box units*. Dialog box units are based on the average size of a character in the font used by the dialog box.

This trick was supposed to make dialog box layouts independent of screen resolutions and font choices. When Windows displays a dialog box, it translates dialog box units into pixels based on the size of the font used by the dialog box. This way text fields, along with all the other controls, are scaled in proportion to the size of the font. In practice this doesn't work very well, even between the Microsoft operating systems. A dialog box designed for Windows 98 will often display truncated text fields on Windows NT or vice versa.

A much better approach to designing dialog boxes would be to specify the layout in a more abstract way. Lessons could be learned from HTML or Java. For instance, in Java AWT (Abstract Window Toolkit) formatting is done dynamically using various Layout objects.

We could make our library more portable, and probably easier to use, by implementing dynamic layout for dialog boxes. Indeed, it is possible in a Windows program to dynamically create a dialog box template and call the API DialogBoxIndirect to display it. This way one could bypass the nonportable resource scripts and gain more flexibility in designing and modifying dialog boxes.

23.3 The Advantages of Porting

I like our calculator program better after this porting exercise. There's a much crisper division between the application code and the library. Even if there was no need to port the calculator I would still keep the modified library interface. And notice how it seems that every time we generalize this program, we end up improving its structure. All throughout this book I've been subjecting our calculator to one transformation after another, and after each transformation the code seemed to become more logical. In many cases generalizations led to simplifications (consider, for instance, the switch to dynamic data structures or the use of the standard library).

This might run counter to common experience. We usually expect modifications to add complexity and break structure, not the other way around. Most programs become less and less maintainable as they go through development cycles. But there is no fundamental law that dooms every software project to keep increasing in entropy until it reaches a thermal death. Complexity can be fought by imposing more structure. If every program transformation is accompanied by appropriate restructuring, a software project can keep evolving virtually forever.

Where most development teams make a mistake is in not being aggressive enough in making structural changes. It seems quicker to modify a program by adding a few more special cases, passing an additional flag, and calling a procedure to do some additional work rather than rethink an abstraction, add a new layer, or rationalize an implementation of a procedure. The latter activity doesn't immediately lead to new functionality, so it might be difficult to squeeze it into an aggressive schedule with looming deadlines and mounting pressure from management. And yet it's this kind of work that is essential in the long run.

So it's really no coincidence that most of this book was dedicated to program transformation. Being able to modify a program not only without sacrificing its structure but actually improving it is probably the most important skill that a programmer can bring to a team.

Bibliography

Cooper, Alan, *About Face: The Essentials of User Interface Design.* Foster City, CA: IDG Books, 1995. A must-read for any programmer who wants to understand the user interfaces.

Ellis, Margaret A., and Bjarne Stroustrup, *The Annotated C++ Reference Manual.* Reading, MA: Addison-Wesley, 1990. A pre-standardization C++ manual.

ISO/IEC 14882:1998(E), *Programming Languages—C++.* The official C++ standard. You can buy the electronic version for $18 directly from the ANSI web site http://webstore.ansi.org. Search for the standard 14882.

Josuttis, Nicolai M., *The C++ Standard Library: A Tutorial and Reference.* Reading, MA: Addison-Wesley, 1999. A comprehensive standard library reference.

Kernighan, Brian W., Ritchie, Dennis M., *The C Programming Language: ANSI C Version.* Prentice Hall, 1988. The official C bible.

Knuth, Donald E., *The Art of Computer Programming.* Reading, MA: Addison-Wesley, 1998. In-depth study of computer algorithms.

Miller, George A., *The Magical Number Seven, Plus or Minus Two: Some Limits on our Capacity for Processing Information.* The Psychological Review, Vol. 63, No. 2, March 1956.

Rector, Brent E., and Joseph M. Newcomer, *Win32 Programming.* Reading, MA: Addison-Wesley, 1997. An excellent description of the Windows API.

Richter, Jeffrey, *Advanced Windows.* Third edition. Redmond, WA: Microsoft Press, 1997. Covers advanced topics in Windows programming like virtual memory, threads, processes, and so on.

Stroustrup, Bjarne, *The C++ Programming Language.* Special edition. Reading, MA: Addison-Wesley, 2000. The official C++ bible.

Stroustrup, Bjarne, *The Design and Evolution of C++.* Reading, MA: Addison-Wesley, 1994. Describes design choices and alternatives in the development of the C++ language.

Appendices

Appendix A
Exercise Solutions

In this appendix you'll find solutions to some of the exercises from the first part of the book. In some cases I went into great detail describing the solutions, in others I provided only a few hints. Source code to some solutions is available on the accompanying CD-ROM. I will be posting more solutions on the Web site www.ReliSoft.com/book.

Chapter 1

1. The first solution is to create the two worlds in a loop:

```
for (int i = 1; i < 3; ++i)
  World world (i);
```

The second possibility is to open a separate local scope for each world:

```
int main ()
{
  {
    World world (1);
  }
  {
    World world (2);
  }
}
```

2. The problem is in the order of initialization of data members. Despite the ordering of initializers in the preamble to the constructor, _hand will be

initialized before _n because that's the order in which they are embedded in Glove. Therefore _n shouldn't be passed as an argument to Hand's constructor because its value hasn't been set at that point. One way to fix this bug is to change the order of embeddings. The other is to use numFingers instead of _n to initialize the _hand.

3. Class Frame

```cpp
class HorBar
{
public:
  HorBar (int n)
  {
    std::cout << "+";
    for (int i = 0; i < n; ++i)
      std::cout << "-";
    std::cout << "+\n";
  }
};

class VerBar
{
public:
  VerBar (int n)
  {
    for (int i = 0; i < n; ++i)
      std::cout << "|\n";
  }
};

class Frame
{
public:
  Frame (int hor, int ver)
  : _upper (hor),
    _ver (ver),
    _lower (hor)
  {}
private:
  HorBar _upper;
  VerBar _ver;
  HorBar _lower;
};
```

4. Class Ladder

```cpp
class Ladder
{
public:
  Ladder (int hor, int ver)
  : _upper (hor, ver),
    _middle (ver),
    _lower (hor, ver)
```

```
    {}
  private:
    Frame     _upper;
    VerBar    _middle;
    Frame     _lower;
  };
```

5. This solution uses only the constructs introduced in Chapter 1.

```
    int main ()
    {
      InputNum num;
      int factorial = 1;
      for (int i = 2; i < num.GetValue (); ++i)
        factorial = factorial * i;
      factorial = factorial * num.GetValue ();
      std::cout << num.GetValue () << "! = "
                << factorial << std::endl;
    }
```

6. Class `Planet`

```
    class Planet: public CelestialBody
    {
    public:
      Planet (double mass, double albedo)
        : CelestialBody (mass),
          _albedo (albedo)
      {
        std::cout << "Creating a planet with albedo"
            << _albedo << std::endl;
      }
      ~Planet ()
      {
        std::cout << "Destroying a planet with albedo"
            << _albedo << std::endl;
      }
    private:
      double _albedo;
    };
```

7. The first part:

```
    class Two
    {
    public:
      Two ()
      {
        std::cout << "Program";
      }
    };
```

```cpp
class Three
{
public:
  Three ()
  {
    std::cout << "objects ";
  }
};

class Four
{
public:
  Four ()
  {
    std::cout << "makes ";
  }
};

class One: public Two
{
public:
  One ()
  {
    Three three;
    std::cout << "with class. ";
  }
private:
  Four    _four;
};
```

The second part can be implemented like this:

```cpp
class One: public Two
{
public:
  One ()
  {
    std::cout << "class ";
  }
  ~One ()
  {
    std::cout << "class ";
  }
private:
  Three  _three;
  Four   _four;
  Five   _five;
};

int main ()
{
  One one;
  std::cout << std::endl;
}
```

where the classes Two, Three, Four, and Five print "Program ", "makes ", "objects ", and "with ", respectively.

8. Class Average

```
class Average
{
public:
  Average ()
    : _sum (0), _count (0)
  {}
  void Put (double n)
  {
    _sum = _sum + n;
    ++_count;
  }
  double Get () const
  {
    return _sum / _count;
  }
private:
  double     _sum;
  int        _count;
};
```

9. The hierarchy of classes should look like this:

```
class LivingBeing {};
class Human: public LivingBeing {};
class Tomato: public LivingBeing {};
class Elephant: public LivingBeing {};
```

or you can be more thorough and separate the flora from the fauna:

```
class LivingBeing {};
class Plant: public LivingBeing {};
class Animal: public LivingBeing {};
class Human: public Animal {};
class Elephant: public Animal {};
class Tomato: public Plant {};
```

10. Here's the sketch of the classes mentioned in the exercise:

```
class NoseHair {};

class Nose
{
...
private:
  NoseHair _noseHair;
};
```

```
class Head
{
...
private:
  Nose _nose;
};

class Human
{
...
private:
  Head _head;
};
class Man: public Human {};
class Woman: public Human {};
```

11. Methods Top and Const

```
int IStack::Top () const
{
  assert (_top > 0);
  return _arr [_top - 1];
}

int IStack::Count () const
{
  return _top;
}
```

12. This example calls Pop on an empty stack, in violation of the contract:

```
int main ()
{
  IStack stack;
  stack.Pop ();
}
```

13. This is the interface of the stack of characters:

```
class CharStack
{
public:
  CharStack () : _top (0) {}
  void Push (char c);
  char Pop ();
  char Top () const;
  int Count () const;
private:
  char _arr [maxStack];
  int  _top;
};
```

This is how you reverse a string using a stack of characters:

```
int main ()
{
  CharStack stack;
  char str [] = "esreveR";
  for (int i = 0; str [i] != '\0'; ++i)
    stack.Push (str [i]);
  while (stack.Count () > 0)
    std::cout << stack.Pop ();
  std::cout << std::endl;
}
```

14. Class `Queue`

```
#include <iostream>
#include <cassert>

const int maxPuts = 8;

class Queue
{
public:
  Queue ();
  double Get ();
  void Put (double x);
private:
  double _arr [maxPuts];
  int    _putIdx;
  int    _getIdx;
};
Queue::Queue ()
: _putIdx (0),
  _getIdx (0)
{}

double Queue::Get ()
{
  assert (_getIdx < _putIdx);
  ++_getIdx;
  return _arr [_getIdx - 1];
}

void Queue::Put (double x)
{
  assert (_putIdx < maxPuts);
  _arr [_putIdx] = x;
  ++_putIdx;
}
int main ()

{
  Queue queue;
```

```
      queue.Put (0.1);
      queue.Put (0.2);
      std::cout << "Getting: " << queue.Get () << ", "
                << queue.Get () << std::endl;
      queue.Put (0.3);
      std::cout << "Getting more: " << queue.Get () << std::endl;
   }
```

15. Class DblArray

```
   #include <iostream>
   #include <cassert>

   const int maxCells = 16;

   class DblArray
   {
   public:
     DblArray ();
     void Set (int i, double val);
     double Get (int i) const;
     bool IsSet (int i) const;
   private:
     double _arr [maxCells];
     bool   _isSet [maxCells];
   };

   DblArray::DblArray ()
   {
     for (int i = 0; i < maxCells; ++i)
       _isSet [i] = false;
   }

   void DblArray::Set (int i, double val)
   {
     assert (i < maxCells);
     assert (!IsSet (i));
     _arr [i] = val;
     _isSet [i] = true;
   }
   double DblArray::Get (int i) const
   {
     assert (i < maxCells);
     assert (_isSet [i]);
     return _arr [i];
   }

   bool DblArray::IsSet (int i) const
   {
     assert (i < maxCells);
     return _isSet [i];
   }
```

```
int main ()
{
  DblArray arr;
  arr.Set (2, 0.2);
  arr.Set (4, 0.4);
  std::cout << "IsSet (0) returns " << arr.IsSet (0) << std::endl;
  std::cout << "IsSet (2) returns " << arr.IsSet (2) << std::endl;
  std::cout << "Get (2) returns " << arr.Get (2) << std::endl;
  std::cout << "Get (4) returns " << arr.Get (4) << std::endl;
}
```

Chapter 2

1. The only tricky operators are:

   - One's complement. It's a unary operator, so you should only pop one argument from the stack.

   - Left and right shifts. These are two-character operators, so after detecting a less than or a greater than sign make sure the next character in the input buffer is the same as the first one. You can simply use the first character as a token.

2. Add a Boolean data member to `Calculator`:
   ```
   bool _isHex;
   ```

   (Remember to initialize it in the constructor.) In the `Execute` method, check for token 'x' and toggle the flag:

   ```
   else if (token == 'x')
   {
     // Toggle hex display
     _isHex = !_isHex;
     status = true;
   }
   ```

   In `main`, check this flag before displaying the contents of the stack:

   ```
   if (TheCalculator.IsHex ())
     std::cout << std::hex;
   else
     std::cout << std::dec;
   ```

3. Wherever values are stored or used in calculations, change the type `int` to `bool`. In particular, rewrite `IStack` (call it `BStack`) to store `bool` values. Here's the relevant fragment of `Calculator::Execute`:
   ```
   bool b2 = _stack.Pop ();
   ```

```
        if (token == '!')
        {
          _stack.Push (!b2);
          status = true;
        }
        else
        {
          bool b1;
          // Special case, when only one number on the stack:
          // use this number for both operands.
          if (_stack.IsEmpty ())
            b1 = b2;
          else
            b1 = _stack.Pop ();

          _stack.Push (Calculate (b1, b2, token));
          status = true;
        }
```

This is the `Calculate` method:

```
        bool Calculator::Calculate (bool b1, bool b2,
                                    int token) const
        {
          bool result;
          if (token == '&')
            result = b1 && b2;
          else if (token == '|')
            result = b1 || b2;
          return result;
        }
```

Chapter 3

1. Here's one possibility:
```
        void StrCpy (char * strDest, char const * strSrc)
        {
          int i = 0;
          char c;
          do
          {
            c = strSrc [i];
            strDest [i] = c;
            ++i;
          } while (c != '\0');
        }
```

2. Notice that in this section the same condition takes care of two cases, str2 being shorter than str1. In general, such optimizations are not recommended because they obscure the code.

```
int StrCmp (char const * str1, char const * str2)
{
  int i = 0;
  while (str1 [i] != '\0')
  {
      int diff = str1 [i] - str2 [i];
      // this also takes care of end of str2
      if (diff != 0)
        return diff;
      ++i;
  }
  if (str2 [i] == '\0')
    return 0;
  // str1 is shorter
  return -1;
}
```

3. Here's one way to do it. However, the specification wasn't complete. It didn't say what to do when the source string's length is greater than or equal to len. Should the destination string then be terminated by a null character at the offset len − 1? What do you think?

```
void StrNCpy (char * strDest, char const * strSrc,
              std::size_t len)
{
  for (std::size_t i = 0; i < len; ++i)
  {
    strDest [i] = strSrc [i];
    // early exit
    if (strSrc [i] == '\0')
      break;
  }
}
```

4.

```
#include <iostream>

int main (int count, char * argv [])
{
  for (int i = 0; i < count; ++i)
  {
    std::cout << i << ": " << argv [i] << std::endl;
  }
}
```

5. You don't want to shrink the stack down to _top, because then the next push would have to grow it again. A reasonable policy is to shrink the capacity of the stack to twice the current _top. We chose to shrink only when _top goes down to 1/3 of the current capacity.

```
int IStack::Pop ()
{
  assert (_top > 0);
  --_top;
  if (_top >= 1 && 3 * _top < _capacity)
    Shrink ();
  return _arr [_top];
}

void IStack::Shrink ()
{
  std::cout << "Shrinking stack from "
            << _capacity << " to " << 2 * _top << ".\n";
  assert (2 * _top < _capacity);
  // Allocate new array
  int * arrNew = new int [2 * _top];
  // Copy all entries
  for (int i = 0; i < _top; ++i)
    arrNew [i] = _arr [i];
  _capacity = 2 * _top;
  // Free old memory
  delete []_arr;
  // Substitute new array for old array
  _arr = arrNew;
}
```

6. Two-deep stack

```
Stack2::Stack2 ()
  : _last (0), _previous (0)
{}

void Stack2::Push (char const * str)
{
  _previous = _last;
  _last = str;
}

void Stack2::Pop ()
{
  _last = _previous;
  _previous = 0;
}

char const * Stack2::Top () const
{
  return _last;
}
```

7. The trick is to keep two pointers: one pointing at the head of the list and the other at its tail. When removing elements, we use the head pointer. We add new elements to the tail. As usual, we are really careful about boundary cases—the queue starting empty and becoming empty.

```
void Queue::Put (int i)
{
  Link * newLink = new Link (i);
  if (_tail == 0)
  {
    _head = newLink;
  }
  else
  {
    _tail->SetNext (newLink);
  }
  _tail = newLink;
}

int Queue::Get ()
{
  assert (_head != 0);
  int i = _head->Value ();
  Link * tmp = _head;
  _head = _head->Next ();
  // Don't delete recursively!
  tmp->SetNext (0);
  delete tmp;
  if (_head == 0)
    _tail = 0;
  return i;
}
```

8. List sequencer for unlinking

```
class UnlinkSeq
{
public:
  UnlinkSeq (List & list)
    : _list (list),
      _cur (list._pHead),
      _prev (0)
  {}
  bool AtEnd () const { return _cur == 0; }
  void Advance ()
  {
    _prev = _cur;
    _cur = _cur->Next ();
  }
  int Id () const { return _cur->Id (); }
  void Unlink ();
private:
  List & _list;
  Link * _cur;
  Link * _prev;
};

void UnlinkSeq::Unlink ()
{
```

```
    assert (_cur != 0);
    if (_prev == 0)
    {
      assert (_cur == _list._pHead);
      _list._pHead = _cur->Next ();
    }
    else
    {
      _prev->SetNext (_cur->Next ());
    }
    delete _cur;
    _cur = 0;
}
```

9. It helps to draw diagrams to see how the pointer manipulations work in these methods.

```
void DLink::Unlink ()
{
  assert (_pNext != 0);
  assert (_pPrev != 0);
  _pNext->SetPrev (_pPrev);
  _pPrev->SetNext (_pNext);
  _pPrev = this;
  _pNext = this;
}

void List::Put (int id)
{
  DLink * pLink = new DLink (id);
  if (_pHead == 0)
    _pHead = pLink;
  else
  {
    pLink->SetNext (_pHead);
    pLink->SetPrev (_pHead->Prev ());
    _pHead->Prev ()->SetNext (pLink);
    _pHead->SetPrev (pLink);
    _pHead = pLink;
  }
}
int List::Get ()
{
  assert (_pHead != 0);
  DLink * pLink = _pHead->Prev ();
  if (pLink == _pHead) // Last one
    _pHead = 0;
  pLink->Unlink ();
  int result = pLink->Id ();
  delete pLink;
  return result;
}
```

10. Notice the implicit conversion from an array of `List`s to a pointer to `List` in the constructor of `HSeq`. This is an example of array/pointer equivalence.

```
class HSeq
{
public:
  HSeq (HTable const & htab)
    : _aList (htab._aList),
      _idx (-1),
      _link (0)
  {
    NextList ();
  }
  bool AtEnd () const
    { return _idx == sizeHTable && _link == 0; }
  void Advance ();
  int Get () { return _link->Id (); }
private:
  void NextList ();

  List const * _aList;
  int          _idx;
  Link const * _link;
};
```

The `Advance` method tries to follow the current link, but if it finds the end of the current list, it searches for the next nonempty list.

```
void HSeq::Advance ()
{
  _link = _link->Next ();
  if (_link == 0)
    NextList ();
}

void HSeq::NextList ()
{
  assert (_link == 0);
  do
  {
    ++_idx;
  } while (_aList [_idx].IsEmpty ());

  if (_idx < sizeHTable)
    _link = _aList [_idx].GetHead ();
  else
    _link = 0;

}
```

11. The implementation is straight forward.

Chapter 4

1. Here are the basic classes:

```cpp
class Sieve
{
public:
  virtual int NextNumber () = 0;
};

class SourceSieve: public Sieve
{
public:
  SourceSieve () : _i (1) {}
  int NextNumber ();
private:
  int _i;
};

class Sieve2: public Sieve
{
public:
  Sieve2 (Sieve & src) : _src (src) {}
  int NextNumber ();
private:
  Sieve & _src;
};
```

Here's the implementation of NextNumber for SourceSieve and Sieve2:

```cpp
int SourceSieve::NextNumber ()
{
  if (_i > 100)
    return -1; // End
  return _i++;
}

int Sieve2::NextNumber ()
{
  int i;
  do
  {
    i = _src.NextNumber ();
  } while (i % 2 == 0 && i != 2 && i != -1);
  return i;
}
```

This is main, which prints all prime numbers less than 100:

```
int main ()
{
  SourceSieve src;
  Sieve2 s2 (src);
  Sieve3 s3 (s2);
  Sieve5 s5 (s3);
  Sieve7 s7 (s5);
  int i;
  for (;;)
  {
    i = s7.NextNumber ();
    if (i == -1)
      break;
    std::cout << i << " ";
  }
}
```

More solutions are available at www.ReliSoft.com/book.

2. The undo method of the NumberCommand should pop a number from the stack. Undo of ArithmeticCommand should pop the result and push back the argument(s). Notice that ArithmeticCommand must store the number of arguments and their values.

Appendix B
Transactions

Imagine using a word processor. You are editing a large document and, after working on it for several hours, you decide to save your work. Unfortunately, there is not enough disk space on your current drive and the save fails. What do you expect to happen?

Option number one is: the program gives up and exits. You are horrified—you have just lost many hours of work. You try to start the word processor again and you have a heart attack—the document is corrupted beyond recovery. Not only have you lost all recent updates, but you lost the original as well.

If horrors like this don't happen, it is because of transactions. A transaction is a series of operations that move the program from one well-defined state to another. A transaction must be implemented in such a way that it either completely succeeds or totally fails. If it fails, the program must return to its original state.

In any professionally written word processor, saving a document is a transaction. If the save succeeds, the on-disk image of the document (the file) is updated with the current version of the document and all the internal data structures reflect this fact. If the save fails, for whatever reason, the on-disk image of the documents remains unchanged and all the internal data structures reflect that fact. A transaction cannot succeed halfway. If it did, it would leave the program and the file in an inconsistent, corrupted state.

Let's consider one more word processing scenario. You are in the middle of editing a document when suddenly all the lights go out. Your computer doesn't have a UPS (uninterruptible power supply), so it goes down too. Five minutes later, the electricity comes back and the computer reboots. What do you expect to happen?

The nightmare scenario is that the whole file system is corrupted and you have to reformat your disk. Of course, your document is lost forever. Unfortunately, this is a real possibility with some file systems. Most modern file systems, however, are able to limit the damage to a single directory. If this is not good enough for you (and I don't expect it is), you should look for a recoverable file system. Such systems can limit the damage down to the contents of the files that were open during the crash. They do it by performing transactions whenever they update the file system metadata (e.g., directory entries). Asking anything more from a file system (e.g., transacting all writes) would be impractical—it would slow down the system to a crawl.

Supposing you have a recoverable file system, you should be able to recover the last successfully saved precrash version of your document. But what if the crash happened during the save operation? Well, if the save was implemented as a transaction it is guaranteed to leave the persistent data in a consistent state—the file should either contain the complete previously saved version or the complete new version.

Of course, you can't expect to recover the data structures that were stored in the volatile memory of your computer prior to the crash. That data is lost forever. (It's important to use the auto-save feature of your word processor to limit such losses). That doesn't mean that the program can't or shouldn't transact operations that deal solely with volatile data structures. In fact, every robust program must use transactions if it is to continue after errors or exceptions.

What operations require transactions? Any failure-prone action that involves updating multiple data structures might require a transaction.

Transient Transactions

A transient, or in-memory, transaction does not involve any changes to the persistent (usually on-disk) state of the program. Therefore a transient transaction is not robust in the face of system crashes or power failures.

We have already seen examples of such transactions when we were discussing resource management. The construction of a well-implemented complex data structure is a transaction—it either succeeds or fails. If the constructor of any of the subobjects fails and throws an exception, the construction of the whole data structure is reversed and the program goes back to the preconstruction state (provided all the destructors undo whatever the corresponding constructors did). That's just one more bonus you get from using resource management techniques.

There are, however, cases when you have to do something special in order to transact an operation. Let's go back to our word processor example. (By the way, the same ideas can be applied to the design of an editor; and what programmer didn't, at one time or another, try to write his or her own editor?) Suppose that we keep text in the form of a list of paragraphs. When the user presses Return in the middle of a paragraph, we have to split the current paragraph into two new ones. This operation involves several steps that have to be done in a certain order:

1. Allocate one new paragraph.
2. Allocate another new paragraph.
3. Copy the first part of the old paragraph into the first new paragraph.
4. Copy the second part of the old paragraph into the second new paragraph.
5. Plug the two new paragraphs in the place of the old one.
6. Delete the old paragraph.

The switch—when you plug in the new paragraphs—is the most sensitive part of the whole operation. It is performed on some master data structure that glues all paragraphs into one continuous body of the document. The master data structure is most likely a dynamic data structure whose modifications might fail—the computer might run out of memory while allocating an extension table or a link in a list. Once the master data structure is updated, the whole operation has been successful. In the language of transactions we say "the transaction has *committed*." But if the crucial update fails, the transaction *aborts* and the program has to *unroll* it. That means it has to get the program back to its original state (which also means that it refuses to split the paragraph) by undoing previous actions.

When designing a transaction it is important to make sure that

- All operations that precede the commit are undoable in a safe manner (although the operations themselves don't have to be—and usually aren't—safe).
- The commit operation is safe.
- All operations that follow it are also safe.

Operations that involve memory allocation are not safe—they may fail, e.g., by throwing an exception. In our case, it's the allocation of new paragraphs that's unsafe. The undo operation is the deletion of these paragraphs. We assume that deletion is safe—it can't fail. So it is indeed okay to do paragraph allocation before the commit.

The commit operation, in our case, is the act of plugging in new paragraphs in the place of the old paragraph. It is most likely implemented as a series of pointer updates. Pointer assignment is a safe operation.

The postcommit cleanup involves the deletion of the old paragraph, which is a safe operation. Notice that, as always, we assume that destructors never throw any exceptions.

The best way to implement a transaction is to create a transaction object. Such an object can be in one of two states: committed or aborted. It always starts in the aborted state. If its destructor is called before the state is changed to committed, it will unroll all the actions performed under the transaction. Obviously, then, the transaction object has to keep track of what's already been done—it keeps the *log* of actions. Once the transaction is committed, the object changes its state to committed and, in that state, its destructor doesn't unroll anything.

Here's how we could implement the transaction of splitting the current paragraph.

```
void Document::SplitCurPara ()
{
  ParaTransaction xact;
  Paragraph * para1 = new Paragraph (_curOff);
  xact.LogFirst (para1);
  Paragraph * para2 = new Paragraph (_curPara->Size () - _curOff);
  xact.LogSecond (para2);
  Paragraph * oldPara = _curPara;
  // May throw an exception!
  SubstCurPara (para1, para2);
  xact.Commit ();
  delete oldPara;
  // Destructor of xact executed
}
```

This is how the transaction object is implemented.

```
class ParaTransaction
{
public:
  ParaTransaction ()
      : _commit (false), _para1 (0), _para2
(0) {}
  ~ParaTransaction ()
  {
    if (!_commit)
    {
      // Unroll all the actions
      delete _para2;
      delete _para1;
    }
  }
  void LogFirst (Paragraph * para) { _para1 = para; }
  void LogSecond (Paragraph * para) { _para2 = para; }
  void Commit () { _commit = true; }
private:
  bool        _commit;
  Paragraph * _para1;
  Paragraph * _para2;
};
```

Notice how carefully we prepare all the ingredients for the transaction. We first allocate all the resources and log them in our transaction object. The new paragraphs are now owned by the transaction. If at any point an exception is thrown, the destructor of the transaction, still in its noncommitted state, will perform a rollback and free all these resources.

Once we have all the resources ready, we make the switch—new resources go into the place of the old ones. The switch operation usually involves the manipulation of some pointers or array indexes but no allocations. Once the switch has been done, we can commit the transaction. From that point on, the transaction no longer owns the new paragraphs. The destructor of a committed transaction usually does nothing at all. The switch makes the document the owner of the new paragraphs and, at the same time, frees the ownership of the old paragraph, which we then promptly delete. All simple transactions follow this pattern:

1. Allocate and log all the resources necessary for the transaction (see Fig. B.1).
2. Switch new resources in the place of old resources and commit (see Fig.B.3).
3. Clean up old resources (see Fig. B.4).

If step one isn't successful, the transaction is aborted and new allocations are cleared up (see Fig. B.2)

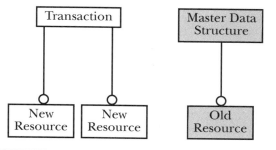

Figure B.1 Prepared transaction. The transaction owns all the new resources. The master data structure owns the old resources

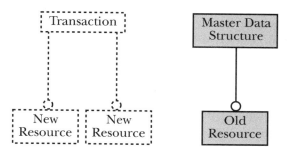

Figure B.2 Aborting a transaction. The transaction's destructor frees the resources

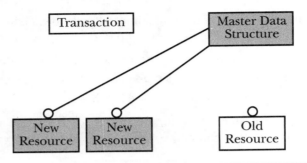

Figure B.3 The switch. The master data structure releases the old resources and takes the ownership of the new resources

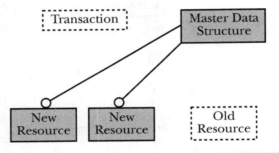

Figure B.4 The cleanup. Old resources are freed and the transaction is deleted

Persistent Transactions

When designing a persistent transaction—one that manipulates persistent data structures—we have to think of recovering from disasters such as system crashes or power failures. In cases like those, we are not so much worried about in-memory data structures (these will be lost anyway), but about the persistent, on-disk data structures.

A persistent transaction goes through similar stages as the transient one.

1. Preparation: New information is written to disk.
2. Commitment: The new information becomes current; the old is disregarded.
3. Cleanup: The old information is removed from the disk.

A system crash can happen before or after commitment (I'll explain in a moment why it can't happen during the commit). When the system comes up again, we have to find all the interrupted transactions (they have to leave some trace on disk) and do one of two things: If the transaction was interrupted before it had a

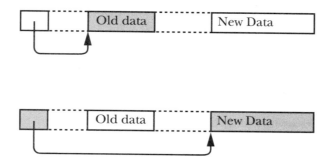

Figure B.5 The switch. In one atomic write operation the on-disk data structure changes its contents

chance to commit, we must unroll it; otherwise we have to complete it. Both cases involve cleanup of some on-disk data. The unrolling means deleting the information written in preparation for the transaction. The completing means deleting the old information that is no longer needed.

The crucial part of the transaction is, of course, commitment. It's the "flipping of the switch." In one atomic operation the new information becomes current and the old becomes invalid (see Figure B.5). An atomic operation either succeeds and leaves a permanent trace on disk, or fails without leaving a trace. That shouldn't be difficult, you say. How about simply writing something to a file? It either succeeds or fails, doesn't it?

Well, there's the rub! It doesn't! In order to understand that, we have to delve a little into the internals of a file system. First of all, writing to a file doesn't mean writing to disk. Or, at least, not immediately. In general, file writes are buffered and then cached in memory before they are physically written to disk. All this is quietly done by the runtime (the buffering) and by the operating system (the caching) in order to get reasonable performance out of your machine. Disk writes are so incredibly slow in comparison with memory writes that caching is a must.

What's even more important: the order of physical disk writes is not guaranteed to follow the order of logical file writes. In fact, the file system goes out of its way to combine file writes based on their physical proximity on disk, so that the magnetic head doesn't have to move too much. And the physical layout of a file might have nothing to do with its contiguous logical shape. Not to mention writes to different files that can be quite arbitrarily reordered by the system, no matter what your program thinks.

Third, contiguous writes to a single file may be split into several physical writes depending on the disk layout set up by your file system. You might be writing a single 32-bit number but, if it happens to straddle sector boundaries, one part of it might be written to disk in one write and the other might wait for another sweep of the cache. Of course, if the system goes down between these two writes, your data will end up partially written. So much for atomic writes.

Now that I have convinced you that transactions are impossible, let me explain a few tricks of the trade that make them possible after all. First of all, there is a file system call, `Flush`, that makes 100% sure that the file data is written to the disk. Not atomically, mind you—Flush may fail in the middle of writing a 32-bit number. But once Flush succeeds, we are guaranteed that the data is safely stored on disk. Obviously, we have to "flush" the new data to disk before we go about committing a transaction. Otherwise we might wake up after a system crash with a committed transaction but an incomplete data structure. And, of course, another flush must finish the committing a transaction.

How about atomicity? How can we atomically flip the switch? Some databases go so far as to install their own file systems that support atomic writes. We won't go that far. We will assume that if a file is small enough, file writes are indeed atomic. "Small enough" means not larger than a sector. To be on the safe side, make it less than 256 bytes. Will this work on every file system? Of course not! There are some file systems that are not even recoverable. All I can say is that this method will work on NTFS—the Windows NT file system. You can quote me on this.

We are now ready to talk about the simplest implementation of the persistent transaction—the three-file scheme.

The Three-File Scheme

An idealized word processor reads an input file, lets the user edit it, and then saves the result. It's the save operation that we are interested in. If we start overwriting the source file, we're asking for trouble. Any kind of failure and we end up with a partially updated (read: corrupted!) file.

So here's another scheme: Write the complete updated version of the document into a separate file. When you finish writing, flush it to make sure the data gets to disk. Then commit the transaction and clean up the original file. To keep a permanent record of the state of the transaction you'll need one more small file. The transaction is committed by making one atomic write into that file.

So here is the three-file scheme: We start with file A containing the original data, file B with no data, and a small one-byte file S (for Switch) initialized to contain a zero. The transaction begins.

1. Write the new version of the document to file B.
2. Flush file B to make sure that the data gets to disk.
3. Commit: Write "1" into file S and flush it.
4. Empty file A.

The meaning of the number stored in file S is the following: If its value is zero, file A contains valid data. If it's one, file B contains valid data. When the program starts up, it checks the value stored in S, loads the data from the appropriate file, and empties the other file. That's it!

Let's now analyze what happens if there is a system crash at any point in our scheme. If it happens before the new value in file S gets to the disk, the program will come up and read zero from S. It will assume that the correct version of the data is still in file A and it will empty file B. We are back to the pretransaction state. The emptying of B is our *rollback*.

Once the value one in S gets to the disk, the transaction is committed. A system crash after that will result in the program coming back, reading the value one from S and assuming that the correct data is in file B. It will empty file A, thus completing the transaction. Notice that data in file B is guaranteed to be complete at that point: since the value in S is one, file B must have been flushed successfully.

If we want to start another *save* transaction after that, we can simply interchange the roles of files A and B and commit by changing the value in S from one to zero. To make the scheme even more robust, we can choose some random (but fixed) byte values for our switch, instead of zero and one (the same trick that was used in the serialization of Boolean values). In this way we'll be more likely to discover on-disk data corruption—something that might always happen as long as disks are not 100% reliable and other applications can access our files and corrupt them. Redundancy provides the first line of defense against data corruption.

This is how we could implement a *save* transaction.

```
class SaveTrans
{
  enum State
  {
  // Some arbitrary bit patterns
      stDataInA = 0xC6,
      stDataInB = 0x3A
  };
public:
  SaveTrans ()
      : _switch ("Switch"), _commit (false)
  {
    _state = _switch.ReadByte ();
    if (_state != stDataInA && state != stDataInB)
        throw "Switch file corrupted";
    if (_state == stDataInA)
    {
        _data.Open ("A");
        _backup.Open ("B");
    }
    else
    {
        _data.Open ("B");
        _backup.Open ("A");
    }
  }
  File & GetDataFile () { return _data; }
  File & GetBackupFile () { return _backup; }
  ~SaveTrans ()
  {
    if (_commit)
        _data.Empty ();
```

```
        else
            _backup.Empty ();
    }
    void Commit ()
    {
      State otherState;
      if (_state == stDataInA)
          otherState = stDataInB;
      else
          otherState = stDataInA;

      _backup.Flush ();
      _switch.Rewind ();
      _switch.WriteByte (otherState);
      _switch.Flush ();
      _commit = true;
    }
  private:
    bool    _commit;
    File    _switch;
    File    _data;
    File    _backup;
    State   _state;
};
```

The same transaction is used here for cleanup. Since we are not calling `Commit`, the transaction cleans up, which is exactly what we need.

The Mapping-File Scheme

You might be a little concerned about the performance characteristics of the three-file scheme. After all, the document might be a few megabytes long and writing it (and flushing!) to disk every time you do a save creates a serious overhead. So if you want to be a notch better than most word processors, consider a more efficient scheme.

The fact is that most of the time the changes you make to a document between saves are localized in just a few places. Wouldn't it be more efficient to update only those places in the file instead of rewriting the whole document? Suppose we divide the document into "chunks" that fit each into a single "page." By "page" I mean a power-of-two fixed-size subdivision. When updating a given chunk we could simply swap a page or two. It's just like swapping a few tiles in a bathroom floor—you don't need to retile the whole floor when you just want to make a small change around the sink.

Strictly speaking, we don't even need fixed-size power-of-two pages, it just makes the flushes more efficient and the bookkeeping easier. All pages may be kept in a single file, but we need a separate "map" that establishes the order in which they appear in the document. Now if only the "map" could fit into a small switch file, we would perform transactions by updating the map.

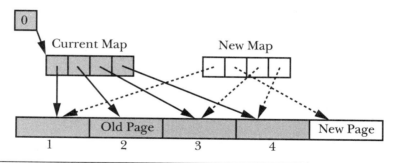

Figure B.6 The Mapping File Scheme: before committing

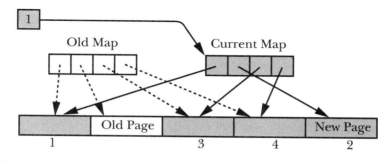

Figure B.7 The Mapping File Scheme: after committing

Suppose, for example, that we want to update page two out of a four-page file. First we try to find a free page in the file (we'll see in a moment how transactions produce free pages). If a free page cannot be found, we just extend the file by adding the fifth page. Then we write the new updated data into this free page. We now have the current version of a part of the document in page two and the new version of the same part in page five (or whatever free page we used). Now we atomically overwrite the map, making page two free and page five take its place.

What if the map doesn't fit into a small file? No problem! We can always do the three-file trick with the map file. We can prepare a new version of the map file, flush it, and commit by updating the switch file (see Figures B.6 and B.7).

This scheme can be extended to a multi-level tree. In fact, several databases and even file systems use something similar, based on a data structure called a B-tree.

Index

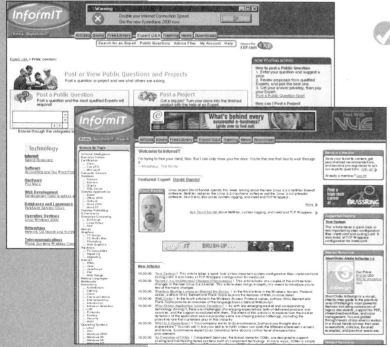

Register
Your Book
at www.aw.com/cseng/register

You may be eligible to receive:
- Advance notice of forthcoming editions of the book
- Related book recommendations
- Chapter excerpts and supplements of forthcoming titles
- Information about special contests and promotions throughout the year
- Notices and reminders about author appearances, tradeshows, and online chats with special guests

Contact us

If you are interested in writing a book or reviewing manuscripts prior to publication, please write to us at:

Editorial Department
Addison-Wesley Professional
75 Arlington Street, Suite 300
Boston, MA 02116 USA
Email: AWPro@aw.com

Visit us on the Web: http://www.aw.com/cseng